LIFE ON THE BRINK

Life on the Brink

Environmentalists Confront Overpopulation

EDITED BY
PHILIP CAFARO AND EILEEN CRIST

THE UNIVERSITY OF GEORGIA PRESS   ATHENS AND LONDON

© 2012 by the University of Georgia Press
Athens, Georgia 30602
www.ugapress.org

Set in Adobe Garamond Pro by
   Graphic Composition, Inc., Bogart, Georgia.
Manufactured by Sheridan Books

The paper in this book meets the guidelines for
permanence and durability of the Committee on
Production Guidelines for Book Longevity of the
Council on Library Resources.

Printed in the United States of America
16 15 14 13 12 P 5 4 3 2 1

LIBRARY OF CONGRESS CATALOGING-IN-PUBLICATION DATA

Life on the brink : environmentalists confront overpopulation /
edited by Philip Cafaro and Eileen Crist.
      p. cm.
Includes bibliographical references and index.
ISBN-13: 978-0-8203-4385-3 (pbk. : alk. paper)
ISBN-10: 0-8203-4385-4 (pbk. : alk. paper)
ISBN-13: 978-0-8203-4048-7 (hardcover : alk. paper)
ISBN-10: 0-8203-4048-0 (hardcover : alk. paper)
1. Overpopulation—Environmental aspects.
2. Environmental ethics.
I. Cafaro, Philip, 1962–
II. Crist, Eileen, 1961–
HB871.I5195 2012
363.7′01—dc23   2012013925

BRITISH LIBRARY CATALOGING-IN-PUBLICATION DATA AVAILABLE

To Edward O. Wilson, Tireless Defender of Nature

*"It is not the Nature of human beings to be cattle in glorified feedlots.
Every person deserves the option to travel easily in and out of the complex
and primal world that gave us birth. We need freedom to roam across land
owned by no one but protected by all, whose unchanging horizon is the same
that bounded the world of our millennial ancestors. Only in what remains of
Eden, teeming with life-forms independent of us, is it possible to experience
the kind of wonder that shaped the human psyche at its birth."*

CONTENTS

TABLES AND FIGURES

PAUL EHRLICH AND ANNE EHRLICH

T HE RECENT UNREST in Arab nations has called the world's attention to some of the political and economic consequences of the West's addiction to petroleum. But sadly, it hasn't brought back into focus two more fundamental and interrelated problems. The first is the population explosion; the second is the expectation of perpetual growth in per capita consumption, not just for several billion poor people, but for the billion or so who are already rich. Happily, there are some encouraging signs of renewed interest in the population-environment nexus, exemplified by this timely book, *Life on the Brink: Environmentalists Confront Overpopulation.*

Over the next forty years, the populations of already water-short Middle East nations are going to increase dramatically, and at the same time their people will be aspiring to catch up with the living standards of today's developed countries. For example, Egypt, with 80 million people today, is projected to grow to some 138 million by 2050. Per capita income in Egypt is now about $5,500, compared with about $47,000 in the United States and $30,000 in the European Union. The aspiration gap is even more stunning in sub-Saharan Africa, where populations are projected to explode from 870 million people to 1.8 billion in the next thirty-nine years.

Per capita income there is now about $2,000, and less than a third of the population has access to a toilet.

The aspiration gap will probably widen further as the poor suffer disproportionately from climate disruption, the spread of toxic chemicals, and an extinction episode unmatched in sixty-five million years, threatening the existence of not just our only known living companions in the universe but also the natural services that they provide, upon which people are utterly dependent. Human agriculture and industry are embedded in and supported by the natural ecosystems of Earth. Among the crucial services and goods supplied free by natural ecosystems are moderation of climates; regulation of the hydrological cycle that supplies fresh water, including control of floods and droughts; cycling of nutrients and replenishment and enrichment of soils; natural disposal of wastes; control of pests and diseases; pollination of plants, including crops; and production of forest products and seafood. Yet modern societies heedlessly displace, poison, overharvest, and directly assault natural ecosystems with little thought for their importance in their own sustenance. Indeed, we have gone so far as to begin destabilizing the gaseous content of the atmosphere and disrupting global climates as well as the natural cycles of vital elements that underpin our food production systems.

Given such a comprehensive (but still largely unappreciated) attack on our global life-support system and the noticeably rising pressures on essential industrial resources such as petroleum, coal, and rare earth minerals, and the consequent need to invest in completely re-engineering the planet's energy-mobilizing and water-handling infrastructure, even maintaining today's standards of living in both rich and poor nations will be increasingly difficult. If projected rates of population and economic growth are fulfilled in the next several decades, safeguarding Earth's precious store of living natural capital, and thereby permitting the support of further billions, will be virtually impossible.

The press is full of stories about problems, most of which are caused at least in part by the conjoined but unmentionable twin elephants of population growth and overconsumption. But spiking food and energy prices, growing water shortages, increasingly severe weather, melting ice caps, dying coral reefs, intersex alligators, disappearing polar bears, collapsing infrastructures, terrorism, and novel epidemics are almost never connected to the elephants. While obviously there are limits to sustainable human numbers and to humanity's aggregate consumption, those limits are almost never mentioned, let alone discussed.

Indeed, when the U.S. Census Bureau announced in 2010 that the United States had passed 308 million people, it was treated as some sort of triumph, with emphasis placed on the decadal redistribution of congressional seats. There was no mention of the expectation that we will add more than 110 million more people by 2050 and then continue growing (don't hold your breath). There was little better media analysis as the global population rocketed past 7 billion in 2011—more than tripling the world's population in our own lifetimes.

The mass media also haven't explained that the two billion additional people expected in the next thirty-five years will do much more environmental damage than the previous two billion. Human beings are smart; they pick the low-hanging fruit first—and we have. Every additional person now, on average, must be fed from more marginal land, supplied with water from sources more distant or difficult to purify, use minerals won from ever-poorer ores, and do without the company and services of many populations of fascinating and useful plants, animals, and microorganisms. This nonlinearity, that results are no longer proportional to effort, has been recognized by scientists since the early 1970s but is unknown to the vast majority of our leaders.

Will technology save us? Obviously, it can help; but its record has been generally dismal. When *The Population Bomb* was published in 1968, there were 3.5 billion people, and we were called alarmist; technology surely could feed, house, clothe, educate, and provide great lives to even 5 billion people! Nuclear agro-industrial complexes or growing algae on sewage would feed everyone! Well, they didn't. Strangely enough, neither technological fix held much appeal for consumers. Instead, the roughly half-billion hungry people of 1968 have increased to about a billion in 2011, and a couple billion more are living in miserable poverty. Why don't the growthmaniacs stop asserting how many billions more people we could care for and focus first on stopping population growth and giving decent lives to all the people already here? And spare us that old bromide about how the next kid may turn out to be the Einstein who saves us; considering the rich-poor gap, he's more likely to be an Osama Bin Laden bent on destroying us. Children need to be well nourished and well educated if they are to contribute as adults to finding ways to create a sustainable society. At the moment the future for both looks bleak, even in rich nations.

Sometimes there is controversy among environmentalists about the relative roles of population size and per capita consumption in causing environmental deterioration. But one can no more separate them than distinguish the multiplicative roles of a rectangle's length or width in contributing to the area of a rectangle. It is, however, possible to determine each one's role in changing the area—or, analogously, in changing the degree of environmental damage. In the past two centuries, population growth and expanding per capita consumption have contributed roughly equally to humanity's assault on its life-support systems. Reducing the assault and transitioning to a sustainable society will require action on *both* factors.

It will take much longer to humanely reduce population size than to alter human consumption patterns. A few decades of moderately reduced average fertility (from today's global average of about 2.5 children per woman to 1.8 or so) would be required to have a significant effect on human numbers and the growth trajectory. Still, moving toward population reduction now in the United States and globally is required if humanity is to attain a sustainable civilization. It could largely be done in a win-win manner, by giving equal rights and opportunities to women and mobilizing to provide all sexually active people with convenient contraception and safe backup abortion services.

Of course, if material overconsumption by the rich continues to escalate, the benefits of ending population growth will be compromised. And if gross underconsumption by the poor is allowed to continue or worsen, then the cooperation we need to resolve the human predicament is unlikely to materialize. Like population and consumption, equity issues and environmental issues are also conjoined twins. So we hope you'll read *Life on the Brink* to help sort out these matters. Then become an activist and work to bring humanity and its leaders to their population senses, before it's too late.

PART I

Introduction

CHAPTER I

Human Population Growth as If the Rest of Life Mattered

EILEEN CRIST AND PHILIP CAFARO

REFLECTING ON THE environmental challenges faced by humanity, political activist and writer Tom Hayden (2010) asks: "Can we continue to overcrowd and over-consume without losing the very things that have given us joy, kept us safe, and provided inspiration for as long as we've been a species?" The answer can only be a resounding "No."

We find joy in the abundant beauty and variety that Earth provides. We find safety in a relatively predictable climate and reliable food sources. We find inspiration in the grandeur of this extraordinary planet. The scale of humanity's presence—let alone our continued growth—imperils these sources of our well-being and the very existence of innumerable other life-forms. We thus are called, even at this late hour, to find the clarity and courage to shift into a new relationship with Earth, before we diminish irrevocably the greater-than-human world, our own lives, and the lives of future generations.

The explosion of humanity has decimated many animal and plant populations, extinguished species and subspecies, and caused collapsing ecologies, spreading bio-homogeneity, and the shrinking and fragmentation of wild places. The engine of this ruin has been the virtually unlimited appropriation of the natural world to serve a human project out of bounds. Ocean life has been reduced to food and bycatch; rainforests razed for meat, soybeans, palm oil, and timber; boreal and temperate forests cut down and exploited for their wood, pulp, and energy resources; mountains and underground shale detonated for coal and natural gas; deep-sea floors punctured for oil; grasslands overgrazed or converted into strictly human breadbaskets; and freshwaters channelized, dammed, dumped in, and overfished. Worldwide, animals are being exterminated at an unprecedented pace, either displaced or killed for their meat and lucrative body parts. Where natural areas and nonhuman beings do not suffer directly, they take indirect hits from climate change and pollution.

The biological heritage of the Holocene has received an enormous blow. In a recent overview, Peter Raven, Jonathan Chase, and J. Chris Pires (2011) write that "biodiversity is diminishing at a rate even faster than the last mass extinction at the end of the Cretaceous Period, sixty-five million years ago, with possibly two-thirds of existing terrestrial species likely to become extinct by the end of this century." If humanity is to avoid committing interspecies genocide in the twenty-first century, we will have to make revolutionary changes in how we live on Earth—including limiting how many of us inhabit it.

While we may disagree about many matters of tactic and strategy, all the contributors to *Life on the Brink: Environmentalists Confront Overpopulation* are committed to such radical change. Above all, we seek to create a civilization that preserves the continued flourishing of wild nature: its biological diversity, ecological complexity, and evolutionary dynamism. In various voices, the contributors affirm that humanity must find its appropriate, limited niche within the larger living world rather than persist on our current biosphere-destroying path. Doing so, we argue, is a matter of basic moral decency.

Typically, population issues are discussed in anthropocentric terms, with a focus on how much people can take from the planet: its "carrying capacity" for human beings. As Joel Cohen (1995) titled his well-received book, the key question is *How Many People Can the Earth Support?* Readers who are environmental activists can probably think of analogous "maximizing" questions: How much water can we take out of that river? How many board feet of lumber can we cut from that forest? How many houses can we shoehorn onto that last undeveloped parcel of land?

Our authors reject the selfishness and conceit of this way of putting matters. It is unjust toward other species. And it points toward a dreary, depauperate future that will be bad for human beings as well. Maximizing the sheer tonnage of human flesh on Earth, by turning the whole world into Resource World, is an ignoble and unjust goal. Humanity can and should pursue a better way. If you believe this too, then you should read on.

※

Between 1960 and 2012, the human population more than doubled, from three billion to over seven billion, while the size of the global economy increased at least sevenfold. Over this same period, we have come to understand that human demographic and economic growth is inversely related to the autonomy, integrity, and diversity of Nature. Yet we have also tended to regard the ecological impacts of "population" and "consumption" as virtually independent factors. Conventional environmental wisdom would have it that overconsumption is the failing of the affluent, as if their numbers were negligible; while overpopulation has been regarded as the plight of the poor, as if they did not consume in ecologically unsustainable ways. As humanity has burgeoned in both affluence and numbers, and the natural world has receded apace, controversies have raged over whether consumption growth or population growth is most culpable.

This has always been a false dilemma. The ecological crisis is the consequence of the consumption patterns of a huge and growing human population. Yet a leftist cadre of the environmental movement has contended that overconsumption in the global North is disproportionately responsible for the biosphere's degradation, leaving the global South, where population is growing most rapidly, largely off the hook. Partly as a consequence of this widely rehearsed reasoning, in the last two decades population growth became a nonissue—or worse, taboo—while Western consumerism, corporate malfeasance, and neocolonial policies have been excoriated as the main drivers of inequity and ecological destruction. While these criticisms contain much truth, the ideology behind them has masked as much as it has revealed. Crucially, it has tended to obscure the detrimental effects of population growth in several ways.

First, little attention has been given to the fact that the rich and the poor often have different *kinds* of environmental impacts. The destructive reach of the affluent is global—the most glaring case being climate change, for which the North does indeed bear primary responsibility. But the destructive reach of the poor tends to be more local or regional, involving, for example, deforestation for subsistence agriculture and fuel, rampant killing of animals for subsistence or markets, overfishing, desertification, and sewage and chemical pollution of fresh waters and coastlines.

Dangerous chemical pollutants originating in the developed world have found their way into the geographically remote flesh of polar bears and the breast milk of Inuit women. But swelling numbers of dispossessed people in Africa and elsewhere have mounted such an aggressive assault on forest animals (*bushmeat*) that conservation biologists coined the term *empty forest syndrome* to describe the ecological reckoning. While the destructiveness of American carbon dioxide pollution cannot be contained within U.S. borders, Madagascar's poverty- and population growth–driven deforestation and species extinctions represent equally tragic and irreversible losses from Earth's commonwealth.

Second, when Western consumers and their corporate and political tools are held culpable for environmental woes, via exploiting the raw materials of poor countries, such exposés regularly omit that the products derived from third-world resources are products for *mass* consumption. Several billion people comprise the upper and middle classes of the world: voracious consumers in the North and now, increasingly, in the global South as well. Sugar, coffee, tea, cocoa, bananas, paper, wood, oil, natural gas, coal, gold, diamonds, iron ore, soybeans, palm oil, meat, shrimp, cut flowers, and so forth—these are or go into commonly used products throughout the world. The stainless steel cookware made in China, sold en masse in big box stores, and found in tens of millions of middle-class households worldwide may well contain iron mined in the Amazon. The oil production degrading Nigeria's coasts and forests fuels large and growing car fleets in the United States, India, Brazil, and Europe. Jewelry donned not just by the gilded class but by all classes, except the dispossessed lowest quintile of humanity, may be made of gold or diamonds extracted at a high ecological price from wild places in Africa and elsewhere. The palm oil in the cosmetics, food, and biodiesels of billions in Asia, Europe, and North America is harvested from slashed-and-burned rainforests in Indonesia and Malaysia.

In brief, to scrutinize the global North and see only the variable of *consumption* is to remain blind to the *mass* that qualifies it. A major factor underlying destructive consumerism is population size: the sheer numbers of consumers around the globe. To propagate the myth that population growth is not itself a problem and to lament, instead, the harmful effects of unsustainable production and consumption bypasses one leading reason that production and consumption *are* unsustainable.

This brings us to the third way that population as a driver of ecological catastrophe has been obfuscated in the last two decades: the fast clip at which Northern consumer ideals are expanding within the global South. Social theorist Juliet Schor calls this the rise of "turbo consumption," in which "a high-end, affluent, media-driven norm of consumption prevails" worldwide, even among the poor (2010, 589). While rich nations with their powerful financial, corporate, and military institutions have wielded enormous influence in the spread of globalization, developing nations (for the most part) are eager to participate in the global economy. Consumer lifestyles have become the hegemonic model, enjoyed by a portion of the world and coveted by the rest.

In a globalized world, where "the end of poverty" has become largely synonymous with the dissemination of a modern high-consumption standard of living, overconsumption and overpopulation are a seamless whole. Consider the rapid escalation of global trade, the worldwide expansion of car culture (in 2009, monthly automobile sales in China surpassed those in the United States), and the swift rise of meat consumption in formerly poor countries. Such trends should dispel any lingering notions that overconsumption can be dealt with while ignoring overpopulation, or vice versa.

By some accounts, during the last fifty years, human beings have consumed as many natural resources as all previous generations put together. That "achievement" came from the wedding of twentieth-century capitalist industrial production and the human population swell, and from their offspring: a mass consumer culture in which ever more people consumed ever more stuff. The levels that resource consumption and pollution might reach during the next fifty years, and the fifty after that, if business as usual prevails, are frightening to contemplate. How many other species, how many wild places, can possibly survive such a century, or the many demands of the ten billion or so increasingly affluent people projected to inhabit Earth by 2100?

⚜

Environmentalists have blundered terribly in failing to face up to growth. As Gustave Speth (2009) puts it, while the worldwide environmental movement has won many victories in recent decades, overall, we are "losing the planet." Certainly the movement has failed to think through population issues, much less address them practically and with the urgency they require. Political correctness and timidity have played a role in this failure; so too, perhaps, has the complacency of the well-paid leaders of major environmental organizations. Yet the message from the scientific community could not be clearer, as stated in the *Millennium Ecosystem Assessment* in 2005, restated in the IPCC's *4th Assessment Report* in 2007, and reiterated in several recent reports on the state of world biodiversity, including the Convention on Biological Diversity's *Global Biodiversity Outlook* published in 2010: simply put, population growth is a major driver of ecological degradation. We cannot create sustainable societies without ending population growth; indeed, as this book argues, without significantly *reducing* the human population. To ignore population matters is to acquiesce in advance to continued ecological decline.

The contributors to *Life on the Brink*—many of them veterans in the fight to protect wild nature—are unwilling to concede defeat. Moreover, we are willing to do the hard work and broach the difficult topics necessary to help lead the environmental movement forward to real and lasting success. In what follows, we discuss the full range of population issues, including the reasons behind mainstream environmental groups' failure to address them. Knowing the necessity to limit human populations if we hope to preserve a vibrant natural world, we have not shied away from controversy or taken refuge in a foolish optimism.

Part 1 introduces our topic. It includes essays by William R. Catton Jr., Albert Bartlett, Martha Campbell, and Dave Foreman. Catton updates his classic work *Overshoot* (1980), identifying the main forces driving ecological degradation, including population growth, and asking whether the environmental movement has what it takes to recognize and overcome those forces. Bartlett provides an accessible tutorial on the mathematics of exponential growth, its power to drive rapid increases in resource use, and the implications for genuine ecological sustainability. Campbell examines why population issues have received little public attention in recent decades from policymakers and the general public, despite continued rapid demographic growth and mounting evidence of this growth's harmful ecological consequences. Dave Foreman, author of the recent *Man Swarm and the Killing of Wildlife* (2011), explores the same topic, with an insider's knowledge of the American environmental movement. While Campbell focuses on declining U.S. funding for international family planning efforts, Foreman also addresses the contentious American immigration debates of a decade ago; readers who compare their accounts will find interesting areas of agreement and divergence.

Part 2 focuses on the ecological impacts of human population growth. Leon Kolankiewicz shows how "a plethora of people produces a paucity of wildlife," emphasizing his own studies and experiences in Central and North America. Jeffrey McKee argues that globally, human population density is the most important variable correlating positively with species endangerment. Taken together, these pieces make a powerful argument that more people equal less biodiversity. Tim Palmer, writing from California, the most populous state in the United States, sees the rivers he has worked so hard to protect threatened by continued population growth. Efficiency improvements in water use could have bought the time and ecological space to create communities that shared water generously with other species; instead, Californians used them to facilitate more demographic and economic growth.

Widening the focus, Lester Brown next alerts us to a "rising tide" of environmental refugees, driven from their homes by a combination of overpopulation and degrading ecosystems. After warning about the dangers of overpopulation for decades, Brown must feel no pleasure to see his predictions beginning to come true. George Wuerthner discusses population growth's potential to drive both famine and agriculture-caused biodiversity loss. And Captain Paul Watson, leader of the Sea Shepherd Conservation Society, explains the toll that population growth takes on the oceans and what we should do about it. Watson's controversial suggestions for population control also serve as a bridge to the next section: "Necessary Conversations."

Part 3 begins with Eileen Crist, who critiques a resourcist worldview and argues that if an "abundant Earth" is to provide for both human and nonhuman flourishing, we must move beyond merely stabilizing the global population at its current bloated level and greatly lower it. Modern contraception methods bring an unprecedented possibility—that parenthood can be a conscious choice, rather than a default option driven by genetic compulsion, cultural expectations, or chance—and the parlous state of Earth demands that we secure this opportunity of conscious parenthood for all. Stephanie Mills, who follows, agrees; she started quite a conversation herself at her college commencement in 1969, when she vowed, for environmental reasons, not to have any children. Looking back on a good life and forward to an ecologically sane future, Mills sees no reason to regret her decision and many reasons for society to encourage less childbearing. Tom Butler, from his perch in Vermont, the forty-ninth least-populous U.S. state, also discusses the social and ecological bene-fits of fewer people. Conventional environmentalism is futile, Butler and many other contributors believe, unless we can reverse population growth.

The following two essays explore the implications of this position for the United States, a country where continued population growth is driven primarily by immigration. Philip Cafaro and Winthrop Staples III provide a comprehensive environmental argument for reducing immigration into the United States and consider some of the moral arguments against doing so. Joe Bish comes to a similar conclusion, from more cosmopolitan ethical premises. With climate change and other global ecological threats loom-ing, the last thing the world needs is more Americans. Ronnie Hawkins asks why so many people fail to appreciate the grave dangers of population growth, finding hope in new ways of seeing, experiencing, and under-standing the biosphere. And Amy Gulick returns us to Earth—in this case, the fjords and temperate rainforests of southeast Alaska—reminding us of what is at stake in our population policies and insisting that it is not too late to create societies that live more harmoniously with Nature.

The essays in part 4 seek to specify "Solutions" to the problem of contin-ued human population growth. Robert Engelman, author of *More: Popu-lation, Nature, and What Women Want* (2008), contends that providing affordable, accessible contraception, securing reproductive freedom, and improving women's economic lives and social status are the keys to reduc-ing fertility rates in developing nations. William Ryerson agrees but argues that in addition, creative efforts to model and incentivize small families are necessary in areas of the world where large families remain the cultural norm. Don Weeden and Charmayne Palomba support Engelman's and Ryerson's proposals, arguing that furthering human rights and limiting human numbers are both necessary, if we hope to create a humane and ecologically sustainable future. Taken together, these three essays provide a fine overview of some of the best recent thinking on global population policy—and a necessary corrective to the widespread belief that the popu-lation problem is solving itself.

Switching the focus back to the American context, Richard Lamm next discusses the inability to confront limits, contending that it undermines clear moral reasoning and effective environmental policymaking. As gov-ernor of Colorado, Lamm showed rare candor in tackling sensitive topics such as immigration and health care rationing; his political success suggests that Americans may be willing to consider limits, when they are discussed honestly. Winthrop Staples III and Philip Cafaro return, making the case that nonhuman species have a right to exist and arguing that such a right implies limits both to human consumption and procreation. Historian Roderick Nash argues that the fragmentation of the global landscape by human expansionism and the population explosion has been a tragic mistake; instead, he believes we should create islands of human settlement within a larger matrix of a vast and restored wild nature. It is an appealing vision, which could only occur gradually and over the long term, and which would require a substantial reduction in human numbers and the humility to rescind civilization's planetary sprawl.

The book concludes with a short epilogue by Philip Cafaro that asks a modest question: Is humanity a cancer on the Earth? It is a modest question, we assert, because other species matter; therefore, the failure to ask it, given humanity's current heading, is a clear indication of selfishness and *im*modesty. We may ignore the question, or even reject it indignantly. But we will answer it with our actions over the next century, as we either work to end the sixth mass extinction in the history of life on Earth, or instead accept it. The book concludes with a select bibliography of essential works on population and the environment and a list of resources for readers interested in learning more and getting involved in efforts to stabilize or reduce human numbers.

࿏

In a 2009 report, the *Economist* articulated the widespread perception that "the population problem is solving itself." Exhibit A was the oft-cited decline in worldwide fertility rates: in 1965 the average woman gave birth to five children; today the worldwide average is just under half of that. According to this "demographic transition" paradigm, modern developments like urbanization, rising incomes, and women's empowerment are reliably accompanied by falling fertility rates; thus, all we need to do is sit back and let globalization solve "the population problem," as we stabilize our numbers decades from now, at around nine or ten billion people. This viewpoint is well captured by the slogan "development is the best contraceptive."

This comforting view suffers from serious flaws. First, it assumes that current downward fertility trends necessarily will continue, and that they will do so automatically. But the causes of changing fertility levels are complex and imperfectly understood, and there are recent examples, from both rich and poor countries, where fertility rates have climbed after earlier declines. Furthermore, while birth rates have declined in recent decades, this has actually taken great effort: to raise the money to provide widespread, affordable contraception; to teach people to trust new contraceptive methods and how to use them effectively; to convince individuals in societies where large families are the norm that smaller families are acceptable, or even preferable. Continuing to drive fertility trends downward will continue to take hard work and substantial resources; it will not happen automatically (Moreland, Smith, and Sharma 2010).

Second, demographic transition theorists commonly assume that current trends are moving fast enough to ward off grave ecological catastrophes—most probably a false assumption, given the speed of global ecological degradation and climate change impacts that we are witnessing. It is true and important that fertility rates are declining, and that the worldwide annual population growth rate has declined along with them, from just over 2 percent in 1970 to its current rate of slightly over 1 percent annually, according to the Population Division of the United Nations Department of Economic and Social Affairs (2011). But in absolute terms, current world population growth is still immense, partly because these lower growth rates are occurring on top of an ever-larger base population. In 1970, the world population grew by seventy-six million people; in 2010, it grew by seventy-eight million (UN 2011). Meanwhile, the latest UN projections are for several *billion* more people to be added over the coming decades. Given that there are abundant ecological signs that *current* human numbers are too high, any significant population increase should be recognized as detrimental, and possibly lethal, to the success of sustainability efforts.

Perhaps the worst aspect of the commonly held view that population growth will take care of itself, however, is its anthropocentric perspective on what counts as an acceptable human population size. It assumes that the world is not already overpopulated, and that any level of appropriation of planetary resources is acceptable, as long as we can make it work for ourselves. Thus, it assumes that stabilizing our numbers in the vicinity of nine or ten billion is unproblematic, as long as we can figure out ways to "feed the world" and take care of our other needs. In its conceit, it completely ignores the fact that even if human beings could thrive under such a scenario, the cost would be global ecological meltdown and the completion of the sixth mass extinction: the treasures of Earth's biological splendor gone or reduced to pitiful remnants.

The truth that complacent demographers and economists regularly bypass—and that mainstream environmentalists have failed to understand or defend—is that with clearly articulated goals and the political will, population growth could be reversed far faster. There is enormous potential to *reduce* our numbers, *within this century and without coercion*, if we take proactive steps to empower individuals and couples who want to have fewer children, and citizens who want to end population growth within their own communities and countries. Many of these steps are described in the articles that follow. Environmentalists should fight for them. The alternative is to give up our proud self-identification as "defenders of Nature" and instead accept a more honest job description: "servants of globalization," making sure all get fed, nobody litters, everyone recycles, and the landscaping by the side of the highway is a little more aesthetically pleasing.

The contributors to this anthology believe that humanity belongs on Earth, but that Earth is not our possession. The human endeavor to make it so, underway and in fact accelerating hard, has scaled our presence way beyond what is ecologically appropriate, morally acceptable, or simply prudent. In order to repair Earth, restore balance to our lives, and preserve options for future generations, humanity must scale back profoundly. Ending population growth and then substantially lowering human numbers will be crucial to this effort. Environmentalists should boldly reengage in population issues. In fact, they should forthrightly advocate for population reduction, all the more so since even many of those who are indifferent to the well-being of other species have good human-centered reasons to support this ambitious goal.

In a paper wryly titled "Population Growth Seems to Affect Everything But Is Seldom Held Responsible for Anything," anthropologist Kenneth Smail proposes that we "imagine any early twenty-first century problem—whether political, economic, environmental, social, or moral—and ask whether its solution would be made easier or more difficult by a rapidly growing population" (1997, 231). Well, let's ask. Sky-high numbers of unemployed youth in the developing and developed worlds? Global climate change? Saving the oceans? Saving the rainforests? Stemming anthropogenic extinction? Providing a quality education to children everywhere?

Securing adequate food for the poor? These are daunting problems. While substantially lowering our population will not guarantee solutions, it will certainly help us address these and other problems more effectively by removing the dimension that scales them up—human numbers. Given that reversing population growth is eminently doable, we should strive to do so now.

Admittedly, a world with fewer people will (for an interim period) provide challenges of its own, such as how to support ballooning numbers of retirees with fewer workers. But these pale in comparison with the global ecological unraveling involved in accommodating, say, ten billion people, all consuming at ever-higher levels. Indeed, it appears that even our current numbers cannot be sustained, as hundreds of millions of people climb out of poverty. We need to start working now not just to end but to reverse population growth, while we still can manage the transition from an endless growth economy with minimal pain and dislocation. We invite readers to join us in thinking through our options and working to achieve a future in which we share the planet generously with all its inhabitants— human and nonhuman. The essays that follow are a great place to start.

BIBLIOGRAPHY

Catton, William. 1980. *Overshoot: The Ecological Basis of Revolutionary Change.* Urbana: University of Illinois Press.
Cohen, Joel. 1995. *How Many People Can the Earth Support?* New York: W.W. Norton.
Economist. 2009. "Falling Fertility: Astonishing Falls in the Fertility Rate Are Bringing with Them Big Benefits." October 29.
Engelman, Robert. 2008. *More: Population, Nature, and What Women Want.* Washington, D.C.: Island Press.
Foreman, Dave. 2011. *Man Swarm and the Killing of Wildlife.* Durango, Colo.: Raven's Eye Press.
Hayden, Tom. 2010. "Introduction to EarthPulse: State of the Earth 2010." *National Geographic* (Special Issue).
Moreland, Scott, Ellen Smith, and Suneeta Sharma. 2010. *World Population Prospects and Unmet Need for Family Planning.* Washington, D.C.: Futures Group.
Raven, Peter, Jonathan Chase, and J. Chris Pires. 2011. "Introduction to Special Issue on Biodiversity." *American Journal of Botany* 98: 333–335.
Schor, Juliet. 2010. "Tackling Turbo Consumption." (An Interview with Jo Littler.) *Cultural Studies* 22 (5): 588–598.

Smail, Kenneth. 1997. "Population Growth Seems to Affect Everything But Is Seldom Held Responsible for Anything." *Politics and the Life Sciences* 16 (2): 231–236.

Speth, Gustave. 2009. *The Bridge at the Edge of the World: Capitalism, the Environment, and Crossing from Crisis to Sustainability.* New Haven, Conn.: Yale University Press.

United Nations Department of Economic and Social Affairs, Population Division. 2011. *World Population Prospects: The 2010 Revision.* New York: United Nations.

CHAPTER 2

Destructive Momentum

Could an Enlightened Environmental
Movement Overcome It?

WILLIAM R. CATTON JR.

ERSTWHILE EXPECTATIONS of perpetual progress have been made
obsolete by changing circumstances. Human actions have been un-
doing much of what the biosphere offers to make this planet suitable to
support a quality human life. Environmentalists' ecological concerns,
linked to new insights about demographic change and technological progress, can clarify our predicament. A growing number of humans, many
equipped with resource-ravenous technology, have exploited a widening
array of natural resources, both renewable and nonrenewable. Ideas about
limits—often shrugged off by statesmen, citizens, and entrepreneurs—are
now vital. One hopeful idea, to which I return at the end of this essay, is
the mandate to so administer nature reserves that human use would "leave
them unimpaired." Tantamount to the quest for sustainability, this idea
needs renewed attention and wider application.

Carrying capacity limits, too often unrecognized, mean that for any
environment there is a rate or amount of resource use that cannot be exceeded without reducing the subsequent ability of that environment to
sustain such use. Much human use of planet Earth has been in defiance
of this principle, so twentieth-century population growth—and technological advances that enabled some *Homo sapiens* to become *Homo colossus*, with huge resource appetites and impacts—turned the past human
carrying capacity surplus into the present carrying capacity deficit.

We, the seven billion humans now trying to live on this finite planet,
are in big trouble. To avoid muddling our way into the future with mis-

guided and piecemeal "remedial" actions that can make the trouble worse, we need to understand its real nature and the causes that have produced it. If we cling to obsolete thoughtways and mistaken notions, even our well-intended efforts to cope can seriously aggravate the difficulties ahead.

I believe the necessary corrective insights are available. Considering the future prospects for living beings and natural ecosystems, life scientist Edward O. Wilson deplored the widespread failure to recognize "environmentalism" as a perspective that is vastly important; indeed, foundational (2002). Environmentalists, he argued, have too often been shrugged off as people who get overly upset about pollution and threatened species, who exaggerate their case in pressing for industrial restraint, and who interfere with economic development when the changes they seek would cost jobs.

Since it first formed roughly four billion years ago Earth has fundamentally changed, acquiring the qualities that made our emergence possible (see Burger 2003). "The soil, water, and atmosphere of its surface," Wilson writes, "have evolved over hundreds of millions of years to their present condition by the activity of the biosphere, a stupendously complex layer of living creatures whose activities are locked together in precise but tenuous global cycles of energy and transformed organic matter" (2002, 39). We humans totally depend on, as Wilson puts it, the "unique, shimmering physical disequilibrium," created and maintained by a diverse biota, that differentiates the living Earth from other planets. Learning to live in full recognition of all this is what environmentalism should mean, he correctly maintains. Can the real core of environmentalist thinking become widely understood and implemented in time to save us from catastrophe?

In 1980 when my book *Overshoot: The Ecological Basis of Revolutionary Change* was published, I was already concerned that the four and a half billion of us were seriously damaging Earth. It was becoming apparent that too few human planet-users—not even most of the so-called alarmists, and certainly few if any political leaders—were availing themselves of ecological concepts and principles that could enable humanity to understand the predicament into which we had already put ourselves. In woeful ecological ignorance, we were failing to see the dire destiny toward which we were racing. The book jacket offered (even to those who might never open my book) some key ideas: we needed to know the all-important concept of *carrying capacity*—the indefinitely supportable number of people extracting resources from the biosphere and putting stuff into it; we needed to know we were living by a *cornucopian myth*, namely the euphoric belief in limitless resources; we needed to understand that by so living we were drawing down Earth's nonrenewable resources and using the renewables faster than their rates of replenishment—*so we were stealing from posterity*; and we needed to overcome the wishful thinking that for all consequent problems there would be a technological fix. We needed to know that, in a nutshell, we had grown beyond Earth's capacity to carry us.

In the book I described instances of other species that multiplied until they overshot the carrying capacity of environments in which they had flourished, and as a result suffered die-off. We need to heed their examples as warnings to ourselves. But to understand carrying capacity, we must define it in sufficient detail. For ranchers, range managers, and ecologically knowledgeable environmentalists, carrying capacity means the population of a given species that a particular environment can support indefinitely: that is, without doing habitat damage that would reduce that environment's future life-supporting capacity. A particular habitat will have different carrying capacities for different species, because each species has a characteristic way of using its environment, in terms of the resources it needs to withdraw from the environment and the metabolic end products it necessarily puts back into the environment. For any livestock species, for example, the members are nearly equivalent to one another as resource users. So a simple head count suffices as a measure of that livestock population's impact on the ecosystem supporting it. This head-counting measure of carrying capacity also works for particular wildlife species, for the same reason.

In the case of humans, however, different societies live different lifestyles. So we have to take account of significant differences between the consumption patterns of different human populations. The definition thus must be refined: human carrying capacity equals the maximum human population *equipped with a given assortment of technology and a given pattern of organization* that a particular environment can support indefinitely—that is, without life-support-reducing habitat damage. This definition takes into account the significantly different ways a given number of people may be equipped and organized, recognizing different ecological loads imposed by people from different cultures. Of course, the strict focus on human carrying capacity usually does not engage the question of whether it is equitable toward other species to maximize human numbers. If we accept that other species have a right to continued existence on Earth, then we must stabilize our growth *well short* of human carrying capacity.

Table 2.1 reveals that biologically we have been a remarkably successful species—so far. Most people today recognize that there are more human beings alive now than ever before, but it is useful to get an overview of how much more numerous we have become. Consider the following comparisons. Shortly after the U.S. bicentennial, my wife and I showed our New Zealand daughter-in-law the view from the ninety-ninth floor of Chicago's Sears Tower (at that time the world's tallest building). She gazed in amazement upon the lights of an urban complex comprising roughly as many people as the entire population of her home country, three million people. Now think of going back to about 35,000 BCE and scattering three million people over several continents. To imagine such scattering is a way of comprehending that, on the entire planet that long ago, there were only about one "Chicago's worth," or one "New Zealand's worth," of human beings.

At that time, all people were living by hunting and gathering; they were foragers like all other animals. Our species continued a hunting-gathering existence for the next twenty-seven thousand years. The descendants of those three million had, by around 8000 BCE, more than doubled their numbers, reaching a total world population of about eight million. That world total can be compared with today's population of one European country (e.g., Switzerland) having the entire planet to themselves. But contrast this slow increase from three to eight million (that spanned twenty-seven millennia) with the fact that two billion Earth inhabitants were living when I was a small boy—and think of the fact that those two billion have more than tripled just within my own lifetime!

Now look at the table's second row. Growth speeded up after people discovered they could manage the local ecosystems on which they depended by planting seeds and tending the growth of crops, while also raising some domesticated animals to provide food, clothing, and transport. Instead of taking an average of over eighteen *thousand* years as foragers to double their numbers, as farmers people now could double themselves in less than eighteen *hundred* years. By the time Columbus sailed across the Atlantic, Earth was home to people numbering about the same as today's population of the portion of North America north of the Rio Grande (the United States and Canada).

Columbus probably gave no thought to demographic concerns, but his voyage revealed to inhabitants of Europe a "New World." This second hemisphere seemed thinly populated—and as Europeans regarded its people as "savages," their prior inhabitance of the hemisphere's lands got

Table 2.1

World population growth to six billion following major breakthroughs in methods of supporting human life

		World population at start and finish of period	Average years to double	Most advanced means of subsistence	Additional special influence	Type of resources mainly relied on
A	35,000 BCE to 8000 BCE	3 million 8 million	18,750	Hunting and gathering		Renewable
B	8000 BCE to 1500 CE	8 million 350 million	1745	Agriculture		Renewable
C	1500 CE to 1800 CE	350 million 969 million	205	Agriculture	Second expansion into New World	Renewable
D	1800 CE to 1865 CE	969 million 1.4 billion	130	Modern industry	Fossil energy exploited	Some nonrenewable
E	1865 CE to 1999 CE	1.4 billion 6 billion	63	Modern industry	Modern sanitation and medical care	Mostly nonrenewable

Sources: Petterson 1960, 872; Durand 1968; Coale, 1974, 43; Boughey 1975, 251; Binyon 1999.

little respect. Europeans presently began to claim the "new" lands and expand into them (as represented in the third row of the table). This sudden increment of human carrying capacity, made available to people of the "Old World," enabled a near-tripling of total human numbers in a little over two centuries. This was so much faster than any previous population increase that growth became a perceptible aspect of human experience. Together with the obvious advantage of living with a fortuitously available carrying capacity surplus, this acceleration of change allowed people (nearly a billion of them) to expect growth and to begin equating growth with "progress."

The Industrial Revolution that followed was also equated with progress. As more and more of the things people used for their increasingly elaborate lives were made in factories with fuel-burning power-driven machines, human beings became ever more dependent on Earth's reserves of solar energy from the distant past—energy from the sun that had been captured by prehistoric vegetation, some of which got buried and was geologically transformed. These deposits were perceived not as safely sequestered carbon that would otherwise have been a troublesome component of the atmosphere, but as abundant usable fuel. Coal, petroleum, and natural gas are combustible, so "of course" people assumed burning is what they were for.

As a consequence, the doubling time for population growth was again shortened (see the fourth row of table 2.1). Even so, there were still "few enough" people so that the damage their new ways of living inflicted upon their *global* habitat remained all too neglected. But then, about the time the U.S. Civil War ended, antiseptic surgery came along as an implementation of the germ theory of disease. That understanding of one important way people get sick enabled human "death control" to emerge as an important new demographic influence—while birth control remained taboo. So population growth once again speeded up: heedless of carrying capacity limits, and ever more rapidly drawing down Earth's nonrenewable resources, particularly fossil fuels.

Shortly after the end of the Second World War, a Swiss-born energy expert at the University of California at Davis published this formula relating the size of animals to their basal metabolism:

$m = W^{3/4}\ 70$ kcal
where m = metabolic rate (kcal/day) and W = weight in kilograms

When the average weight of an animal is known, the formula can be applied to calculate (from that weight's 3/4 power) that animal's daily caloric sustenance requirement. But going the other way, if we know an animal's total daily energy use, we can solve for its apparent size (in kilograms). I applied this formula to estimates of total human energy use—by our bodies and our technological apparatus combined—in the different historic eras represented by the rows in Table 2.1. As readers could see from a chart of "Cetacean Equivalents" that I published in the journal *BioScience* seven years after *Overshoot* came out (Catton 1987), our hunting-gathering ancestors were the energy-using equivalents of common dolphins. But Americans today are each equivalent—through our direct personal, plus indirect societal, use of energy—to an adult sperm whale, a much larger species.

Alternatively, since we don't spend most of our time swimming in an ocean and since paleontologists have come to regard dinosaurs as possibly having been warm-blooded, I applied Kleiber's formula to derive another startling comparison. An American today is, on average, equivalent in energy use to a forty-one-metric-ton dinosaur. The dinosaur derived energy for its muscular activity from what it ate; we derive the energy we use for our bodies, and for the mechanical extensions by which we do many marvelous things today, from food plus fuel.

The United States is inadequately understood ecologically if seen as simply comprising some three hundred million two-legged, clothed, speaking individuals we see as fellow *Homo sapiens*. On a per capita average, Americans have become the energy-using equivalent of huge dinosaurs. And there are more than five dozen of us *Homo colossi* per square mile foraging for our sustenance, including food, fuels, and many kinds of materials. By having allowed ourselves to become so dependent on enormous quantities of energy extracted from Earth's reserves, we have reverted to being "foragers." Modern people have become not only hypernumerous but also hypervoracious. We forage on a colossal scale, and not just on territory we can legitimately claim as our own. To get the fuel and materials we "need," we now reach to other parts of the world, and even out into mile-deep ocean waters, where we set up platforms to drill two miles into the ocean bottom—as the recent calamity in the Gulf of Mexico reminded us.

Now look at table 2.2 (a modified version of table 2.1) and notice how I have separated the top three (preindustrial) rows from the fourth and fifth (industrial era) rows. The upper three rows represent the experience of "ordinary" (i.e., noncolossal) *Homo sapiens*, while the bottom two rows

Table 2.2
World population growth to six billion—by two categories of humans

	World population at start and finish of period	Average years to double	Most advanced means of subsistence	Additional special influence	Type of resources mainly relied on
Homo sapiens (non colossal)					
			Foraging		
A	35,000 BCE to 8000 BCE	3 million 8 million	18,750	Hunting and gathering		Renewable
			Farming		
B	8000 BCE to 1500 CE	8 million 350 million	1745	Agriculture		Renewable
C	1500 CE to 1800 CE	350 million 969 million	205	Agriculture	Second expansion into New World	Renewable
Homo colossus					
			Foraging again		
D	1800 CE to 1865 CE	969 million 1.4 billion	130	Modern industry	Fossil energy exploited	Some nonrenewable
E	1865 CE to 1999 CE	1.4 billion 6 billion	63	Modern industry	Modern sanitation and medical care	Mostly nonrenewable

represent the shift into the *Homo colossus* era. Our use of fossil fuels makes us a race of giants—giving us colossal per capita resource appetites and making our per capita environmental impacts also colossal.

The change from row A to row B represented a crucial advancement by our species. Previously, in row A, humans had been foragers, depending upon finding nutrients that were available to them only where nature happened to put them, in quantities that nature, not the forager, had contrived. With the advent of agriculture, when foraging was largely superseded among many groups, supplies of sustenance could (in principle) at last be made more nearly sustainable, because farming enabled some control over local ecosystem processes.

Now we can see that the change from row C to rows D and E was, in this respect, a huge step backward, even though our uncritical belief in perpetual progress has made us unable or unwilling to recognize this (Heinberg 2003). By becoming *Homo colossus* we reverted to being foragers—dependent upon *finding* vast quantities of resources we have come to need. We are subject once again to the provision of needed resources by nature's processes not under our control. Substances we have come to depend on (in ever-increasing quantities during the last two centuries) were deposited underground long ago with no regard for how many of us would be coming along with technology that required extracting and using them. Foraging by *Homo colossus* has become truly ravenous, and we have already extracted and used up the most accessible portions of Earth's carboniferous legacy. That is why, in increasingly desperate efforts to perpetuate colossal lifestyles, we have allowed our corporate agents to punch hazardous holes in the ocean bottom, working robotically under seawater two miles deep; and we have condoned other corporate bodies to destroy mountain ecosystems and pollute their human and nonhuman surroundings for our endless consumption of "black gold."

By such extravagant means, we have continued being fruitful and have further multiplied, until we now people the whole planet, in many places very densely and almost nowhere with clear-minded regard for carrying capacity limits, let alone nonhuman species. We still imagine we can use the atmosphere of this finite planet both as breathable air and as a limitless repository for the gaseous effluents from our colossal activities. Sadly, we continue to get more agitated about monetary deficits in national budgets than about the much more fundamental and devastating carrying capacity deficit in humanity's ecological budget. As the years go by, we modern people keep recklessly enlarging that deficit. We also obscure reality by talking merely of "developed" and "developing" countries, not recognizing the ominous significance of the fact that we have become two kinds of people: those equipped with a resource-hungry technological apparatus and those not so equipped (who are speedily in the process of becoming thus equipped). The planet is now being called upon to feed not only huge numbers of people but also their vast array of machines. Earth is called upon to support both *Homo colossus* and not-yet-colossal *Homo sapiens*—with most of the latter desiring transmutation to *colossus* status. Therefore, as a necessary sequel to *Overshoot*, I wrote another book arguing that we have waited too long after there was reason to know we were living with a carrying capacity deficit (Catton 2009). Humanity now faces a "bottleneck" of narrowing opportunities and the real possibility of massive die-offs due to degradation of essential ecosystem services.

Is there a basis for hope that we may yet humanely cope with the horrendous difficulties entailed in passing through the ecological bottleneck? Occasionally human beings do show a nobler side, as expressed, for example, on a bronze plaque displayed unobtrusively in all U.S. national parks. It eulogizes Stephen Mather, founding director of the National Park Service, quoting a member of Congress who stated that "there will never come an end to the good that he has done." The plaque tells park visitors that in 1916, Mather's new bureau in the Interior Department was mandated to "provide for the enjoyment of the [parks and other natural areas under its jurisdiction] in such manner and by such means as will leave them unimpaired for the enjoyment of future generations" (Albright and Schenck 1999, 275–277). This difficult task of combining use with preservation is often referred to as the dilemma of national park management. Considering national parks as areas for human recreation, this mandate was tantamount to recognizing a concept of recreational carrying capacity and managing parks' use so as to preserve all their biological, geological, and historical legacies. The dilemma would become aggravated as visitor numbers increased, with greater publicity, improved transportation, and ongoing population growth (Sontag 1990; Simon 1995).

Still, the park concept has inspired many people and helped protect many wild places, spreading around the world. Over a hundred nations have followed the American example and established national parks, protecting specimens of their natural treasures. A national parks movement became a significant part of the global environmental movement, and the establishment of new national parks and protected areas became a key tool in worldwide efforts to preserve biodiversity (Riley and Riley 2005).

Crucially, the establishment and ongoing protection of national parks has always involved an appreciation of limits to growth. Recently, for example, an opinion piece in *The Press* of Christchurch, New Zealand, argued against government plans to explore mining possibilities in that country's national parks. Such a proposal, the author contended, "confuses short-term measures of GDP with long-term national wellbeing." Minerals, he said, even if abundant, "are not the source of our national wealth," and extracting them is not what makes "New Zealand an enviable country to live in" (Hayward 2010). The writer went on to endorse views expressed in a British government report called *Prosperity without Growth* and argued that continued economic growth that focused on extraction and consumption of natural resources overlooks our planet's limits.

Despite the popularity of the national park idea, there has always been resistance to setting lands aside; that is, to significantly curtailing the possibilities for their economic exploitation. This ambivalence can be understood as an example of *cultural lag* (Ogburn 1966). As different aspects of a culture change at different rates, change in one cultural element may lag behind more rapid change in another, leading to societal maladjustments and stress among a society's members. The national park idea exemplifies ecological wisdom, but cultural lag has stalled its full implementation. And if combining preservation with use by too many people is indeed a dilemma, it is not unique to parks. We face this dilemma throughout the world, not just in the more pristine places sometimes grudgingly "set aside."

The need to inhabit our planet in a way that does not diminish its suitability—and, indeed, its beauty—for future generations has to become what we truly mean when we seek sustainability. Although sustainability may have become a buzzword in our time, it is an essential concept, and environmentalists do well to promote its use. Persistent uncertainties in our knowledge about ecosystem interconnections are no warrant for the reckless pretense of limitlessness. Limits of knowledge call for prudence, and prudence requires striving to inhabit this planet in ways that minimize damage to its future ability to support not only ourselves and our posterity but also other species upon whose coexistence we may be more dependent than we have yet learned to recognize.

Some may suppose it absurd to suggest that the future well-being of humanity could depend on thinking of the preservation ideal as a model for ensuring the future of the whole planet. Do we dare even imagine treating Earth as one big natural park? What a marvelous achievement it was when some influential people a century ago conceived the idea of conserving designated portions of this amazing world "in such manner and by such means as will leave them unimpaired for the enjoyment of future generations" (U.S. National Park Service Organic Act, qtd. in Dilsalver 1994). Must the fact that few could then imagine applying such a standard of sustainability more globally be dismissed with an "of course, we were wise not to overgeneralize"? Or will our twenty-second-century posterity look back on this century's sad undergeneralization—our failure to preserve ecosystems unimpaired—as a tragic instance of cultural lag?

BIBLIOGRAPHY

Albright, Horace, and Marian Albright Schenck. 1999. *Creating the National Park Service*. Norman: University of Oklahoma Press.

Binyon, Michael. 1999. "Now We Are Six Billion." *The Times* (London), October 13.

Boughey, Arthur. 1975. *Man and the Environment: An Introduction to Human Ecology and Evolution*. 2nd ed. New York: Macmillan.

Burger, William. 2003. *How Unique Are We?* Amherst, N.Y.: Prometheus Books.

Catton, William R., Jr. 1980. *Overshoot: The Ecological Basis of Revolutionary Change*. Urbana: University of Illinois Press.

———. 1987. "The World's Most Polymorphic Species: Carrying Capacity Transgressed Two Ways." *BioScience* 37 (June): 413–419.

———. 2009. *Bottleneck: Humanity's Impending Impasse*. Bloomington, Ind.: Xlibris.

Coale, Ansley. 1974. "The History of Human Population." *Scientific American* 231 (September): 41–51.

Dilsaver, Lary, ed. 1994. *America's National Park System: The Critical Documents*. Lanham, Md.: Rowman and Littlefield.

Durand, John. 1968. "The Modern Expansion of World Population." *Proceedings of the American Philosophical Society* 111 (June): 136–145.

Hayward, Bronwyn. 2010. "Parks Key to Kiwi Wellbeing." *The Press*, Christchurch, New Zealand, May 6.

Heinberg, Richard. 2003. *The Party's Over: Oil, War and the Fate of Industrial Societies*. Gabriola Island, B.C.: New Society.

Kleiber, Max. 1947. "Body Size and Metabolic Rate." *Physiological Reviews* 27 (October): 511–541.

Ogburn, William F. 1966. *Social Change: With Respect to Cultural and Original Nature*. New York: Dell. (Orig. pub. 1922.)

Petterson, Max. 1960. "Increase of Settlement Size and Population since the Inception of Agriculture." *Nature* 186 (June): 870–872.

Riley, Laura, and William Riley. 2005. *Nature's Strongholds: The World's Great Wildlife Reserves*. Princeton, N.J.: Princeton University Press.

Simon, Noel. 1995. *Nature in Danger: Threatened Habitats and Species*. New York: Oxford University Press.

Sontag, William, ed. 1990. *National Park Service: The First 75 Years*. Philadelphia: Eastern National Park and Monument Association.

Wilson, Edward O. 2002. *The Future of Life*. New York: Alfred A. Knopf.

CHAPTER 3

Reflections on Sustainability and Population Growth

ALBERT BARTLETT

SUSTAINABILITY

In the 1960s and 1970s, it became apparent to many thoughtful individuals that populations, resource use, and environmental degradation were increasing at rates that could not long continue. Perhaps most prominent among the publications that discussed these problems in quantitative terms was the book *Limits to Growth* (Meadows et al. 1972), which simultaneously evoked admiration and consternation. The rush to rebut the concept of limits was immediate and urgent, prompted perhaps by the thought that the message of ecological and hence economic limits was too terrible to be true.

Shortly thereafter, *sustainability* began to be spoken of as a key environmental goal. A commonly used definition of sustainability can be found in the report of the World Commission on Environment and Development (commonly called the Brundtland Commission) from 1987: "Sustainable development is development that meets the needs of the present without compromising the ability of future generations to meet their own needs" (Brundtland et al. 1987). We need to examine this statement.

"Future generations" (plural) implies "for a very long time," where "long" means "long compared to a human lifetime." This focus on good stewardship for future generations is what makes the concept appealing to environmentalists. But as we see below, steady growth of populations or resource consumption for modest periods of time leads to populations or rates of resource consumption so large as to become unmanageable, unrealistic, and ultimately impossible.

The long time implied by the concept of sustainability plus the simple arithmetic of growth lead us to the First Law of Sustainability: *Population growth and/or growth in the rates of consumption of resources cannot be sustained* (Bartlett 2006). Hence *sustainable growth*, a phrase beloved by politicians, is an oxymoron. In a world of finite size, with limited resources, sustained growth of any material thing, such as a population or an economy, is not possible. Physical objects or processes cannot grow forever in a finite world. Understanding this simple fact is central to any understanding of sustainability.

AN INTRODUCTION TO THE ARITHMETIC OF GROWTH

According to the Intergovernmental Panel on Climate Change (IPCC), population growth and economic growth are the two main causes of global climate change. As the IPCC's *Fourth Assessment Report* from 2007 puts it: "GDP/per capita and population growth were the main drivers of the increase in global emissions during the last three decades of the 20th century. . . . At the global scale, declining carbon and energy intensities have been unable to offset income effects and population growth and, consequently, carbon emissions have risen" (IPCC 2007, 107).

In fact, whether we study air pollution, water shortages, sprawl, biodiversity loss, or any other major environmental problem, we find that growth is the fundamental cause of all of them. To gain a better understanding of these problems and their possible solutions, we need to understand the fundamentals of growth.

Let's look at steady growth. This is growth in which the fractional increase in the size of a growing quantity per unit time is constant (Bartlett 2004). As an example, consider 5 percent growth per year. The 5 percent is a fixed fraction, and the "per year" is a fixed length of time. This is what we want to talk about, ordinary steady growth. The technical name for this growth is *exponential*.

Since it takes a fixed length of time to grow 5 percent, it follows that it takes a longer fixed length of time to grow 100 percent. This longer time is called the *doubling time*, T(2). We need to know how to calculate the doubling time. It's easy, using "the rule of 70"[1]:

Table 3.1

Doubling times for different rates of steady growth

Percent growth per year	Doubling time in years
Zero	Infinity
0.5	139
1.0	70
1.5	46
2.0	35
3.0	23
4.0	17
5.0	14
10.0	7.0
20.0	3.5

$$T(2) \text{ in years} = 70 \text{ / (the percent growth per year)}$$

At 5 percent growth per year, $T(2) = 70 / 5 = 14$ years. Table 3.1 gives the doubling times for several annual growth rates.

I wish we could get everyone to make this simple calculation every time we see a percent growth rate of anything. For example, if you saw a story that said crime had been growing 7 percent per year over the past ten years, you might not bat an eyelash. But if you saw a headline saying "Crime Doubles in a Decade," you would probably ask, "My heavens, what's happening?" What's happening is 7 percent growth per year. Divide the 7 into 70 and the doubling time is ten years!

Something growing 7 percent per year will double in size in ten years. It will double twice (quadruple) in size in two doubling times (twenty years), and in four doubling times (forty years) it will be $2 \times 2 \times 2 \times 2 = 16$ times its original size. In ten doubling times (one hundred years) the growing quantity will increase by a factor of $2 \times 2 \times 2 \times 2 \times 2 \times 2 \times 2 \times 2 \times 2 \times 2 = 1024$.

This last calculation shows that it's a good approximation to remember that in ten doubling times the growing quantity will grow to approximately a thousand times its initial size. One dollar in a savings account at an interest rate of 7 percent per year compounded continuously will grow in one hundred years to $1024! *The key point is that modest growth rates can produce enormous increases in just a few doubling times.* The following story makes this point nicely.

LARGE NUMBERS FROM A MODEST NUMBER OF DOUBLINGS

Legend has it that the game of chess was invented by a mathematician who worked for a king. The king was very pleased and said, "I want to reward you." "My needs are modest," the mathematician replied. "Please take my new chess board and on the first square, place one grain of wheat. On the next square, double the one to make two. On the next square, double the two to make four. Just keep doubling till you have doubled for every square; that will be an adequate payment." The king thought, "This foolish man! I was ready to give him a real reward, and all he asked for was a few grains of wheat."

How much wheat is this? We know there are eight grains on the fourth square. We can get this number, eight, by multiplying three twos together. It's 2 × 2 × 2; it's one 2 less than the number of the square. That continues for each square, so on the last square, we would find the number of grains by multiplying sixty-three 2s together.

Now let's look at the way the totals build up. When we place one grain on the first square, the total on the board is one. We add two grains on the second square and now the total on the board is three. We put four grains on the third square and now the total on the board is seven. Seven is a grain less than eight, one grain less than three 2s multiplied together. Fifteen (on the fourth square) is one grain less than four 2s multiplied together. That continues in each case, so when we are done, the total number of grains on the board will be one grain less than the number we get by multiplying sixty-four 2s together. This filling process is illustrated in table 3.2.

Now the question is, by the time we cover square sixty-four, how much wheat has our inventor accumulated? Would it make a nice pile in your living room? Would it fill your house or school? Would it cover the county to a depth of two meters? How much wheat are we talking about?

The answer is, it is roughly four hundred times the worldwide harvest of wheat in the year 2000. This could be more wheat than humans have harvested in the entire history of Earth! You ask, "How did we get such a big number?" It was simple. We started with a single grain; then we let the number grow steadily until it had doubled a mere sixty-three times. Steady growth (doubling) quickly leads to enormous numbers.

Table 3.2
Doubling on a chess board

Number of square	Grains on that square	Total grains on the board thus far
1	1	1
2	2	3
3	4	7
4	8	15
5	16	31
6	32	63
64	2^{63}	$2^{64} - 1$
n	2^{n-1}	$2^n - 1$

One key point before we leave our chessboard: *the growth in any one doubling time is greater than the total growth during all the preceding doubling times.* For example, when we put eight grains on the fourth square, eight is a larger number than the total of seven that were already on the board. When we put thirty-two grains on the sixth square, thirty-two is a larger number than the total of thirty-one that were already there. Every time the growing quantity doubles, it takes more grains to cover that square than it did to cover all the preceding squares.

This has important implications for resource use. For example, from 1870 to 1970, world production of petroleum grew steadily by approximately 7 percent per year. Because a century is about ten doublings at 7 percent annual growth, petroleum production (barrels per year) in 1970 was approximately a thousand times larger than it was a century earlier in 1870. Furthermore, in each succeeding decade of continued 7 percent annual growth, more oil was produced worldwide than had been produced in all of the previous history of steady growth of global petroleum production.

Similarly, the power of doubling has obvious implications regarding environmental stressors. We have good evidence that *current* populations, rates of consumption, and pollution levels are pushing ecosystems around the world to the breaking point and are driving many species to extinction. Further growth, no matter how slow, will make all of these problems worse, and with each continued doubling time we can expect that there will be approximately as much destruction of the environment as has happened in all preceding human history. This is clearly unsustainable.

POPULATION GROWTH

Throughout human history up to about the start of the Industrial Revolution, the worldwide birth rates and death rates were approximately equal (both were high), and consequently the growth rate of the Earth's human population was near zero. With the advent of improved medicine and sanitation, death rates dropped while birth rates remained high. This led to rapid and unprecedented growth of the human population.

The population growth rate peaked at approximately 2 percent per year around the year 1970 and has declined to approximately 1 percent per year in 2010. Even with the slowly declining growth rates, the world population is increasing by about 80 million every year (in 2010), and projections show the world population growing from about 7 billion in late 2011 to 9 to 11.5 billion in 2100. Some simple calculations can illustrate the impossibility of continuing the current growth rate of around 1 percent per year for any length of time.

Suppose that the world population growth rate had been 1 percent per year (doubling time of seventy years) since the time of the legendary Adam and Eve. A population of one person would grow to a population of about 4.3 billion in thirty-two doubling times, so a population of two (Adam and Eve) would have to double thirty-one times to become a population of 4.3 billion. Starting with a population of two, the population would grow to seven billion in a little over thirty-one doubling times. If each doubling time is seventy years (for 1 percent annual growth), then 31 × 70 = 2170 years ago would be our estimate of when Adam and Eve lived. The human species has been living for much more than 2170 years, so we conclude that the average growth rate of the Earth's human population has been much less than 1 percent per year. In fact, throughout essentially all of human history, the rate of growth of Earth's human population has been very close to 0 percent per year.

In the past two centuries, we have seen a surge in Earth's human population. Modern medicine and sanitation have caused death rates to drop below birth rates, while industrialized, fossil fuel–based agriculture has allowed nations to feed much larger populations. As of 2010, the global birth rate stood at 267 per minute with the global death rate at 108 per minute. That is a gain of 159 people per minute across the whole Earth, or about an eighty million population increase every year! But today's high world population growth rate is an anomaly, which must soon come to an end.

Earlier, we calculated doubling times based on annual percentage increases; we can also do the inverse calculation, using changes in total population size to find the rate of growth. If the population is P(o) at time t(o) and is P(1) at time t(1), then we can find the average growth rate from the following formula:

Growth rate = [100 / (t(1) − t(o))] × ln[P(1) / P(o)]

Here "ln" means "the natural logarithm" of the quantity following in square brackets.

Let's consider an example. The population of Boulder, Colorado, my hometown, was 19,999 in 1950; twenty years later, in 1970, it was 66,870. The average rate of growth of Boulder's population for this twenty-year period was

R = [100 / 20] × ln[66,870/19,999]
= 5 × ln[3.344]
= 5 × 1.207
= 6.035 percent per year

The doubling time T(2) for this rate of population growth was 70 / 6.035 = 11.48 years.

This growth rate could not continue for long, because in just ten doubling times, or 115 years, the population would be about *a thousand times* as large as it was in 1970. That is, by 2085, it would rise to over sixty-six *million* people.

There is not enough space in the Boulder Valley for this many people, nor are there the resources to serve them. Boulder's growth has slowed, and eventually it will stop. The key question people in Boulder need to ask is whether we will be able to stop the growth in a timely and sensible manner, or will we wait until there are wall-to-wall people and we are all drowning in our own effluents.

Essentially the same question confronts many towns, cities, and nations around the world. In 2010, the growth rate of the world population was a little over 1 percent per year, driven primarily by high birth rates in the developing world. The growth rate of the United States population was also a little over 1 percent per year, driven primarily by high immigration rates from some of those same countries.

Common sense and numerous declining ecological indicators suggest that this population growth, in the United States or in the world, cannot continue for long. In fact, since our population today is unsustainable, we must go further and find humane ways to make births per year come out lower than deaths per year, until the world population declines to a size that can be sustained. The key questions are, first, whether the nations of the world can choose to stabilize and then reduce their populations to a sustainable level; and, second, whether we can limit resource consumption and waste generation to levels that allow us to not just live, but live well, and to share resources generously with the other human and nonhuman inhabitants of Earth.

Most thinking people support the concept of a sustainable future. After all, given the possible harms involved, it seems only rational to try to avoid potentially disastrous ecological overshoot. But a big part of *rationality* is *numeracy*, which is the mathematical equivalent of literacy, and this kind of numeracy seems to be absent from our policy decisions.

STEADY GROWTH IN A FINITE ENVIRONMENT

Bacteria grow by doubling. One bacterium divides to become two, the two divide to become four, the four become eight, sixteen, and so on. Suppose we had bacteria that doubled in number this way every minute. Suppose we put one of these bacteria in an empty bottle at 11:00 in the morning and then observe that the bottle becomes full at precisely noon. There is our case of ordinary, steady growth, with a doubling time of one minute in the finite environment of one bottle.

Here are three questions.

First: at what time was the bottle half full? Answer: at 11:59, one minute before 12:00, because with steady growth the bacteria double in number every minute.

Second: if you were an average bacterium in that bottle, at what time would you first realize you were running out of space? Well, consider the last few minutes in the bottle. At 12:00, it's full; one minute before noon, it's half full; two minutes before noon, it's a quarter full; before that, an eighth; then a sixteenth. At five minutes before noon, when the bottle is only 3 percent full and is 97 percent open space, just yearning for development, would you realize there might be a looming problem? (In the ongoing controversy over growth in my hometown, someone wrote in to the newspaper: "Look, there's no problem with population growth in Boulder, because we have fifteen times as much open space as we've already used." But when the open space was fifteen times the amount of space that we had already used, the time in Boulder Valley was four minutes before noon.)

Now suppose that at two minutes before noon some of the bacteria realize they are running out of space, and they launch a great search for new bottles. They search offshore on the outer continental shelf and in the overthrust belt and in the Arctic, and they find three new bottles. That is an incredible discovery; it's three times the total amount of resource they had ever known about. They now have four bottles, where before their discovery there was only one. Surely this will help them create a sustainable society, won't it?

Now for my third question: how long can growth continue as a result of this magnificent discovery? Well, look at the score; at 12:00, one bottle is filled, there are three to go; 12:01, two bottles are filled, there are two to go; and at 12:02, all four are filled, and that's the end of the line.

You do not need any more arithmetic than this to evaluate the absolutely contradictory statements that we have all heard from politicians, who tell us in one breath that we can go on increasing our populations, our effluents, our rates of consumption of fossil fuels or water, and in the next breath they say, "Don't worry, we will always be able to discover the new resources and technologies that we will need to meet the requirements of that growth."

A little arithmetic is all that is needed to show that "sustainable growth" is an impossibility. But this seems beyond most politicians and most sustainability "experts," who advocate all manner of efficiency improvements which, taken together, cannot achieve sustainability, because they do not include stopping growth in population and rates of consumption (Bartlett 2008). See the First Law of Sustainability.

AND A LITTLE GEOMETRY

There was a time, long ago, when people thought that the Earth was flat, but now for several centuries we have known that the Earth is spherical. However, there are problems with a spherical Earth. A sphere is finite in extent, which implies limits. In particular, it implies that there are limits to growth of the things that live on the Earth and consume its resources. Today, many people believe that the resources of the Earth and the powers of the human intellect are so enormous that population growth can continue indefinitely and that there is no danger that we will ever run out of anything.

Perhaps our greatest proponent of limitlessness was the late economist Julian Simon (1981). In one article, he wrote:

> Technology exists now to produce in virtually inexhaustible quantities just about all the products made by nature—foodstuffs, oil, even pearls and diamonds . . .

> We have in our hands now—actually in our libraries—the technology to feed, clothe and supply energy to an ever-growing population for the next 7 billion years . . .

> Even if no new knowledge were ever gained . . . we would be able to go on increasing our population forever. (Simon 1995)

This is nonsense, of course. Even one *million* years of 1 percent population growth—let alone seven billion—would lead to more people than the estimated number of all the atoms in the known universe (Bartlett 1996). But this nonsense is widespread and bipartisan among politicians and policymakers.

After a United Nations report predicted future shortages of natural resources because of continued population growth, Jack Kemp, secretary of the Department of Housing and Urban Development under President George H. W. Bush, is reported to have said: "Nonsense, people are not a drain on the resources of the planet" (*High Country News* 1992).

Lawrence Summers, Treasury secretary in the Clinton administration (and later chief economic advisor to President Obama) stated that the administration "cannot and will not accept any 'speed limit' on American economic growth. It is the task of economic policy to grow the economy as rapidly, sustainably, and inclusively as possible" (McKibben 2007, 9). Note the oxymoronic implication of this assertion.

These people believe that perpetual growth is desirable; consequently, it must be possible. A friend recently returned from an international conference in Germany and reported that whenever he brought up the subject of limits, the angry rebuttal was: "We're tired of hearing of limits to growth! We're going to grow the limits!"

A spherical Earth is finite and hence unappealing to the devotees of perpetual growth. In contrast, a flat Earth can accommodate growth forever, because a flat Earth can be infinite in the two horizontal dimensions and also in the vertical downward direction. The infinite horizontal dimensions forever remove any fear of crowding as population grows, and leave plenty of habitats for other species, somewhere "out there." The infinite downward dimension assures people an unlimited supply of all of the minerals, fossil fuels, and other raw materials that will be needed by a human population that continues to grow forever. The flat Earth removes any need for worry about limits.

So, let us think of the proponents of "sustainable growth," the "we're going to grow the limits!" people, as members of the New Flat Earth Society. After all, a flat Earth is the only Earth that has the potential to allow the human population to grow indefinitely.

NOTES

I wish to thank Phil Cafaro for guidance and patience as I prepared this text.

1. Where, you might ask, does the 70 come from? The answer is that it is approximately 100 multiplied by the natural logarithm of two ($100 \times \ln 2 = 69.3 = \sim 70$). To find the time for the growing quantity to triple in size, you would use the natural logarithm of three. If you would like to work through the mathematics in detail, see "The Arithmetic of Growth: Methods of Calculation" (Bartlett 1993), which is available at www.albartlett.org.

BIBLIOGRAPHY

Bartlett, A. A. 1993. "The Arithmetic of Growth: Methods of Calculation." *Population and Environment* 14: 359–387.

———. 1996. "The New Flat Earth Society." *Physics Teacher* 34 (6): 342–343.

———. 2004. *The Essential Exponential: For the Future of Our Planet.* Lincoln: Center for Science, Mathematics and Computer Education, University of Nebraska.

———. 2006. "Reflections on Sustainability, Population Growth and the Environment." In *The Future of Sustainability*, edited by Marco Keiner, 17–37. Dordrecht: Springer.

———. 2008. "Why Have Scientists Succumbed to Political Correctness?" *Teachers Clearinghouse for Science and Society Education* 27 (Spring): 21.

Brundtland, G. H., et al. 1987. *Our Common Future.* (Report of the World Commission on Environment and Development.) Oxford: Oxford University Press.

High Country News. 1992. Paonia, Colo., January 27: 4.

Intergovernmental Panel on Climate Change (IPCC). 2007. *Climate Change 2007: Mitigation: Technical Summary.* Cambridge: Cambridge University Press.

McKibben, Bill. 2007. *Deep Economy: The Wealth of Communities and the Durable Future.* New York: Henry Holt Books.

Meadows, Donella H., et al. 1972. *Limits to Growth.* New York: Universe Books.

Simon, Julian. 1981. *The Ultimate Resource.* Princeton. N.J.: Princeton University Press.

———. 1995. "The State of Humanity: Steadily Improving." *Cato Policy Report* 17 (5).

CHAPTER 4

Why the Silence on Population?

MARTHA CAMPBELL

I N THE 1960S AND 70S much attention was paid to the world's rapidly growing human population. The number of people on this planet
stood at three billion in 1960 and doubled before the end of the century.
By 2050 that number is projected to expand to between 8 and 10.5 billion
people. In spite of this rapid change, little media or policy attention has
been paid to population growth since the 1980s, and since 1994 the subject
has all but disappeared from the press and academia, even regarding the
circumstances and projections of the fastest growing countries.

By 2050 Uganda is projected to grow from 33.8 million to 91.3 million, Niger from 16 to 58 million, and Afghanistan from 29 to 73 million
(PRB 2010). Asia will add 430 million people between 2010 and 2020—a
single decade. India is growing by over a million people every 23 days
(UNPD 2009); nearly all this growth is in the lowest-income regions of the
country, where the level of nutrition available to the poor has not changed
over the last 15 or 20 years. In 1950 Pakistan had a total population of
41 million (UNPD 2009); today it is 185 million and projected to grow to
335 million by 2050 (PRB 2010). The implications for water needs in this
largely arid country, only 20% larger than Texas, are a serious concern. In
1900 Ethiopia had 5 million people, in 1950 it had 18.4 million, and in
2000 it had 65.5 million (UNPD 2009). By 2010 Ethiopia had a population
of 85 million, and it is projected to reach 173 million by 2050—nearly a
tenfold increase in one century (PRB 2010). This rapid population growth
has played a major role in the decimation of nearly all of Ethiopia's forests
and consequently in its climate change.

In some ways lack of attention to population has been combined with actual hostility toward raising the population question. Many young people on university campuses have been taught over the past 15 years that the connection between population growth and the environment is not an acceptable subject for discussion. Indeed, in many circles it is politically incorrect to say that slowing population growth will help to make it possible to preserve the environment for future generations. The question is why, and the answer is far from simple, although some generalizations are possible (Campbell 1998).

A DELICATE, MISUNDERSTOOD SUBJECT

Population growth, which I will refer to in this paper as simply population, has always been a delicate, easily misunderstood subject, because it involves sex, reproduction, cultures, religion, and severe inequities around the world. The global population has been growing rapidly over the past 200 years. In 1999 the population was 6 billion, rising to 7 billion by late 2011 (table 4.1). The rapid population growth over the past 200 years has been driven by increased survival, and not by higher fertility. More babies, children, as well as adults have survived because of improved nutrition, cleaner water, better hygiene, and vaccination. Improved nutrition included new forms of transportation, mainly trains, which could carry farm produce to where people lived. Canals and railroads were important for reducing local famines. Improved hygiene was driven by new knowledge about bacteria and disease. Looking at the driving forces of population growth, on the whole, what occurred during this 200-year period was the arrival of new and welcome technologies, as well as information for improving health and increasing survival.

The new technologies and information that dramatically reduced mortality have not spurred controversy. Everyone wants to save children's lives. But the idea of enabling women to have control over their childbearing is widely treated as a sensitive, often controversial subject. For this reason, access to technologies, information, and even the scientific underpinning of the technologies that women need to manage their own fertility has been severely constrained (Potts 2003). In many countries these are still difficult for many women to obtain today.

The fact that the world's population of 3 billion people in 1960 may triple to 9 billion by 2050 has received little public attention over nearly

Table 4.1
Population growth over the last 210 years

Year	Population	Time needed to add the next billion
1800	1 billion	~200,000 years
1930	2 billion	130 years
1960	3 billion	30 years
1975	4 billion	15 years
1987	5 billion	12 years
1999	6 billion	12 years
2011	7 billion	12 years

Source: Scheidel 2003.

two decades. There are six reasons for this silence, which together might be seen as a "perfect storm": visibility of actual fertility decline in the developed countries as well as a number of the developing ones; well-justified attention to the impact of high levels of consumption on the environment; an implicit welcome by conservative political and religious forces to reduced needs for family planning; the tragedy of AIDS dominating international health concerns; the 1994 Cairo conference's focus on examples of coercive family planning, while largely overlooking the coercion of women forced into unwanted childbearing; and the popular assumption in standard demographic theory that couples naturally want many children. This sixth, theoretical reason for the silence has made it difficult to see the many barriers blocking women's options for managing their childbearing. In what follows, I explore these six reasons for the recent silence on population, which together have worked to obscure population growth as a social and environmental problem.

A PERFECT STORM

First, as a whole, birth rates have fallen around the world (figure 4.1), and this change has frequently been reported in the press. In many developing countries, family planning programs have had a real impact since the 1950s, bringing down the world's fertility from 5.5 to 2.5 children per woman (PRB 2010). (In this paper, the term "fertility" is used in the demographic sense, meaning "the number of children born to a woman," in contrast to its biological meaning of "the ability to reproduce.") Average family size

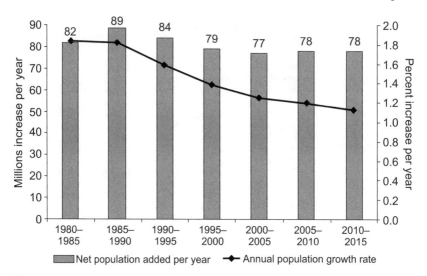

Figure 4.1
Trends in world population growth, 1980–2015
Source: UNPD 2010.

has fallen to very low levels in Europe and Japan, and much media attention has focused on the challenge of an aging population structure.

Second, patterns of overconsumption are a highly visible factor adversely affecting the environment and natural resources—including greenhouse gas emissions, deforestation, and biodiversity losses. It is easy to see that we need to consume less. It is more difficult for most people to recognize the effect of population growth on the environment and its connection with increased consumption.

Many people argue that consumption in the developed world, rather than population growth in the developing world, causes environmental decline. To a large extent, and concerning certain impacts (including climate change), they are correct. However, population is an important factor as well, and in some places it is the principal driver of resource loss and environmental stress. The Nile is an excellent case in point. The demand for water is increasing in all ten countries of the Nile Basin, as these countries all have agricultural economies and rapidly growing populations (table 4.2).

The Blue Nile from Ethiopia and the White Nile from Uganda merge at Khartoum, Sudan, and by the time this great river reaches the Mediterranean it is severely depleted. The populations of Ethiopia, Sudan, and the remaining countries in the Nile Basin together are projected to double by

Table 4.2
Actual and projected population sizes (in millions) of countries of the Nile Basin

Country	2010	2025	2050
Burundi	8.5	11.6	16.8
Democratic Republic of Congo	67.8	101.4	166.3
Egypt	80.4	103.6	137.7
Eritrea	5.2	7.4	10.8
Ethiopia	85	119.8	173.8
Kenya	40.1	51.3	65.2
Rwanda	10.4	15.8	28.3
Sudan	43.2	56.7	75.9
Tanzania	45	67.4	109.5
Uganda	33.8	53.4	91.3
Total	419.4	588.4	875.6

Source: PRB 2010.

2050, and the amount of Nile water available for Egypt is likely to decline. Various studies have produced a range of possibilities from an 80% decline by the year 2060 to an actual gain of 22% if global warming results in more rainfall in the region (Sokka 2004, 2; King 2006, 15). The difficulty is that Egypt's population is also growing rapidly, as an earlier decline in the fertility rate has stalled at about 3.0, and projections show that the population will go from 80 million in 2010 to 137 million in 2050 (PRB 2010).

Population is the multiplier of everything we do and everything we consume. While we need to consume less, it is actually easier to change family size around the world than it is to change patterns of consumption. There is a large unmet need for family planning today, while it is likely to take a long time for people to *want* to reduce their consumption. The trend is moving in the opposite direction: people everywhere aspire to consumer lifestyles, and the global consumer class is on the rise.

The third element contributing to the perfect storm of silence has a very different origin. Anti-abortion activists, religious leaders, and conservative think tanks have been influential in reducing attention to population growth. They tend to welcome the idea perpetrated in the media—namely, that the population explosion is "over" (Lutz, Sanderson, and Scherbov 2001). It is also worth remembering that the most extreme and vocal advocates against abortion are not supportive of family planning.

The fourth reason that contributed to silence about population has been the sheer scale of the AIDS epidemic that captured the world's attention. People often cynically ask, isn't AIDS "taking care of" the population growth problem? The answer is no. In Uganda (population 5 million in 1950) fertility is 6.5 per woman, and in spite of the AIDS epidemic the population is expected to rise to over 91.3 million by 2050 (PRB 2010). Eight countries in Southern or East Africa have an HIV prevalence in the adult population estimated to be 12% or more (PRB 2009). In six of these (Botswana, South Africa, Namibia, Swaziland, Zimbabwe, and Lesotho), fertility has also fallen, and thus population growth is now modest and may become negative. In the remaining two (Zambia and Mozambique) fertility is still high and population growth is close to 2% per annum (Cleland 2006).

Even if the demographic impact of HIV/AIDS were greater, solving a problem one dying parent at a time, one dying child at a time, is not any kind of solution we would welcome. Indeed, strong advocacy for family planning is driven by the desire to avert catastrophic events like famine, disease, and conflict that are exacerbated, or made more probable, by population growth. In all of the fast-growing countries there is a well-documented need for family planning, which is often difficult for many women to obtain. Two hundred and fifteen million women around the world do not want another child either ever or in the next two years, but are not using modern contraception (Singh et al. 2009).

The fifth factor in this "perfect storm" concerns certain policy developments. The 1994 United Nations International Conference on Population and Development (ICPD, or "Cairo" for short) was the turning point in removing the population subject from policy discourse. The important difference between Cairo and the previous decadal UN population conferences was its emphasis on the needs of women around the world, especially low-income women in low-resource settings. In the run-up to the two-week conference in Cairo, talking about population became politically incorrect in many circles. Drawing attention to any connection between population growth and environmental destruction became taboo—again, because such a connection was viewed, or promoted, as disadvantageous to women. It became inappropriate to say that slowing population growth will make it more possible to preserve the environment for future generations and reduce poverty. "Malthusian" and even "demographic" became derogatory terms describing anyone still concerned about population growth.

Cairo recognized that in many societies large numbers of women are marginalized, often lacking equal treatment under the law, separated from educational and economic opportunities, doing large portions of the agricultural work while lacking the freedom to own or control property, and too often being victims of domestic violence. As part of the Cairo effort to help women, attention was also drawn to episodes of coercion in family planning for which there was a history in India in the 1970s and in China's one-child policy later. Ironically, the domestic and cultural coercion women experience when they cannot have control over how many children to have, or whether to have children and when, has been far more overlooked than government-driven coercion in family planning programs. The strategy adopted at Cairo for addressing issues about pregnancy and childbearing was to combine family planning with all aspects of health that are particular to women, calling it "reproductive health." The leadership of this movement promoted the new language of reproductive health in lieu of family planning, which was now to be subsumed under this new term. Intentionally or inadvertently, they promoted the idea that all family planning efforts before 1994 were "coercive," labeling them "population control," a term henceforth viewed as purely derogatory. Addressing a hearing of the UK Parliament on Population and the Millennium Development Goals, the President of the International Planned Parenthood Federation said of the Cairo conference, "the taboo about population . . . was the result of a mythology . . . that equated population policies with coercion" (Sinding 2006).

A strategy that was meant to improve women's health led to a false generalization about all past efforts in family planning, entirely incongruent with the good work of more than a hundred family planning associations (FPAS) around the world, which had been established and organized long before 1994. In reality, the vast majority of the national family planning programs were designed to make obtaining family planning easier for women and men, not to force them to control their fertility. The concerted effort among the FPAS since the 1950s was often instigated by relatively rich women who already enjoyed the privilege of being able to manage their family size, and who were painfully aware that the poor women around them had no such option.

The shift of language from family planning to reproductive health, in particular, contributed to the substantial reduction of financial support for family planning budgets in foreign aid agencies. The term "reproductive health" was well understood in the broad women's health movement, and in agencies working in these international arenas, but it was less well understood, and more difficult to identify with, in the U.S. Congress, European parliaments, and even the broad public. A survey of insiders in the field of population studies sought to understand factors contributing to the declining international visibility of the family planning movement, and found that the term "reproductive health" was neither a well-defined nor a compelling concept (Blanc and Tsui 2005).

The strategy to promote silence on population and family planning was meant to benefit women's health and well-being. However, this strategy may well have been counterproductive to both sets of goals, as access to family planning options did not expand with growth in the number of women who wanted them, and women's reproductive rights and choices have thus not been implemented on a large scale. After Cairo, in a number of countries the disparity in fertility rates between the richest and poorest economic quintiles increased (Fotso 2006). While Cairo may have produced some benefits, expansion of access to family planning was not among them. This has been a serious failure, as the "ability of women to control their own fertility is absolutely fundamental to women's empowerment and equality" (UKDID 2006).

The sixth factor deflecting attention from population concerns has been classic demographic transition theory (Potts and Campbell 2005). Ironically, the dominant paradigm in understanding human fertility decline has helped to write population growth off the public agenda, out of public discussion, and generally out of sight. This paradigm has implicitly fostered the idea that couples around the world have always wanted many children, and that the only way they change their minds is when some change occurs in their societies. The assumption is that when people become wealthier or more educated then change occurs, and somehow couples will shift their predilection for many children in favor of a smaller family size. The belief that it is "natural" for couples to want many children leads to the inference that they have to be induced to want a smaller family. And this belief fuels the apprehension of entering the slippery slope toward "population control," implying some form of inappropriate persuasion, or even outright coercion.

The classic theory of the demographic transition (attempting to explain the shift from high mortality and fertility, to lower mortality while fertility stayed high, followed by the eventual decline in fertility) was that some external force was required to induce people to have smaller families. This theoretical framework for understanding fertility decline was accepted in the 1950s and has been adhered to tenaciously, even in the face of numerous exceptions to the basic model. The widely accepted assumption built into this theory is that the last stage of the demographic transition to lower fertility occurred when factors of modernization, such as urbanization, caused a reduction in parents' natural desire for many children (Notestein 1953). Over time, aspects of modernization other than urbanization have variously been seen by demographers as the main instigators of this change, including socio-economic change, education, and opportunities for women's employment.

At the core of the classic theory was the assumption that the demand for limiting family size was necessarily a change brought about by some societal shift exogenous to the personal experience of the parents making reproductive decisions. The justification for this paradigm was provided through innumerable comparisons of fertility decline and large datasets describing socio-economic growth and related modernization factors, showing significant correlation, which was interpreted as causality. But as family planning spread in East Asia and Latin America in the 1970s and 1980s, more and more exceptions to the demographic transition theory arose.

Like the geocentric model of the universe before Copernicus, the classic explanation of fertility decline has been sinking under the weight of an ever-increasing number of anomalies. For example, this classic explanation does not explain why surveys show that women's desired family size on average declines ahead of the decline of actual family size. The demographic transition model does not explain why where family planning is made easy to obtain, as in Thailand, women with no education use birth control as much as educated women; while in the Philippines, where the government makes family planning hard to get—largely because of the influence of the Catholic church—uneducated women have a very low use of contraception. Demographic transition theory also does not mesh well with the biology of human reproduction, where, because of frequent sexual intercourse of couples in virtually all societies, easy access to fertility regulation methods is simply a requirement to reduce average family size (Potts 1997).

The barriers standing between low-income women and effective family planning include the sheer absence of important method options in clinics in 96 countries; a large number of medical rules and practices not based

on medical evidence which make contraception difficult for women to obtain (such as unnecessary tests before contraception is permitted); provider
bias wherein women are often given incorrect and inadequate information about birth control; insufficient supplies of contraceptive commodities; national rules against sterilization (even though a number of Muslim
countries, including Iran and Bangladesh, offer this option); old colonial
abortion laws brought to Africa in the 19th century and never changed
while the colonizers changed their own in Europe; the prescription status
of oral contraceptives, which is not needed for safety purposes; and misin-
formation—mainly the widely held, incorrect belief by many uneducated
women that contraception is more dangerous than another pregnancy
(Campbell, Sahin-Hodoglugil, and Potts 2006; Campbell and Bedford
2009). Social and cultural pressures play a significant role as well, but they
appear to have less influence on women once contraception becomes easily
available and socially normal.

Many things we have now in our consumer lives—from photocopy
machines to garage door openers and television remote controls—we did
not want until they showed up as real, available options (Campbell 2006).
Women's decision-making processes around the use of family planning,
and around having a smaller family, may well follow a similar "consumer"
pattern. In brief: when accessible and affordable family planning services
are brought to women, and these services become the new norm within
their societies, women use them and fertility rates decline.

Because of the very large number of barriers to fertility regulation, and
the low birth rates that ensue wherever these barriers are removed, there
is good reason to suspect that the principle driver of fertility decline is
simply relatively easy access to the means and information women need to
manage their own fertility. Childbirth has been dangerous since time im-
memorial, and maternal mortality rates are extremely high in low-resource
settings. It is logical to believe that virtually all women would like to have
some control over their own childbearing.

BREAKING THE SPIRAL OF SILENCE

It is important to ask: Which among the six reasons for the silence on
population growth are most amenable to change? One thing we should
recognize is that *perceptions* of current situations, easily derived from the
way the situations are presented in the press, are often more important
than the realities on the ground. Thus, regarding the first reason, attention

to the substantial fall in birth rates around the world has not been accompanied in the press by news that fertility in the world's poorest countries, such as Niger, Uganda, and Nigeria, is persistently high. Much has been written on poverty since 1994, but with little mention of the population growth factor. This has started to change in the UK since the 2007 release of the report of the UK Parliamentary hearings on population growth in low-income countries in connection with the Millennium Development Goals (APPG 2007). It includes expert testimony that no country (with the exception of a small number of anomalous oil-rich states) has gotten out of poverty while maintaining high fertility rates.

The second reason for the silence, that the impacts of high levels of consumption on the environment are more visible than the effects of population growth, is similarly spurred by the absence of public information that population growth is a major factor in the competition among Egypt, Ethiopia, and Sudan for the waters of the Nile; among Turkey, Syria, and Iraq for the Euphrates, and at least 6 other large anticipated trouble spots around the world over the critical resource of water. This situation could be changed if we could educate the media to see the role of population growth in these trouble spots.

Anti-abortion activists, religious leaders, and conservative think tanks, which represent reason three for the silence on population, appear intransigent in their beliefs and related values about population. But the rest of the world is not as fanatical as these groups in the United States, and some important changes are occurring in Ethiopia, Colombia, Portugal, and Mexico City, which have all recently liberalized their abortion laws.

Regarding the fourth reason, some people have observed that attention to the AIDS problem grew when advocates for therapeutic drugs for HIV-infected people developed an effective strategy: they recognized that parliaments and foreign aid agencies cared less about health than about poverty, and thus centered their publicity on the effect of the disease on poverty. John Cleland and Steven Sinding pointed out in *The Lancet* that population growth might have an even larger harmful impact on poverty in Africa than AIDS (Cleland and Sinding 2005). We cannot know where this debate will lead, but it seems reasonable that as the connection between high fertility and poverty becomes better understood, attention to the population factor will follow.

The fifth element in the "perfect storm" involves policy decisions which will support the empowerment of women. Their success, however, will partly depend on recognizing and discussing the connections between population growth, the very large unmet need for family planning in many countries, in addition to the more widely recognized need for women's rights. This change is happening gradually, but the velocity depends on reducing the influence of the sixth contributor to silence, namely, the theoretical framework which currently guides (I believe incorrectly) how people think about population. As long as the received theory of the demographic transition remains the basis of public understanding, it will be easy to continue seeing population levels and family planning as derivative outcomes of other changes, and unacceptable subjects for candid discourse and active policy planning.

It is important not to wait for modernization processes to influence the shift toward smaller families—while the world's population burgeons, along with its global and local destructive effects. But if, in contrast, we can show that what is required to reduce fertility is not coercion, but freedom for women to have control over whether and when to have a child, then the silence can end once and for all, and the need for policies that enable women to manage their child-bearing decisions can come to the fore.

The close link between absence of media communication and misperceptions that initiated that silence easily converted into a spiral of silence (Noelle-Newman 1984; Brasted 2007). The challenge is to break the spiral with greater clarity, showing that:

(1) Continuing population growth in the world's poorest countries makes it impossible to escape from poverty and ecological degradation;

(2) High fertility is not due to women's desire to subject themselves repeatedly to the extremely dangerous process of childbirth; and

(3) Fertility can decline when women are given the freedom to have control over their childbearing—which strengthens their own health and the health and wellbeing of their living children as well.

A WIN-WIN STRATEGY

Use of family planning prevents death from unintended pregnancies and from induced abortions. There is excellent evidence that, given the same level of health care, a child born less than 18 months after a sibling has a death rate *two to four* times that of a baby born after a longer interval (Rutstein 2005). Children from smaller families are more likely to enter and stay in school, even when all other socio-economic variables are fixed (Knodel and Woogsith 1991). There is also a new recognition that falling fertility offers an economic dividend (Birdsall, Kelly, and Sinding 2001), as countries no longer need to support the health and educational needs of ever greater numbers of children; and that it is difficult or impossible for any developing country to escape from poverty while fertility remains high (APPG 2007). Given the benefits of family planning to women, to their children, and to preserving the environment, we hope to see the day very soon when the silence on population can be ended and the subject will be addressed openly and with the compassion it deserves.

NOTE

This chapter is reprinted from the article of the same name with kind permission of Springer Science and Business Media, from *Population and Environment* 28, nos. 4–5 (2007): 237–246. I wish to express my thanks to Rachel Weinrib for her assistance in preparing this revised manuscript.

BIBLIOGRAPHY

All Party Parliamentary Group on Population, Development and Reproductive Health (APPG). 2007. *Return of the Population Factor: Its Impact on the Millennium Development Goals.* London: House of Commons.

Birdsall, N., A. C. Kelly, and S. Sinding, eds. 2001. *Population Matters: Demographic Change, Economic Growth, and Poverty in the Third World.* London: Oxford University Press.

Blanc, A. K., and A. O. Tsui. 2005. "The Dilemma of Past Success: Insiders' Views on the Future of the International Family Planning Movement." *Studies in Family Planning* 36 (4): 263.

Brasted, M. 2007. "Protest in the Media." *Peace Review* 17 (4): 383–388.

Campbell, M. 1998. "Schools of Thought: An Analysis of Interest Groups Influential in International Population Policy." *Population and Environment* 19 (6): 487–512.

———. 2006. "Consumer Behavior and Contraceptive Decisions: Resolving a Decades-Long Puzzle." *Journal of Family Planning and Reproductive Health Care* 32 (4): 241–244.

Campbell, M., and K. Bedford. 2009. "The Theoretical and Political Framing of the Population Factor in Development." *Philosophical Transactions of the Royal Society B* 364: 3101–3113.

Campbell, M., N. Sahin-Hodoglugil, and M. Potts. 2006. "Barriers to Fertility Regulation: A Review of the Literature." *Studies in Family Planning* 37 (2): 87–98.

Cleland, J. 2006. Oral testimony in U.K. All-Party Parliamentary Group Hearings. May 8. Transcripts available from www.appg-popdevrh.org.uk.

Cleland, J., and S. Sinding. 2005. "Viewpoint: What Would Malthus Say about AIDS in Africa?" *Lancet* 366 (9500): 1899–1901.

Fotso, J. 2006. "The African Population and Health Research Center (APHRC), Kenya." Oral evidence to All Party Parliamentary Group on Population, Development and Reproductive Health, June, p. 6. Transcripts available from www.appg-popdevrh.org.uk.

King, David. 2006. Oral evidence to All Party Parliamentary Group on Population, Development and Reproductive Health. July 3.

Knodel, J., and M. Woogsith. 1991. "Family Size and Children's Education in Thailand: Evidence from a National Sample." *Demography* 28: 119–131.

Lutz, W., W. C. Sanderson, and S. Scherbov. 2001. "The End of World Population Growth." *Nature* 412: 543–545.

Noelle-Newman, E. 1984. *Spiral of Silence: Public Opinion—Our Social Skin*. Chicago: University of Chicago Press.

Notestein, F. 1953. "Economic Problems of Population Change." *Proceedings of the Eighth International Conference of Agricultural Economists*. London: Oxford University Press. 13–31.

Population Reference Bureau (PRB). 2009. *2009 World Population Data Sheet*. Accessed from www.prb.org/DataFinder.aspx.

———. 2010. *2010 World Population Data Sheet*. Accessed from www.prb.org/DataFinder.aspx.

Potts, M. 1997. "Sex and the Birth Rate: Human Biology, Demographic Change, and Access to Fertility-Regulation Methods." *Population and Development Review* 23 (1): 1–39.

———. 2003. "Two Pills, Two Paths: A Tale of Gender Bias." *Endeavor* 27: 127–130.

Potts, M., and M. Campbell. 2005. "Reverse Gear: Dependence on a Disappearing Paradigm." *Journal of Reproduction and Contraception* 16 (3): 179–186.

Rutstein, S. O. 2005. "Effects of Preceding Birth Intervals on Neonatal, Infant and under Five Years Mortality and Nutritional Status in Developing Countries: Evidence from the Demographic and Health Surveys." *International Journal of Gynaecology and Obstetrics* 89, Suppl. 1: s7–24.

Scheidel, W. 2003. "Ancient World, Demography of." In *Encyclopedia of Population*, edited by P. Demeny and G. McNicoll. New York: Macmillan Reference. 1: 44–48.

Sinding, S. 2006. Oral testimony in U.K. All-Party Parliamentary Group Hearings. May 8. Transcripts available from www.appg-popdevrh.org.uk.

Singh, S., J. E. Darroch, L. S. Ashford, and M. Vlassoff. 2009. "Adding It Up: The Costs and Benefits of Investing in Family Planning and Maternal and Newborn Health." New York: Guttmacher Institute and United Nations Population Fund.

Sokka, L. 2004. "Population Network Newsletter." *Popnet*, no. 36, Autumn.

United Kingdom Department for International Development (UKDID). 2006. Written evidence to All Party Parliamentary Group on Population, Development and Reproductive Health. March, p. 16. Accessed from www.appg -popdevrh.org.uk.

United Nations Population Division (UNPD). 2009. "World Population Prospects: The 2008 Revision." New York: United Nations, Department of Economic and Social Affairs.

United Nations Population Division (UNPD). 2010. "World Population Prospects: The 2010 Revision." New York: United Nations, Department of Economic and Social Affairs.

CHAPTER 5

The Great Backtrack

DAVE FOREMAN

> *Unlike plagues of the dark ages or contemporary diseases we*
> *do not yet understand, the modern plague of overpopulation*
> *is soluble by means we have discovered and with resources*
> *we possess. What is lacking is not sufficient knowledge of*
> *the solution but universal consciousness of the gravity of the*
> *problem and education of the billions who are its victims.*
> —Rev. Martin Luther King Jr., 1966

UNLOOKED-FOR but swift, we have come on like a swarm of locusts: a wide, thick, darkling cloud settling down like living snowflakes, smothering every stalk, every leaf, eating away every scrap of green down to raw, bare, wasting earth.

It's painfully straightforward. There are too many men for Earth to harbor.[1] At nearly seven billion of us, we have overshot Earth's carrying capacity. The Man swarm yet swells like the black, living, withering mouthclouds that have ransacked fields since the first digging stick scratched a line in dirt. The crippling of Earth's life support system by such a flood of upright apes is bad news for us.

But it is much worse news for the other Earthlings—animals and plants, wildeors and worts—who are taking a far worse beating than are we for our devil-may-care childishness and greed.[2] Long ago we overshot Earth's carrying capacity for keeping wild things hale and hearty. For many years it has been the booming and spreading overflow of naked apes that has been the greatest threat to brimming, many-fold life on Earth. The bedrock work of conservation—shielding wildlands and keeping all kinds of wildlife alive—is impossible without freezing and then lowering the population of Man.

Soon after I was born, Aldo Leopold, to my mind the top conservation thinker of the twentieth century, wrote in the beginning of his wonderful book *A Sand County Almanac*, "[T]here are those who can live without wild things, and there are those who cannot." For as long as I can recall, I've been one of those cannots. I have no wish to live in a world without wild things.

More of our kind means fewer wild things. A stabilized human population means hope for wild things. A shrinking human population means a better world for wild things. And for men and women and children. Population stabilization should be a bedrock conservation and environmental care—once again.

WHY THE RETREAT?

Over the last thirty years, there have been many shifts in the conservation, environmental, and resource camps. Maybe the most striking and deep rooted is that these camps worked hard to spotlight the booming Man swarm in the 1960s and 1970s, yet today overpopulation worry is kicked into the corner and shunned like an old, smelly dog. This is a tectonic shift.

In today's world, population growth is overlooked as the mainspring of ecological and social woes. I've been clipping news stories about wretchedness and starvation in Africa for a long while. Most of these reports don't tip a hat to population growth as the root (or even a rootlet) or look at how population stabilization could help lessen the woes. In the fall of 2005 there was much ado about starvation in Niger. Left unsaid about this forlorn land was that according to the United Nations, it has the highest birthrate in the world. The beaten-down souls highlighted in the news all seemed to have nine kids more or less. Could this have anything to do with why Niger was a heartbreaking, hopeless wreck? It didn't seem as though any of the reporters were asking.

Likewise, environmentalists in the United States lambaste suburban and exurban sprawl, as they should. But do they acknowledge that over half of sprawl is driven by population growth, that the United States is the only big, wealthy land with third-world growth rates, and that our growth is mostly goosed along by immigration? Not that I've heard lately. This head-in-the-sand mood showed itself further in the fall of 2006 when the United States snapped the three-hundred-million-head wire. Environmentalists and conservationists should have been marching in the streets to warn that we must freeze our population and stop growth. But those who should understand that there are limits to growth mostly overlooked this frightful benchmark. When environmentalists did say something about it, they seemed to shrug it off as small potatoes. A spokesperson for the Environmental Defense Fund said that population growth itself wasn't what was wrong, that it was where people chose to live (*New York Times* 2006). I shook my head in disbelief. No, that's not true. I yelled at the paper, balled it up in my hands, and threw it against the wall, cussing up a blue streak all the while. Later, I smoothed it out so I could clip the article. There are more than one or two articles in my files that look like they've gone through the same treatment.

How far conservationists and environmentalists have come from what now seem to me to be the golden years of the 1960s and 1970s. If conservationists are going to keep the wildworld, we must deeply and truthfully ask why we've backed away from the overpopulation fight.

Historian Samuel Hays, in his landmark book *Beauty, Health, and Permanence*, wrote that in the 1970s, "It was rather widely agreed that population growth should be limited" (1987, 224). Widely, indeed; good heavens, former president Eisenhower in 1968 said, "Once, as president, I thought and said that birth control was not the business of our Federal Government. The facts changed my mind. . . . I have come to believe that the population explosion is the world's most critical problem." Keep in mind that Ike said this as Vietnam was blowing up and when the Cold War was about as hot as it got. Three years earlier, President Lyndon Johnson had told the United Nations that "five dollars invested in population control is worth one hundred dollars invested in economic growth" (Ehrlich and Ehrlich 1970, 259, 295). That wisdom should be chiseled into marble above the main door of the World Bank. A Gallup poll in 1976 showed that in North America "84 percent said that they did not want more people in their country and 82 percent not in their community" (Hays 1987, 224). Today we seem happy to wallow together cheek to jowl, butt to butt in an endless sardine can. U.S. population in 1976 was a little over 200 million; now it is around 310 million. Juggle those two numbers in your head and think through what they mean.

Leon Kolankiewicz and Roy Beck, in their two papers, "The Environmental Movement's Retreat from Advocating U.S. Population Stabilization" (Beck and Kolankiewicz 2000) and "Forsaking Fundamentals"

(Kolankiewicz and Beck 2001), have undertaken the most thorough look at why U.S. environmental and conservation bodies have shunned population quandaries. William Ryerson, president of the Population Media Center, described in *Wild Earth* how political correctness led to the international backing off on overpopulation (Ryerson 1998/99). These researchers are unsparing truth seekers and unafraid of spooking a stampede of frothing, red-eyed sacred cows. Kolankiewicz and Beck see five drivers behind the "American environmental movement's retreat from population advocacy": (1) dropping fertility; (2) anti-abortion politics; (3) emergence of women's issues as a priority concern of population groups; (4) a rift between conservationists and New Left roots; and (5) immigration becoming the chief growth factor (2001, 3–4). In his weighing of how international population stabilization work was torpedoed and left to sink, Ryerson (1998/99) spotlights lowering U.S. fertility rates, the Catholic stand against contraception and abortion, the feminist shift to pronatalism, and the Reagan administration's dropping of U.S. leadership. I would add to these the belief that overconsumption is much more to blame for ecological ills than overpopulation. There are deeper roots still, having to do with Man's nature. And then there is how population Cassandras have warned about the wrong things.

FERTILITY RATE DROP IN WEALTHY COUNTRIES

Although population had been growing by frog leaps in the West since 1800 and the world over after 1900, soldiers coming home after World War Two lit the fuse of the population bomb in the United States and other wealthy countries—the baby boom. The total fertility rate (TFR— the average number of children per woman) for American women in the 1950s was 3.5, while approximately 2.1 is the TFR to keep a population stable, without growing. We were bustin' our britches with that 3.5 TFR. I was born in 1946, the first year of the baby boom, and I recall that my class throughout school was always twice as big as the year before us and much smaller than the year after us. By 1969, President Richard Nixon warned, "One of the most serious challenges to human destiny in the last third of this century will be the growth of the population. Whether man's response to that challenge will be a cause for pride or for despair in the year 2000 will depend very much on what we do today" (Kolankiewicz and Beck 2001, 12). Knock Nixon all you want, but in this he was a great, farsighted statesman, brimming with truth, and the world's leaders today are chicken-hearted, head-in-the-sand pipsqueaks handing us sweet little lies bubbling in golden champagne flutes.

Also in 1969, Stephanie Mills, in her commencement address at Mills College on the east side of the bay from San Francisco, said that "the most humane thing for me to do is to have no children at all" (1989, 51). Mills was thrust into national celebrity-hood for her selfless oath. She was not alone in her feelings, as I and others of our generation picked childless-ness, too.[3] Others chose to have only one or two children.

Then something striking happened: "[T]he birth rate in the United States dropped dramatically. . . . By 1973, the fertility rate had fallen to replacement level." In 1975, the TFR was only 1.7. The news media bally-hooed the drop with headlines blaring "Population Problem Solved" and "U.S. Arrives at Zero Population Growth" (Ryerson 1998/99, 101). How-ever, it was a sweeping misunderstanding that getting to replacement-level fertility meant that zero population growth had been gained. "Population momentum" keeps the population climbing for "up to 70 years after the replacement-level fertility is reached," write Kolankiewicz and Beck (2001, 16). Moreover, it was only wealthy countries that had gained replacement-level fertility. Elsewhere, babies were still coming down like hailstones in a High Plains thunderbuster. But many folks in the United States and other wealthy lands believed the population threat was over. Even many environmentalists and conservationists so believed and shoved population to the back burner.

Nonetheless, lowering the birth rate in the United States, Europe, Japan, and elsewhere was an awesome deed. Have you thanked a non-breeder today?

A stabilized U.S. population of no more than 250 million was in our grasp in 1975. As we shall see shortly, though, we let that hope fall through our fingers. Without taking strong steps now, the United States will have a population in 2100 that is over 750 million—three times beyond where our population could have stabilized, had we not stumbled since the late 1970s. I sit here in my recliner chair with a stiff drink in my hand. Even that, the fire crackling in the fireplace, the snow swirling outside, and a big, ol' gray tabby cat purring in my lap can't chase away the gloom and the shame that in my conservation life this happened. We failed. What else can I say? We failed because we didn't pay enough heed to what was happening in Washington, D.C., with immigration legislation at the time.

ANTI-ABORTION POLITICS

The Catholic Church sneered at worry about population growth owing to their gruesome belief that contraception is a sin. When the pope of Rome finally okayed the rhythm method, H. L. Mencken wrote, "It is now quite lawful for a Catholic woman to avoid pregnancy by resort to mathematics, though she is still forbidden to resort to physics or chemistry" (VanDe-Veer and Pierce 1994, 370). With the Supreme Court's *Roe vs. Wade* ruling in 1973 making abortion lawful, the Catholic Church heaped up wrath about "baby killing" to their spurning of family planning. Catholics got into bed with their erstwhile blood foes, fundamentalist Protestants, in an anti-abortion storm that helped lead to today's authoritarian Right (Lowi 1995). Bill Ryerson writes, "Recognizing that concern with population growth was one of the reasons many people supported legalized abortion, the Right to Life movement evolved a strategy to cast doubt on the existence of a population problem." It was their hold on Ronald Reagan that led him to end the international leadership of the United States on population stabilization at the 1984 UN population conference in Mexico City (Ryerson 1998/99, 102). The old men of the Catholic hierarchy swore that those worried about overpopulation were anti-Catholic. Moreover, the church set out "to disprove that rising population size had anything to do with deterioration of natural or human environments or the ability of poor countries with rapidly growing populations to develop economically" (Kolankiewicz and Beck 2001, 18–19). Unlike Nixon, the popes and cardinals have been shortsighted old men, deaf to the whimpering of millions of hungry babies headed for slow deaths or crippled lives. Wrapping themselves in overproud blood-red robes, they are answerable for untold woe and hurt.

The ugliness of the Catholic nobility's damnation of birth control was laid out by the head of Catholics for a Free Choice, Frances Kissling, in an op-ed in the *Baltimore Sun*. A Ugandan cardinal, Emmanuel Wamala, told Catholics in Africa that it would be better for women to get AIDS from their husbands than to use condoms. The president of the Pontifical Council of the Family, Cardinal Alfonso Lopez Trujillo, told BBC that HIV can go through a condom (it can't); and Kissling writes that a priest told her on CNN's *Crossfire* that "it was worse to lose your soul and go to hell because you used a condom to prevent AIDS than to die of AIDS" (Kissling 2006).

Even Islam, in so many ways mired in the Dark Ages, is not against contraception and can even abide some abortions. Abortion is legal in Turkey and Tunisia, both Muslim countries. Until recently, Iran had strong and quite progressive family planning, where subsidies were cut after a third child, and both men and women had to take a class about modern contraception practices before they could get a marriage license.[4] I wish the United States was that far ahead.

EMERGENCE OF WOMEN'S ISSUES AS A PRIORITY CONCERN

Some social activists became upset by population stabilization work in China and India, both of which were growing by leaps and bounds in the 1970s. By yelling about "coercion," such do-gooders killed family planning talk at the third UN population conference in Cairo in 1994. There, they flipped the goal from putting the brakes on growth to the empowerment of women. Family planning experts, writing in the British medical journal the *Lancet*, state, "The recommendations of the Cairo Conference replaced the hitherto dominant demographic-economic rationale for family-planning programmes with a broader agenda of women's empowerment and reproductive health and rights." Funding for international family planning dropped. By 2000, the drafters of the UN's Millennium Development Goals pretty much trashed worry about overpopulation and overlooked family planning (Cleland et al. 2006).

Feminist and human-rights groups were the big dogs in this shift. Outsiders from such outfits even were brought in to take over the population committee of the Sierra Club. Such folks had to quickly buy Sierra Club memberships after being asked to be on the committee. As a Sierra Club board member and member of the conservation governance committee then, I threw a hissy fit when the population committee's draft goal for the Sierra Club on population was written out as the empowerment of women.[5] No, I said, you are scrambling means and ends. The goal of the Sierra Club must be population stabilization and then reduction; empowering women may be a key path to that goal, but it is not the goal itself. I won for a while but soon left the Sierra Club board because of the club's backing off on population.

Kolankiewicz and Beck write, "Now centered in a feminist rather than environmental mission, many population, family planning, and women's groups would support no talk of stopping growth or reducing average family size because that implied restrictions on what they considered a universal right of women to choose their number of children entirely free of the merest hint of official or informal pressure" (2001, 21). In this, what had been the family planning/population movement showed itself to be blind to limits to growth—and to the worth of other Earthlings. To say that women have the right to have as many children as they want is much the same as saying that men have the right to as many gas-guzzling, land-ripping suvs as they want. Except it is worse. Either way, it says that it is okay for anyone to act on selfish whims that ransack wild things. As in so many things, we scramble rights with irresponsibility. Freedom becomes no better than a two-year-old's temper tantrum.

SCHISM BETWEEN CONSERVATIONISTS AND THE NEW LEFT ROOTS

As with other political ideologies, some on the Left are at odds with conservation. Population is one of the flash spots. In the Earth Day era, socialist environmentalists like Barry Commoner shunned the thought that population growth was behind any "environmental" plights (many anti-establishment bunches then, such as the Berkeley Ecology Center, were strong on the need to lower population, however). Most environmental and conservation groups brushed aside the cornucopian Lefties on over-population, but the class-struggle Left bided its time. They believed that conservative conservationists "hijacked Earth Day" with population worrying and thereby weakened the environmental movement. In the 1998 Sierra Club election on immigration policy, the Far Left cavalry rode to the rescue under the flag of a Bay Area Marxist outfit called the Political Ecology Group (PEG) to kill the immigration-lowering initiative (Foreman 1997/98; Kolankiewicz and Beck 2001).

Internationally, Leftist environmentalists sidelined overpopulation early on; for example, the 1972 United Nations Conference on the Human Environment in Stockholm, Sweden, did not deal with overpopulation. For one thing, social justice Leftists felt that talk about overpopulation blamed the world's poor for the "environmental" plight; instead, they said, we should target high living in wealthier countries. Then and later, they were also upset by China's one-child policy and India's widespread sterilization as raids on freedom. Some of those writing on international overpopulation have underlined these so-called human-rights wrongs as explaining why work on overpopulation was dropped by international agencies. China was able to keep its one-child policy going and slowed its population growth markedly. India, after the assassination of Indira Gandhi, shoved its program into a back room. The upshot now is that China has "sharply reduced child malnutrition" and only "7 percent of its children under 5 are underweight." Sad India, however, has an "epidemic" of childhood malnutrition, with 42.5 percent of its children under five underweight (Sengupta 2009). There are other drivers behind deep hunger in India (a World Food program report in 2009 said that India had 230 million hungry folks, or one-quarter of the world's total), but bungled population work is a leading one. India is now set to become the world's most populous country. In doing so, it will gain a landslide of woe.

I am no lover of Chinese tyranny, mind you. Besides progressive knee-jerkers, some thoughtful population-freeze workers see that while China's one-child policy was a boon for China, it may have helped lead to shutting down family planning work elsewhere, leading to more births outside of China. Who knows? Now that China's per capita affluence is growing by leaps and bounds, though, I hope that it will stick to the one-child policy, lest it have even greater impact on the wild Earth.

IMMIGRATION BECAME THE CHIEF CAUSE OF U.S. GROWTH

Recall that by the mid-1970s, the TFR in the United States, as in Japan and many European countries, had come down below 2.1 children per woman. Our population was set to even out. We had clipped the wires on the population bomb—in the United States, at least. But then we threw our win away, without wilderness/wildlife keepers, including me, understanding what was happening.

Kolankiewicz and Beck write: "When most Americans began to focus on U.S. growth in the 1960s, immigration was an almost insignificant fraction of growth. . . . At the very time that American fertility fell to a level that would have allowed population stabilization within a matter of decades, immigration levels were rising rapidly. . . . By the end of the 1990s, immigrants and their offspring were contributing nearly 70 percent of U.S. population growth" (2001, 28). While Americans of breeding age were doing our share to stabilize growth, Congress cut us off at the knees by greatly raising immigration. Kolankiewicz and Beck further write: "If immigration and immigrant fertility had been at replacement level rates since 1972—as has native-born fertility—the United States would never have grown above 250 million. Instead, U.S. population passed 273 million before the turn of the century" (2001, 28). Unless we do a quick U-turn, our population will shoot past 400 million before we know it. Former Colorado governor Richard Lamm, a Democrat and a liberal and conservationist, asks: "Given present realities, why do we want our children to face an America of 400 million people?" (1994). Why, indeed?

In the forty years after 1925, immigration into the United States ran at about two hundred thousand people a year. After immigration law "reforms" in 1965, yearly immigration leapt up to one million—or five times what it had been earlier. It gets worse. Since 1990, the immigration flood has swelled to one and a half million every year, or more than seven times what it was when I was a child (Cafaro and Staples 2009). I can't help but think that only a year after the federal government passed the Wilderness Act in 1964, it opened the floodgates to a new threat to wilderness— exponential growth instead of population stabilization. What makes the 1965 immigration law so bitter is that the Wilderness Act put population growth at the forefront of threats to wilderness:

> In order to assure that *an increasing population*, accompanied by expanding settlement and growing mechanization, does not occupy and modify all areas within the United States and its possessions, leaving no lands designated for preservation and protection in their natural condition, it is hereby declared to be the policy of the Congress to secure for the American people of present and future generations the benefits of an enduring resource of wilderness. (U.S. Congress 1964, Section 2a, emphasis added)

Here is where things get nasty. Because immigration is now the driver of population growth in the United States, the herd mindset of political correctness stops any unruffled, thoughtful talk about population in this country. Just acknowledging that immigration is behind population growth gets one keelhauled for racism. This only became so in the 1990s— in the late 1980s, as earlier, the Sierra Club's stand was that "immigration to the U.S. should be no greater than that which will permit achievement of population stabilization in the U.S" (Sierra Club 1989). Former friends of mine in the Sierra Club drove me away when they hinted that backers of the 1998 immigration ballot initiative were anti-immigrant and therefore racist. No one called me racist to my face, but the hint was there. I laid out this sorry tale in "Progressive Cornucopianism" in *Wild Earth* and won't dwell on it here (the article is at www.rewilding.org). By the way, my nieces and nephews have the last names of Pacheco, Serna, and Montoya.

Kolankiewicz and Beck show how immigration stopped conservationists from working to freeze population in the United States. For one thing, the way environmental and conservation clubs see themselves as a wing of progressivism makes them fear nettling Leftist friends and leaders of racial-advocacy outfits by acknowledging what more immigration will lead to. Moreover, when some (most?) of the environmental and conservation funding community was taken over by social activists, foundations more and more ended funding to groups that spotlighted immigration and then overpopulation at all. Don Weeden, tough-nosed and fearless executive director of the Weeden Foundation, can't get the Environmental Grantmakers Association to even talk about population growth.[6]

Although the growthmongers of the *Wall Street Journal* bliss-out have helped elbow folks away from worrying about growth, it has been the politically correct bludgeoning by the Leftist Gestapo of Paul and Anne Ehrlich, the late Garrett Hardin, Dick Lamm, and other population-freeze boosters that has undercut good population work among conservation and environmental clubs. Many true liberals like Wisconsin secretary of state Doug LaFollette and former senator Gaylord Nelson have long spoken out on the threat of overpopulation and worked for population stabilization, but the politically correct crowd has undercut freeze work.

EHRLICH VS. SIMON . . . SIMON WINS?!

After the drop in American, European, and Japanese fertility rates, many believed that growth was no longer a worry. Thanks somewhat to *Population Bomb*'s scenarios of widespread starvation leading to world war, which have not happened (yet), people reckon that growth is not something to fear. Now breathless warnings are coming from those who worry about falling populations—the birth dearthers. The fuzzy feeling that Paul Ehrlich was wrong has shifted the minds not only of right-wing economists and fast-buck hustlers, it has swayed—to a degree I didn't truly understand until recently—the thinking of conservationists and environmentalists. Although these beliefs may bubble along just below mindfulness, they lead some environmentalists and conservationists to downplay population growth or to forget about it altogether.

Because the dazzling, breathtaking, continent-sweeping starvation and out-and-out resource wars did not happen by 1980 and still have not occurred, old warnings from *The Population Bomb* and other books and articles of that time are shrugged off. Never mind that today many, if not most, of the blood-fights within and between nations are tied to overpopulation and resource shortages, as Michael Klare (2002) shows well. Moreover, tens of millions have starved and are starving, but the linkage of resource wars and starvation to overpopulation is dim at best to most folks.

HUMAN NATURE

Now let's dig a little deeper to understand why we backed off on overpopulation. Maybe we are even asking the wrong thing when we ask, "Why has society-at-large and the environmental and conservation teams backed off from forthright work on population growth?" Perhaps we should ask instead: "Why did folks for a short while between the end of World War Two and the mid-1970s worry about population growth?" In other words, maybe the lackadaisical feeling of today is the everyday mood, and the worried days of the population movement are the oddity. I think Man's nature is where conservationists must look to understand the carefree way in which we think about growth today. In our evolutionary biology, we might learn why it is so hard to reckon well with growth.

First of all, we love babies. We can't help it. If we didn't love babies (or making babies) we wouldn't be here. Our burning yearning to have babies and to ward them from all harm comes from evolution. Not wanting offspring is odd. My wife Nancy Morton and I are evolutionary misfits and losers since we do not swoon over babies and children, and because we have steadfastly not made any. Were everyone like us, *Homo sapiens* would go pffftt.

Then there is that old devil, tribalism. Archaeologists and primatologists show how we humans and our forebears have worked to kill off nearby bands since at least our last shared forebear with chimpanzees five or more million years ago. In the age-old struggle for *lebensraum* and goodies, one's own band needed to be stronger than the neighboring bands. The quickest path for being mightier than your neighbors was to have a bigger gang of throwaway young males. We see this wanting of population overlordship playing out in the immigration wars today in Europe, North America, and Australia. Throughout the world, leaders of ethnic (tribal) immigra-

tion outfits flatly say that they want more immigration of their bunch
for greater political might that will lead to takeover. Sociopolitical foes of
wide-open immigration warn that the traditional American (or European)
ethnic blend is being swamped by the ethnic makeup of immigrants. This
worry in the United States comes from blacks and non-Hispanic whites. I
also hear it from native New Mexicans of Spanish background about those
coming from Mexico. Moreover, we see the war club of more bodies being
swung today in Israel-Palestine, in Sunni-Shia-Kurd Iraq, in Tibet, in Bo-
livia, in Ukraine, in Darfur, in Rwanda-Eastern Congo, in Fiji . . . We also
see it in the pin-striped-suit crowd at Foggy Bottom and other geopolitical
lairs who believe that by keeping our population high, the United States
can go on being *the* world power.

Julian Simon further wins the day against Paul Ehrlich because he offered uplifting words against warnings, smiley faces against furrowed
brows. Optimism may well be part of human nature. People want to believe that everything is going to be okay, that we are going to keep making
headway in every way, that each generation will have a better life than
mom and dad—even when all the warnings flash "No!" The cornucopi-
ans shun carefulness as a social pathology. David Ehrenfeld sheds light on
why this is so: "The motive for their constant insistence on being opti-
mistic and 'positive' is simply the converse of this; optimism is necessary
for those who are attempting the impossible; they could not continue to
function without it" (1978, 235). Were they to face the dark pit before us,
they would lose their will to live. They would have to come nose to nose
with their madness. This they know. To keep the dread from their minds,
they curse the truth tellers. Such is the root of the mean-spirited optimism
of Dick Cheney and his button-down goons. They are snarling at us: "Do
not pop our fantasy!" I can almost forgive conservationists and environmentalists who, after chewing on all this, feel that population stabilization
is hopeless and think that their sweat is better spent on other work.

CONCLUSION

The best beacons for the harm done by population growth are right before
our noses: wholesale extinction, wrecked and plowed wildlands, and climate weirdness. But too many who are worried about such things do not
see—or do not want to see—that it is the flood of new mouths that makes
them happen. Or if they see, they are afraid on political grounds to say so,
or they do not have enough like-minded friends to do anything about it.

And when we get right down to it, just freezing world and U.S. population is not nearly enough. Stout-hearted J. Kenneth Smail, an anthropology professor at Kenyon College in Ohio, has shown that there is really no choice but to sharply lower the population of Man over the next one or two hundred years. Smail (1997) lays out what I think is an unassailable argument that we must work to bring the population of Man down to about two billion, else we face utter ruin. I think we who love wild things and who know that the population explosion is killing them and their wildworld now need to grab Smail's work and build on it. For the sake of wild things we must bring our population down to roughly two billion. For those of us now on Earth, we can begin to lay the groundwork for such a campaign. There is no better work before us.

NOTE

This essay is based on chapter 9 of Dave Foreman's *Man Swarm and the Killing of Wildlife* (Durango, Colo.: Raven's Eye Press, 2011).

The chapter epigraph is drawn from a Martin Luther King Jr. speech given after he received the Margaret Sanger Award in Human Rights in 1966. Quoted in Ehrlich and Ehrlich 1970, 211.

1. I use *Man* or *Men* capitalized for the species *Homo sapiens, woman* for the female of the species, and *man* uncapitalized for the male. This is more in keeping with earlier English, which had another word for male *Homo sapiens*: *wer*, which lives on today in *werewolf*. Today's English, oddly for a modern tongue, does not have a straightforward word for our kind that is also not the gendered word for the male. To have to call ourselves by a Latin word, *human*, is cumbersome and abstract. I do not write *Man* in a sexist way, but for the goodness of the English tongue.

2. A key insight of Charles Darwin's is that all life kinds can track their beginnings back to a shared forebear. Biologists today call this forebear the last common ancestor or LCA. We—plants, animals, fungi, and microorganisms—are kin. Thus we all should share the name "Earthling." Some think *wildlife* means only mammals, but all untamed living things, plants and fungi, too, should be called wildlife. *Wildeor* is an earlier English word for wild animal. I write *wildlife* with a broad brush for all untamed life and *wildeor* only for wild animals. I'll also use the lovely old word for plants: *wort*. Such words make me feel as though my fingernails are full of damp dirt and my nose is down in the duff. To my ears, plants sound potted and animals brushed.

3. Off the top of my head I can name nearly one hundred friends within fifteen years of my age who have never had children. Then there is my family. My grand-

mother had four children and eleven grandchildren. But those eleven grandkids have had only fifteen children—less than replacement by far.

4. Unfortunately, in late 2010, Iran's President Ahmadinejad reversed Iran's forward-looking population policy and reinstated a pronatalist policy.

5. In the Sierra Club's volunteer hierarchy, the conservation governance committee oversaw the population committee; any resolutions or draft policies from population and other committees had to first go through conservation governance before going to the board of directors.

6. My book *Take Back Conservation* deals with how conservation is harmed by seeing it as a wing of progressivism, while my more recent *Man Swarm and the Killing of Wildlife* (2011) presents an extended argument for reining in human population growth to protect wild nature.

BIBLIOGRAPHY

Beck, Roy, and Leon Kolankiewicz. 2000. "The Environmental Movement's Retreat from Advocating U.S. Population Stabilization (1970–1998): A First Draft of History." *Journal of Policy History* 12 (1): 123–156. (PDF also available from www.rewilding.com.)

Cafaro, Philip, and Winthrop Staples. 2009. "The Environmental Argument for Reducing Immigration into the United States." *Environmental Ethics* 31: 3–28.

Cleland, John, Stan Bernstein, Alex Ezeh, Anibal Faundes, Anna Glasier, and Jolene Innis. 2006. "Family Planning: The Unfinished Agenda." *Lancet*, November 18.

Ehrenfeld, David. 1978. *The Arrogance of Humanism*. New York: Oxford University Press.

Ehrlich, Paul, and Anne Ehrlich. 1970. *Population Resources Environment: Issues in Human Ecology*. San Francisco: W. H. Freeman.

Foreman, Dave. 1997/98. "Progressive Cornucopianism." *Wild Earth* 7 (4): 1–5. (Also available from http://rewilding.org/rewildit/.)

———. 2011. *Man Swarm and the Killing of Wildlife*. Durango, Colo.: Raven's Eye Press.

Hays, Samuel. 1987. *Beauty, Health, and Permanence: Environmental Politics in the United States, 1955–1985*. New York: Cambridge University Press.

Kissling, Frances. 2006. "Ban on Contraceptives Antiquated, Dangerous." *Baltimore Sun*, November 14.

Klare, Michael. 2002. *Resource Wars: The New Landscape of Global Conflict*. New York: Henry Holt.

Kolankiewicz, Leon, and Roy Beck. 2001. "Forsaking Fundamentals: The Environmental Establishment Abandons U.S. Population Stabilization." Wash-

ington, D.C.: Center for Immigration Studies. (PDF also available from www
.rewilding.com.)

Lamm, Richard. 1994. "The Real Bind Is Too Many People Everywhere." *High
Country News*, Paonia, Colo., September 5.

Lowi, Theodore. 1995. *The End of the Republican Era*. Norman: University of
Oklahoma Press.

Mills, Stephanie. 1989. *Whatever Happened to Ecology?* San Francisco: Sierra Club
Books.

New York Times. 2006. "U.S. Population on Track to 300 Million." October 14.

Ryerson, William. 1998/99. "Political Correctness and the Population Problem."
Wild Earth 8 (4): 100–103.

Sengupta, Somini. 2009. "As Indian Growth Soars, Child Hunger Persists." *New
York Times*, March 13.

Sierra Club. 1989. "Sierra Club Population Report." San Francisco: Sierra Club.

Smail, J. Kenneth. 1997. "Beyond Population Stabilization: The Case for Dramatically Reducing Global Human Numbers." *Politics and the Life Sciences* 16 (2):
183–192.

VanDeVeer, Donald, and Christine Pierce, eds. 1994. *The Environmental Ethics
and Policy Book: Philosophy, Ecology, Economics*. Belmont, Calif.: Wadsworth.

U.S. Congress. 1964. *The Wilderness Act*, PL 88–577, Statement of Policy. Washington, D.C.: Congressional Record.

PART II

Impacts

CHAPTER 6

Overpopulation versus Biodiversity

How a Plethora of People Produces a Paucity of Wildlife

LEON KOLANKIEWICZ

I N 1988, JUST AS I was finishing my three-year stint as a Peace Corps
volunteer in Honduras, I was invited to help organize and lead a fact-
finding expedition into the heart of the remote and legendary region
known as La Mosquitia—the largest remaining rainforest wilderness of
this ecologically beleaguered Central American country. La Mosquitia
had the lowest human population density of Honduras, with subsistence
villages scattered hither and yon among large expanses of virtually un-
inhabited virgin tropical rainforest and pine savanna. This biological Eden
contained intact ecosystems that still teemed with jaguars, pumas, ocelots,
scarlet macaws, toucans, harpy eagles, tapirs, peccaries, anteaters, iguanas,
and manatees, all imperiled elsewhere in overpopulated, overexploited
Central America.

Alas, the chainsaws, axes, machetes, explosives, bulldozers, logging
trucks, guns, bullets, and the humans who wield these powerful and destructive implements were encroaching rapidly. Thus a sense of urgency
pervaded our expedition. In a country whose population was mushroom-
ing by 3.5 percent annually—on a trajectory to double every twenty years
and quadruple every forty—demographic pressures would only continue
to intensify until every wild landscape was subjugated or laid to waste.

Our mission was to investigate disquieting rumors reaching Teguci-
galpa, the Honduran capital, that illicit loggers and squatters were invad-
ing with impunity the supposedly inviolate *zona nuclear*, the fully protected core zone, of the 975,000-acre Río Plátano Biosphere Reserve. In

1980, the Río Plátano was the first such reserve to be established in Central America, under UNESCO's Man and Biosphere Program, in cooperation with the Honduran government.

Thirteen of us set out from the edge of the frontier into the untamed wilderness. Half of our group hailed from indigenous communities— Pesch, Miskito, and Garífuna—living more or less sustainably, but also impoverished, within the Biosphere Reserve. Tragically, only twelve of us survived the harrowing journey, as Omar Hernandez vanished forever into the maw of El Subterraneo, a deep and treacherous canyon.

The disappearance and death of our companion was not the only tragedy that haunted this mission. In a microcosm, we also witnessed firsthand the unfolding tragedy of humanity's relentless and accelerating assault on the Earth's remaining wilderness, wildlife, habitat, and biodiversity. Furthermore, we saw that contrary to the politically correct conventional wisdom of the contemporary environmental movement, the perpetrators of this assault included not only the rich and powerful but also the poor and powerless.

As we left the settled frontier behind and plunged deeper into the jungle, advancing first by jeep and then on foot with machetes and mules, disturbing rumors of destruction that had reached our ears beforehand became disturbing facts before our eyes. We discovered unchecked penetration by illegal logging roads into the Biosphere Reserve's core zone, officially protected but obviously on paper only. We also encountered massive migration along these new access routes by mestizo *campesinos* (i.e., Spanish-speaking, nonnative, rural peasants) from the heavily populated southern parts of Honduras to the reserve's sparsely populated *tierras vírgenes* (virgin lands).

The most powerful family in the area, the Zelayas—one with a history of violence against uppity land reformers and defenders of the *campesinos*—was building the logging roads. Mahogany and other valuable, exportable tropical hardwoods were luring illegal loggers ever deeper into the rainforest, and the few pathetic boundary posts of an unguarded reserve offered no defense. In the wake of the logging trucks followed the land-hungry *campesinos*, applying traditional slash-and-burn agriculture: sustainable when population density is low, but destructive when it is too high. These desperate settlers were claiming and clearing any patch of standing forest. The Honduran government lacked the resolve, interest, or means to deal with *reforma agraria* (land reform), logging, or unauthorized settlement. It also lacked the *huevos* (no translation needed) to confront intransigent Catholic Church opposition to contraceptives and educational efforts to slow population growth. In essence, the *tierras vírgenes* of the Biosphere Reserve served as an escape valve for a society incapable of coming to grips with its own internal contradictions. The rape of officially protected virgin lands was the sorry outcome.

With sinking hearts, we observed a defaced boundary post; behind it, within the reserve, stretched a vast clear-cut of sterile stumps where just a year earlier had stood lush rainforest. We encountered a truck hauling three massive mahogany logs out of the reserve, accompanied by well-armed bosses. Whole families of *campesinos* were flooding into the reserve on foot. Many had already cleared forest and planted crops. One logging boss ventured that some eight thousand migrants had already settled here in the five years since the road first penetrated this territory. Our Miskito Indian guide, who had explored here seven years earlier, was shocked and dismayed at just how quickly the clear-cutting and unauthorized settlement had encroached on the very heart of the reserve.

A virtual slaughter of the area's wildlife was in progress. Animals like deer were shot for food; others like the jaguar were killed because they were a perceived menace to livestock and children. We observed *campesinos* fishing with homemade *dinamita*, an indiscriminate, destructive method all too common in Honduras. Unsurprisingly, the fish harvest was shrinking.

I visited the rudimentary home of one very friendly young man in his twenties, hoping to rent a mule from him. His wife was so busy slapping together *tortillas de maíz* that she scarcely had time to glance up at the odd visitor and send one of her sons off to fetch his *papá*, working in the fields. On the dirt floor played another toddler, his scrawny legs caked with a layer of dust and grime. The mother politely beckoned me to sit down on her lone piece of furniture—a crude wooden stool. On the hills all around were corn stalks shooting up among the blackened stumps of trees. A year earlier, it had been virgin rainforest.

Stretched on the wall of this palm-thatched hut—home to a growing family of five—were the spotted skins of several former denizens of the fallen jungle: stealthy jaguars and ocelots that had ventured within shooting range of the pioneer and his rifle. It was a poignant testimonial to what was taking place in this region: extermination. Humans displacing wildlife. One species, *Homo sapiens*, was expanding at the expense of most other creatures and bankrupting biodiversity in the process. A few favored domesticated species like cows, chickens, and dogs and opportunistic hangers-on like rats and cockroaches accompany us as we trample and tame wild nature. In any case, the wildcat hides hanging on my host's wall were souvenirs of a disappearing world.

This simple home with walls of cane and a dirt floor, enclosed only on three sides, offered less security from the elements and foraging wild beasts than many a trail shelter in which I've camped. It would offer scant protection to a youngster from a prowling wildcat. Against malaria-carrying *Anopheles* mosquitoes and that nearly invisible biting plague known as *jejenes* ("no-see-ums") there was no protection at all.

I couldn't help but admire the hardiness of these folks toiling to tame the wilderness, as well as their humility, hospitality, and hard work. They shared what precious little they had with me: black unsweetened coffee, stumpy bananas, and a crude stool on which to sit. If only their burgeoning numbers weren't hacking down the tropics' dwindling forests and wildlife habitat! As I wrote at the time, "with each woman giving birth to seven or eight kids on the average, in just 30 years this place will have gone from wilderness to metropolis."

COUNTING THE COST OF MOUNTING NUMBERS

Measuring the impact of human population size and growth on wildlife and biodiversity is more complex than the foregoing account might suggest. While there is a causal relationship between human overpopulation and declining biodiversity, it is not necessarily direct or inversely proportional. Even the useful formula IPAT (Impact = Population × Affluence × Technology; Ehrlich and Holdren 1971) is more a mental tool for conceptualizing the relative roles of population and other factors in generating aggregate environmental impact than a precise, proven mathematical model expressing a fundamental law of nature, like $E = MC^2$. What we do know is that more people generally equal less wildlife.

As of late 2011, there are 7 billion people on Earth and 312 million people in the United States, growing by some 70–80 million and 3 million every year, respectively (for the latest estimates, visit the U.S. Census Bureau population clocks at www.census.gov). Yet these enormous but abstract numbers do not in and of themselves adversely impact wildlife and biodiversity. It is not the mere existence per se of billions of human beings but what all these billions *do* in the process of surviving and prospering that actually causes impacts. At the most basic level, each of us imposes a load or exerts a force on our biophysical milieu: that complex web of biotic and abiotic entities called an ecosystem. We extract inputs of low-entropy energy and matter from environmental "sources" (aka resources) and excrete outputs or waste into environmental "sinks" (e.g., land, water, air). Merely pursuing the most fundamental processes of animal life—inhaling, exhaling, eating, drinking, defecating, urinating, moving, reproducing, and securing garments and warmth—entails certain environmental consequences. Every single human organism inevitably impacts his or her environment, though the magnitude of that impact can vary significantly.

Even primitive hunter-gatherers "living lightly on the land," at the barest threshold of survival, can profoundly influence surrounding ecosystems. Hunter-gatherers used fire to manipulate vegetation and habitats, benefiting certain species of flora and fauna while adversely affecting others. Early humans also caused direct mortality of hunted wildlife, killed for meat, hides, or other useful body parts. Wildlife populations would often be reduced from hunting pressure in the vicinity of human settlements, hence the need to periodically move camps and villages into virgin territory. Over thousands of years, this tendency eventually led to the peopling of virtually the entire planet, save Antarctica.

A SHORT HISTORY OF HUMANS AND WILDLIFE IN NORTH AMERICA

When it comes to wildlife, North America was already depauperate—biologically bereft—millennia before aggressive Europeans and Euro-Americans began to tame the continent and expel or exterminate its indigenous inhabitants. Boasting iconic Pleistocene (Ice Age) megafauna such as mammoths, mastodons, giant sloths, giant beavers, giant condors, giant polar bears, dire wolves, saber-toothed cats, and the like, much of North America must have been as rich as Africa's Serengeti before the arrival of the first Paleo-Indian *Homo sapiens* some thirteen thousand to twenty thousand years ago.

In recent decades, circumstantial evidence has strongly implicated Paleolithic migrants to North America in the well-documented extinctions of mammalian megafauna. Not long after their initial arrival, overall mammalian diversity plummeted at least 15–42 percent below the diversity baseline that had endured millions of years (Carrasco, Barnosky, and

Graham 2009). More than half of large mammals vanished in an unrivaled "cataclysmic extinction wave" at the close of the Pleistocene due to the direct effects of human predation (Alroy 2001). For eons, the great mammals had survived epochal climatic shifts, vast glacial and interglacial cycles sweeping away biomes like so many autumn leaves. These shifts rivaled those of the late Pleistocene, but this time the great shaggy beasts could not survive the spears, strategies, and supreme tenacity of this cunning new predator.

What causes consternation, in the context of the IPAT formula, is that this tragic, unprecedented, and irrevocable loss of North American biodiversity occurred at a time when human population, affluence, and technology were all relatively miniscule. Yet given enough time, our primordial ancestors were apparently capable of wreaking havoc on biodiversity even before the advent of agriculture. They were pursuing immediate survival imperatives rather than stewardship and sustainability, doing what comes naturally to any organism.

In seeming contrast to this dreadful story of extinction and loss is the recent history of qualified success in wildlife conservation in America. This story too cautions against assigning blame for the demise of North American biodiversity solely to overpopulation in too hasty or facile a manner. Since President Theodore Roosevelt set aside Pelican Island National Wildlife Refuge in Florida in 1903, more than 550 national wildlife refuges have been established throughout the country, conserving more than ninety-five million acres under the slogan of "Wildlife Comes First." While a dedicated conservationist himself, Roosevelt was also responding to popular outrage at the carnage taking place in America at the time.

A century ago, whitetail deer had been all but extirpated from many states, wild turkeys were scarce, and market hunters were threatening edible waterfowl for their flesh and elegant wading birds for their feathers. Populations of charismatic birds like the California condor, ivory-billed woodpecker, trumpeter swan, and whooping crane were in freefall. The passenger pigeon, the single most abundant bird in North America and perhaps the world—Audubon described their immense migrating flocks darkening the sky for hours—was on the verge of extinction. The American buffalo (bison) had barely escaped this fate as railroads and ruthless gunners pushed westward into Indian Territory. Mountain lions, wolves, elk, and bison had been eliminated in the East, and the grizzly bear all but wiped out of the Golden Bear State (California). The fabled and ferocious plains grizzly that had chased fearless Meriwether Lewis into the Missouri River was no more. In the second half of the twentieth century, majestic birds of prey—the American bald eagle, peregrine falcon, brown pelican, and osprey—were all threatened with annihilation from the widespread use of DDT and its chemical cousins.

Today, several decades after the worst pesticides were banned and ambient concentrations have diminished, these raptors have all rebounded. Whitetail deer have become so numerous that they are considered a scourge to gardeners and a hazard to motorists in many places. Protected wading birds (herons and egrets) and managed waterfowl are far more abundant and enjoy stable populations. Bison, grizzly, and wolf populations, while not regaining their former glory, have at least stabilized and reclaimed some old haunts; their continued survival, for the time being, seems secure.

With major investments of money, technology, expertise, and tender loving care, the California condor and whooping crane have taken impressive if tenuous steps away from the brink of extinction; they still number only in the hundreds, but this beats numbering in the dozens, single digits, or zero.

What a change a genuine commitment to conservation makes! America took to heart the moving prose and pleas of venerated activists and authors like John Muir, John Burroughs, Aldo Leopold, Olaus Murie, Rachel Carson, and many other naturalists. Of course, one also needs the economic means and technical wherewithal to convert commitment into action and results. And in the twentieth century, as America grew wealthy and better educated, specialized new fields like wildlife management and conservation biology were able to develop into full-fledged (if not always well-funded) professions.

AN INCOMPLETE FORMULA, OTHER MEASURES,
AND A BROAD CONSENSUS

The point is that, here in the United States, the current status and future prospects for many prominent and beloved species of wildlife have improved even as the three main drivers of environmental degradation—population, affluence, and technology, according to the IPAT formula—have all expanded enormously. U.S. population alone more than quadrupled from 75 million in 1900 to 312 million in 2011. According to at least a superficial understanding of IPAT, the status of wildlife should have worsened considerably, not improved. What gives? Is IPAT mistaken, or incomplete? Is a perpetually growing human population compatible with wildlife and biodiversity conservation after all?

The short answer is, "No way." While IPAT is a useful concept, it is an oversimplification of a complex reality. It is also easily misunderstood and misinterpreted. In particular, regarding wildlife, to assume that the affluence and technology factors are necessarily negative is mistaken. Rather, they are a mixed blessing, and sometimes they can mitigate rather than exacerbate a larger population. The greater resource consumption and waste generation that accompany affluence are indeed generally inimical to wildlife. Yet under the right circumstances and inspired leadership, affluence and associated higher educational levels can nurture an enlightened ethics that values wildlife and biodiversity. This is crucial to the generous support that successful public and private wildlife conservation programs require. And while some technologies like pesticides, chainsaws, coal-fired power plants, and bulldozers are generally damaging, many others, such as radio telemetry, satellite imagery, binoculars, computers, artificial insemination, and geographic information systems (GIS) can be crucial tools in modern wildlife management and endangered species recovery.

The bottom line is that we humans can wipe out wildlife even at relatively low levels of population size, affluence, and technological power, if good stewardship is not a priority. That was the case, for example, in the United States until about a century ago. However, once we become better stewards, attempting to avoid adverse impacts on wildlife, allowing for only sustainable rather than uncontrolled harvests and so forth, then we have the potential to really improve the situation, as we have to some degree. However, at that point we then reach another plateau in the pursuit of sustainable conservation. For no matter how well we excel as managers, the amount of wildlife we can save is constrained by the amount of uncontaminated, uncompromised, intact habitat remaining. If we continue to increase the number of people, levels of consumption, and aggregate demands on the land, we will inevitably decrease the abundance and diversity of wildlife. Enlightened management and cutting-edge technologies can only do so much; they cannot work miracles, hoodwink nature, or cram a thousand species onto the head of a pin. We can't game the system.

Furthermore, the situation is not as sanguine for wildlife as the heartwarming examples above might suggest. The dire state of biodiversity in besieged, overpopulated California is instructive. California has more native species than any other state, as well as more endemics, those unique life forms found nowhere else on Earth. This extraordinary biodiversity is already stressed by the state's enormous population, thirty-nine million and counting, and further threatened by continuing growth.

The 2007 report *California Wildlife: Conservation Challenges* (Bunn et al. 2007) by the California Department of Fish and Game (CDFG) tallied more than eight hundred imperiled species, including half of all mammals and a third of all birds. *California Wildlife* identified the major "stressors" impacting California's wildlife and habitats. It emphasized: "Increasing needs for housing, services, transportation, and other infrastructure place ever-greater demands on the state's land, water, and other natural resources." Of course, all of these are linked directly to population size. California's bloated population surged by nearly 50 percent from 1970 to 1990 and swelled another 14 percent in the 1990s; official projections— more a nightmare than a preview—foresee 60 million residents by 2050. The relentless spread of one life form, our own, is riding roughshod over hundreds of fellow living creatures that have been part of California far longer than humans have.

Globally, the situation is just as grim. In a dismal 2010 report card based on thirty-one indicators, the journal *Science* reported that "the rate of biodiversity loss does not appear to be slowing," in spite of the 2002 Convention on Biological Diversity in which world leaders had committed to achieving a significant reduction in the rate of biodiversity loss by 2010 (Butchart 2010).

Eminent biologists and authors like Jared Diamond, E. O. Wilson, and Norman Myers all agree that population growth and the forces it multiplies or unleashes on the landscape are devastating biodiversity. Diamond refers to an "Evil Quartet" of habitat destruction, fragmentation, overharvesting, and introduced species (Sanderson and Moulton 1998). Wilson touts the acronym HIPPO—habitat destruction, invasive species, pollution, population, and overharvesting. He estimates that at least twelve thousand wild species are going extinct annually (Biello 2008).

Wilson has written: "The pattern of human population growth in the 20th century was more bacterial than primate. When *Homo sapiens* passed the six-billion mark we had already exceeded by perhaps as much as 100 times the biomass of any large animal species that ever existed on the land. We and the rest of life cannot afford another 100 years like that" (Wilson

2002). There is no more stinging indictment of human hypergrowth, or what Wilson calls "our reproductive folly."

The Conservation Measures Partnership is a collaborative effort of a dozen prominent conservation groups dedicated to improving international wildlife conservation. The partnership's "Threats Taxonomy" lists direct threats to biological diversity. Their main categories include (1) residential and commercial development; (2) agriculture and aquaculture; (3) energy production and mining; (4) transportation and service corridors; (5) biological resource use; and (6) human intrusions and disturbance. Clearly, each of these is a direct function of population size and, of course, affluence (Conservation Measures Partnership 2010).

Yet another measure that quantifies the troubling extent to which *Homo sapiens* is commandeering the natural world is human appropriation of net primary production (HANPP). Net primary production is the annual growth of all plant matter, from hardy lichens to towering redwoods, plus cultivated crops like corn and wheat. It is the plant kingdom's annual output. Austrian researchers note at the online *Encyclopedia of the Earth*, "empirical studies increasingly demonstrate that HANPP is a major indicator of human pressures on ecosystems and may have adverse effects on biodiversity" (Haberl, Erb, and Krausmann 2010).

HANPP is what is harvested by people for our own consumption, plus the share of natural production lost to environmental degradation. Another portion of HANPP occurs from development that replaces living vegetation with pavement and buildings. In effect, the share of NPP co-opted by humans is unavailable to wildlife, which must then survive on less. Growing numbers of omnivorous human consumers with growing appetites are leaving only the leftovers—and ever fewer leftovers, at that—for the millions of creatures that inhabit the biosphere with us. The bottom line is that if HANPP continues to increase, more species will be snuffed out of existence permanently. The collective appetite of *Homo colossus*, as William Catton dubs our resource-devouring species, has grown so titanic that not even all of Planet Earth can satisfy it anymore.

This is also borne out by ecological footprint (EF) analysis. EF measures aggregate human demands, or the human load imposed on the biosphere. According to EF analysis, since about the 1980s, humanity as a whole has been living beyond the ecological means of the biosphere; we are already in ecological overshoot, an unstable and unsustainable condition. Yet even as our aggregate EF continues to increase, the Earth's biocapacity—the ability of available terrestrial and aquatic areas to provide ecological services—is being degraded by excessive human activity. We humans now use the equivalent of about 1.4 Earths (Ewing et al. 2009). But how is it even possible to use more than one Earth at any one time? Only by using up vast stores of fossil fuels, which were created over tens of millions of years. In effect, temporarily, we have at our disposal more than one planet, or what Catton refers to as the "ghost acreage" of "phantom carrying capacity" (Catton 1980). Our biodiversity-besieging population and economic explosion have been ignited by a one-time jolt of "ancient sunshine."

EF analysis also helps reveal the extent to which massive numbers of massively consuming Americans are impacting the entire biosphere. In 2006, our EF was 22.3 global acres per capita, while our biocapacity was only 10.9 global acres per capita, for an ecological deficit of 11.3 global acres per capita (Ewing et al. 2009). This means we have exceeded the nation's carrying capacity. In other words, we gargantuan Americans are living beyond our ecological means, boosting our vaunted living standards and nonnegotiable lifestyles only by drawing down biocapacity and degrading irreplaceable biodiversity across the planet. We may be able to preserve remnants of nature here, but by importing carrying capacity we are exporting nature destruction around the world. The only way out of this conundrum without risking economic unraveling or collapse—which all too many unemployed Americans have gotten a bitter taste of in the "Great Recession" of 2008–2010 and afterward—is by transitioning to a steady-state economy and sharply increasing the efficiency with which we consume energy and resources. Even then, it will take ingenuity and innovation to avoid the Jevons paradox, the counterintuitive result by which aggregate resource consumption increases even as efficiency improves.[1]

LIMITING OUR NUMBERS TO HELP OTHER
SPECIES SURVIVE

In analyzing environmental effects, environmental scientists refer to direct, indirect, and cumulative impacts. Human population growth impacts biodiversity in all three ways. The most significant direct impact occurs when we eliminate or fragment wildlife habitat by converting it into farmland to feed ever more humans and livestock (fed to humans "moving up the food chain") and, increasingly, vehicles (i.e., ethanol and biodiesel derived from crops). Overpopulation-related habitat damage and loss also occur with the construction of reservoirs, power lines, roads, mines, logging operations, overgrazing, bottom trawling, and urban sprawl.

Invasive species that accompany growing, spreading human populations exemplify an indirect impact. Exotic plants, animals, and microbes unleashed by humans are wreaking havoc on native terrestrial and aquatic ecosystems, flora, and fauna around the world. More people are linked to more travel, more trade, and more spread of exotics. The notorious zebra mussel, native to Eastern Europe, hopped across the Atlantic in 1988 when an ocean-going vessel dumped ballast water into Lake St. Clair, between Lake Huron and Lake Erie. It now infests and is radically altering the ecology of lakes and rivers across vast swaths of North America. This aggressive, adaptable bivalve also threatens our already besieged native freshwater mussel diversity, the richest in the world, at about three hundred species.

The ultimate cumulative impact is anthropogenic climate change, from the steady accumulation of human-emitted greenhouse gases in the atmosphere. This could end up having a greater adverse impact on wildlife and biodiversity than all other malevolent forces combined. According to the Intergovernmental Panel on Climate Change, increasing greenhouse gas emissions are primarily a function of rising populations and increased affluence.

As a consultant to the U.S. Fish and Wildlife Service, I have been privileged to help prepare comprehensive conservation plans (CCPs) on more than forty national wildlife refuges from the Caribbean to Alaska. In diverse ecosystems, I have witnessed the myriad impacts of voracious human demands on wildlife. Yet I have also seen the uplifting results of dedicated, indefatigable efforts to save biodiversity.

In the U.S. Virgin Islands, managers and concerned citizens are working hard to protect Sandy Point, Green Cay, and Buck Island National Wildlife Refuges. Population growth is not their friend. As noted in a recent CCP that I helped draft:

> [The Caribbean] ecosystem is home to 78 threatened and endangered
> species (29 animals and 49 plants), including species of birds, reptiles,
> and amphibians, as well as unique and diverse habitats ranging from coral
> reefs, sandy beaches, and mangrove forests to limestone hills and forested
> mountains. . . .
>
> Since the end of the Second World War, human population has increased
> dramatically on almost every island . . . negative ecological trends have all

accelerated as a result of the demands explosive human growth has placed on the environment.

> Within the U.S. Virgin Islands, the demands for space and land created by a rapidly growing human population of over 100,000 have resulted in extensive loss and degradation of natural ecosystems, especially on densely populated St. Thomas. (USFWS 2009b)

Two of the many "critters" inhabiting this ecosystem—one tiny and one humongous—exemplify the threats and hopes facing wildlife in this brave, new, human-dominated world.

Three decades ago, the world's surviving population of the tiny, critically endangered St. Croix ground lizard (*Ameiva polops*) on fourteen-acre Green Cay National Wildlife Refuge could probably have fit into two buckets. The disappearance of this six-inch, inconspicuous reptile from the nearby island of St. Croix is believed due to human disturbance, land development, and the introduced Indian mongoose, which preyed on it. Determined recovery efforts at the refuge and nearby Buck Island Reef National Monument, to which it has been translocated, offer hope that *A. polops* will yet endure. Even so, it is disconcerting that the entire existing population still probably weighs less than a single adult human. Globally, the ratio of our species' aggregate biomass to theirs exceeds seven billion to one (7,000,000,000:1).

The lumbering leatherback turtle (*Dermochelys coriacea*) nests on beaches at Sandy Point National Wildlife Refuge not far from the ground lizard but outweighs it 10,000:1. At up to eight feet in length and a ton in weight, the leatherback is the largest, deepest diving, and widest ranging of all sea turtles. It is endangered because of overexploitation by people for its eggs and meat, incidental take by commercial fisheries, disorientation of hatchlings by beachfront lighting, and excessive nest predation (USFWS 2009a). Yet at Sandy Point National Wildlife Refuge, nesting leatherbacks have increased from fewer than twenty in 1982 to more than a hundred in recent years; average hatchling production has quintupled. This success is due to the tireless efforts of refuge manager Mike Evans and biologist Claudia Lombard and their supporting cast of conservationists and volunteers.

Limiting human numbers both locally and globally is crucial to saving these two endangered reptiles. Locally, population stabilization would reduce pressure to poach sea turtle eggs and trample the ground lizard's habitat; it would give them vital breathing room. Globally, it would help curb the unremitting buildup of greenhouse gases that threatens the Caribbean with more frequent and ferocious hurricanes, sea level rise, coral-killing warmer waters, and coral-dissolving acidifying waters. Humanely stabilizing and reducing the human population is a necessary condition for saving biodiversity and halting the brutal wave of extinction breaking over the Earth.

LEST WE FORGET

The late Donella Meadows, lead author of *The Limits to Growth,* used to write a syndicated newspaper column called *The Global Citizen.* In 1999, on the fiftieth anniversary of the conservation classic *A Sand County Almanac,* Meadows wrote a tribute to its author, Aldo Leopold, pioneering wildlife scientist and wilderness advocate.

Meadows noted that while environmentalists are sometimes accused of disliking people, Leopold wasn't like that at all. Rather, he saw us humans as the only creatures endowed with the ability to love nature and understand our connection to it. Leopold once spoke at the dedication of a monument to the passenger pigeon, and his remarks are telling: "For one species to mourn the death of another is a new thing under the sun. The Cro-Magnon who slew the last mammoth thought only of steaks. The sportsman who shot the last pigeon thought only of his prowess. The sailor who clubbed the last auk thought of nothing at all. But we, who have lost our pigeons, mourn the loss. Had the funeral been ours, the pigeons would hardly have mourned us" (Meadows 1999).

Our species is unique, because here and now only we have the ability to destroy, or to save, biodiversity. Only we have the ability to care one way or the other. The destiny of all wild living things is in our hands. Will we crush them or let them be wild and free? Limiting human population will not guarantee success, but not doing so means certain failure.

NOTE

1. The Jevons paradox is named for the English economist William Stanley Jevons, who first commented on this phenomenon in 1865. Jevons had observed that technological improvements in the efficiency of coal use in various industries actually increased overall coal consumption, rather than reducing it, as one might

expect. The Jevons paradox is a particular example of what modern economists call the "rebound effect." Higher efficiency reduces the relative cost of using energy and resources, thereby stimulating demand and thus offsetting potential savings. Moreover, increased efficiency encourages economic growth, further increasing demand for energy/resources. Since the Jevons paradox applies to technological improvements, it may be possible to circumvent by means of green taxes or conservation standards such as nationwide caps on carbon emissions.

BIBLIOGRAPHY

Alroy, J. A. 2001. "A Multispecies Overkill Simulation of the End-Pleistocene Megafaunal Mass Extinction." *Science* 292 (5523): 1893–1896.

Biello, David. 2008. "Population Bomb Author's Fix for Next Extinction: Educate Women." *Scientific American*, August.

Bunn, David, Andrea Mummert, Marc Hoshovsky, Kirsten Gilardi, and Sandra Shanks. 2007. *California Wildlife: Conservation Challenges: California's Wildlife Action Plan.* (Prepared by the UC Davis Wildlife Health Center for the California Department of Fish and Game.) Sacramento: California Department of Fish and Game.

Butchart, Stuart, et al. 2010. "Global Biodiversity: Indicators of Recent Declines." *Science* 328, (5982): 1164–1168.

Carrasco M. A., A. D. Barnosky, and R. W. Graham. 2009. "Quantifying the Extent of North American Mammal Extinction Relative to the Pre-Anthropogenic Baseline." *PLoS ONE* 4 (12): e8331. DOI:10.1371/journal.pone.0008331.

Catton, William R., Jr. 1980. *Overshoot: The Ecological Basis of Revolutionary Change.* Urbana: University of Illinois Press.

Conservation Measures Partnership. 2010. "Threats Taxonomy." Accessed from www.conservationmeasures.org/initiatives/threats-actions-taxonomies/threats-taxonomy.

Ehrlich, Paul, and John Holdren. 1971. "Impact of Population Growth." *Science* 171 (3977): 1212–1217.

Ewing, B., S. Goldfinger, A. Oursler, A. Reed, D. Moore, and M. Wackernagel. 2009. *The Ecological Footprint Atlas.* Global Footprint Network. Accessed from www.footprintnetwork.org.

Haberl, H., K. Erb, and F. Krausmann. 2010. "Global Human Appropriation of Net Primary Production (HANPP)." *Encyclopedia of the Earth.* Accessed from www.eoearth.org.

Meadows, Donella. 1999. "Sand County Almanac Fifty Years Later." Donella Meadows Archive, Sustainability Institute. Accessed from http://www.sustainer.org/dhm_archive/index.php?display_article=vn783leopolded.

Sanderson, James, and Michael Moulton. 1998. *Wildlife Issues in Our Changing World*. 2nd ed. Boca Raton: CRC Press.

U.S. Fish and Wildlife Service (usfws), Department of the Interior. 2009a. "Leatherback Sea Turtle Fact Sheet." usfws North Florida Ecological Services Office, Jacksonville, Fla.. Accessed from www.fws.gov/northflorida/SeaTurtles/Turtle%20Factsheets/leatherback-sea-turtle.htm.

————. 2009b. "Sandy Point, Green Cay, and Buck Island National Wildlife Refuges: Draft Comprehensive Conservation Plan and Environmental Assessment." usfws Southeast Region, Atlanta, Ga. Accessed from www.fws.gov/southeast/planning/PDFdocuments/VirginIslandsDraftCCP/Edited%20Draft%20CCP%20Virgin%20Islands%20Refuges.pdf.o.

Wilson, Edward O. 2002. "The Bottleneck." *Scientific American*, February.

CHAPTER 7

The Human Population Footprint on Global Biodiversity

JEFFREY MCKEE

T HE TERM *footprint* has become a common expression for various types of human environmental impacts on both urban and natural environments. Architects refer to the *footprint* of a building, the *carbon footprint* was launched into the political domain, and the more general term *ecological footprint* is spreading from the academic world to the general public. What is often lacking is discussion of the *human population footprint*. To be sure, the general effects of human population growth are discussed in terms of urbanization and suburban sprawl, for example, but not so much in terms of environmental impact and, particularly, the effects of human population density on biological diversity. There is now a growing body of academic literature (reviewed by Luck 2007) establishing a scientific link between human population density and growth and increased extinction threats for plants and animals, yet this key footprint remains on the outskirts of conservation dialogue.

Contemporary trends among threatened species, as gauged by long-term paleontological data, confirm that Earth is experiencing its sixth mass extinction of plant and animal species (Barnosky et al. 2011). Although the causes of the current mass extinction are complex and mediated by human behavior, there is clearly a strong connection between the density of the human population and threats of further extinctions. Moreover, both human population and threatened species are growing in numbers.

Here I pursue the hypothesis that human population density alone is a key factor in threats of extinction to other animals. This is not to say that it is the only factor, for indeed human behavior and a host of other factors are important as well. But population density appears to be at the core of the matter. I further argue that without ending human population growth, the mass extinction we are experiencing will accelerate, despite the most noble conservation efforts. I conclude that all conservation strategies in which biologists and planners engage must continue, but that they should integrate the realities of the effects of human population density and growth.

MASS EXTINCTION IN PERSPECTIVE

The fossil record has revealed five mass extinctions in the past, including the one 65 million years ago in which most of the dinosaurs met their demise. With such knowledge from the fossil record, extinction rates can be gauged paleontologically. For example, in southern Africa, prior to 1.8 million years ago when the mammalian biodiversity deficit began, every 100,000 years would see the extinction of four large mammals, balanced out by the evolutionary origin of four large mammals (McKee 1995, 2001, 2003). But in the past 10,000 years alone, southern Africa has seen the extinction of at least sixteen mammal species, nine of which have gone extinct in historic times (Klein 2000). As this is typical of other places and time frames since the origins of humans and their ancestors, such an extinction rate increase warrants the claim of a sixth mass extinction in the world today.

Despite the African extinctions, Africa is often referred to as the "living Pleistocene" because large mammals such as elephant and rhino have persisted into the present, while their counterparts have gone extinct on other continents, largely at the hands of humans. One explanation for this persistence of African megafauna comes from our knowledge of hominin origins in Africa. Our prehuman ancestors there gradually moved into a hunting niche, so the likes of elephants, hippos, and rhinos had more time to adapt to the new predators. Elsewhere the arrival of skilled human (and prehuman) hunters had a more immediate and devastating effect.

On this basis it could be argued that once humans have had their initial impact, animals might adapt and survive alongside our growing human populations. But there are problems with this argument, for indeed there remain many threatened species, even in Africa. Although the rate of human population growth is steadily declining, our overall numbers are still growing exponentially as the number of threatened species continues to climb. So we must look at both extinction rates and extinction threats as our population grows.

Extinction rates during historic times are difficult to gauge. Only a thousand or so species have been *recorded* as having gone extinct since 1600. Indeed, no good correlation has been found between known extinctions and human population densities (Luck 2007). But as wildlife populations dwindle in the wake of our expansion, one can infer that biodiversity is being diminished at genetic levels. As Darwin presciently noted, "rarity precedes extinction; and we know that this been the progress of events with those animals which have been exterminated, either locally or wholly, through man's agency" (1859, 319–320). So whereas we might not see species extinctions per se, we can measure with a wide gauge the effects of human population density on nonhuman species by looking at species *threatened* with extinction.

THREATENED SPECIES AND HUMAN POPULATION DENSITY

We must look at threatened species together with elements of the human enterprise, particularly human population density and growth. Taking a broad view of current ecological trends, McKee et al. (2004) analyzed data on threatened species per nation, comprising critically endangered, endangered, and vulnerable species of mammals and birds from the International Union for Conservation of Nature (IUCN) Red List (based on threats in 2000). Data from continental nations, excluding exceptionally small nations, were also compiled on human population densities and "species richness"—defined for the analyses as the number of known mammal and bird species per unit area. Using a stepwise multiple regression analysis, a mathematical model was discovered that explained 88 percent of the variability in current threats to mammal and bird species per country on the basis of just two variables: human population density and species richness. Clearly "species richness" is not the root cause of the threats— these diverse ecosystems persisted through climatic changes and ecosystem shifts over many thousands of years. That leaves the other variable in the equation, human population density, as the likely causal factor leading to global increases in threatened species. It appears that the greater concentration of species set the conditions for the human population impact to be more intense.

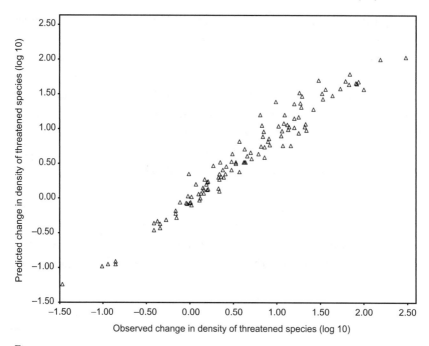

Figure 7.1

Correlation between predicted and observed changes in the density of threatened species per nation between 2000 and 2010

Has the trend continued? Predictions of extinction threats for mammal and bird species in 2010, on the basis of projections from the 2000 model, were strongly correlated with the observed data, with the model predicting 83.8 percent of species threat levels (McKee, Chambers, and Guseman forthcoming). On the other hand, this was somewhat expected, given the time span of just one decade, so it was worth looking at how *change* over the decade might relate to our observations. There we found that the model's predicted change in densities of threatened species had a 95.6 percent correlation with observed changes in human population density alone (figure 7.1).

In order to test how much of the change over one decade was attributable to human population growth as opposed to other potential factors, we used a stepwise multiple regression to find the most statistically significant variables accounting for the changes in species threat levels. Human population density change was the most statistically significant variable entered by the analysis, accounting for 96.4 percent of the change

(McKee, Chambers, and Guseman forthcoming). Gross national product (GNP) was the only other variable adding any explanatory power to the residual variation in levels of threatened species. Other variables, including agricultural land use and species richness, were not as strongly correlated with the changes in densities of threatened species and added nothing to the model. In other words, once one accounts for population density and GNP, other variables just become statistical noise.

ADDRESSING THE ISSUES FOR THE FUTURE

Human population growth and the environmental dominance that has characterized the human enterprise set in motion a global mass extinction that is now accelerating due to continued human population growth. Whereas we can document past extinctions and current threats of species extinctions, this measure is not the sole indicator of a compromised ecosystem. There is also a significant depletion of genetic biodiversity, which puts species at an even greater risk of extinction, as adaptability and evolvability are compromised. At the other end of the spectrum, ecosystem diversity is also jeopardized by human population growth. This comes from both ecosystem collapse as well as homogenization of habitats due to invasive species, thereby compounding threats to sustainability even further.

It is odd that many environmentalists have been reluctant to address human overpopulation as an important issue, as it is at the core of understanding what is happening to biodiversity. Any cogent conservation strategy must include an agenda to curb population growth, lest it be doomed to ultimate failure. Why are we willing to cull elephants in South Africa to protect the environment but are not willing to even open a dialogue on the conservation imperative of curbing human population growth?

This is not to say that common conservation strategies cannot be effective. There are a number of countries, such as Kenya, that have achieved success, with declining numbers of threatened species despite continued population growth. These countries can temporarily buck the trends relating biodiversity loss to increased population density by implementing sound and scientifically based conservation strategies. But there is always a potential reversal of fortunes if human population growth continues to mount further pressure. And many countries do not have the economic incentive of countries like Kenya, where ecotourism is important, to do all they can for the species that inhabit their lands.

All else being equal, the future looks bleak for wild animals, plants, and ecosystems if we do nothing about human population growth. Using population projections with the 2010 model, the average nation with a growing population can expect a 3.3 percent increase in the number of threatened mammals and birds by 2020, based on population growth alone, and a 10.8 percent increase by 2050, when it is projected that global population will exceed nine billion people (McKee, Chambers, and Guseman forthcoming). Amelioration of population threats to some species by 2050 in the twenty-one countries with projected *declining* human populations are predicted to be more modest, with an average reduction in threats of 2.5 percent; in those nations, that amounts to a maximum of four fewer threatened species and a mean of only about one fewer per nation.

However, there are opportunities to combine conservation strategies with knowledge of human population dynamics. The nation-by-nation data show that of the twelve countries with declining human populations from 2000 to 2010, nine had a concomitant reduction in the number of threatened animal and bird species. This does not appear to be a mere correlation, suggesting yet again both the validity of the human population/ biodiversity connection and the potential for a novel conservation strategy. Nations and areas with shrinking populations could be targeted for wildland reclamation and proactive introduction and restoration of native species, besides the ones that are making a comeback on their own.

Our population footprint has become increasingly evident and must be urgently addressed. In his classic essay on the "tragedy of the commons," Garrett Hardin (1968) stated that "a finite world must have a finite population." It is up to our generation to define "finite population" and to do something about it. Nine billion people in 2050 would go far beyond what is sustainable for Earth's ecosystems. If we are to stave off further losses in the first mass extinction to be induced by a single sentient species, then swiftly stabilizing and humanely reducing our oversized population will have to become integral to conservation strategies.

BIBLIOGRAPHY

Barnosky, Anthony, Nicholas Matzke, Susumu Tomiya, Guinevere Wogan, Brian Swartz, Tiago Quental, Charles Marshall, Jenny McGuire, Emily Lindsey, Kaitlin Maguire, Ben Mersey, and Elizabeth Ferrer. 2011. "Has the Earth's Sixth Mass Extinction Already Arrived?" *Nature* 471 (March): 51–57.

Darwin, Charles. 1859. *On the Origin of Species by Means of Natural Selection.* London: John Murray.

Hardin, Garrett. 1968. "The Tragedy of the Commons." *Science* 162 (3859): 1243–1248.

International Union for Conservation of Nature (IUCN). 2010. *The IUCN Red List of Threatened Species.* Accessed from www.iucnredlist.org/about/summary-statistics.

Klein, Richard. 2000. "Human Evolution and Large Mammal Extinctions." In *Antelopes, Deer, and Relatives, Present and Future: Fossil Record, Behavioral Ecology, Systematics, and Conservation,* edited by Elisabeth Vrba and George Schaller. New Haven, Conn.: Yale University Press. 128–139.

Luck, Gary. 2007. "A Review of the Relationships between Human Population Density and Biodiversity." *Biological Reviews* 82: 607–645.

McKee, Jeffrey. 1995. "Turnover Patterns and Species Longevity of Large Mammals from the Late Pliocene and Pleistocene of Southern Africa: A Comparison of Simulated and Empirical Data." *Journal of Theoretical Biology* 172 (2): 141–147.

———. 2001. "Faunal Turnover Rates and Mammalian Biodiversity of the Late Pliocene and Pleistocene of Eastern Africa." *Paleobiology* 27 (3): 500–511.

———. 2003. *Sparing Nature: The Conflict between Human Population Growth and Earth's Biodiversity.* New Brunswick, N.J.: Rutgers University Press.

McKee, Jeffrey, Erica Chambers, and Julie Guseman. Forthcoming. "Human Population Density and Growth Validated as Extinction Threats to Mammal and Bird Species."

McKee, Jeffrey, Paul Sciulli, David Fooce, and Thomas Waite. 2004. "Forecasting Global Biodiversity Threats Associated with Human Population Growth." *Biological Conservation* 115: 161–164.

CHAPTER 8

Beyond Futility

TIM PALMER

F OUR DECADES of environmentalism have changed America. The
citizens involved in this historic movement have protected landscapes
and rivers, cleaned up air and water, and transformed the way people
think about their relationship with Earth. It's been a wild ride that many
thousands of us have been privileged and thrilled to join.

But there's one big problem. We're still losing ground (Heinz Center
2008). And for most of the places and values we have safeguarded, we are
soon forced to fight again. With no relief, the challenges continue to reap-
pear as the threats return ever stronger.

My first awareness of this bitter futility came through a hero of my
youth: Jim McClure, a city councilman where I went to college. Jim and
an army of courageous residents took up the fight against a freeway that
would have sliced through the heart of the region, eliminating farmland, displacing people, transforming commercial districts, and disabling
whole ecosystems. They won a hard battle. But twenty years later, after
the region's population grew by half again, the pressure to relieve conges-
tion became overpowering. The freeway was built. All their work simply
bought a little time, and not much of it.

Here is an example from my own career in river conservation. After
thousands of dams had been built through the 1960s, people began to
realize the tremendous detrimental effects on rivers, fish, and whole landscapes, and a movement grew to protect the best rivers that remained.
A powerful political alliance was driven away from the old pork-barrel

politics and spending on dams (Palmer 2004). The demand for water was still enormous and expanding with no end in sight, but rather than make more water available via new dams or take it from other people, a strategy was pursued to make improved use of the water we already had. These efficiency efforts paid off, and per capita use of water declined by 20 percent nationally between 1980 and 1995 (Jehl 2002). In California, per capita use was halved during a forty-year period.

But here's the catch: population growth has rendered the savings almost meaningless. In the same 1980–1995 period, the national population increased by 16 percent, and in California's last forty years the population nearly doubled (California Department of Finance 2011). Water shortages have increased and require unpopular adjustments by farmers and consumers, while still spelling ruin to whole ecosystems from the Sacramento Delta to Florida's Apalachicola Bay.

Even though much of the low-hanging water-saving fruit has been picked, we can probably cut the current use in half once again (Gleick, Cooley, and Groves 2005). But by the time we do that the population is likely to double for a second time. With the numbers of people outstripping the amounts of water saved, we'll be back in the same place where we started, except with less potential for further conservation and with a lot more people waiting in line for water. In the end, we will not have protected wild rivers, spared endangered species, or saved public money as we had intended, but we will have principally served to make more population growth possible. Then, the momentum to grow will be even greater. I can't help wonder if saving water is like four-wheel drive. It simply enables us to get stuck deeper.

The point here is that many people sought to do something good in conserving water, something of lasting value. But nothing can truly be protected if the source of the threat continues to grow.

The same kind of story is told by a friend who works to protect farmland, which is being lost to sprawl at the rate of a million acres per year (Daniels and Bowers 1997). Counting farmlands and wildlands together, sprawl consumes 2.2 million acres per year, according to the Natural Resources Conservation Service. My friend's motivation is simple: we need farmland in order to eat. She labors to keep the best soils from being lost to development. A key strategy is to reduce property taxes on farmers through ten-year agreements not to develop. But many eventually sell for housing, once the payoffs are high enough. Because the population continues to grow, the effort to save farms ends up being little more than an efficient phasing-in of new subdivisions.

Consider one of today's biggest ecological problems: climate change. With only about 4 percent of the world population, the United States is responsible for about 20 percent of the greenhouse gas emissions that cause global warming. Radical reductions are needed to bring the problem even somewhat under control (IPCC 2007). While fully knowing this, we continue to burn more fuel and cause more emissions. That's bad enough. But here is the important part: within sixty years or so, at current population growth rates, there will be twice as many Americans. If we can't do what's needed now with the consumption demands generated by three hundred million Americans, how will we succeed with six hundred million?

On good days, Jim McClure and I and hundreds of thousands of others who labor for a better future know that our country would be worse off today if we had not done this work. But on bad days we know that everything we've done has only delayed and in some cases facilitated growth that's now poised to undo all our efforts.

Would we have given up if we had known that the benefits would last only twenty years? Fifty years? I think the answer is no. I would still have worked to save the Kings River as one of the most remarkable places I've ever known, hoping that others would have the ability to save it again in the future. A more important question is this: If we had known that the fruits of our labor were only temporary, would we have worked on the source of the problem, rather than only on the symptoms?

Working for efficiency, better resource management, the "greening" of development, and other reforms are all important. But I've concluded that little can be accomplished in the long term if the most fundamental pressure behind the problems—population growth—continues. Perhaps you've seen the cartoon of a bathtub, overflowing on all sides. A distressed homeowner mops furiously with a pathetic little towel while the faucets keep blasting out water full force. Not only is turning down the tap on population the essential step to succeed if we want a livable and quality environment, but it is the *only* measure that will ultimately work.

Recognizing the worldwide implications of population growth, people have striven to reduce the rate of growth in many ways, including education for women, information about birth control, and increasing availability of contraception. In response to these efforts and to changing times, birth rates in many places are going down (Weeks 1990). But the numbers of people are still going up, and the United Nations forecasts that world population will grow from nearly 7 billion to 9.2 billion by 2075 (UNPD 2004; some estimates are higher). At that point, population may plateau, but any sigh of relief will still be unfounded. Environmental destruction, overconsumption of resources, global warming, human suffering, hunger, water shortages, crowding, and scarcity-induced wars are all with us today and are likely to be worse when the world is nearly 30 percent more crowded than it already is.

While world population gets some attention, growth in the United States often goes unconsidered, under the myth that population is solely a problem of developing countries. Yet America is growing faster than any other large industrialized nation and faster than many developing countries, including Jamaica, El Salvador, Namibia, Sri Lanka, and Thailand (CIA 2011). Most important, from a planetary perspective, growth here is what really counts; Americans are by far the biggest consumers of the Earth's resources. Furthermore, population growth in the United States is something about which we citizens in the United States can actually do something. This is the place for which we are most responsible, where we must live with the consequences, where we make the laws, and where we have an opportunity to be a model for others. Recognizing all this, it seems imperative to address population growth in the United States.

American population is growing, with projections for another 110,000,000 people in the next forty years (U.S. Census Bureau 2011). At current rates of growth, America will double its current population in about sixty years and keep on doubling.

Our population's pattern of doubling at roughly regular time intervals is what statisticians call exponential growth. It is not a steady change that marches on in increments as if 2 new students were added to a classroom each year. In that case, called linear growth, even in the tenth year there would still be only 2 more students added. This alone would eventually overcrowd any classroom, but exponential growth is alarmingly different. If the number of new students is doubled each year, in the tenth year there would be not 2 new students but 1,024. This is what is occurring in America, and the repercussions are profound.

To understand exponential growth better, a biological analogy may be helpful. If duckweed on a farmer's pond is doubling every day, the initial growth rate will not be alarming. One square foot of coverage will be only two square feet on the second day. But recognizing that the weed will inevitably cover the pond in a given number of days—say thirty-seven, in this example—it is interesting to ask, when will the pond be half-covered? Half-covered doesn't sound like much; think about a concert auditorium with half its seats empty. Half might be just enough to prompt the farmer to think about doing something to control the duckweed. But the pond will be half-covered on the thirty-sixth day. The entire second half will be covered up on the very last day of the cycle.

One could argue that our country is "full" of people now, given current levels of crowding, resource overuse, and biodiversity loss. Consider the ecological footprint model. This says that beyond the space we directly occupy, each of us needs a predictable amount of area for food production, water supplies, transportation systems, energy sources, and so forth. The footprint of Americans has been calculated at 12.6 acres per person (Wackernagel and Rees 1998). Considering lands that are unsuited to both habitation and support activities, America is arguably already more than full: the present population is only possible by mining the accumulated energy of fossil fuels and by causing unsustainable environmental damage nationally and globally (Ehrlich and Ehrlich 1991). But if you disagree with that and think that the country is only half-full, then remember that it *will* be full in just one more doubling cycle. And remember, owing to the momentum of growth—all the people now having children—it takes time to slow the process down. Until several generations reproduce at a lower level, younger age cohorts that are larger than older age cohorts continue to have kids and cause the population to grow.

Growth rates can, of course, subside. But even with a slower growth *rate*—the number that makes the news—actual growth continues. Just 1 percent per year, which sounds small, will double the population in seventy years. In 2010, headlines in California proclaimed that the state's growth rate dropped to 1 percent, as if the state's perpetual boom were past. But 1 percent growth in California is 350,000 more people every year: the size of Saint Louis or New Orleans. Data show similar historic dips in growth rates, but they've never lasted for long.

At recent rates of growth, the United States would reach a billion people by 2100—the size of China in the 1980s. But *how* is our population growing? Births to native-born residents of the United States are below two children per family, the level of "zero population growth" that would lead to a stabilized population within about fifty years. But that's not happening. According to census data, most recent growth in the United States has come through immigration, while 82 percent of the growth projected for the next forty years will be immigration driven (Passel and Cohn 2008). In California, virtually 100 percent of the growth is from immigration (Bouvier 2003). Today immigration—including the children of the immigrants, who must be counted, because obviously they would not be here if their parents hadn't come to America—is the main driver of U.S. population growth. Net legal and illegal immigration into the United States has totaled about 1.2 million per year in recent years (Camarota 2007).

This puts many of us in a difficult spot. We do not want to deny the opportunity of immigration to other people. But we don't want to deny other opportunities, either, such as the opportunity for our children and grandchildren to have a healthy environment, or the opportunity for other species to live and thrive, and for our kids and grandkids to see them. While efficiency improvements might limit the damage in some cases, two times the number of people tends to double the amount of sprawl and open space consumed, the wildlife habitat destroyed, the water used, the oil and coal burned.

Given all that's at stake, I'm dismayed that we rarely even talk about the U.S. population growth. But I'm outraged when I think about this from another point of view. Imagine yourself, for a moment, on the side of the people who want unrestricted economic growth and typically resist environmental protection. What would you do you if you wanted to make sure that unlimited amounts of land were available for development no matter what the loss, that every drop of oil and bucket of coal would be extracted and burned no matter what the consequences, that every rule for the environment would be stretched, ignored, or rescinded? You could work case by case, as happens every day all across America. But if you wanted to win the war and not just particular battles against environmentalists— plus along the way, enjoy a perpetual source of cheap labor based on an oversupply so large that it makes bargaining or unionizing impossible—if you wanted all this, then all you would need is an ever-increasing population. You wouldn't have to do anything except make sure that population growth did not stop. In the end, people will demand to be accommodated; endangered frogs are no match against human suffering, real or imagined. The losses might be resisted for a while, the way they were by Jim McClure, but not for long. A growing population is, in fact, so important to anti-environmentalists' success that they would be well served if there were a taboo on even discussing population growth and the ways to limit it.

Indeed, now that immigration drives growth, it has become difficult to discuss the issue, because it is entwined with race and ethnicity. It just so happens that most of the current growth comes from Mexico, Central and South America, and Asia. Our history of immoral racism rightly makes us cautious about repeating past mistakes. But accusations of racism, even when false, are one of the most effective conversation stoppers in our culture. Yet discussions about the numbers are needed, no matter where people come from.

Imagine, once again, that you were a foe to the kinds of political action for environmental protection that the Sierra Club espouses. Now think about the glee with which you would regard that group's self-imposed taboo on the discussion of American population growth and immigration. In highly publicized cases, the Club in recent years has rejected proposals by some members to simply consider the issue (Kolankiewicz and Beck 2001).

What happens when you do discuss population growth and immigration in the United States? Here are just a few of the questions that come up in my conversations, along with my responses.

Isn't overconsumption by Americans the real problem? It is inexcusable and needs to be changed, but the guilt associated with inequities here cannot be assuaged no matter how many more people come to partake in overconsumption. The difficulty of getting Americans to reduce consumption is no reason to increase the population of American consumers even more. Splitting our efforts equally between the reduction of consumption and the stabilization of population might be a reasonable approach, given Paul Ehrlich and John Holdren's formula: population × consumption = environmental impact. Because even if by some cultural and marketing miracle we cut consumption in half (back to 1950s levels), remember, the gain would soon be undone by the increase in population at current growth rates.

Isn't immigration needed to fill jobs that Americans don't want? Unemployment in America in 2011 is a severe problem, owing to economic recession. It is in the news every day. What is not in the news is that 112,000 new immigrant workers are legally allowed to enter the country *per month*, consigning America's unemployed, including recent immigrants, to deepening joblessness (Camarota and Jensenius 2009). Many additional workers arrive illegally. Americans want jobs, but a surplus of labor means that jobs failing to meet safety laws, with horrible working conditions and unfairly low wages, will be filled by desperate people, and it means that all bargaining possibilities by workers will be foregone. This model may serve unscrupulous employers, but it does not serve workers, either native born or immigrant.

Don't we have an obligation to help other people? Yes, as a member of a wealthy society, I feel an obligation to help the less fortunate. But I also feel an obligation to protect the places where the next generation of Americans will live. I see no advantage in filling up our country until it offers no appeal to people searching for something better than the poverty-stricken countries where they now live. Rather than letting immigration run its course, I believe our obligation is to help the people of the world to make the changes they need, in their own countries, for all of their residents.

Beginning with the Reagan administration, funding for family planning aid, especially for such agencies as the United Nations Population Fund and Planned Parenthood, was cut back sharply. In his foreword to *A Pivotal Moment: Population, Justice, and the Environmental Challenge*, Tim Wirth, president of the United Nations Foundation, notes that since 1995 the United States has decreased its support for international population programs by almost 40 percent (2009). Among many others, Wirth advocates that through financial and technical support, the United States should strongly promote family planning programs around the world. This would be an important way to lead the world toward global sustainability and a stabilized world population.

Efforts of this type have the potential to be far more effective and sustainable than allowing a tiny fraction of the world's needy to become American consumers by immigrating into the United States. Worldwide about eighty million additional people are added to impoverished countries per year. Even at immigration levels that would overwhelm America in every respect, such immigration would be insignificant help compared to world needs. Immigration is not going to solve the problems of other countries and can, in many ways, exacerbate them (Krikorian 2008).

We are all in this together, and isn't world population a zero-sum game, with equal effects being felt no matter where the people are? Yes, we are, and no, it isn't. Immigrants who come to America don't come to be poor; they reasonably aspire to the American "standard of living." That means becoming American consumers, which increases energy use, carbon emissions, and other problems for the Earth. Americans, eventually including the new ones, consume resources at forty times the rate of people in India, so the *global* ecological effects of U.S. population increases are far greater than increases in India or in most other countries.

The questions are many, and all need to be addressed in greater detail, but space is limited. So let me return to my key point: if we do not conserve the great support systems of nature, there will be no life on Earth as we know it, let alone lives of decency for people inside or outside the United States, today or tomorrow, native or immigrant. If we are to limit global warming, maintain enough farmland to grow our food, protect enough wildlands to sustain other creatures, provide healthy water to all people, and also have fish be supported by those waters—if we are to sustain our lives without the crush of personal freedoms that are extinguished in an anthill world of crowding—then we must address the issue of population growth. For the world, that means embracing effective family planning programs and women's empowerment to rein in population growth. For the United States, it means reducing immigration. If we do not pursue these related goals, our environmental efforts will be futile, as the savings of today are simply spent tomorrow, and tomorrow, until nothing remains.

The fate of our country and the world can be changed in time to leave something of value for all those who are yet to be born. But to do that, the population and immigration discussion must begin.

BIBLIOGRAPHY

Bouvier, Leon. 2003. *California's Population Growth,, 1990–2002: Virtually All from Immigration.* Santa Barbara, Calif.: Californians for Population Stabilization.
California Department of Finance. 2011. "State of California Total Population, 1850 to 2010." Department of Finance, Demographic Research Unit, Sacramento, Calif. Accessed July 2011 from www.dof.ca.gov/research/demographic/documents/California-HistoricalPop-Seats1850-2010.pdf.
Camarota, Steven. 2007. "100 Million More: Projecting the Impact of Immigration on the U.S. Population, 2007–2060." Washington, D.C.: Center for Immigration Studies.
Camarota, Steven, and Karen Jensenius. 2009. "Worse Than It Seems: Broader Measure of Unemployment Shows Bleak Picture." Washington, D.C.: Center for Immigration Studies.
Central Intelligence Agency (CIA). 2011. "Population Growth Rate: Country Comparison." *The World Factbook.* Accessed July 2011 from https://www.cia.gov/library/publications/the-world-factbook/rankorder/2002rank.html.

Daniels, Tom, and Deborah Bowers. 1997. *Holding Our Ground.* Washington, D.C.: Island Press.

Ehrlich, Paul R., and Anne H. Ehrlich. 1991. "The Most Overpopulated Nation." *NPG Forum*, January. Rpt. 1996, available from www.npg.org/forum_series/ TheMostOverpopulatedNation.pdf.

Gleick, Peter, Heather Cooley, and David Groves. 2005. *California Water 2030: An Efficient Future.* Oakland, Calif.: Pacific Institute.

Heinz Center for Science, Economics, and the Environment. 2008. *The State of the Nation's Ecosystems, 2008.* Washington, D.C.: Island Press.

Intergovernmental Panel on Climate Change (IPCC). 2007. *Climate Change 2007: Synthesis Report for Policymakers.* Accessed from www.ipcc.ch/publications_ and_data/ar4/syr/en/spms1.html.

Jehl, Douglas. 2002. "Running Dry." *New York Times*, September 28.

Kolankiewicz, Leon, and Roy Beck. 2001. *Forsaking Fundamentals: The Environmental Establishment Abandons U.S. Population Stabilization.* Washington, D.C.: Center for Immigration Studies.

Krikorian, Mark. 2008. *The New Case against Immigration, Both Legal and Illegal.* New York: Penguin/Sentinel Press.

Palmer, Tim. 2004. *Endangered Rivers and the Conservation Movement.* 2nd ed. New York: Rowman and Littlefield.

Passel, Jeffrey, and D'Vera Cohn. 2008. "U.S. Population Projections: 2005–2050." Washington, D.C.: Pew Research Center.

Pimentel, David, and Marcia Pimentel. 1990. "Land, Energy, and Water: The Constraints Governing Ideal U.S. Population Size." *NPG Forum*, January.

United Nations Department of Economic and Social Affairs, Population Division (UNPD). 2004. *World Population to 2300.* New York: United Nations.

U.S. Census Bureau. 2011. "Projected Population of the United States, by Race and Hispanic Origin: 2000 to 2050." Washington, D.C. Accessed July 2011 from www.census.gov/population/www/projections/usinterimproj/natprojtab01.pdf.

Wackernagel, Mathis, and William Rees. 1998. *Our Ecological Footprint: Reducing Human Impact upon the Earth.* Philadelphia: New Society.

Weeks, John. 1990. "How to Influence Fertility: The Experience So Far." *NPG Forum*, September.

Wirth, Timothy E. 2009. Foreword to *A Pivotal Moment: Population, Justice and the Environmental Challenge*, edited by Laurie Mazur. Washington, D.C.: Island Press.

CHAPTER 9

Environmental Refugees

The Rising Tide

LESTER BROWN

IN LATE AUGUST 2005, as Hurricane Katrina approached the U.S. Gulf Coast, more than one million people were evacuated from New Orleans and the small towns and rural communities along the coast. The decision to evacuate was well taken. In some Gulf Coast towns, Katrina's powerful twenty-eight-foot-high storm surge did not leave a single structure standing. New Orleans survived the initial hit, but it was flooded when the inland levies were breached and water covered large parts of the city—in many cases leaving just the rooftops exposed, where thousands of people were stranded (Brown 2006).

Once the storm passed, it was assumed that the million or so Katrina evacuees would, as in past cases, return to repair and rebuild their homes. Some seven hundred thousand did return, but close to three hundred thousand did not. Nor do they plan to do so. Most of them have no home or job to return to. They are no longer evacuees. They are climate refugees. Interestingly, the first large wave of modern climate refugees emerged in the United States—the country most responsible for the rise in atmospheric carbon dioxide that is warming Earth. New Orleans is the first modern coastal city to be partly abandoned (Grier 2005; Brown 2006; Louisiana Recovery Authority 2007; World Resources Institute 2009).

One of the defining characteristics of our time is the swelling flow of environmental refugees: people displaced by rising seas, more destructive storms, expanding deserts, water shortages, and dangerously high levels of toxic pollutants in the local environment.

Over the longer term, rising-sea refugees will likely dominate the flow of environmental refugees. The prospect for this century is a rise in sea level of up to six feet. Even a three-foot rise would inundate parts of many low-lying cities, major river deltas, and low-lying island countries. Among the early refugees will be millions of rice-farming families from Asia's low-lying river deltas, those who will watch their fields sink below the rising sea (Pfeffer, Harper, and O'Neel 2008). The flow of rising-sea refugees will come primarily from coastal cities. Among those most immediately affected are London, New York, Washington, Miami, Shanghai, Kolkata, Cairo, and Tokyo. If the rise in sea level cannot be checked, cities soon will have to start either planning for relocation or building barriers that will block the rising seas.

The movement of millions of rising-sea refugees to higher elevations in the interior of their countries will create two real estate markets—one in coastal regions, where prices will fall, and another in the higher elevations, where they will rise. Property insurance rates are already rising in storm- and flood-prone places like Florida (Larsen 2006).

River deltas contain some of the largest, most vulnerable populations. These include the deltas of the Mekong, Irrawaddy, Niger, Nile, Mississippi, Ganges-Brahmaputra, and Yangtze Rivers. For example, a six-foot sea level rise would displace fifteen million Bangladeshis living in the densely populated Ganges-Brahmaputra delta (Young and Pilkey 2010). The London-based Environmental Justice Foundation reports that "a one meter [three foot] sea-level rise would affect up to 70 percent of Nigeria's coastline affecting over 2.7 million hectares. Egypt would lose at least 2 million hectares in the fertile Nile Delta, displacing 8 to 10 million people, including nearly the entire population of Alexandria" (2009, 23).

Low-lying islands will also be hit hard. The thirty-nine members of the Alliance of Small Island States stand to lose part or all of their territories as sea level rises. Among the most immediately threatened are Tuvalu, Kiribati, and the Marshall Islands in the Pacific Ocean and the Maldives in the Indian Ocean. Well before total inundation, islanders face saltwater intrusion that can contaminate their drinking water and make it impossible for deep-rooted crops to survive. Eventually, all crops will fail (Alliance of Small Island States 2010). Some three thousand of Tuvalu's ten thousand people have already migrated to New Zealand, seeking work under a labor migration program. Larger populations, such as the three hundred thousand people in the Maldives, will find it more difficult to migrate elsewhere. The president of the Maldives is actively pursuing the possibility of purchasing land for his people to migrate to as the sea level inches upward and makes island life untenable (Warner et al. 2009; CIA 2010; UNPD 2009).

Meanwhile, following the 2004 tsunami that so memorably devastated Indonesia, the government of the Maldives decided to organize a "staged retreat" by moving people from the lower-lying islands, some two hundred in total, to a dozen or so slightly higher islands. But even the highest of these is only about eight feet above sea level. And in anticipation of higher seas, the Papua New Guinea government moved the one thousand residents of the Carteret Islands to the larger island of Bougainville (Fritz 2010; Environmental Justice Foundation 2009). Aside from the social upheaval and the personal devastation of people losing their country to the rising sea, there are also legal issues to be resolved. When does a country cease to exist legally, for example? Is it when there is no longer a functioning government? Or when it has disappeared beneath the waves? And at what point does a country lose its vote in the United Nations? In any event, rising sea level is likely to shrink UN membership as low-lying island states disappear.

How far might the sea level rise? Rob Young and Orrin Pilkey note in *The Rising Sea* that planning panels in Rhode Island and Miami assume a minimum rise of 3.5 feet by 2100. A California planning study uses a 4.6-foot rise by century's end. The Dutch, for their coastal planning purposes, are assuming a 2.5-foot rise for 2050 (Young and Pilkey 2009, 2010).

If the Greenland ice sheet, which is well over a mile thick in places, were to melt completely, sea level would rise twenty-three feet. And if the West Antarctic ice sheet were to break up entirely, sea level would rise sixteen feet. Together, the melting of these two ice sheets, which scientists believe to be the most vulnerable, would raise sea level thirty-nine feet. And this does not include thermal expansion as ocean water warms, an important contributor to sea level rise (UNEP 2007; 2009, 9, 27).

A study published by the International Institute for Environment and Development has analyzed the effect of a ten-meter (thirty-three-foot) rise in sea level. The study begins by noting that 634 million people currently live along coasts at ten or fewer meters above sea level, in what they call the Low Elevation Coastal Zone (McGranahan, Balk, and Anderson 2007). The most vulnerable country is China, with 144 million potential climate refugees. India and Bangladesh are next, with 63 million and 62 million respectively. Viet Nam has 43 million vulnerable people, and

Indonesia 42 million. Also in the top ten are Japan with 30 million, Egypt with 26 million, and the United States with 23 million. Some of the refugees could simply retreat to higher ground within their own country. Others—facing extreme crowding in the interior regions of their homeland—would seek refuge elsewhere (McGranahan, Balk, and Anderson 2007).

The second category of environmental refugees is also closely related to elevated global temperatures. A higher surface water temperature in the tropical oceans means there is more energy to drive tropical storm systems, which can lead to more destructive storms. The combination of more powerful storms and stronger storm surges can be devastating, as New Orleans discovered. The regions that are most at risk for more-powerful and destructive storms are Central America, the Caribbean, and both the Atlantic and Gulf coasts of the United States. In Asia, where hurricanes are called typhoons, it is East and Southeast Asia, including Japan, China, Taiwan, the Philippines, and Viet Nam, that are most vulnerable. The other region in danger is the Bay of Bengal, particularly Bangladesh.

In the fall of 1998, Hurricane Mitch—one of the most powerful storms ever to come out of the Atlantic, with winds approaching two hundred miles per hour—hit the east coast of Central America. As atmospheric conditions stalled the normal northward progression of the storm, more than six feet of rain fell on parts of Honduras and Nicaragua within a few days. The deluge collapsed homes, factories, and schools, leaving them in ruins. It destroyed roads and bridges. Seventy percent of the crops in Honduras were washed away, as was much of the topsoil. Huge mudslides destroyed villages, sometimes burying local populations (Abramovitz 2001). The storm left eleven thousand dead, and thousands more were never found (National Climatic Data Center 2004). The basic infrastructure—the roads and bridges in Honduras and Nicaragua—was largely destroyed. President Flores of Honduras summed it up this way: "Overall, what was destroyed over several days took us 50 years to build" (quoted in Chavez et al. 2001). The cost of the damage from this storm exceeded the annual gross domestic product of the two countries and set their economic development back by twenty years.

The first decade of this century has brought many other destructive storms. In 2004, Japan experienced a record ten typhoons that collectively caused $10 billion worth of losses. The 2005 Atlantic hurricane season was the worst on record, bringing fifteen hurricanes, including Katrina, and $115 billion in insured losses (Smith and Helft 2004; Doering 2010).

A third source of refugees is advancing deserts, which are now on the move almost everywhere. The Sahara Desert is expanding in every direction. As it advances northward, it is squeezing the populations of Morocco, Tunisia, and Algeria against the Mediterranean coast. The Sahelian region of Africa—the vast swath of savannah that separates the southern Sahara Desert from the tropical rain forests of central Africa—is shrinking as the desert moves southward. As the desert invades Nigeria, Africa's most populous country, from the north, farmers and herders are forced southward, squeezed into a shrinking area of productive land. Some desert refugees end up in cities, many in squatter settlements, and others migrate abroad. A 2006 UN conference on desertification in Tunisia projected that by 2020 up to sixty million people could migrate from sub-Saharan Africa to North Africa and Europe (Federal Republic of Nigeria 1999; UN News Centre 2006; UNPD 2009).

In Iran, villages abandoned because of spreading deserts or a lack of water number in the thousands. In the vicinity of Damavand, a small town within an hour's drive of Tehran, eighty-eight villages have been abandoned (Iranian News Agency 2002). In Latin America, expanding deserts are forcing people to move in both Brazil and Mexico. In Brazil, some 250,000 square miles of land are affected, much of it concentrated in the country's northeast (Matallo 2006; Brown 2004, 86–87). In Mexico, many of the migrants who leave rural communities in arid and semiarid regions of the country each year are doing so because of desertification. Some of these environmental refugees end up in Mexican cities; others cross the northern border into the United States. U.S. analysts estimate that Mexico is forced to abandon four hundred square miles of farmland to desertification each year (Schwartz and Notini 1994; Faist and Alscher 2009).

In China, desert expansion has accelerated in each successive decade since 1950. Desert scholar Wang Tao reports that over the last half century or so some twenty-four thousand villages in northern and western China have been abandoned either entirely or partly because of desert expansion. China's Environmental Protection Agency reports that from 1994 to 1999 the Gobi Desert grew by 20,240 square miles, an area half the size of Pennsylvania. With the advancing Gobi now within 150 miles of Beijing, China's leaders are beginning to sense the gravity of the situation (Wang Tao et al. 2004).

The U.S. Dust Bowl of the 1930s, which was caused by overplowing and triggered by drought, forced more than two million "Okies" to leave the land, many of them heading west from Oklahoma, Texas, and Kansas to California. But the dust bowl forming in China is much larger, and so is the population: during the 1930s the U.S. population was only 150 million, compared with China's 1.3 billion today. Whereas U.S. migration was measured in the millions, China's may measure in the tens of millions. And as a U.S. embassy report entitled *Grapes of Wrath in Inner Mongolia* noted, "unfortunately, China's twenty-first century 'Okies' have no California to escape to—at least not in China" (Montgomery 2007, 145–58; UNPD 2009; U.S. Embassy 2001).

The fourth group of people who will be forced to leave their homes are those in places where water tables are falling. With the vast majority of the three billion people projected to be added to the world by 2050 being born in such countries, water refugees are likely to become commonplace. They will be most common in arid and semiarid regions where populations are outgrowing the water supply and sinking into hydrological poverty. Villages in northwestern India are being abandoned as aquifers are depleted and people can no longer find water. Millions of villagers in northern and western China and in northern Mexico may have to move because of a lack of water (Shah et al. 2000; UNPD 2009).

Thus far the evacuations resulting from water shortages have been confined to villages, but eventually whole cities might have to be relocated, such as Sana'a, the capital of Yemen, and Quetta, the capital of Pakistan's Baluchistan province. Sana'a, a fast-growing city of more than two million people, is literally running out of water. Wells that are thirteen hundred feet deep are beginning to go dry. In this "race to the bottom" in the Sana'a valley, oil-drilling equipment is being used to dig ever deeper wells. Some are now over half a mile deep (UNPD 2008; Laessing 2010; UNFAO 2009c). The situation is bleak because trying to import water into this mountain valley from other provinces would generate tribal conflicts. Desalting sea water on the coast would be expensive because of the cost of the process itself, the distance the water would have to be pumped, and the city's altitude of seven thousand feet. Sana'a may soon be a ghost city (Lyon 2009). Quetta, originally designed for fifty thousand people, now has a population exceeding one million, all of whom depend on two thousand wells pumping water from what is believed to be a fossil aquifer. In the words of one study assessing its water prospect, Quetta will soon be "a dead city" (Integrated Regional Information Networks 2002).

Two other semiarid Middle Eastern countries that are suffering from water shortages are Syria and Iraq. Both are beginning to reap the consequences of overpumping their aquifers, namely irrigation wells going dry

(UNFAO 2009a, 2009b). In Syria, these trends have forced the abandonment of 160 villages. Hundreds of thousands of farmers and herders have left the land and pitched tents on the outskirts of cities, hoping to find work. A UN report estimates that more than a hundred thousand people in northern Iraq have been uprooted because of water shortages (Brown and Crawford 2009, 26; De Schutter 2010; Lightfoot 2009). Hussein Amery, a Middle East water expert from the Colorado School of Mines, puts it very simply: "Water scarcity is forcing people off the land" (quoted in Amos 2010).

The fifth category of environmental refugee has appeared only in the last fifty years or so: people who are trying to escape toxic waste or dangerous radiation levels. During the late 1970s, Love Canal—a small town in upstate New York, part of which was built on top of a toxic waste disposal site—made national and international headlines. Beginning in 1942, the Hooker Chemical Company had dumped twenty-one thousand tons of toxic waste, including chlorobenzene, dioxin, halogenated organics, and pesticides there. In 1952, Hooker closed the site, capped it over, and deeded it to the Love Canal Board of Education. An elementary school was built on the site, taking advantage of the free land. But during the 1960s and 1970s people began noticing odors and residues from seeping wastes. Birth defects and other illnesses were common. Beginning in August 1978, families were relocated at government expense and reimbursed for their homes at market prices. By October 1980, a total of 950 families had been permanently relocated (U.S. EPA 2010a).

A few years later, the residents of Times Beach, Missouri, began complaining about various health problems. A firm spraying oil on roads to control dust was using waste oil laden with toxic chemical wastes. After the U.S. Environmental Protection Agency discovered dioxin levels well above the public health standards, the federal government arranged for the permanent evacuation and relocation of the town's two thousand people (EPA 2010b).

Another infamous source of environmental refugees is the Chernobyl nuclear power plant in Kiev, which exploded in April 1986. This started a powerful fire that lasted for ten days. Massive amounts of radioactive material were spewed into the atmosphere, showering communities in the region with heavy doses of radiation. As a result, the residents of the nearby town of Pripyat and several other communities in Ukraine, Belarus, and Russia were evacuated, requiring the resettlement of 350,000 people. In 1992, six years after the accident, Belarus was devoting 20 percent of its national budget to resettlement and the many other costs associated with the accident (Cherp et al. 2002).

While the United States has relocated two communities because of health-damaging pollutants, the identification of 459 "cancer villages" in China suggests the need to evacuate hundreds of Chinese communities (Liu 2010). China's Ministry of Health statistics show that cancer is now the country's leading cause of death. The lung cancer death rate, also boosted by smoking, has risen nearly fivefold over the last thirty years (Xue-jun and Huan-zhong 2007; Xinhua 2008).

With little pollution control, whole communities near chemical factories are suffering from unprecedented rates of cancer. The World Bank reports that liver cancer death rates among China's rural population are four times the global average. Their stomach cancer death rates are double those for the world. Chinese industrialists build factories in rural areas where there is cheap labor and little or no enforcement of pollution control laws. Young people are leaving for the city in droves, for other jobs and possibly for better health. Yet many others are too sick or too poor to leave (World Bank 2007, 45–46; Liu 2010).

Separating out the geneses of today's refugees is not always easy. Often the environmental and economic stresses that drive migration are closely intertwined. But whatever the reason for leaving home, people are taking increasingly desperate measures. The news headlines about refugees who try to cross the Mediterranean tell the story: a 2009 BBC story entitled "Hundreds Feared Drowned off Libya," a 2008 *Guardian* piece with the headline "Over 70 Migrants Feared Killed on Crossing to Europe," and an Associated Press story from 2008—"Spain: 35 Reported Dead in Migrant Ordeal" (BBC News 2009; Hooper 2008; Associated Press 2008).

Some of the stories are heartrending beyond belief. In mid-October 2003, Italian authorities discovered a boat bound for Italy carrying refugees from Africa. After being adrift for more than two weeks and having run out of fuel, food, and water, many of the passengers had died. At first the dead were tossed overboard. But after a point, the remaining survivors lacked the strength to hoist the bodies over the side. The dead and the living shared the boat, resembling what a rescuer described as "a scene from Dante's Inferno" (Cowell 2003). The refugees were believed to be Somalis who had embarked from Libya, but the survivors would not reveal their country of origin lest they be sent home. We do not know whether they were political, economic, or environmental refugees. Failed states like Somalia produce all three. We do know that Somalia is a lawless entity and an ecological basket case, with overpopulation, overgrazing, and the resulting desertification destroying its pastoral economy (Cowell 2003).

In April 2006, a man fishing off the coast of Barbados discovered a twenty-foot boat adrift with the bodies of eleven young men on board, bodies that were "virtually mummified" by the sun and salty ocean spray. As the end drew near, one passenger left a note tucked between two bodies: "I would like to send my family in Basada [Senegal] a sum of money. Please excuse me and goodbye." The author of the note was apparently one of a group of fifty-two who had left Senegal on Christmas Eve aboard a boat destined for the Canary Islands, a jumping off point for Europe (Leitsinger 2006; Roman 2006; Bruni 2002; Botsford 2002; Agence France-Presse 2003).

Each day Mexicans risk their lives in the Arizona desert, trying to reach jobs in the United States. Some four hundred to six hundred Mexicans leave rural areas every day, abandoning plots of land too small or too eroded to make a living. They either head for Mexican cities or try to cross illegally into the United States. Many of those who try to cross the Arizona desert perish in its punishing heat; scores of bodies are found along the Arizona border each year (Jordan and Sullivan 2003; McLeman and Smit 2004; Myers 2010).

The potentially massive movement of people across national boundaries is already affecting some countries. India, for example, with a steady stream of migrants from Bangladesh and the prospect of millions more to come, is building a ten-foot-high fence along their shared border. The United States is erecting a fence along the border with Mexico. The current movement of Chinese across the border into Siberia is described as temporary, but it will likely become permanent. Another major border, the Mediterranean Sea, is now routinely patrolled by naval vessels trying to intercept the small boats of African migrants bound for Europe (Sullivan 2007; Stout 2006; Radyuhin 2003; Thorne 2006; Frontex 2010).

In the end, the question is whether governments are strong enough to withstand the political and economic stress of extensive migration flows, both internal and external. Some of the largest flows will be across national borders and are likely to be illegal. As a general matter, environmental refugees will be migrating from poor countries to rich ones, from Africa, Asia, and Latin America to North America and Europe. In the face of mounting environmental stresses, will the migration of people be limited and organized or will it be massive and chaotic?

People do not normally leave their homes, their families, and their communities unless they have no other option. Maybe it is time for governments to consider whether it might not be cheaper and far less painful in human terms to treat the causes of migration rather than merely respond to it. This means working with developing countries to restore their economy's natural support systems—the soils, the grasslands, the forests—and it means accelerating the shift to smaller families to help people break out of poverty. Treating symptoms instead of causes is not good medicine. Nor is it good public policy.

❧

When it comes to population growth, the United Nations has three primary projections. The medium projection, the one most commonly used, has world population reaching 9.2 billion by 2050. The high one reaches 10.5 billion. The low projection, which assumes that the world will quickly move below replacement-level fertility, has population peaking at 8 billion in 2042 and then declining. If the goal is to eradicate poverty, hunger, and illiteracy, as well as achieve sustainability, then we have little choice but to strive for the lower projection (UNPD 2009).

Slowing world population growth means ensuring that all women who want to plan their families have access to family planning services. Unfortunately, this is currently not the case for 215 million women, 59 percent of whom live in sub-Saharan Africa and the Indian subcontinent. These women and their families represent roughly one billion of Earth's poorest residents, for whom unintended pregnancies and unwanted births are an enormous burden (Singh et al. 2009, 4). Former U.S. Agency for International Development (AID) official Joseph Speidel notes that "if you ask anthropologists who live and work with poor people at the village level . . . they often say that women live in fear of their next pregnancy. They just do not want to get pregnant" (quoted in APPG 2007, 22).

The United Nations Population Fund and the Guttmacher Institute estimate that meeting the needs of these 215 million women who lack reproductive health care and effective contraception could each year prevent 53 million unwanted pregnancies, 24 million induced abortions, and 1.6 million infant deaths (Singh et al. 2009, 4–5, 19). Along with the provision of additional condoms needed to prevent HIV and other sexually transmitted infections, a universal family planning and reproductive health program would cost an additional $21 billion in funding from industrial and developing countries (UNFPA 2008, 2009; Joseph Speidel, personal communication, October 8, 2010; Population Action International 2004; Haddock et al. 2008).

The good news is that governments can help couples reduce family size very quickly when they commit to doing so.

NOTE

This paper is based on chapter 6 of Lester R. Brown's *World on the Edge: How to Prevent Environmental and Economic Collapse*, Earth Policy Institute (New York: W. W. Norton, 2011).

BIBLIOGRAPHY

Abramovitz, Janet. 2001. "Averting Unnatural Disasters." In *State of the World 2001*, edited by Lester R. Brown et al., 123–142. New York: W. W. Norton.

Agence France-Presse. 2003. "Boat Sinks Off Coast of Turkey: One Survivor and 7 Bodies Found," 22 December.

Alliance of Small Island States. 2010. "Members and Observers." Accessed July 15, 2010, from www.sidsnet.org/aosis/members.html.

All Party Parliamentary Group on Population, Development and Reproductive Health (APPG). 2007. *Return of the Population Growth Factor: Its Impact on the Millennium Development Goals*. London: Her Majesty's Stationery Office.

Amos, Deborah. 2010. "Mideast Water Crisis Brings Misery, Uncertainty." *National Public Radio*, January 8.

Associated Press. 2008. "Spain: 35 Reported Dead in Migrant Ordeal." August 26.

BBC News. 2009. "Hundreds Feared Drowned off Libya." March 31.

Botsford, Flora. 2002. "Spain Recovers Drowned Migrants." BBC News. April 25.

Brown, Lester R. 2004. *Outgrowing the Earth: The Food Security Challenge in the Age of Falling Water Tables and Rising Temperatures*. New York: W. W. Norton.

———. 2006. "Global Warming Forcing U.S. Coastal Population to Move Inland." *Eco-Economy Update*. Washington, D.C.: Earth Policy Institute.

Brown, Oli, and Alec Crawford. 2009. *Rising Temperatures, Rising Tensions: Climate Change and the Risk of Violent Conflict in the Middle East*. Winnipeg: International Institute for Sustainable Development.

Bruni, Frank. 2002. "Off Sicily, Tide of Bodies Roils Immigrant Debate." *New York Times*, September 23.

Central Intelligence Agency. 2010. *The World Factbook*. Accessed from https://www.cia.gov/library/publications/the-world-factbook/index.html.

Chavez, Arturo, Michael A. Dunn, Pamela A. Monroe, Todd F. Shupe, Lakshman

Velupillai, and D. Vlosky. 2001. "After the Hurricane: Forest Sector Reconstruction in Honduras." *Forest Products Journal* 51 (November/December): 18–24.

Cherp, Aleg, Angelina Nyagu, Fedor Fleshtor, Keith Baverstock, Marina Khotouleva, and Patrick Gray. 2002. *The Human Consequences of the Chernobyl Nuclear Accident*. New York: United Nations Development Programme (UNDP) and United Nations International Children's Fund (UNICEF).

Cowell, Alan. 2003. "Migrants Found off Italy Boat Piled with Dead." *International Herald Tribune*, October 21.

De Schutter, Olivier. 2010. *UN Special Rapporteur on the Right to Food: Mission to Syria from 29 August to 7 September 2010*. Preliminary conclusions. Accessed from www.srfood.org.

Doering, Christopher. 2010. "Government Warns of Worst Hurricane Season since 2005." *Reuters*, May 27.

Environmental Justice Foundation. 2009. *No Place Like Home: Where Next for Climate Refugees?* London: Environmental Justice Foundation.

Faist, Thomas, and Stefan Alscher. 2009. *Environmental Factors in Mexican Migration: The Cases of Chiapas and Tlaxcala*. Case study report on Mexico for the Environmental Change and Forced Migration Scenarios Project. Bielefeld, Germany.

Federal Republic of Nigeria. 1999. *Combating Desertification and Mitigating the Effects of Drought in Nigeria*. National Report on the Implementation of the United Nations Convention to Combat Desertification. Nigeria, November. Accessed from www.unccd.int/cop/reports/africa/national/1999/nigeria-eng.pdf.

Fritz, Carolina. 2010. "Climate Change and Migration: Sorting through Complex Issues without the Hype." Migration Policy Institute Feature. Washington, D.C.. Accessed from www.migrationinformation.org/Feature/display.cfm?ID=773.

Frontex. 2010. *General Report 2009*. Warsaw. Accessed from http://www.frontex.europa.eu/annual_report.

Grier, Peter. 2005. "The Great Katrina Migration." *Christian Science Monitor*, September 12.

Haddock, Sarah, Karen Hardee, Jill Gay, Piotr Macie, J. Pawlak, and Christina Stellini. 2008. *Comprehensive HIV Prevention: Condoms and Contraceptives Count*. Washington, D.C.: Population Action International.

Hooper, John. 2008. "Over 70 Migrants Feared Killed on Crossing to Europe." *Guardian*, August 28.

Integrated Regional Information Networks. 2002. "Pakistan: Focus on Water Crisis." *IRIN News*, May 17.

Iranian News Agency. 2002. "Official Warns of Impending Desertification Catastrophe in Southeast Iran." *BBC International Reports*, September 29.

Jordan, Mary, and Kevin Sullivan. 2003. "Trade Brings Riches, But Not to Mexico's Poor." *Washington Post*, March 22.

Laessing, Ulf. 2010. "Yemen's Water Crisis Eclipses Al Qaeda Threat." Reuters, February 17.

Larsen, Janet. 2006. "Hurricane Damages Soar to New Levels: Insurance Companies Abandoning Homeowners in High-Risk Coastal Areas." *Eco-Economy Update*. Washington, D.C.: Earth Policy Institute.

Leitsinger, Miranda. 2006. "African Migrants Die an Ocean Away." *Washington Post*, June 2.

Lightfoot, Dale. 2009. *Survey of Infiltration Karez in Northern Iraq: History and Current Status of Underground Aqueducts*. Paris: UNESCO, September.

Liu, Lee. 2010. "Made in China: Cancer Villages." *Environment*, March/April.

Louisiana Recovery Authority. 2007. *Migration Patterns: Estimates of Parish Level Migrations Due to Hurricanes Katrina and Rita*. Baton Rouge, La.: August.

Lyon, Alistair. 2009. "Water Crisis Threatens Yemen's Swelling Population." Reuters, August 30.

Matallo, Heitor. 2006. "General Approach to the Costs of Desertification." Presentation at the International Workshop on the Cost of Inaction and Opportunities for Investment in Arid, Semi-Arid, and Dry Sub-Humid Areas, Rome, December 4–5.

McGranahan, Gordon, Deborah Balk, and Brigit Anderson. 2007. "The Rising Tide: Assessing the Risks of Climate Change and Human Settlements in Low Elevation Coastal Zones." *Environment and Urbanization* 18 (1): 17–37.

McLeman, Robert, and Barry Smit. 2004. "Commentary No. 86: Climate Change, Migration and Security." Canadian Security Intelligence Service. Accessed from www.csis.gc.ca/pblctns/cmmntr/cm86-eng.asp.

Montgomery, David. 2007. *Dirt: The Erosion of Civilizations*. Berkeley: University of California Press.

Myers, Amanda. 2010. "Immigrant Deaths in Arizona Desert Soaring in July." Associated Press, July 16.

National Climatic Data Center, National Oceanic and Atmospheric Administration, U.S. Department of Commerce. 2004. "Mitch: The Deadliest Atlantic Hurricane since 1780." Accessed from www.ncdc.noaa.gov/oa/reports/mitch/mitch.html.

Pfeffer, W. T., J. T. Harper, and S. O'Neel. 2008. "Kinematic Constraints on Glacier Contributions to 21st-Century Sea-Level Rise." *Science* 321 (5894): 1340–1343.

Population Action International. 2004. "Why Condoms Count in the Era of HIV/AIDS." Fact sheet FS21. Washington, D.C.: Population Action International, June 1. Accessed from http://209.68.15.158/Publications/Fact_Sheets/FS21/Summary.shtml.

Radyuhin, Vladimir. 2003. "A Chinese 'Invasion.'" *World Press Review* 50 (12).

Roman, Mar. 2006. "A New Record for Africans Risking Boat Route to Europe." *Washington Post*, September 4.

Schwartz, Michelle Leighton, and Jessica Notini. 1994. *Desertification and Migration: Mexico and the United States*. Research Paper. Washington, D.C.: U.S. Commission on Immigration Reform. San Francisco.

Shah, Tushaar, David Molden, R. Sakthivadivel, and David Seckler. 2000. *The Global Groundwater Situation: Overview of Opportunities and Challenges*. Colombo, Sri Lanka: International Water Management Institute.

Singh, Susheela, Jacqueline E. Darroch, Lori S. Ashford, and Michael Vlassoff. 2009. *Adding It Up: The Costs and Benefits of Investing in Family Planning and Maternal and Newborn Health*. New York: Guttmacher Institute and United Nations Population Fund (UNFPA).

Smith, Michael, and Daniel Helft. 2004. "Bad Weather, Climate Change Cost World Record $90 Billion." Bloomberg, December 15.

Stout, David. 2006. "Bush, Signing Bill for Border Fence, Urges Wider Overhaul." *New York Times*, October 27.

Sullivan, Tim. 2007. "Neighbor India Quietly Fencing Out Bangladesh." Associated Press, June 26.

Thorne, John. 2006. "Europe, Africa Seek to Limit Immigration." Associated Press, July 10.

United Nations Environment Programme (UNEP). 2007. *Global Outlook for Ice and Snow*. Nairobi: UNEP.

———. 2009. *Climate Change Science Compendium 2009*. Nairobi: UNEP.

United Nations Food and Agriculture Organization (UNFAO). 2009a. "Iraq." AQUASTAT country profile. Accessed from www.fao.org/nr/water/aquastat/countries/iraq/index.stm.

———. 2009b. "Syrian Arab Republic." AQUASTAT country profile. Accessed from www.fao.org/nr/water/aquastat/countries/syria/index.stm.

———. 2009c. "Yemen." AQUASTAT country profile. Accessed from www.fao.org/nr/water/aquastat/countries/yemen/index.stm.

United Nations News Centre. 2006. "Scientists Meeting in Tunis Called for Priority Activities to Curb Desertification." June 21. Accessed from www.un.org/apps/news/story.asp?NewsID=18950&Cr=desert&Cr1.

United Nations Population Division (UNPD). 2008. *World Urbanization Prospects: The 2007 Revision Population Database*. Accessed from http://esa.un.org/unup/.

———. 2009. *World Population Prospects: The 2009 Revision Population Database*. Accessed from http://esa.un.org/wup2009/unup/index.asp?panel=5.

United Nations Population Fund (UNFPA). 2008. *Donor Support for Contraceptives and Condoms for STI/HIV Prevention 2007*. New York: UNFPA.

———. 2009. *Flow of Financial Resources for Assisting in the Implementation of the Programme of Action of the International Conference on Population and Develop-*

ment. Report of the secretary-general for the UN Economic and Social Council, Commission on Population and Development. New York.

U.S. Embassy, Beijing. 2001. *Grapes of Wrath in Inner Mongolia.* Report. Beijing, May.

U.S. Environmental Protection Agency (EPA). 2010a. "Love Canal." Superfund Redevelopment Initiative. Accessed from www.epa.gov/r02earth/superfund/ npl/0201290c.pdf.

———. 2010b. "Times Beach One-Page Summary." Superfund Redevelopment Program. Accessed from www.epa.gov/superfund/programs/recycle_old/success/ 1-pagers/timesbch.htm.

Wang Tao, Wei Wu, Xian Xue, Qingwei Sun, and Guangting Chen. 2004. "A Study on Spatial-Temporal Changes of Sandy Desertified Land during Last 5 Decades in North China." *Acta Geographica Sinica* 59: 203–212.

Warner, Koko, Charles Ehrhart, Alex de Sherbinin, Susana Adamo, and Tricia Chai-Onn. 2009. *In Search of Shelter: Mapping the Effects of Climate Change on Human Migration and Displacement.* Atlanta: CARE International.

World Bank. 2007. *Cost of Pollution in China: Estimates of Physical Damages.* Conference Edition. Washington, D.C.: World Bank.

World Resources Institute. 2009. *Climate Analysis Indicators Tool (CAIT) Version 6.0.* Washington, D.C. Accessed from http://cait.wri.org.

Xue-jun, Qin, and Shi Huan-zhong. 2007. "Major Causes of Death during the Past 25 Years in China." *Chinese Medical Journal* 120 (24): 2317–2320.

Xinhua. 2008. "Death Caused by Lung Cancer Soars in China." *China View,* April 29.

Young, Rob, and Orrin Pilkey. 2009. *The Rising Sea.* Washington, D.C.: Island Press.

———. 2010. "How High Will Seas Rise? Get Ready for Seven Feet." *Yale Environment 360,* January 14. Accessed from http://e360.yale.edu/content/feature .msp?id=2230.

CHAPTER 10

Population, Fossil Fuels, and Agriculture

GEORGE WUERTHNER

THE GLOBAL POPULATION reached seven billion toward the end of 2011, up from six billion in 1999. It only took a dozen years to increase our population by that one billion. In another fifteen years or so, we may have an additional billion people inhabiting the planet, and projections place the population between nine and ten billion by 2050. Feeding Earth's population is going to be one of our greatest challenges, even as the environmental costs associated with intensive agricultural production are already staggering. According to the World Bank, global food production will have to rise by about 70 percent between now and 2050 to feed nine billion people (*Economist* 2011). This bodes ill for biological diversity and the world's remaining wildlands.

Currently an astounding 75 percent of Earth's land mass (excluding Greenland and Antarctica) is used by and directly affected by humans. Of this amount approximately 1 percent is urbanized, 11.7 percent is cropland, 36 percent is grazed by domestic livestock, with 26 percent in managed forests (Erb et al. 2009). Of the 25 percent or so of Earth unaffected by humans, more than half is bare rock, desert, or ice, while much of the rest is still near-pristine forests, primarily in the tropics and boreal zones.

Agriculture can be understood as the concentration of solar energy and nutrients into one or a few species of domesticated plants and animals. Not surprisingly, agriculture is a major driver of biodiversity destruction. A field of corn is a biological desert from a biodiversity perspective. Industrial agriculture involves stripping the land of its native species of animals, plants, fungi, and other organisms and replacing them with large-scale monocultures. Some project that to feed growing human populations, croplands will need to be expanded to as much as 18 percent of terrestrial landscapes by 2050, at the expense of native ecosystems (Tilman 1999). Because agriculture affects almost half of the planet's land area, it is the largest single contributor to many environmental ills, including soil erosion, deforestation, species' extirpations and range contractions, and ground and surface water pollution. It is also a major contributor to the greenhouse gases responsible for global climate change.

Historically, agricultural production permitted human populations to grow well beyond the limits imposed by a hunter-gatherer lifestyle. Agriculture allowed the first huge jump in human population and the development of cities. In preindustrial societies, agriculture was largely driven by solar inputs in the form of wood, water power, wind power, and animal power. The next great population jump came when fossil fuels were marshaled to provide energy to human society. Agriculture underwent a revolution in output with this utilization of fossil fuel energy, exploiting ancient carbon reserves. Beginning in the 1800s, coal was the energy source that powered steam engines that allowed farmers to get their produce to markets in distant cities and provided the fuel to run early tractors and other farm machinery. Then in the early 1900s, the development of artificial nitrogen fertilizer, using natural gas as a major component, greatly increased agricultural production. Indeed, half of the world's population today may be fed as a consequence of synthetic fertilizers (Erisman et al. 2008).

In the United States, it is estimated that soil erosion is occurring at seventeen times the rate of soil formation, with fully 90 percent of croplands losing soil above sustainable rates. Soil erosion is even higher in most of Africa and Asia (IUGS n.d.). While artificial fertilizers may make up for some soil nutrient losses, it is at the cost of steep levels of pollution from producing and transporting them, as well as from nitrous oxide emissions and runoff, respectively implicated in global warming and coastal dead zones. Using fertilizers as a fix for soil depletion simply encourages its continuance, hurrying us toward a future where soil is further degraded and synthetic fertilizer pollution escalates.

Fossil fuels power tractors and other farm vehicles, transport food long distances, sometimes power irrigation pumps, and in many other ways subsidize modern agriculture. While there are many unconventional sources of fossil fuels left to exploit, including gas hydrates, new sources available through gas-fracking techniques, and large reserves of coal accessible through traditional mining and mountaintop removal, all of these sources and new technologies are hugely damaging to the environment. Similar high ecological costs are associated with newly exploited oil sources like tar sands and oil shales.

In other words, it is becoming more and more ecologically destructive to maintain the infrastructure that supports industrial agriculture. But David Pimentel, a Cornell University researcher, suggests that corn production would decline as much as 80 percent in the absence of modern farm equipment, fertilizers, and pesticides. All this shows why we cannot grow food in an ecologically sustainable manner and, at the same time, maintain and grow a huge human population.

Despite the recent movement toward buying local produce, which typically involves the sale of fresh vegetables and fruits, most of the calories people consume on a daily basis are cereal grains or grain-based foods. These are typically grown on large monoculture acreages far from urban centers. Corn, soy, wheat, and rice are the grain staples for most of the world's population, and a good portion of these grains becomes feed for animals; in the United States, for example, the majority of corn grown feeds livestock, not people.

Growing vast amounts of grain to feed humanity—especially an increasing global population with a growing taste for meat and other animal products—is a huge challenge (Brown 2011). To date, it has been possible primarily due to the input of fossil fuels in one form or another. The clearing of new land, particularly in the tropics by removal of forests with chain saws, bulldozers, and other machinery, the ripping up of native grasslands with giant tractors, and the plowing of enormous acreages are only possible on the present-day scale with fossil fuel subsidies. The so-called Green Revolution that vastly increased yields was, in essence, a fossil fuel revolution. More dangerous is that in much of the world we have forgotten how to grow food without these technological and energy inputs.

Some studies suggest that it may be possible to feed a population of over nine billion with completely organic methods; however, this assumes that cropland acreage increases by 20 percent, that people significantly limit their intake of meat, and that food is distributed equally (Erb et al. 2009). Most of this new cropland will be in tropical rainforests where biodiversity is greatest; thus, new agricultural production will destroy a significant amount of the world's remaining biodiversity. So even if it proves possible to support an enormous population via sustainable, organic farming, the cost to ecosystem services, biodiversity, and wildlands will be immense, because of the sheer acreage of land required.

A wild card in all speculation about the future of food production is climate change. Most knowledgeable observers believe climate change will challenge production capacity, becoming another factor compromising agricultural output. Ironically, agriculture itself is one of the major contributors to global climate change. It is estimated that 25 percent of CO_2 is produced by agriculture—mainly via deforestation for new agricultural production, burning of fossil fuels in production, and biomass burning (Climate Institute n.d.). Agriculture, particularly livestock production, is also one of the leading sources of non-CO_2 greenhouse gases, contributing 54 percent of methane emissions and nearly 80 percent of nitrous oxide emissions (Climate Institute n.d.).

Exacerbating the growing impact of agriculture on the world's native ecosystems is the simultaneous increase in the consumption of meat and dairy products around the planet (Bittman 2008). Since World War II, global meat consumption has grown fivefold (Nierenberg 2005). And demand is rising fastest where population is also growing fastest: in the last twenty years alone, meat consumption in the developing world has doubled. Meat and dairy production is projected to double again by 2050 (UNFAO 2006).

Demand for meat is rising worldwide with the spread of affluence and the related expansion of confined animal feeding operations. The bulk of croplands worldwide are planted to grow livestock feed crops. An estimated 30 percent of Earth's ice-free land is directly or indirectly involved in livestock production, according to the United Nation's Food and Agriculture Organization (2006). It is surprising how little land is used to grow crops consumed directly by humans. For example, all fruits, nuts, and vegetables harvested in the United States are grown on about nine million acres, or 2.5 percent of the total acreage used for croplands. The bulk of

U.S. cropland is devoted to grain such as corn and other crops that are largely fed to livestock (O'Brien 2009).

Providing a diet rich in meat requires approximately ten times the fossil fuel caloric input of a largely vegetarian diet. Roughly half of the greenhouse gas emissions attributed to human diets come from meat, even though beef, pork, and chicken together account for only about 14 percent of what people eat (Raloff 2009). Indeed, 18 percent of all greenhouse gases globally are attributed to livestock production—more than the entire world transport sector (UNFAO 2006).

Livestock production is also a tremendous driver of biodiversity loss. It is estimated that domestic livestock now make up 20 percent of all animal biomass on the planet (UNFAO 2006). Domestic animals grazing on rangelands negatively impact native species, since every blade of grass going into cattle or sheep is that much less forage for native species, from grasshoppers to larger mammals such as elk or gazelles (Freilich et al. 2003). Livestock are also one of the main reasons that wild predators have been vilified and slaughtered the world over. For example, not only is the rapid increase of livestock degrading Mongolia's grasslands today, but Mongolia's wolves have been killed rampantly because of the threat that they represent to livestock. In addition, though initially largely driven by subsistence farmers practicing slash and burn agriculture, the vast majority of forest destruction today is for cattle ranching and for growing crops like soybeans, which are largely used as cattle feed (Union of Concerned Scientists 2010).

Not surprisingly, given the number of acres of land devoted to livestock production, there are significant impacts on water resources as well. Globally, livestock production is the largest source of water pollution, dead zones at the mouths of rivers, and the degradation of coral reef systems. Livestock also harm water quality by reducing the ability of soils and riparian zones to hold moisture through soil compaction and trampling by hooves (Belsky, Matzke, and Uselman 1999). This increases erosion and reduces late-season flows, just when many wild species are most threatened by insufficient water. In the United States, the only region where fully reliable statistics are available, livestock are responsible for 55 percent of soil erosion and sedimentation, 37 percent of pesticide use, 50 percent of total antibiotic use, and 33 percent of the nitrogen and phosphorus loads in freshwater supplies (UNFAO 2006).

To sum up: livestock production may well be the largest single cause of biodiversity losses worldwide, since it is responsible for the bulk of deforestation and for large percentages of sedimentation of coastal areas, water pollution, land degradation, and climate change. For example, Conservation International has identified 35 worldwide biological hot spots; of these, 23 are negatively impacted by livestock production. An analysis of Red-Listed species by the World Conservation Union shows that most of them are adversely affected to some degree by livestock production. The World Wide Fund for Nature has identified livestock production as a major threat to 306 terrestrial ecoregions out of 825 that are found globally (UNFAO 2006).

Of course, in many parts of the world, including some desert regions, high mountain areas, and grasslands regions, livestock production is the least impactful or only agricultural enterprise possible and provides many people's livelihoods. Nevertheless, much of this grazing is nonsustainable, particularly in arid regions where 73 percent of the rangelands have been degraded to some extent. Here population pressure plays a key role, making it more likely that additional people will push the landscape beyond its regenerative abilities.

The convergence of population growth, expanding agriculture, and climate change is likely to create immense challenges for humanity, and it is certain to deepen the biodiversity crisis. Without a significant reduction in the global population, in combination with a change in diet and fossil fuel subsidies, the deleterious impact of agriculture on global ecosystems will only mount. Human population growth must be swiftly ended and ultimately reversed to maintain a healthy planet for people, and a viable planet for all other life on Earth. Without a commitment to population reduction and a scaling back of industrial agriculture, the planet's ecological integrity remains in serious jeopardy.

BIBLIOGRAPHY

Belsky, A. J., A. Matzke, and S. Uselman. 1999. "Survey of Livestock Influences on Stream and Riparian Ecosystems in the Western United State." *Journal of Soil and Water Conservation* 54 (1): 419–431.
Bittman, Mark. 2008. "Rethinking the Meat Guzzler." *New York Times*, January.

Brown, Lester R. 2011. "The New Geopolitics of Food." *Foreign Policy*, May/June.

Climate Institute. N.d. "Agriculture." Accessed July 5, 2011, from www.climate .org/topics/agriculture.html.

Economist. 2011. "Now We Are Seven Billion." October.

Erb, Karl-Heinz, Helmut Haberl, Fridolin Krausmann, Christian Lauk, Christoph Plutzar, Julia Steinberger, Christoph Müller, Alberte Bondeau, Katharina Waha, and Gudrun Pollack. 2009. "Eating the Planet: Feeding and Fueling the World Sustainably, Fairly and Humanely—A Scoping Study." Social Ecology Working Paper no. 116. Institute of Social Ecology and Potsdam Institute for Climate Impact Research. Vienna.

Erisman, J. W., M. A. Sutton, J. Galloway, Z. Klimont, and W. Winiwarter. 2008. "How a Century of Ammonia Synthesis Changed the World." *Nature Geoscience* 1: 636–639. doi:10.1038/ngeo325.

Freilich, Jerome E., John M. Emlen, Jeffrey J. Duda, D. Carl Freeman, and Philip J. Cafaro. 2003. "Ecological Effects of Ranching: A Six-Point Critique." *BioScience* 53 (8): 759–765.

International Union of Geological Sciences (IUGS). N.d. "Geoindicators: Soil and Sediment Erosion." Accessed July 5, 2011, from www.lgt.lt/geoin/doc .php?did=cl_soil.

McKibben, Bill. 2010. "The Only Way to Have a Cow." *Orion*, March/April.

Nierenberg, Danielle. 2005. "Happier Meals: Rethinking the Global Meat Industry." Worldwatch Paper no. 171. Washington, D.C.: Worldwatch Institute.

O'Brien, Daniel. 2009. "U.S. Crop Acreage Trends and Soybean/Corn Price Ratios." December 9. Accessed July 5, 2011, from http://www.agmanager.info/ marketing/outlook/newletters/archives/GRAIN-OUTLOOK_12-10-10.pdf.

Pimentel, D., L. E. Hurd, A. C. Bellotti, M. J. Forster, I. N. Oka, O. D. Sholes, and R. J. Whitman. 1973. "Food Production and the Energy Crisis." *Science*: 182 (4111): 443–449. DOI: 10.1126/science.182.4111.443.

Raloff, Janet. 2009. "AAAS: Climate-Friendly Dining . . . Meats: The Carbon Footprints of Raising Livestock for Food." *Science News*, February 15. Accessed from www.sciencenews.org/view/generic/id/40934/title/Science_%2B_the_Public__ AAAS_Climate-friendly_dining_%E2%80%A6_meats.

Tilman, David. 1999. "Global Environmental Impacts of Agricultural Expansion: The Need for Sustainable and Efficient Practices." *Proceedings of the National Academy of Sciences* 96: 5995–6000.

Union of Concerned Scientists. 2010. "Deforestation Today: It's Just Business." Union of Concerned Scientists, Cambridge, Mass. Accessed July 5, 2011, from www.ucsusa.org/about/1992-world-scientists.html.

United Nations Food and Agriculture Organization (UNFAO). 2006. *Livestock's Long Shadow: Environmental Issues and Options.* Rome: UNFAO.

CHAPTER II

The Laws of Ecology and Human Population Growth

CAPTAIN PAUL WATSON

THE EARTH, OR more accurately the Ocean, is a planet, but because it contains complex ecosystems and living entities on a celestial body hurtling through space, it may also be metaphorically described as a spaceship. The living entities that crew this spaceship are millions of species working within diverse ecological niches to maintain the complex life-support system of the ship. The foundation for this life-support system is made up of the species that most human beings regard as the lowest life forms: bacteria, insects, plankton, plants, invertebrates, and fish. We could call them the custodians or the working crew of Spaceship Earth. The spaceship in reality belongs to them, not us. They run it. We so-called higher forms of life are merely the passengers. The custodians do not need us, but we need the custodians. We humans suffer under the delusion that we own this planet. We do not. We never have and never will. We have not been here long, and we will not be here much longer if we continue to operate in contempt of the rules of ecology and in total disrespect of the ship's crew.

An essay I wrote a few years back caused a great deal of anger and outrage; it was even discussed in the national media. The reason for the outrage was that I stated that earthworms are more important than human beings. It is an ecological truth, because we humans need earthworms, but earthworms do not need us. Earthworms are a necessity for our survival, but we are of virtually no use to earthworms. This is an easy concept to comprehend for an ecologist, but unacceptable from an anthropocentric perspective. It challenges the mythologies that we as a species have constructed to validate our existence. It reinstates what we consider to be the "lowest" forms of life as the most important forms of life.

A life-support system requires some essential engineering. Of course we must breathe, and thanks to trees, plants, bacteria, and plankton we can. Another necessity, water, has its quality maintained by wetlands, estuaries, plankton, and bacteria. Eating is another component of our life-support system, and our gratitude must extend to the bacteria, earthworms, bees, beetles, ants, plants, and other animals for that privilege. We also must have a comfortable temperature gradient in which to live. Plankton, plants, and animals ensure the integrity of a global climate is maintained. Finally, there must be a mechanism for recycling waste. Bacteria, plants, insects, fungi, and animals can all take credit for this vital and often overlooked function.

The ecological reality is that no species can survive long outside of the laws of ecology. A violation of these laws leads to extinction. An extreme violation of these laws leads to a major extinction event. That is the situation in which we find ourselves at the moment. One species, our own, has radically violated the basic laws of ecology, placing us in the midst of a major extinction event. Between the year 2000 and the year 2065, we will lose more species of plants and animals than the planet has lost in the last sixty-five million years. The last major extinction event was caused when a comet or an asteroid collided with our spaceship. This emerging extinction event is being caused by the collective ecological ignorance and anthropocentric arrogance of one of the passenger species. We humans are the greatest threat to biological diversity and to our own survival.

It is hard to comprehend the enormity of the catastrophe we are creating, especially on a spaceship where the majority of the human passengers are slaughtering the more important nonhuman crew because of greed, apathy, collective denial, and a sense of self-designated superiority. It is like the passengers on an ocean liner partying in luxury, while slaughtering and feeding upon the engineers, navigators, and crew, only to find themselves adrift, with no place to go and nothing to eat or drink, and wondering where the crew went as they slowly starve.

The laws of ecology are (1) the law of diversity, (2) the law of interdependence, (3) the law of ecological niches, and (4) the law of finite resources. The law of diversity means that the integrity and strength of an ecosystem depends upon the diversity of species within the system:

the greater the diversity, the stronger the system. The law of interdependence means that all species within an ecosystem are dependent upon all other species within the system. The law of ecological niches means that within every ecosystem all species have a role to play. The law of finite resources means that there is a limit to growth within the system—a limit to carrying capacity. When a species exceeds carrying capacity, it begins to steal carrying capacity from other species, leading to a diminishment in biodiversity and resilience.

A major extinction event means a grave loss of biological diversity, and that is what is happening to our planet now. Biodiversity destruction is the single greatest threat to human survival on this planet because it weakens and removes our custodians, the species that make it possible for us to be the passengers. What we are in effect doing is eroding the immune system of the planet, compromising the functioning of Earth's life-support system. We have become like a deadly autoimmune disease to Earth, killing the essential crewmembers as we overload our spaceship with human passengers. This is not something that most people want to hear, and of course the anthropocentric response is outrage. That is understandable, but it does not make it an untruth.

I am a ship's captain. If I were to descend into the engine room of my ship below the waterline and discover my engineers gleefully popping rivets out of the ship's hull, I would be shocked and angry. "What the hell are you doing?" I would ask. They would look up at me with a smile and say: "Well, Captain, we get a buck apiece for these rivets when we get back to port, and we have families to feed and we need the money." An irresponsible captain would reply: "Really, well cut me in for some of that loot, boys." And they would continue their rivet popping until they popped one rivet too many, and the hull would collapse, the ship would sink, and the crew would drown.

Every species on the planet is a living rivet in the living hull of the biosphere. If we lose one rivet too many, our life-support system will crash, and we will become victims of our own engineered mass extinction event. The captains of the ships of state could intervene, but governments for the most part are made up of leaders who have been funded by rivet-poppers, elected by rivet-poppers, or are powerful rivet-poppers themselves who simply seized control. The catastrophe in the Gulf of Mexico that began in April 2010 illustrates this distinctly, when the corporation that caused the problem was delegated to solve the problem by a government that largely capitulated to the demands of the corporation. So whereas most Americans believe that this two-party system supported by corporate campaign funding is a democracy, it is, in practice, an oleaginous oiligarchy. In other words, government by the oil companies acting in the interest of the oil companies. This is not surprising considering that oil is the reason for human overpopulation and thus the cause of diminishment of biodiversity.

If oil were to disappear tomorrow, there would be a drastic and agonizing reduction in human numbers. Oil is used to grow and transport vast amounts of food. Oil moves huge numbers of people from location to location, enabling humanity to spread across the planet using oil to construct habitations, to manufacture clothing, tools, and lots of essentially useless products for entertainment purposes. The problem for humanity with regard to oil and other fossil fuels is that they are finite substances. Oil's most important function is to safely store carbon, and it happens to be extremely toxic to life, but ironically the lack of oil would be more toxic to the survival of billions of people. So if it does not poison us or kill us through global heating and climate change, it will kill billions of us when it simply is all used up.

The problem is that we are addicted. Oil is a drug. We need it, we want it, we crave it, and we all use it. So not only do we have a problem of a growing population, but we also have a growing population of a dangerous substance-addicted species. This is not promising for an enlightened future. And the biggest problem is that people for the most part don't care. What we have is collective apathy fuelled by distractions and diversions. This is evident in what human societies consider important. Religion, sports, and entertainment are the three most notable forms of collective mass escapism from the realities of ecology. Consider that the video game World of Warcraft has over eleven million subscribers, and there is not a single environmental or conservation organization in the world that can equal that number of supporters. Millions of people are living in these fantasy worlds, ignoring the reality of the world in which they actually live.

Yes, I know, I'm one of those dour gloom and doom Cassandras predicting the fall of humankind and, like Cassandra, being cursed to have my predictions ignored. I am not, however, standing on the street corner with a sign saying the world is going to end. I have chosen to fight for Earth and not to lament for it. And thus, in my life, I helped to create the Greenpeace Foundation and to establish the Sea Shepherd Conservation

Society because defending diversity, especially in the oceans, is defending the future and gives us hope that we can survive.

Despite this, like all other humans I am a hypocrite. Hypocrisy is unavoidable, due to the complexity of the anthropocentric reality we have created that requires being in the paradigm in order to shift it. My ships burn oil, and I trade that off for the lives of whales, sharks, dolphins, turtles, birds, and marine invertebrates. You can't fight a whaling ship with a kayak. All environmentalists must acknowledge their own hypocrisy, but we must strive to mitigate our impacts, and that is the reason my ships are run as vegan vessels. The raising, slaughter, and transportation of livestock and fish utilize more fossil fuels than the entire automobile industry. We could eat organic, but this is highly unlikely for all seven billion of us growing in number every day. Without petroleum-based fertilizers, hundreds of millions of people would starve to death. We can drive hybrids and electric cars and pretend that we have solved the problem, or ease our consciences by recycling or joining Greenpeace. But that would be naive.

It all comes down to this: there are too many of us and too few of everything else. The solution is more of everything else—except cows, pigs, dogs, cats, and our other domestic animals—and fewer of us. But how do we achieve that? There are no easy answers.

Intelligent and ecologically concerned people cut right to the chase and declare they will have no children. Considering that such people would be hard pressed to outnumber the regular players of World of Warcraft, this does not bode well as a solution. Ecologically intelligent men and women refraining from reproduction leave the world in the hands of the ecologically ignorant and the anthropocentrically arrogant. If the biocentrically oriented refrain from having children, while the ecologically ignorant reproduce, the self-sacrificing people would act like cuckoo birds, paying taxes to raise the children of people who will do little to solve our problems. The population will grow even larger, with a higher proportion in the eco-idiocracy.

Then there is immigration, which enables less responsible countries like Catholic Mexico and Muslim Pakistan, for example, to export their surplus numbers to other countries. Mexicans and Pakistanis continue to have too many children, fueling further population growth. And since rich countries consume many times more resources per capita than poor countries, immigrants moving from poor nations to rich nations increase their consumption enormously, making global ecological problems even worse.

Social justice advocates will be angered by this, but the reality is that the laws of ecology are unconcerned with how humans treat each other. Alleviating poverty, promoting socialism or democracy, and empowering minorities are noble endeavors but irrelevant to the basic fact that resources are finite and there are limits to growth. Rich nations should be striving to lower their consumption rates, but instead poorer nations are being encouraged to increase theirs. North America, Japan, and Europe have benefited the most from exploiting the world's resources, but India and China are rapidly catching up. Poor nations strive to be rich. China was relatively poor a few decades ago but is now the foremost consumer of energy in the world. So what is the solution? The Chinese experiment of legislating just one child succeeded in slowing population growth but failed to do so justly and fairly, because a cultural preference for boys sometimes led to the abandonment or killing of baby girls and resulted in the dangerous social situation of a grossly imbalanced sex ratio.

Any solution to too many people will most likely be ethically problematic, but that is all the more reason to act now, while we still have relatively good options, rather than waiting until we are forced to act in even more unappealing ways by dire necessity. As populations increase and carrying capacity is reduced, the costs of food and commodities will continue to rise. The present policy of subsidizing production costs is likely to cease, and poverty will increase considerably. Societies will also not be able to keep up the charade of "sustainability," a word that has been used to mask the destruction of resources. Before we are faced with potential collapse, especially when fossil fuel resources are diminished and overall global carrying capacity is reduced, concerted attempts should be made to lower our populations. Rather than endure genocide, war, famine, or pestilence, societies may choose to implement a more humane answer, although one that is in opposition to what is often falsely seen as a fundamental human right: the right to unlimited procreation.

Instead of an unlimited right, having children should be seen as a limited right with commensurate responsibilities. There are various ways this could be implemented. One possibility would be to limit parenthood to those who are able to show that they can provide financially and educationally for their offspring and to discourage all couples from having more than two children. Children should not be raised in abject poverty or ignorance, nor should *future* children be forced to live in a crowded, ecologically barren world. Such a policy would help end population growth and eventually lead to a decrease of the human population. This would not only reduce our current excessive demands on the biosphere but also prepare us for a future balanced relationship between humanity and an ecologically restored Earth. It would also help ensure that couples a few centuries from now can exercise *their* right to have a child or two of their own.

While the outline of the above policy sounds authoritarian, the alternative of unrestricted procreation is leading to disastrous consequences for the entire human species. Making parenthood a limited right could be the only humane solution in a world with ever-expanding human populations and rapidly diminishing resources. A finite resource base cannot sustain unrestricted growth—that is a basic law of ecology and cannot be changed to suit human desires. Such a solution will be violently opposed, especially by religious institutions where common sense is almost always sacrificed to the irrationality of superstitious faith. However, what seems ethically unacceptable now may be appreciated and deemed necessary in a world of obviously declining resources. Human populations must be reduced, and doing so consciously is the truly ethical choice for humanity's future on Earth.

The world one hundred and two hundred years from now will be vastly different from what we see today. The end of oil will be the end of civilization as we know it and the beginning of a new relationship between humans and nature. The alternatives to fossil fuel energy are not practical; at least not if we expect them to provide the sort of cheap, abundant energy we have gotten used to in recent years. Solar and wind power probably cannot satisfy the needs of seven or eight billion people. Nuclear energy requires vast amounts of fossil fuel to extract finite resources of uranium ore, process and transport the uranium, and build the reactors; and there is no way to safely and securely store the nuclear waste. Humans may turn the clock back to the age of sail and horsepower. Large cities may become unsustainable and be replaced by towns and villages. Reducing our numbers could be deemed essential for the survival of the human species, and such survival, in the face of life-threatening obstacles, will probably require real sacrifices in what we have come to think of as a "high standard of living." If these sacrifices are not voluntary and rationally acceded to, nature may provide the more aggressive and painful enforcement.

It is all very bleak, but the numbers relative to resources are daunting. There simply are not enough water, food, and fuel resources and pollution "sinks" to continue to support growing numbers of consumer-status-aspiring humans. And as more resources are consumed, more of the caretaker crew species will be driven to extinction, thus undermining the life-support systems of Earth even more.

It's time to back off from the all-you-can-eat passenger buffet. The crew of this magnificent spaceship needs our respect and our support. They also need to be given some rights; most importantly, the right to survive, flourish, and continue to do what they do best: keep us all alive. If the plankton, the invertebrates, bacteria, and the fish die, the oceans will die, and if the oceans die, we will die. The value of a fish swimming in the ocean, maintaining the integrity of the oceanic ecosystem, is far more important than its value on a plate in a restaurant. It's as simple as that.

The needs of the crew are more important than the needs of the passengers, and we humans have been enjoying first-class service at the expense of the crew for too long. We will survive only by rejecting the anthropocentric perspective in favor of a biocentric point of view, and by living in harmony with all other species. We must realize that any species, including our own, survives as part of a collective whole, in accordance with the laws of diversity, interdependence, and finite resources.

PART III

Necessary Conversations

CHAPTER 12

Abundant Earth and
the Population Question

EILEEN CRIST

I N *ONE WITH NINEVEH,* Paul and Anne Ehrlich identify "civilization's most fundamental challenge" in two parts: one, "making it possible for everyone in a growing population to have an adequate diet while [two] reducing human impacts on the global environment" (2004, 25). Indeed, food production will have to roughly double by midcentury in order to meet rising demand (Gillis 2011). This necessity, however, makes the second part of civilization's challenge—"reducing impacts on the global environment"—all but unrealizable, since meeting people's needs invariably takes precedence over the protection of nonhumans and their homelands. Therefore, providing "an adequate diet for all" will inevitably be achieved (if it *can* be achieved) through the ongoing displacement and extermination of nonhumans that human food procurement, production, and transportation entail.

As unpromising as this looks for Nature, it is barely the first chapter of the future swiftly coming our way. What must be added to the picture is the present-day trend well beyond the provision of an adequate diet for people: namely, the heavy footprint of the global consumer class—which has been growing by hundreds of millions of people in recent decades— coupled with the social objective that the standard of living of the world's poor be raised. While "raising the standard of living" may be nebulous shorthand for the worthy aim of ending severe deprivation, translated into shared understanding and policy the expression is a euphemism for the global dissemination of consumer culture—the unrivaled model of what a "high standard of living" looks like. But to feed a growing population *and* enter increasing numbers of people into the consumer class is a formula for completing Earth's overhaul into a planet of resources: for ever more intensified uses of land and waterways for habitation, agriculture, and farming; for the continued extraction, exploitation, and harnessing of the natural world; and for the magnification of global trade and travel.

The concomitant of Earth's human zoning (and receiving virtually no mention in mainstream media or the leftist and social justice literature) is the genocide of Earth's wild nonhumans. I use the word *genocide* here in its literal sense: the mass violence against and extermination of non-human nations, negating not only their own existence but also their roles in Life's interconnected nexus and their future evolutionary unfolding. This planet-wide holocaust is marching on virtually unabated, despite its extensive and decades-long documentation, driven by the lifeways of *both* the world's rich and poor, and most especially by their Faustian economic partnerships. The ongoing and escalating genocide of nonhumans is shrouded in silence, a silence signifying disregard for the vanquished. Silence is how power talks down to the subjugated. Silence is how power disdains to talk about their extinction (see Jensen 2006).

To talk back to power from the standpoint of nonhumans has proven extremely difficult. Part of the difficulty lies in the fact that *one* constituency—for example, men, Western culture, or corporations—cannot be held solely accountable for the dire plight of the greater-than-human world. The domination of Nature cannot be pinned on a particular constituency that derives power and profit from it. Rather, culpability lies in broad human participation, exceeding any particular group or (at this historical juncture) culture, and crossing class, race, religious, national, ethnic, and gender boundaries. Thus, those who have defended the non-human world against the violence and destruction it has suffered have sought to place the blame on anthropocentrism: the omnipresent set of taken-for-granted sensibilities and orientations that always prioritize (ethically, pragmatically, and usually unreflectively) human interests.

Anthropocentrism can be described as a worldview rather than an ideology, because human-centeredness is far more encompassing and consensual than a set of ideas that serve some dominant group. Identifying this particular culprit, however, has not turned out to be medicine for curing humanity's rampage. Given the ubiquity of anthropocentrism, it has been impossible to find the Archimedean point—the place outside the dominant normative order—from which to launch a critique that can actually touch, let alone move, the whole. *Nothing* seems to sway the global social collective from its presumptuous intent to constitute the entire planet as a human resource domain and to reify and impose that constitution as reality.

While the anthropocentric worldview can be held accountable for the historical trajectory into the present ecological catastrophe, the magnitude of Life's crisis today, in conjunction with the deafening silence enveloping it, renders the idea of anthropocentrism too feeble and academic for the critical-analytic task of opposing the human domination of the natural world. Undergirding the tyranny of this domination is something more deadly than anthropocentrism, or a highly virulent strain of it: the open or tacit stance of human supremacy. The foundational pillar of human supremacy is the belief that human beings are the superior life form of the planet and Earth's entitled owners. From the foundation of this lived, widespread belief flow the ruling conceptions of and actions toward the greater-than-human world. Human supremacy fuels the top-down conceptualization of Nature as a resource base, a domain to be used for our ends.

The standpoint of human supremacy is incapable of conceptualizing the world in its ontological self-integrity: rather, it always grasps the world in terms of how it can serve the needs and wants to which we presume ourselves entitled. Indeed, the foundational belief of supremacy, in its interlocked conceptual and action-orientation dimensions, manifests most clearly in the attitude of total entitlement: an entitlement, moreover, that can hardly be challenged because it claims both consensual power *and* morality on its side. Human supremacy is so deeply entrenched, so taken for granted, that the concept of *resources* has attained the epistemic status of a *natural kind*:[1] calling soil, water, forests, coal, oil, livestock, fisheries, wildlife, and so on resources appears as a realistic, normal description of some aspect of the world. The toxic import of the very idea of resources is masked by its normality—a normality instilled by the mode of existence humanity has constructed in accordance with the shared belief in our superiority. Thus the tyranny of viewing and treating the natural world as

composed of resources is shrouded through the latter's tacit metaconcep-
tualization as a normal and realistic description.

The assumption embedded in the concept of resources is that the
natural world always is graspable in terms of its disposability to human
ends: conceptually, actionably, open-endedly, and in perpetuity. The pervasive use of the concept reflects its entrenchment; even those who regret
human unrestraint feel compelled to talk about resources as a counterfeit
referent for things, living beings, and natural conditions on Earth. The
concept of resources is an abstraction, for it says nothing specific about
any real aspect of the world. It pretends to point at real things, but it
points at nothing except back at the pointer: us. The concept of resources
inscribes the world, conceptually and instrumentally, as a usable field, and
by refusing all concreteness it makes itself all-inclusive and endlessly ra-
pacious. It serves human colonialist attitudes and ends, and all of us are
complicit in its ubiquity and ramifications.

The concept of resources is composed of *re* and *sources*. What various
sources are reduced to ostensibly having in common is that they can be
earmarked as reservoirs of things (living or dead, simple or complex, big
or small, readily available or technologically accessible) that are useful or
profitable for people. *Re* as a prefix of sources suggests that such reservoirs
can be disposed of over and over again. The abstraction of resources—
being merely functional diction for human-user purposes—governs most
ideas and actions related to the living world.

The very idea of resources, however, prefigures the living world's *physical*
erasure. The plunder of the oceans, for example, has been ideationally pre-
figured in the resource-derivative words *fisheries* and *fish stock*. The same
goes for the word *livestock*, which has conceptually anticipated the infernal
treatment of animals in the industrial food system. Similarly, the worldwide devastation of freshwater life (Dudgeon et al. 2006) is utterly un-
surprising, given that rivers and lakes have been conceptually conflated
with, and instrumentally reduced to, *freshwater*. Fisheries, livestock, freshwater—they are all for the taking, and our ability to take them is testimony to our superior nature, and our superior nature entitles us to the
taking, and the rightfulness of the taking is ciphered to be reflected back
to us in our very words.

The process of objectification of living beings and their homelands is
a sine qua non of human domination, always accomplished linguistically
along with its real-world destruction and infliction of suffering. The con-

cept of resources works as a discursive incarceration of the living world, because it does not present itself as a renaming but rather, in feigned innocence, offers itself as a realistic and normal referent. As a renaming with denotative pretensions, the concept of resources inscribes human totalitarianism upon the biosphere. Thus, resources along with its sundry cousins (such as *natural capital*) substantially evacuate the living world of its immanent ontological substance. The concept of resources has become a gaping wound on the face of language that has engraved the delusion of human supremacy into commonsense, science-sense, technocratic, and political thinking, policy discourse, and other social arenas.

The transfiguration of the world into resources shapes the human understanding of reality in such a way, and at such a pervasive level, that we end up perceiving the totality of what is through resource-laden thought. This not only devastates the living world but also vastly diminishes humanity as well by boxing us into a virtually inescapable way of life through structuring our collective experience on Earth. (Martin Heidegger called this self-inflicted constriction "the danger" [1977]). In other words, the aggressive and parochial claim that human beings make on Nature by renaming it *resources* lays a suffocating claim upon humanity itself, by constricting thought, cutting us off from the wonders of the biosphere, and extinguishing the possibility of yet-to-be-imagined (sane, harmonious, beautiful) ways of being on Earth.

It is within this resource-saturated collective mindset that "the population question" gets framed: How many people can Earth support?[2] This is the ruling question. Implicit in the question, and explicit in most quarters in which it is posed, is the quandary: What is the maximal number of people for whom Earth can provide resources without severely degrading those resources for future people? This question menaces Earth. The question we should be asking instead is, How many people, and at what level of consumption, can live on Earth without turning Earth into a human colony founded on the genocide of its nonhuman indigenes? The latter is rarely posed because the genocide of nonhumans is something about which the mainstream culture, including the political Left, observes silence. Academics largely follow suit, perhaps because they view raising an issue about which silence is observed as a non sequitur. Instead, the standard query we encounter is, How many people can Earth support? and its spinoffs. For example: How many people can Earth feed? Can Earth support nine billion people? Ten billion people? More?

The prevailing question takes as given that our numbers will keep climbing, even though the strategies for reversing population growth are well understood. An international financial, technological, knowledge, and informational campaign to bring the full range of modern contraceptive methods, safe abortion, professional counseling, and sex and health education throughout the world—and especially to the places where they are most urgently needed—would make a difference of billions within this century (see Potts 2009). Stabilizing and then reducing our numbers, *globally*, demands proactive measures, implemented at the grassroots level so as to reach people in all places and walks of life.[3] These measures involve two dimensions: delivering services that enable people to plan their childbearing choices and removing obstacles that prevent people from accessing such services.

Wherever modern family planning is made available and barriers to access are lifted, women and their partners almost universally choose to have far fewer children. As Robert Engelman puts it, "few people are aware that easy access to good family planning services is most of what's needed to achieve a sustainable world population" (2008, 210). This trend is so striking that leading-edge population analysts like Engelman and Martha Campbell propose that women are, by nature, mostly disinclined to have many children but are rather intent on successfully raising the child or children they already have.[4] Campbell discusses a "latent desire" in women for fewer children, which swiftly surfaces when women are given affordable access to family planning, reliable counseling for modern contraception options, safe abortion services, and, last but far from least, a sociocultural climate receptive to the choice of fewer or no children (see Campbell and Bedford 2009).

The implications are profound: the most important dimension of addressing population growth is simply to make resources for the control of fertility a political, economic, social, and cultural top priority, while also acting to remove or preempt financial, informational, cultural, and normative barriers to access. In numerous countries where such measures have been spearheaded by governments, backed financially and implemented competently, fertility rates swiftly declined. Iran is perhaps the most striking case of the results of a successful population policy: from an average of 5.5 children per woman in 1988, fertility declined to 1.7 in 2009. The catalyst of this transition was the reinstitution of Iran's family planning program in 1989, coupled with an educational, cultural, and healthcare crusade to encourage and enable the choice of smaller families. Among other measures, this all-out effort included the creation of fifteen thousand health clinics to service rural populations, a campaign to raise women's literacy, media programming to raise consciousness and disseminate information, and the provision of all forms of birth control free of charge (Brown 2011).[5]

I offer the Iranian case as a dramatic example of how drastically, in Lester Brown's words, "a full-scale mobilization of society can accelerate the shift to smaller families" (2011, 159). Indeed, *immediate full-scale mobilization* is what the Earth's forests, prairies, oceans, rivers, animals, and climate are crying for (see Foreman 2011). And population growth everywhere would decelerate as soon as this were made the concerted goal of an international campaign, involving the partnership of aid organizations, financial and UN institutions, governments, and grassroots healthcare providers and activists. Instead of the estimated nine or ten billion people of UN demographic projections, we would peak at eight billion and then take the road to declining numbers—perhaps thereby averting the sixth mass extinction, a dilapidated global ecosystem, climate catastrophes, and the real possibility of immense human suffering.

Making voluntary family planning available, affordable, safe, and culturally normal is an achievable intervention that can be implemented immediately (Prata 2009). But instead of pursuing this rational, ethical, and prudential path—that would foster ecological protection and restoration, support women's right to plan their childbearing, and, additionally, possibly preempt or alleviate famine, disease, and resource wars—mainstream discourse and the political Left hold the population increase in the pipeline, under current policies, as our inexorable fate.

As a consequence, the question How many people can Earth support? morphs into the quest to "resourcify" Earth in new and ever intensified ways. Thus, for example, the quandary of whether more than nine billion people can be fed becomes the pursuit (already fully underway) of a second Green Revolution, with its extensions and technological innovations beyond the first. For Earth to meet the subsistence demands of many billions of current and future people—let alone the demands made when these billions achieve modern consumer lifestyles—involves scaling up the rational-instrumental enterprise of late modernity: increasing the efficiency of crop cultivation and rotation, maximizing arable land (both already in use and new), stretching out water supplies via, for example, adopting irrigation-efficient technologies, optimizing fertilizer and pesticide applications, proliferating industrial fish farms, scaling up animal confinement and through-put operations, and creating higher-yield or stress-resistant crops by traditional breeding or genetic engineering. The entire face of Earth, in other words, with nary a thought for the self-integrity of the greater-than-human world, must be harnessed to provision however many billions we end up becoming: but heaven forbid that we should collectively consider the possibility of reducing our numbers.

Regarding Earth as our resource base embeds the reigning belief that Earth is our *property*: humanity's commonwealth. The affiliated presumption is that Earth can, and even should, be maximally populated by people, as long as the consequent exploitation of resources does not endanger people themselves. Because humans are spellbound by the idea that Earth is our planetary real estate, cognitive and pragmatic activity is funneled into working with the *plasticity* of resources. As Julian Simon (1981) rightly pointed out, with much anthropocentric pomposity, resources are highly malleable. Consider the ways. The resource base can be enlarged: for example, more land under the plough, more groundwater discovered, more oil and mineral reserves found. The services of previously depleted or forsaken resources can be accessed through new or alternative ones: for example, biofuels, tar sands, wind energy, electric cars, artificial meat, hydroponics. Resource-use efficiency can be intensified or revolutionized: for example, by eliminating food waste, dematerialization, recycling industries. Resources can be technologically manipulated to amplify or prolong their productivity: for example, hydrofracking, genetic engineering of crops and animals, fish factory farms, genetically modified bacteria for mineral extraction. And the pricey extraction or conversion of resources might eventually be made affordable: for example, desalinization, solar fuel cells, extraterrestrial mining.

As long as such a "resource enhancement portfolio" can be developed and implemented, then an increasing and eventually very large stable population *might* be supportable; maybe such a large population can even be provided with a high-consumption way of life. Environmentalists' objection to this Simonian reverie, of billions of people enjoying a global consumer culture and expanding the human empire to the universe at large, is that limitlessly enhancing the resource base eventually results in breaching biophysical limits, with consequences like climate change, agricultural and industrial pollution, peak oil, and the severe degradation or loss of ecological services. This critique is more than justified, no longer as a set of projected forecasts but by the daily realities of droughts, floods, mudslides, environmental cancers, and oil and food price hikes. But a response to this oft-rehearsed critique is that the very civilization at work prospecting, expanding, and diversifying the resource base is also increasingly engaged in the parallel work of correcting the side effects of its own excesses. This is the reason that Julian Simon embraced recycling, solar energy, environmental remediation, and pollution cleanup as important components of the civilizational toolkit for moving forward. We could update Simon's "ecofriendly" list by adding the imminent possibilities of geoengineering, synthetic biology, genetic engineering, laboratory-made meat, and sundry adaptation projects to keep climate change under control and food on the table. More serious than modern society's potential ability to technologically fix or muddle through problems of its own making is people's apparent willingness to live in an ecologically devastated world and to tolerate dead zones, endocrine disruptors, domestic animal torture (aka concentrated animal feeding operations or CAFOs), and unnatural weather as unavoidable concomitants of modern living.

I am presenting a picture of the present and intensifying human-colonized world. But in contrast with many of my colleagues, I do not necessarily foresee a world that collapses by undermining its own life-support systems. It may instead turn into a world that is molded and propped up by the strengths that advanced industrial civilization has at its disposal: the rational-instrumental means of technical management, heightened efficiency, and technological breakthrough. It is possible that by such means a viable "civilization" might be established upon a thoroughly denatured planet. What is deeply repugnant about such a civilization is not its potential for self-annihilation, but its totalitarian conversion of the natural world into a domain of resources to serve a human supremacist way of life and the consequent destruction of all the intrinsic wealth of its natural places, beings, and elements. "Project Human Takeover" has proceeded acre by acre, island by island, region by region, and continent by continent, reaching its current global apogee with the final loss of wild places and the corollary sixth mass extinction underway. What the near future heralds, if we stay on the present trajectory, is the sealing of this nonhuman genocide by means of Earth being *put to work*, 24/7, to serve a master, populous race. The proverbial water will be squeezed out of stone, metaphorically and literally, not only to bring people bread but circuses too. As Max Horkheimer and Theodor Adorno foresaw decades ago, the culmination of what we have come to call *civilization* "radiates disaster triumphant" (1972, 3).

The dominant culture (pardon the repetition: including the Left) is so myopically centered on human affairs that Earth has become merely a stage for humanity's dramas. Human supremacy has ensconced widespread indifference toward the plight of nonhumans and their homes; it ignores, and keeps itself ignorant of, the question of *their* reproductive rights, as individuals and as species. The dominant culture thus seems unable to grasp the moral evil of erasing wild nature just to accommodate more and more people to live, *all at once*, on a planet occupied as a resource satellite. Our conceit has made us so imagination-poor that we cannot fathom that future people, disabused perhaps of our own species-small-mindedness, will desire to live in a world rich in kinds of beings and kinds of places.

Hope lies in humanity's coming to realize the immensity of what we are irretrievably losing, which is *not* resources. Hope lies in the fact that we are native to Earth: we have the potential of understanding that we are losing our own family.

So, "How many people can Earth support?" It depends on what we mean when we say "Earth." The Earth transmogrified into a resource domain, I would wager, can support many billions of people. It already does. But Earth as a biosphere with abundant numbers and kinds of free nonhumans, with connected and thriving wild places, with a richly textured biogeography, with domesticated Earthlings not chained to a sickening industrial "food" system, with horticultures healthy for people and friendly to wildlife, with human denizens not living in terror of the specters of hunger, war, and rape, and with the world's oceans allowed to rebound into a semblance of their former largesse and beauty: *that* Earth can support far fewer than billions of people—people who will, almost undoubtedly, want to enjoy many of the amenities of the consumer age. Let's call the first *Resource Earth* and the second *Abundant Earth*.

If human beings choose Abundant Earth, then we also choose embarking on a speedy journey toward a declining world population. In the straight and simple words of Alan Weisman, "the intelligent solution would require the courage and the wisdom to put our knowledge to the test. It would be poignant and distressing in ways, but not fatal. It would henceforth limit every human female on Earth capable of bearing children to one" (2007, 272; see also McKibben 1998). It is an elegant solution— and not an authoritarian one, because in a global human society *actually awakened* to the precipice of Life's collapse, many women and men may well choose none, while others chose one, and a few choose two. It is the average that needs to be one child per woman: by 2100 the human population could be on the way to, give or take, two billion (Weisman 2007, 272).[6] Abundant Earth could then return; not in its former splendor but splendorous enough. By starting on this road today, at the very least we will give future people the choice between Resource Earth and Abundant Earth. They can always choose to be fruitful and multiply and subdue Earth into a resource base all over again.

But hopefully that choice will be as likely as future people deciding to reinstitute human slavery or take away women's vote. For there will yet come a time when the call for freedom resounds with all its magical potency not just for all people, but for Earth's animals, rivers, grasslands, mountains, oceans, and forests too.

NOTES

1. The philosophical term *natural kind* corresponds to a classification of things or entities that do not depend on humans for their existence (see Hacking 1999). The concept of resources is pervasively used with the epistemic force of a natural kind, as though the things and beings we identify as resources are actually and objectively "out there," as such.

2. See, for example, Cohen (1995), Waggoner (1996), and the *Economist* (2011). A recent example of the popularity of this question is David Attenborough's 2009 documentary *How Many People Can Live on Planet Earth?* Attenborough clearly believes humanity should leave room for other species, yet he winds up posing the population question anthropocentrically.

3. I approach the population question as a global question and not a national one because I do not regard "nations" as real entities in the way that Earth is a real entity, and because I support a bioregional, cosmopolitan future in which we inhabit Earth so sparsely and equitably that human migration choices, as such, should have virtually no ecological impact.

4. Given plausible natural selection pressures against a female "reproductive strategy" for numerous offspring (childbearing and pregnancy have carried high

mortality risks for most of our natural history as a species), from an evolutionary biology perspective, this suggestion is cogent.

5. That Iran has recently backtracked and embraced a pronatalist policy does not make a difference to my argument that rapid declines in fertility are possible.

6. The number of two billion, as a first goal in the quest for an optimal global population, is one on which Gretchen Daily and Anne and Paul Ehrlich have also converged (1994). More recently, the Ehrlichs elucidate the rationale for this ball-park figure as follows: "[A]n optimal population size would be one for which the minimal physical necessities of a decent life could be guaranteed for everyone . . . and basic human social and political rights could be ensured for all. . . . [P]opu-lation should be large and dispersed enough to encourage maintenance and de-velopment of humanity's cultural diversity and to provide critical mass in numer-ous areas of high density so that intellectual, artistic, and technological creativity would be stimulated. But the population should be small enough to permit the preservation of natural ecosystems and biodiversity at a level that could sustain natural services. Hermits and outdoor enthusiasts would find plenty of wilderness to hide in or enjoy; lovers of opera, theater, and fine food could have large vibrant cities" (2004, 184). Of course, no "optimal" population number can be decided once and for all. But a goal of about two billion people is possible and a good one to move toward in the course of the twenty-first century. For a similar estimate and argument, see Smail (1997).

BIBLIOGRAPHY

Attenborough, David. 2009. "How Many People Can Live on Planet Earth?" BBC Horizon special.

Brown, Lester R. 2011. *World on the Edge: How to Prevent Environmental and Eco-nomic Collapse*. Earth Policy Institute. New York: W. W. Norton.

Campbell, Martha, and Kathleen Bedford. 2009. "The Theoretical and Political Framing of the Population Factor in Development." *Philosophical Transactions of the Royal Society B* 364: 3101–3113.

Cohen, Joel E. 1995. *How Many People Can the Earth Support?* New York: W. W. Norton.

Daily, Gretchen C., Anne H. Ehrlich, and Paul R. Ehrlich. 1994. "Optimum Human Population Size." *Population and Environment* 15 (6): 469–475.

Dudgeon, David, et al. 2006. "Freshwater Biodiversity: Importance, Threats, Status and Conservation Challenges." *Biological Review* 81: 163–182.

Economist. 2011. "Special Report on Feeding the World: The 9-Billion People Question." March.

Ehrlich, Paul, and Anne Ehrlich. 2004. *One with Nineveh: Politics, Consumption, and the Human Future*. Washington, D.C.: Island Press.

Engelman, Robert. 2008. *More: Population, Nature, and What Women Want.* Washington, D.C.: Island Press.

Foreman, Dave. 2011. *Man Swarm and the Killing of Wildlife.* Durango, Colo.: Raven's Eye Press.

Gillis, Justin. 2011. "A Warming Planet Struggles to Feed Itself." *New York Times*, June 5.

Hacking, Ian. 1999. *The Social Construction of What?.* Cambridge, Mass.: Harvard University Press.

Heidegger, Martin. 1977. "The Question Concerning Technology." In *The Question Concerning Technology and Other Essays*, 3–35. New York: Harper.

Horkheimer, Max, and Theodor W. Adorno. 1972. *Dialectic of Enlightenment.* Translated by John Cumming. New York: Seabury Press.

Jensen, Derrick. 2006. *Endgame.* Vol. 1: *The Problem of Civilization* and vol. 2: *Resistance.* New York: Seven Stories Press.

McKibben, Bill. 1998. *Maybe One: A Case for Smaller Families.* New York: Penguin.

Potts, Malcolm. 2009. "Where Next?" *Philosophical Transactions of the Royal Society B* 364: 3115–3124.

Prata, Ndola. 2009. "Making Family Planning Accessible in Resource-Poor Settings." *Philosophical Transactions of the Royal Society B* 364: 3093–3099.

Simon, Julian. 1981. *The Ultimate Resource.* Princeton. N.J.: Princeton University Press.

Smail, Kenneth. 1997. "Beyond Population Stabilization: The Case for Dramatically Reducing Global Human Numbers." *Politics and the Life Sciences* 16 (2): 183–192.

Waggoner, Paul. 1996. "How Much Land Can 10 Billion People Spare for Nature?" *Daedalus* 125 (3): 73–93.

Weisman, Alan. 2007. *The World without Us.* New York: St. Martin's Press.

CHAPTER 13

Nulliparity and a Cruel Hoax Revisited

STEPHANIE MILLS

A WHILE BACK AT my regular weekly women's meeting, I sat among friends. One woman, lacking child care, had brought her new baby daughter. While Mom ventilated the emotional strains she was experiencing as a single parent, baby Felicia captured every heart in the room. Most of the women could barely restrain themselves from snatching her out of the arms of whoever was cuddling her at the moment. It was a sweet, primal disturbance of our adult conversation. Then another woman, a tough-minded news hen and something of a jock, spoke of the pangs she felt putting her youngest child on the school bus for the first time and wept.

Clearly, mother love is a force of nature, easily trumping mere reason. Dave Brower used to say that you couldn't reason prejudice out of a person because it didn't get in that way. Reason is a pipsqueak, the melting tip of the iceberg of mentality. Which kind of makes me wonder why, back in 1969, I was so sure that I could and would get through my natural female life without becoming a mother.

I became a notorious nonmother when I shocked the media and my classmates at our graduation ceremonies with a commencement address titled "The Future Is a Cruel Hoax." I declared that given the seriousness of all the ecocatastrophes then gaining momentum, "the most humane thing for me to do would be to have no children at all." An amazing amount of uproar ensued, but my gesture manifestly didn't launch a mass anti–mass movement—not if all the baby-having going on around me, and the absence of overpopulation as a subject of concern in the public mind, are any indication.

While I consider myself to be a staunch feminist, the largest system about which I can care is not womankind or humankind but Earth's evolutionary processes. Because it's axiomatic that wilderness preservation, restoration, and expansion are the minimum conditions necessary for this process to continue, my ultimate loyalty is to the wild.

Ecocentric, biocentric, animist, alone in a world of wounds—strange is the lot of those who chance into the deep ecological mindset, who believe that "our community" means the ecosystem, watershed, bioregion, biome, continent, planet—all our relations; that every living thing is as important as any person; that they all could get along fine without *Homo sapiens* but not us without them. It's humbling and troubling; makes one feel like a grinch and superfluous all at once.

Population is, let's face it, a horrible issue. It's quantitative, parsing the richness and pathos of human life on Earth in incomprehensibly large numbers. It's an observable reality, but because exponential growth is not a sudden event, overpopulation remains somehow below the threshold of being perceived as catastrophic. As Garrett Hardin observed, "Nobody ever dies of overpopulation."

Here in northwest Lower Michigan our pretty rural landscape—never mind the howling wilderness—is dying of overpopulation. Perhaps it's progress that nobody around here is in favor of just plain growth any more. They want the sustainable kind. I'm about the only person I ever hear wishing that people would quit having children. And because it really is an offensive thing to say, I do so only rarely.

In my community, baby-having and childrearing automatically justify all manner of hyperconsumerism, including the use of disposable diapers, the acquisition of a family van, trips to Disney World, and a succession of pairs of $100 sneakers. In the utterly atomized nuclear family, *parenting* seems to have become a major job of work for mothers mostly, and therefore warrants such indulgence. Whereas among those unselfconscious, backward ecosystem peoples we hear that babies weren't the individual's or couple's property, privilege, or sole responsibility. There were fewer, happier, less fashionable babies (and slicks of baby poop on the cave floor, probably).

I have found that not having children is a great time-saver and an easy way to shrink one's ecological footprint. In conjunction with authorhood, a notoriously unremunerative calling, nonmotherhood has kept my eco-logical footprint positively dainty.

In an interconnected world, the decision to bear a child isn't only a personal matter, nor does it pertain only to one's moment. Won't even the wanted, cared-for children feel betrayed to discover (assuming that such thoughts are still thinkable in the future) that previous generations ignored the problem of overpopulation and dodged the difficult choices in favor of a comfortable, conventional existence whose price included migratory songbirds, large mammals, old-growth forests, and polar ice shelves?

I bite my tongue a lot. I don't want to risk alienating my friends, or nowadays their daughters, by arguing against their childbearing, except in the obliquest ways. Regardless of which birth it is, first, second, or third, I wind up congratulating new parents, especially mothers, warmly. At that point the horse is out of the barn. New parents have plenty of crap to deal with, even without a population bomber's disapproval, and children need and deserve to feel welcome once they're here.

As I push my grocery cart down supermarket aisles of sugar-frosted fiber puffs, overlit thoroughfares grid-locked with parents often rudely and sometimes abusively attempting to appease or curb the advertising-inculcated desires of their TV-transmogrified kids, I find myself wishing that it were somehow possible to get my fellow Americans to be at least as thoughtful and caring about these children they've already had as they are about their cars.

In my youth I came across a women's magazine interview with illustri-ous nonmom Katherine Hepburn. In it Hepburn said she didn't think she could be as good as she wanted at being an actress and a mother both, so she felt she had to choose between them. Fortunately for film fans, she went with acting. It struck me as eminently reasonable that one should assess oneself and one's society realistically and then make a considered decision as to the likeliest way to spend one's life.

Thus when women of my cohort and younger bewail the difficulty of combining motherhood and a career, or how hopeless it is to get their husbands (if said husbands are still around) to take on some responsibil-ity for doing the wash or schlepping the kids around, I have to bite my tongue prit'near off. I'm sure that parenthood is exhausting. I agree totally that in contemporary circumstances the gender-based division of labor is grossly exploitative of women. But I have to wonder whether these women

imagined that the revolution would be accomplished before the end of
their pregnancy.

꙰

People refuse to believe the rules apply to us, that human beings are subject to biological constraints. The reasons for this exceptionalism are various—theological, ideological, technotopian. Me, I'm a Rules Girl. And,
minus human exceptionalism, things are looking grim.

As the most hard-nosed population biologists have been patiently
pointing out all along, if we do not address overpopulation by using birth
control, Nature will deal with it by overriding death control. Given global
climate change, sprawling megacities, declining nutrition, assaults on our
immune systems, drug-resistant pathogens, and, with WTO, the prospects
of no impediments to the worldwide movement of agricultural commodities and their hitchhiking pests, to say nothing of the possibility of rogue
bugs bolting from germ warfare or genetic engineering labs, an awful lot
of epidemics may be in store. The current opinion seems to be that death
itself should be curable, and whenever it befalls, it's a tragedy. When the
myth that modern medicine has or can cure infectious disease is shattered,
we will have a lot of philosophical maturing to do.

"Fear of individual death and grief," wrote Gregory Bateson in *Mind and
Nature*, "propose that it would be 'good' to eliminate epidemic disease and
only after 100 years of preventive medicine do we discover that the population is overgrown" (247). These days, as forensic anthropology attempts
to probe our deep past, some say that the growth of human population has
steadily driven the series of technological changes: extinction of Pleistocene
megafauna, thus hunting and gathering, then agriculture, and civilization,
industrialization, and globalization—now approaching apogee.

Checking epidemic disease is only the most recent factor in the long,
lurching history of the expansion of our species. However, Bateson's insight that "fear of individual death and grief" are driving forces of our dis-
proportion with the rest of life illuminates the core dilemma of overpopulation. Among individual human beings, birth brings joy and death brings
sorrow. Forgoing children and accepting death as natural will always be
very tough to sell, given the abstract, almost absent nature of the rewards
for such an ethic.

❧

If a lot more women—say 90 percent—would follow my sterling example of nulliparity, it would unravel the biological family, that seed-syllable and basic unit of human culture, and make for a wrenching, possibly disastrous discontinuity for our kind. Yet the need to contain, restrain, and minimize our species vis-à-vis more than human nature is extreme. Earth's in a highly unnatural state of affairs. Can we be unnatural enough to regain our just proportion to all the rest of life? Which is the greater distortion of human essence: not to reproduce or to live in a completely anthropogenic environment, every terrain dominated and depleted by the human species?

Deep down inside, population is nothing if not a women's issue. Personally, I wish that billions of women would just say no to motherhood and set up Amazon republics instead. All men have to do then is take their matters into their own hands. Of course, it would be marvelous if ecocentric men would organize "snip-ins"—mass vasectomy festivals. To reinforce and reward this behavior, urologists could tattoo a beauty mark on the vasectomee's face above the beard line once he's flunked the sperm test. Kind of an antithesis to the semiotics of the wedding ring.

Once birth control and abortion are universally and freely available and the various pronatalist policies tucked away in the tax code have been abolished, but artfully, so that children don't wind up deprived as a result, propaganda might be the one acceptable means of civic action available to deal with overpopulation: an all-out attempt to change public opinion about reproductive behavior. And I'm not talking about a "stop at two" or even "one is plenty" campaign, but "Just Don't Do It!" There needs to be a steep decline in human numbers. Our last chance for it to be volitional rather than apocalyptic is for the vast majority of people now on Earth not to reproduce.

The trouble with propaganda for nonparenthood is that it has tended to be tacky and materialistic, dissing children and gushing about all the fun you can have (read "money to spend") if you're not buying magnetic alphabets for your refrigerator door. Economic calculus has yet to vanquish the drive for procreation. For just about everyone but the Amish, children are a major expense, noncontributors to the household economy. Still *Homo economicus* keeps on making babies. I would like to think that this means that our hearts are still flesh, even if everything else about us is bent by economism.

Of course, if the idea of persuading people not to reproduce is too heartless and objectionable, another way to attack the problem would be to promote, even insist on, breathairianism: drawing your sustenance from breath alone. Although to date its most prominent practitioners have been unmasked as fakers, not fakirs, given to gobbling candy bars off-camera, genuine breathairianism might be a way to dodge the birth control bullet. OK—no more gloomy talk about overpopulation. Have all the children you want, just nobody eat anything. Or go outside.

NOTE

This essay was first published in the journal *Wild Earth* 7 (4) in 1997.

CHAPTER 14

Colossus versus Liberty

A Bloated Humanity's Assault on Freedom

TOM BUTLER

> *Democracy cannot survive overpopulation. Human dignity*
> *cannot survive it. Convenience and decency cannot survive it.*
> *As you put more and more people onto the world, the value of*
> *life not only declines, it disappears.*
> —Isaac Asimov, 1988 interview with Bill Moyers

I AM SKIING IN the woods behind my house. It has been a good old-fashioned New England winter, one of the snowiest on record. The storm that passed over the region yesterday dumped more than two feet of powder, and the snowpack is far deeper than typical for mid-March here in the foothills of Vermont's Green Mountains.

Most afternoons, just before dusk, I ski these informal, neighbor-maintained trails to the top of the ridge, a place I call Coyote Knoll because the old logging road we use as a ski and walking path is a major travel corridor for *Canis latrans*. Their sign is pervasive; throughout the winter wild canids and other animals frequently save energy by walking on my tracks. With successive storms and our various comings and goings, the animals and I construct a palimpsest of paw prints and ski tracks, a layered travel record captured in a stratigraphy of snow.

From atop Coyote Knoll, a name not found on any official map, one sees Mount Mansfield, the state's highest peak, twenty or so miles to the north. To the east, just across the valley carved by the Huntington River, rises Camel's Hump, arguably Vermont's best-loved mountain. Its distinctive profile appears on the back of the state quarter.

The quality of the waning light this afternoon is extraordinary. It slants through the trees, causing ice crystals on the branches to sparkle and prompting the maple, birch, and ash trees to cast long shadows. The alpenglow turns Camel's Hump a dusky purple. If "the true end of philosophy" is to "love your home," as the badger counseled in *The Sword in the Stone* (White 1939, 285), then my philosophical training is daily made anew, for I love this spot. But Yosemite, it's not. This landscape's beauty is prosaic, the unflashy loveliness of typical northern hardwood forest slowly recovering its health since agricultural settlement destroyed most of northern New England's forest cover, replaced native wildlife with Merino sheep (and later dairy cows), and caused the region's rivers to run brown with silt.

There is another notable sight from atop Coyote Knoll: No houses. No roads. No human structures of any kind, and the chances of running into another person here are low. My town was chartered in 1763, and yet, in this long-settled landscape, I am free to experience solitude, natural beauty, and the spiritual and physical rejuvenation that comes from muscle-powered recreation in the great outdoors. Virtually every resident, even here in the state's most populous county, can enjoy this experience either out one's back door or with a short trip by car or bike. Why? Because Vermont is still an overwhelmingly rural place, with a total population ranking forty-ninth in the United States.[1]

Due to the state's low population and largely undeveloped character—ranging from farmland to designated wilderness, dotted with small towns and only one significant urban area—Vermont's citizens have the liberty to live, work, and play close to nature. But population growth and exurban development patterns, now popularly called "rural sprawl," increasingly threaten that freedom by degrading the qualities that make this area appealing, as well as reversing the past century's general trend of landscape rewilding.

The stonewalls, cellar holes, and other historical artifacts mouldering about these hills record an unlovely history in which an unsuited agricultural regime was imposed onto a landscape that had evolved a complex web of ecological relationships since the retreat of the glaciers some twelve thousand years ago. Dramatic simplification and loss of ecological integrity ensued. Remarkably, however, the eastern U.S. forest is unique among temperate forests of the world for the reason that over the past century it has been expanding, not shrinking (McKibben 1995). The trajectory of land health has been toward wildness.[2]

I regularly see the spoor of whitetail deer, moose, fisher, red fox, and other creatures, and sometimes see the creatures themselves, in these woods. On various rambles I've startled a black bear, crossed paths with a coyote, and nearly stepped on a porcupine, all within a hundred yards of Coyote Knoll. The amazing resurgence of species whose populations were either extirpated or drastically reduced here 150 years ago is the result of large historical trends, such as the opening of the American West to European settlement, which allowed marginal agricultural lands across northern New England to be abandoned and begin reforesting; also, the resurgence is a result of conscious actions by conservationists.[3] These have included species reintroductions and augmentation, as well as habitat protection. Apex predators such as wolves and catamounts are missing, but practically all of the region's other native creatures are present.

But just as macro phenomena—such as the global extinction crisis, climate change, collapsing fisheries—point to the hard truth that humanity has overshot Earth's carrying capacity, the apparent end of this forest recovery cycle in the Northeast reflects the problem of growth. A recent report released by Harvard Forest researchers highlights the fact that the 150-year progression of reforestation is now concluded, and population pressures are causing forest cover to decline in all six New England states (Foster et al. 2010, 5). While just one metric for measuring the overall health of the region, forest loss and degradation is a key factor in understanding anthropogenic impacts on a regional scale. When considered along with other measures of ecological integrity, it is another signpost that population growth and concomitant resource exploitation are a growing menace.

Few people, however, recognize that menace, whether it is extrapolated from a single data stream or from a host of measurable trends. Quantifying the deleterious effects of population growth has not proven to be a potent strategy for stimulating behavioral or political change. It seems that demographics is, except to demographers, a generally ignored abstraction.

Is there another way of communicating about these topics that prompts an emotional reaction in individuals? Perhaps there is. Clearly, at this particular moment in American politics, with the rise of the Tea Party, and in global politics, with democratic reform movements agitating across the Middle East, there is a groundswell of rhetoric positing freedom as the central objective of human striving.

Unfortunately, in its current incarnation the emergent Tea Party movement appears to be primarily libertarian rather than traditionally conservative in its orientation and seems hostile to individual or collective actions that might turn back the assault on wild freedoms described here. But for any social change movement that purports to champion the cause of freedom, what goal could be more important than to stabilize and begin reducing human population? A strong case can be made that this task is key to reinvigorating genuine democratic values, far more important to genuine liberty than cutting taxes or reforming entitlement programs.

If Garrett Hardin (1993, 297) was correct—and I believe he was—when he wrote that "loss of freedom is an inevitable consequence of unlimited population growth in a limited space," then a bloated humanity's ultimate impact is the inexorable diminishment of liberty. In Vermont, where we have the last best example of participatory democracy—an annual town meeting at which local government and school budgets are debated and passed, with any resident having the right to speak and offer amendments from the floor—we see the direct connection between small population size and the ability of citizens to govern themselves. And with our part-time, nonprofessional legislature, every Vermonter has ready access to state lawmakers, and even regular folks have frequent opportunities to personally interact with the governor and members of our congressional delegation. This level of access becomes impossible in large population states such as New York and California.

With legislative bodies relatively fixed in their size but representing a growing population, there is a steady erosion in democracy, a point that Professor Albert Bartlett (Wooldridge 2011) highlights using the example of his hometown city council: "In 1950 the population of Boulder [Colorado] was approximately 20,000 and there were nine members of the Council. In 2011 Boulder's population is approximately 100,000 and there are still just nine members of the Council. Today there are five times as many constituents per member of the Council as there were 60 years ago. As a consequence, we have only one-fifth of the democracy that we had 60 years ago."

In practice freedom is being given away, or rather dribbled away demographically, by a populace that has unthinkingly absorbed the mantra that all growth is good. Freedom has been incompletely protected even while universally celebrated in the American experience. Questions about the expansion or erosion of liberty have real cultural power. The idea that individual citizens should be free to enjoy a high quality of life linked to the natural character and aesthetics of their home place is a nonthreatening, and perhaps even politically resonant, spot to begin a conversation about human overpopulation.

Transcending anthropocentrism and broadening that conversation to include the liberty of nonhuman nature, such as the freedom of wildlife populations to rebound in concert with the reforestation of New England, is crucial. Broader still is the idea that the ever-growing human footprint on the biosphere poses a grave threat to the freedom of wilderness areas (both designated and de facto) to persist and thrive across the landscape. It is fundamental to stress this assault on liberty, because wilderness is "the arena of evolution" (Foreman 2004, 114), and the defining characteristic of wilderness is freedom.

Wilderness is self-willed land (Vest 1985) where natural processes, not human agency, direct the ebb and flow of life. The word *pristine* does not appear in the Wilderness Act of 1964, which established America's National Wilderness Preservation System. Howard Zahniser, the primary author of the Wilderness Act, was a Pennsylvania native who spent considerable time at his family's cabin in New York's Adirondack Park, where much of the forest had been scalped by timber butchers in the nineteenth century before the park's creation. Zahniser was widely traveled in the West and Alaska, but as an easterner knew that wilderness could grow as well as shrink. He consciously avoided absolute terms such as *virginal* and *untouched* when drafting the Wilderness Act, choosing to use the less familiar word *untrammeled* as the key modifier in the statute's definition of *wilderness*. A *trammel* is a net or hobble for a horse, something that impedes free movement. Untrammeled lands, then, are not necessarily pristine but are unyoked to human will, not manipulated to produce resources, and free to follow their own evolutionary course.[4]

The wilderness idea is a remarkable concept to have emerged from American society, with its utilitarian orientation to the landscape and devotion to "progress" borne of economic growth. While likely descended from ancient cultural traditions (the sacred grove), the modern wilderness movement that arose here was a reaction to decimated forests and wildlife and loss of scenic beauty as European settlement reshaped, and degraded, natural landscapes. These changes were closely linked to burgeoning human populations, affluence, and technology. While the nascent conservation movement generally did not challenge directly the growth economy's underlying assumptions (Krall 2011), from its beginning some wilderness movement leaders recognized growth as an existential threat to wildlands and wildlife. "There is just one hope of repulsing the tyrannical ambition of civilization to conquer every niche on the whole earth," wrote Wilderness Society cofounder Robert Marshall (1930). "That hope is the organization of spirited people who will fight for the freedom of the wilderness."

Nearly a century after conservation movement pioneers worried about American economic expansion's "tyrannical ambition" to conquer the wild, the technological means available to achieve that end are more sophisticated, but the worldview driving the ambition remains the same. That view stems from and contributes to a particular kind of society. Borrowing a metaphor from biology, we might say that population growth is *allelopathic*, helping to create conditions favorable to itself and toxic to competitors, in this case the idea that a small, stable human population is desirable for ecological and cultural reasons.

Let's unpack this metaphor a bit. The population growth treadmill is a positive feedback loop. Following the invention of agriculture, human numbers rose to a size and density that allowed new kinds of social organization, especially economic specialization and hierarchy that were impossible during the vast majority of human history when we lived in dispersed clans of hunters and gatherers. In turn, these more complex, stratified societies set the stage for industrialization and modernity, from which sprang the present, techno-industrial growth society based on corporate capitalism. Growth begets a culture of growth, and that culture has now become the dominant force globally, wiping out biological and cultural diversity.

Moreover, in the case of the overdeveloped world, increasingly children grow up in a cognitive landscape where corporations begin inculcating the desire to consume practically from birth (Schor 2004). The physical layout of communities, paltry green space, and overblown concern about stranger danger keep children inside, addicted to technologically mediated rather than direct experience, and ripe for marketing (Louv 2005). More people, less nature, more people with nature-deficit disorder, less empathy for the wild: all perfect social conditions, created by growth, that mold people into cogs of the "megamachine," to use Lewis Mumford's term.

Just as the ancient world's greatest statue, the Colossus of Rhodes, could not have been constructed until Greek society reached a certain level of affluence and technology, our society's ability to commence the final assault on wildness needed to wait until the present time, when technical knowledge, an anthropocentric worldview, and hubris aligned. Now that moment of synergy has arrived. And ironically, the crises facing humanity—which, of course, are symptoms of overpopulation—are being used to justify radical proposals to reshape the biosphere. At the macro scale, advocates of geoengineering believe they can reset Earth's temperature through a techno-fix (Bronson, Mooney, and Wetter 2009). Geoengineering boosters tend to affect the demeanor of reluctant global repairmen and cite all manner of noble ecological and social objectives (Goodell 2010). Call it noblesse oblige, planetary edition, with the high priests of techno-savvy as lords of the global manor.

Equally sweeping in its arrogance, the emerging field of synthetic biology, most famously promoted by genome-mapping pioneer Craig Venter, seeks to construct new life-forms from the ground up. In 2010, Venter's team successfully "booted up" the first synthetic organism, which was designed on a computer and assembled by machines. At least in the eyes of the public relations team at the J. Craig Venter Institute (2010), "the ability to routinely write the software of life will usher in a new era in science, and with it, new products and applications such as advanced biofuels, clean water technology, and new vaccines and medicines." In public remarks Venter has noted, "our pace of digitizing life has been increasing at an exponential" rate; he goes on to assert that synthetic biology is about to "create a new version of the Cambrian explosion where there's massive new speciation based on this digital design." Undoubtedly, any critics who worry about the unintended consequences of manufacturing new species and reengineering the global climate will be scorned as Luddites, naysayers to the brave new world of human-created biodiversity on a climate-controlled planet.

But what does it say about our species, the misnamed "wise ape," that we think such a course of action is wise? In more than three billion years of organic evolution on Earth, every species that has ever lived owed its existence to *context*: genes and structures and behaviors were shed or accreted over time in relation to other organisms and environmental factors. All of life is about interaction, and every creature moves within a web of ecological relationships. Assembling bits of genetic code, like software, to create new species that serve human desires (most especially profitability!) is something new under the sun. These life-forms are wholly shorn of context—they spring from the minds and whims of technocrats and will not have the rough and tumble, deep-time lineage of all other evolved creatures. As with geoengineering, synthetic biology is a decidedly different level of manipulation than, say, traditional plant breeding. The hubris of this campaign to assume Godlike control of Earth is breathtaking. It is domestication at its most facinorous. It is the last, great assault on liberty, the freedom of life itself to march on its own evolutionary path, creating beauty along the journey.

For those of us who seek to address the root causes of the ecosocial crisis, including overpopulation, by overturning the anthropocentric worldview and its religion of growth, these developments in mega- and nanotechnology are a depressing reminder that society is far from endorsing a Leopoldian land ethic that places the "integrity, stability, and beauty of the biotic community" foremost in our deliberations (Leopold 1949). But to the boosters and acolytes of these new technologies, the possibilities for human power and profit are as mesmerizing as Colossus must have been to the local Rhodians or visitors sailing their ships into Mandraki Harbor more than twenty centuries ago.

Surely the giant statue was perceived as an enduring monument when it was built. But it stood watch over the port for a mere fifty-six years before an earthquake felled it in 226 BC. Apparently its ruins lay scattered for more than eight hundred years before the bronze plates were sold for scrap. Today, humanity faces an earthquake of resource limits precipitated by exponential growth. Will our shiny civilization be as brittle as the Colossus when the tremors begin? How much of the diversity of life will be crushed by the wreckage of our modern colossus, the industrial growth society, as it tumbles?

Prominent individuals, including James Hansen, Bill McKibben, and Al Gore, continue to agitate for public policy actions to confront climate change, arguing that there is still time enough to forestall the worst scenarios for human-caused climate chaos. The vast bulk of attention to the issue by mainstream environmental groups has centered on energy policy. Anthropogenic climate change is, like the global extinction crisis (Eldredge 2001), a biological cataclysm unprecedented in the past sixty-five million years, merely a symptom of ecological overshoot by an obese humanity, yet rarely is the underlying disease discussed by influential nongovernmental organizations (NGOs), the media, or politicians. Sustaining economic and demographic growth but powering it with low-carbon power sources is the stated objective of practically all large nonprofits and progressive government leaders. Criticizing the industrial growth economy and corporate capitalism is as taboo as public advocacy for stabilizing and then dramatically lowering our global population numbers.

The chance of reining in exponential population growth through intentional and vigorous—yet humane and noncoercive—policies becomes ever less likely, because there is not yet even a national conversation about the problem of growth. James Howard Kunstler (2005, 249) has written persuasively about how the "psychology of previous investment" is a powerful barrier to individuals thinking clearly about the crowded, ecologically devastated, and possibly energy-scarce future, and making rational behavioral changes. The psychology of previous investment operates at the community and societal level, too. It is exceedingly difficult to abandon past behaviors or infrastructure when so much effort has gone into creating them.

In America we have now spent more than two centuries constructing a national narrative of expansion and progress based on growth. That mythic story is so thoroughly imbedded in common discourse and conventional wisdom that it goes largely unrecognized and uncritiqued.[5] Social critics, including conservationists, who have the temerity to challenge the religion of growth are ignored and marginalized. And so even the activist community has become balkanized in recent decades, with NGOs focused on overpopulation being essentially shunned by conservation and environment-related nonprofits that should be their natural allies. This history of the mainstream conservation movement abandoning overpopulation concerns has been well analyzed (Beck and Kolankiewicz 2000).

Despite the innovative efforts of some NGOs to address the cultural norms that contribute to high fertility and mass immigration,[6] I am not sanguine about our chances to make the needed changes before various horses of the apocalypse (war, famine, and plague) dramatically reduce human numbers. Humans, as tribal, small group animals, have little in our evolutionary heritage to help us cope with the challenge of understanding the peril of exponential growth. But if there is any chance to even have a reasonable conversation across the political spectrum about the dire need to address overpopulation, then a more robust dissection of how that growth affects liberty, for nature and people, perhaps can be useful.

One can take comfort, at least, in beauty—the late-afternoon light in snowy woods, or spending time in wild and semiwild settings like Coyote

Knoll and working for their permanent protection. Taking the long view offers solace too, for the power of wildness to rebuild life's richness and diversity following previous mass extinction episodes is undeniable. While the loss of beauty and complexity precipitated by humanity's demographic explosion is cause for sadness beyond words to communicate, those of us who love self-willed lands and creatures and who fight the tyranny of mindless growth at least surely recognize that the bumper sticker oracle spoke sagely when she proclaimed, Nature Bats Last. Ultimately, wild freedom will prevail.

NOTES

1. Long Vermont winters are followed by mud season, the blackflies can be pesky, and wages are low. Please don't move here.

2. Critics may note that the trend I celebrate here has been underway even while Vermont's human population increased. This is true. Whereas nineteenth-century inhabitants primarily depended upon a local agricultural economy that radically deforested the state, subsequent industrialization and economic globablization have allowed modern Vermonters' ecological footprint to stretch around Earth. The vast bulk of our food and manufactured goods comes from outside the state's borders. Because of our continued population growth, the rewilding of Vermont has coincided with an increase in the total demands that Vermonters place on wild nature globally. Such population growth here is no more sustainable or just toward nature than population growth elsewhere.

3. The Northeast has a very low percentage of its area protected in state or federal wilderness areas, in part because of the relative paucity of public lands compared to the West. The region does have a vibrant land trust movement, however, and one regional organization, the Northeast Wilderness Trust, exclusively dedicated to conserving wilderness areas (www.newildernesstrust.org). The scrappy conservation group RESTORE: The North Woods (www.restore.org/index_noflash .html) has been advocating for a new Maine Woods National Park that would expand federal public land in the region.

4. Space constraints preclude a substantive exploration of this idea, but obviously the extent to which lands can be "self-willed" stretches along a continuum. America's largest protected area, the Arctic National Wildlife Refuge, can operate as a self-regulating ecosystem, and therefore be more fully self-willed, than can small eastern wilderness areas, which are typically disjunct islands of intact habitat in a sea of degraded land, where natural processes are impaired.

5. This may be beginning to change, and none too soon. For example, see

Richard Heinberg's *The End of Growth: Adapting to Our New Economic Reality* and John Greer's *The Wealth of Nature: Economics as If Survival Mattered*. Leading-edge think tanks critiquing the growth paradigm include the Center for the Advancement of the Steady State Economy (www.steadystate.org) and the New Economics Institute (http://neweconomicsinstitute.org).

6. The Population Media Center (www.populationmedia.org) is the most notable example of an NGO using innovative mass media programs in the developing world to affect cultural norms about family size and other social issues. Numbers USA (www.numbersusa.com) is the most influential group working to educate voters about how mass immigration is driving rapid U.S. population growth.

BIBLIOGRAPHY

Beck, Roy, and Leon Kolankiewicz. 2000. "The Environmental Movement's Retreat from Advocating U.S. Population Stabilization (1970–1998): A First Draft of History." *Journal of Policy History* 12 (1): 123–156.

Bronson, Diana, Pat Mooney, and Kathy Jo Wetter. 2009. "Retooling the Planet? Climate Chaos in a Geoengineering Age." Stockholm: Swedish Society for Nature Conservation.

Eldredge, Niles. 2001. "The Sixth Extinction." *ActionBioscience.org*. Reston, Va.: American Institute of Biological Sciences.

Foreman, Dave. 2004. *Rewilding North America: A Vision for Conservation in the 21st Century*. Washington, D.C.: Island Press.

Foster, David, et al. 2010. "Wildlands and Woodlands: A Vision for the New England Landscape." Petersham, Mass.: Harvard Forest, Harvard University. Accessed from www.wildlandsandwoodlands.org.

Goodell, Jeff. 2010. *How to Cool the Planet*. New York: Houghton Mifflin.

Greer, John Michael. 2011. *The Wealth of Nature: Economics as If Survival Mattered*. Gabriola, B.C.: New Society.

Hardin, Garrett. 1993. *Living within Limits: Ecology, Economics, and Population Taboos*. New York: Oxford University Press.

Heinberg, Richard. 2011. *The End of Growth: Adapting to Our New Economic Reality*. Gabriola, B.C.: New Society.

Krall, Lisi. 2011. "Remembering History: Comment to Tim Murray and Tom Butler." *Daly News: Steady State Commentary and Related News*. Arlington, Va.: Center for Advancement of the Steady State Economy. Accessed from http://steadystate.org/remembering-history.

Kunstler, James Howard. 2005. *The Long Emergency: Surviving the Converging Catastrophes of the Twenty-First Century*. New York: Atlantic Monthly Press.

Leopold, Aldo. 1949. *A Sand County Almanac*. New York: Oxford University Press.

Louv, Richard. 2005. *Last Child in the Woods: Saving Our Children from Nature-Deficit Disorder*. Chapel Hill, N.C.: Algonquin Books.

Marshall, Robert. 1930. "The Problem of the Wilderness." *Scientific Monthly* 30: 141–148.

McKibben, Bill. 1995. *Hope, Human and Wild*. New York: Little, Brown.

Schor, Juliet B. 2004. *Born to Buy: The Commercialized Child and the New Consumer Culture*. New York: Scribner.

Venter Institute. 2010. "First Self-Replicating Synthetic Bacterial Cell." J. Craig Venter Institute, La Jolla, Calif. Accessed July 2011 from www.jcvi.org.

Vest, Jay Hansford C. 1985. "Will-of-the-Land: Wilderness among Primal Indo-Europeans." *Environmental Review* 9 (4): 323–329.

White, T. H. 1939. *The Sword in the Stone*. New York: G. P. Putnam's Sons.

Wooldridge, Frosty. 2011. "Dr. Albert Bartlett Exposes Overpopulation in America." March. Accessed July 2011 from www.rense.com/general93/alb.htm.

CHAPTER 15

The Environmental Argument for Reducing Immigration into the United States

PHILIP CAFARO AND WINTHROP STAPLES III

T HIS ESSAY ARGUES that a serious commitment to environmentalism entails ending America's population growth and hence a more restrictive immigration policy. The need to limit immigration necessarily follows when we combine a clear statement of our main environmental goals—living sustainably and sharing the landscape generously with other species—with uncontroversial accounts of our current demographic trajectory and of the negative environmental effects of U.S. population growth, nationally and globally.

At the current level of about 1.5 million immigrants per year, America's population of 310 million is set to increase to over 700 million people by 2100. "Reform" proposals such as those floated in recent years by the Bush and Obama administrations could increase immigration to over 2 million annually, with the potential to nearly triple our population to over 850 million by the end of the century. Conversely, scaling back immigration to 200,000 per year would greatly reduce America's population growth, according to studies by the U.S. Census Bureau.

Given the many issues with which environmentalists must deal and the contentious nature of immigration debates, it is understandable that many of us would prefer to avoid them. But the reality is that across the country, environmentalists are losing the battle to create a sustainable society and protect wild nature. Sprawl development destroys 2.2 million acres of wildlands and agricultural lands each year; over thirteen hundred plant and animal species remain on the endangered species list, with more added each year; water shortages in the West and Southeast are being used to justify new river-killing dams and reservoirs; and U.S. carbon emissions continue to rise. Obviously, we haven't figured out how to create a sustainable society with three hundred million inhabitants. It is not plausible to think we will be able to do so with two or three times as many people. The United States should enact policies to end population growth in our own country and back international policies that discourage it elsewhere.

THE ARGUMENT

The environmental argument for reducing immigration into the United States is relatively straightforward:

(1) Immigration levels are at a historic high, and immigration is now the main driver of U.S. population growth.

(2) Population growth contributes significantly to a host of environmental problems within our borders.

(3) A growing population increases America's large environmental footprint beyond our borders and our disproportionate role in stressing global environmental systems.

(4) In order to seriously address environmental problems at home and become good global environmental citizens, we must stop U.S. population growth.

(5) We are morally obligated to address our environmental problems and become good global environmental citizens.

(6) Therefore, we should limit immigration into the United States to the extent needed to stop U.S. population growth.

This conclusion rests on a straightforward commitment to mainstream environmentalism, easily confirmed empirical premises, and logic. Despite this, it is not the consensus position among American environmentalists.

Some environmentalists support continued high levels of immigration, while most are uncomfortable with the topic and avoid discussing it. So strong is this aversion that groups such as the Sierra Club, which during the 1970s prominently featured strong commitments to U.S. population stabilization, have dropped domestic population growth as an issue (Kolankiewicz and Beck 2001). Several years ago, the group Zero Population Growth went so far as to change its name to Population Connection ("PC" for short).

In 2006, the United States passed the three-hundred-million mark in population—that's ninety-five million more people than were here for the first Earth Day in 1970—with little comment from environmentalists. In 2007, as Congress debated the first major overhaul of immigration policy in several decades, leaders from the principal environmental organizations remained silent about proposals that could have added hundreds of millions more Americans during the twenty-first century.

Like immigration policy for the past fifty years, immigration policy for the next fifty looks likely to be set with no regard for its environmental consequences. We believe this is a bad course of action. As committed environmentalists, we would like to see our government set immigration policy (and all government policy) within the context of a commitment to sustainability. We don't believe that the goals we share with our fellow environmentalists and with a large majority of our fellow citizens—clean air and clean water; livable, uncrowded cities; sharing the land with the full complement of its native flora and fauna—are compatible with continued population growth. It is time to rein in this growth—or forthrightly renounce the hope of living sustainably here in the United States.

DEFENDING THE ARGUMENT

Our claim, then, is that "the environmental argument" is sound and that America should scale back immigration. Some readers will disagree. So let's look at the argument in more detail, starting with premise (1) that *immigration levels are at a historic high, and immigration is now the main driver of U.S. population growth.*

Consider some demographic history. Between 1900 and 2000, the U.S. population almost quadrupled, from 76 million to 281 million people. The largest decadal population increase during the previous century was also the most recent: a 32.7 million increase between 1990 and 2000 (U.S. Census Bureau 1900–2000). This population growth resulted from a mixture of natural increase and immigration, which, as figure 15.1 shows, has varied widely over the past century.

From 1880 to the mid-1920s, America experienced an immigration boom, the Great Wave, during which immigration averaged six hundred

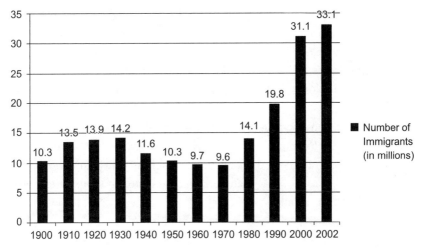

Figure 15.1
U.S. immigrant population, twentieth century
Source: Camarota 2002, 2.

thousand annually. U.S. population numbers grew rapidly in these years, due to a combination of high birth rates and high levels of immigration. For the next forty years, from 1925 to 1965, the United States had a relatively restrictive immigration policy, which allowed two hundred thousand people into the country annually, on average. The U.S. population grew substantially during this time, too, from 115 million to 194 million, primarily due to high rates of natural increase. During the 1950s, for example, American women had an average of 3.5 children apiece, far above the 2.1 total fertility rate (TFR) necessary to maintain the population of a nation with modern health care and sanitation.

By the 1970s, American women were averaging fewer babies—in 1975 the TFR stood at a lowest ever 1.7—and the United States was well positioned to transition from a growing to a stable population. One study found that without post-1970 immigration, the U.S. population would have leveled off below 250 million in the first few decades of this century (Bouvier 1998). It didn't happen, however, because in 1965 and several times thereafter, Congress greatly increased immigration levels. Between 1965 and 1990, immigration averaged 1 million people annually—*five times the average in the previous four decades.* Since 1990, immigration has increased even more, to approximately 1.5 million annually (one million legal and half a million illegal)—the highest sustained rate in history.

For these reasons, the U.S. population has continued to grow, resulting in a missed opportunity to get one key aspect of sustainability—human numbers—under control. Germany, France, Japan, and most industrialized countries now have stable or slowly growing populations. Meanwhile, the U.S. population stands at 313 million people and continues to grow rapidly.

Such is our demographic past; what of our demographic future? The Grand Council of the Iroquois famously looked "seven generations" out concerning the impacts of their decisions. Looking four generations into the future, in 2000 the U.S. Census Bureau released the population projections shown in table 15.1.

Each of the three projections or "series" holds fertility rates steady while varying immigration levels, so annual immigration rates make the main difference between them. Under the zero immigration projection, the U.S. population continues to grow throughout the twenty-first century, adding over a hundred million people by 2100. Under the middle projection, with immigration a little less than one million annually, we instead add nearly three hundred million people and almost double our population by 2100. And under the highest scenario, with annual immigration over two million, our population nearly triples by 2100, adding almost six hundred million more people by the end of the century. Obviously, according to the Census Bureau, immigration makes a *huge* difference to future U.S. population numbers.[1] Premise (1) is true.

What of premise (2) that *population growth contributes significantly to a host of environmental problems within our borders?* Here, unfortunately, we're faced with an embarrassment of riches. From many potential examples, let us briefly discuss one: urban sprawl.

In the past two decades, sprawl, defined as new development on the fringes of existing urban and suburban areas, has come to be recognized as an important environmental problem in the United States. Between 1982 and 2001, the United States converted 34 million acres of forest, cropland, and pasture to developed uses, an area the size of Illinois. The average annual rate of land conversion increased from 1.4 million acres to 2.2 million acres over this time and continues on an upward trend (Natural Resources 2001). Sprawl is an environmental problem for lots of reasons, including increased energy consumption, water consumption, air pollution, and habitat loss for wildlife. Habitat loss is by far the number one cause of species endangerment in the United States (Wilcove et al. 1998). Unsur-

Table 15.1
Projected U.S. population, in millions

Year	Zero series	Middle series	Highest series
2000	**274**	**275**	**276**
2010	288	300	309
2020	302	325	347
2030	313	351	391
2040	321	377	443
2050	**328**	**404**	**498**
2060	335	432	558
2070	343	464	625
2080	354	498	697
2090	366	534	774
2100	**377**	**571**	**854**

Source: Hollmann, Mulder, and Kallan 2000, table F.

prisingly, some of the worst sprawl centers, such as southern Florida and the Los Angeles basin, also contain large numbers of endangered species.

What causes sprawl? Transportation policies that favor building roads over mass transit appear to be important sprawl generators. So are zoning laws that encourage "leapfrog" developments far out into the country and tax policies that allow builders to pass many of the costs of new development on to current taxpayers rather than new home buyers. Between 1970 and 1990, these and other factors caused Americans' per capita land use in the hundred largest metropolitan areas to increase 22.6 percent. In these same areas during this same period, however, the amount of developed land increased 51.5 percent (Beck, Kolankiewicz, and Camarota 2003, 5).

What accounts for this discrepancy? The number one cause of sprawl, by far: population growth. New houses, new shopping centers, and new roads are being built for new residents. As figures 15.2a and 2b illustrate, in recent decades cities and states with the highest population growth rates have also shown the most sprawl.

The most comprehensive study to date on the causes of sprawl in the United States analyzed several dozen possible factors. Grouping together all those factors that can increase per capita land use and comparing these with the single factor of more "capitas," it found that in America between 1982 and 1997, 52 percent of sprawl was attributable to popu-

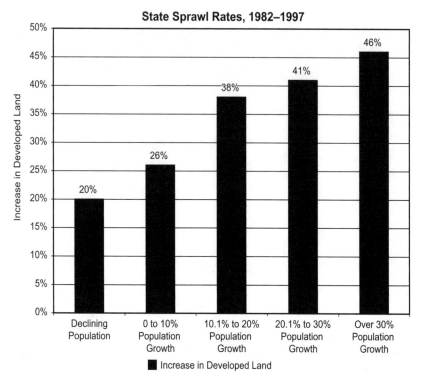

Figures 15.2a and 15.2b
Sprawl rates, U.S. states and cities
Source: Beck, Kolankiewicz, and Camarota 2003, 6, 8.

lation increase, while 48 percent was attributable to misguided policies that increased land use per person (Beck, Kolankiewicz, and Camarota 2003, 5).

Some "smart growth" advocates resist the conclusion that population growth is an important sprawl factor: partly because they don't want to obscure the need for good planning, partly due to political correctness. But the bottom line is that if we want to stop sprawl, we must change the transportation, tax, zoning, *and population* policies that encourage it. We will not stop sprawl if we simply accept as inevitable that factor—population increase—which the best research shows accounts for half of the problem. Nor will we solve our other major domestic environmental problems. That is because premise (2) is true.

As environmentalists, though, we need to "think globally." So what of premise (3) that *a growing population increases America's large environ-*

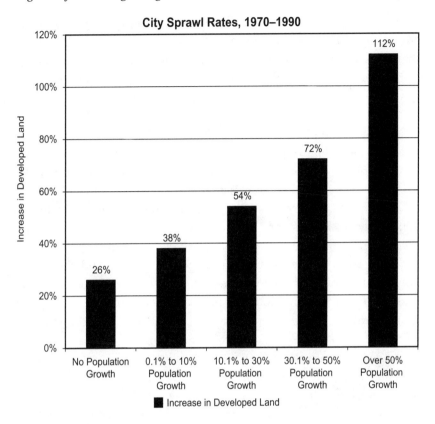

City Sprawl Rates, 1970–1990

mental footprint beyond our borders and our disproportionate role in stressing global environmental systems? Consider global warming, arguably the most important environmental challenge facing the world in the twenty-first century. Nothing mortifies American environmentalists more than our country's failure to show leadership in combating global warming. As the world's largest economy and historically largest greenhouse gas emitter, the United States has a moral obligation to lead the world in meeting this challenge (Singer 2004, chapter 2). Instead, in addition to doing nothing ourselves to solve the problem, the U.S. government has worked hard to undermine international solutions.

The most recent *Assessment Report* from the Intergovernmental Panel on Climate Change (IPCC 2007) and more recent scientific studies (Hansen et al. 2008) suggest that the industrialized nations will have to cut emissions by approximately 80 percent over the next four or five decades in order to keep global climate change from reaching potentially disastrous proportions. Meeting this objective will be difficult for the United States, given the stranglehold Big Oil and King Coal have on U.S. energy policy, under both Republican and Democratic administrations. Crucially, if our population continues to grow, success becomes even less likely.

Look at the numbers. In order to cut greenhouse emissions 80 percent in the next half century, we will have to cut emissions an average of 80 percent per person *at our current population*. But if we double our population, as we are on track to do over roughly the same period, we will have to decrease per capita emissions *90 percent* in order to reduce emissions sufficiently. Such reductions will be more expensive and demand greater sacrifice from Americans. They are thus less likely to happen.

"Hold on a minute," critics may respond. "We can and should cut our carbon emissions by four-fifths or more. The technologies exist, and America is wealthy enough to meet our moral obligation to address global warming. The problem, above all, is Americans' hoggish overconsumption."

We agree (Cafaro 1998, 2011). Limiting consumption must play an important role in addressing global warming. American environmentalists should work to enact policies that reduce our fossil fuel consumption as much as possible. Such policies should include increased taxes on fossil fuels, redirecting transportation funding from highway construction to mass transit, heavy subsidies for wind and solar power, large increases in auto fuel standards, improved building codes that reduce the energy needed for heating and cooling, and more.

However, re-engineering the world's largest economy and changing the consumption patterns of hundreds of millions of people are immense undertakings that will be difficult, expensive, and (we may assume) only partly successful. Al Gore has stated that global warming is "the moral challenge of our time"; many of us agree with him. But if Americans are serious about doing our part to limit global warming, the "multiplier effect" of population growth is too important to ignore.

Again, look at the numbers. Between 1990 and 2003, U.S. *per capita* CO_2 emissions increased 3.2 percent, while *total* U.S. CO_2 emissions increased 20.2 percent (Carbon Dioxide Information Analysis Center 2010). Why the discrepancy? During that same period, America's population increased 16.1 percent (U.S. Census Bureau 2010). More people drove more cars, built more houses, and so on. Population growth greatly increased total emissions, and it is *total* emissions, not *per capita* emissions, that quantify our full contribution to global warming.

Before we go on, please note: we do not claim that, by itself, halting U.S. population growth will solve sprawl or meet our global warming responsibilities. On the contrary, Americans must reduce our per capita consumption of land and energy in order to meet these challenges. On the other hand, the evidence clearly shows that recent population growth has increased Americans' total land and energy consumption and made these problems even worse. Americans must address both overconsumption and overpopulation if we hope to create a sustainable society and contribute to a sustainable world.[2]

Clearly premises (2) and (3) are true: U.S. population growth contributes significantly to both domestic and global environmental problems. Can we go further and state, with premise (4), that *in order to seriously address environmental problems at home and become good global environmental citizens, we must stop U.S. population growth?*

Yes, we can. It is of course possible to spin out scenarios in which America's population doubles, triples, or quadruples, and yet we still manage, through miracles of technological creativity or ethical self-sacrifice, to become ecologically sustainable. Perhaps, as techie magazines like *Discover* and *Wired* periodically suggest, we may begin building farms in high rises and let the rest of the landscape return to nature. Perhaps Americans will start taking seriously Jesus's sayings about the unimportance of wealth and material possessions and focus instead on what is really important in life ("for where your treasure is, there will your heart be also"; Matt. 6:21).

Meanwhile, back in the real world, such scenarios are implausible. They are therefore morally suspect as a basis for action, or inaction. Given the difficulties of getting three hundred million Americans to curb their consumption, there is no reason to think we will be able to achieve sustainability with two or three times as many Americans. Indeed, there are good reasons to think that three hundred million Americans is already much too high. Scientists David and Marcia Pimentel suggest a U.S. population of forty to one hundred million might be truly sustainable, given the right environmental policies and consumption levels (Pimentel and Pimentel 1990).

Environmentalists too often assume an infinite elasticity in our ability to reduce environmentally harmful consumption. This might have made sense thirty years ago, when our paradigm for such consumption was burning leaded gasoline or spraying deodorants that contained ozone-depleting chlorofluorocarbons (CFCs). We could spend some money, remove lead or CFCs from those particular products, and continue happily consuming, minus the negative environmental effects.

Today, as human beings cook the Earth and cause the sixth great extinction episode in our planet's history, we measure environmentally harmful consumption in terms of our carbon footprints and the hectares of land necessary to sustain our consumption choices—land that is then *not* available as habitat for other species. Our per capita impacts can and should be reduced. But because many of our consumption acts generate carbon emissions and use other resources, these impacts cannot be reduced to zero. As the cost of greener substitutes increases, the general public and then environmentalists refuse to pay them. As we move beyond *changing* consumption patterns in ways that perhaps more efficiently provide the benefits people want, and instead ask people to *reduce* consumption of goods and services that they desire or enjoy, sustainability becomes a much harder sell. Even environmentalists tend to fade to a lighter shade of green, when consuming less would decrease what we consider our quality of life.

Consider your humble authors. We like to think of ourselves as serious environmentalists. One of us bicycles to work every day and recently spent tens of thousands of dollars to retrofit his house with a super-efficient heating system. The other lives in a small apartment with few extraneous possessions and has spent much of the last few decades working to protect endangered wildlife. Still, we drive our cars, when that is necessary or convenient. We eat fairly conventional diets. We occasionally fly on airplanes to visit relatives or attend scholarly conferences. We would be willing to do without some of these amenities, in order to help create a sustainable society. Still, there are limits . . . and we suspect that long before we reach ours, our fellow citizens will have reached theirs.

In other words, we can imagine Americans consuming at the levels of western European or Japanese citizens. We see this as a goal worth striving for politically. We cannot imagine Americans (or western Europeans or Japanese, for that matter) voluntarily living and consuming at the levels of the average citizen from Mexico, much less the average Nigerian or Bangladeshi. Barring universal enlightenment or dire catastrophe, these aren't live political options, and it is pointless to pretend otherwise. Nevertheless, it is urgent that the United States move toward creating a sustainable society. That means consuming less *and locking in the environmental gains made possible by less consumption*, not negating them through increased population.

Such considerations suggest that premise (4) is true: we must stop U.S. population growth in order to meet our environmental responsibilities. Of course, population stabilization or reduction would not guarantee sustainability, but in tandem with serious efforts to decrease per capita consumption, they would make it possible. In philosophical terms, ending population growth is a necessary but not a sufficient condition for creating a sustainable society. If we are good environmentalists, that should be good enough to convince us to agree to premise (4).

That we are good environmentalists is captured by premise (5): we believe that *we are morally obligated to address our environmental problems and become good global environmental citizens*. We will not argue for this premise here or provide a detailed statement of what it amounts to in practice. Environmentalism means many things to many people. Still, there are two general goals to which most environmentalists subscribe: creating societies that leave sufficient natural resources for future human generations to live good lives; and sharing the landscape generously with nonhuman beings. Let us call this *generous sustainability* to differentiate it from more selfish, anthropocentric conceptions of sustainability, such as that developed by the Brundtland Commission on Environment and Development: "sustainable development is development that meets the [human] needs of the present without compromising the ability of future [human] generations to meet their own needs" (World Commission 1987, chap. 2). Numerous surveys in recent decades have shown that a large majority of Americans, from across the political spectrum, support these environmental goals. Here, then, we take this moral commitment as given, for the purpose of our argument.[3]

To sum up, we claim that premises (1) through (5) of "the environmental argument for reducing immigration" are true. But our conclusion necessarily follows from them. Therefore, that conclusion (6) is also true: *we should limit immigration into the United States to the extent needed to stop U.S. population growth.*

OUR POLICY PROPOSAL — AND THE ALTERNATIVE

We propose, then, that the United States reduce immigration by taking the following measures:

- Cut legal immigration from one million to two hundred thousand per year (the level allowed during the middle of the last century).

- Reduce illegal immigration by strictly enforcing sanctions against employers who hire illegal workers (it is fruitless to try to lower legal immigration levels while ignoring or condoning illegal immigration).

- Rework trade agreements, and increase and improve development aid, to help people live better lives and rein in population growth in their own countries.

Such a policy would allow some of the benefits of immigration to continue (provide asylum for political refugees, allow small influxes of workers with special skills, etc.), while helping the United States move toward population stabilization. Because our current TFR of 2.05 is right around "replacement rate" (2.1) and because reducing immigration would likely help drive our TFR even lower, such stabilization is no wild eco-fantasy. The United States is nearly there, if we are willing to limit immigration (this also holds true for other developed nations, whose fertility rates tend to be even lower than the U.S. rates).

This proposal is solidly within the mainstream of the best thinking on sustainability. As the President's Council on Sustainable Development put it in 1996: "Managing population growth, resources, and wastes is essential to ensuring that the total impact of these factors is within the bounds of sustainability. Stabilizing the population without changing consumption and waste production patterns would not be enough, but it would make an immensely challenging task more manageable. In the United States, each is necessary; neither alone is sufficient." One of the council's ten major suggestions for creating a sustainable society was: "Move toward stabilization of U.S. population" (President's Council 1996, iii).

Reducing immigration should be part of a comprehensive U.S. population policy, designed first to stabilize and then to reduce human numbers, slowly and humanely, both at home and abroad. As part of this effort, in addition to reducing immigration, we propose that the federal government do the following:

- Increase funding for family planning clinics and take other steps to improve easy, inexpensive access to contraception domestically.

- Preserve the right to abortion (forcing women to bear children they do not want is unjust, and forcing them to have illegal abortions is dangerous).

· End tax breaks and other government subsidies that encourage American citizens to have more children.

Meanwhile, in our foreign policy, the United States should act as follows:

· Increase funding for international family planning efforts, to help secure safe, affordable contraception in other countries.

· Vigorously support women's reproductive rights (including abortion rights) and girls' equal rights to primary and secondary education, worldwide.

· Deny all foreign aid and any immigration slots to nations that fail to commit to stabilizing their populations or sharing wealth fairly among their citizens.

Such policies would make a strong statement that the age of endless growth is over and that the United States will no longer act as a "safety valve" for failed or unjust societies that cannot or will not provide decent opportunities for their own citizens. It will spread the message that people who want to create good lives for themselves and their families need to do so where they are, and that those nations that fail to keep their populations from ballooning will themselves have to suffer the consequences. This approach seems best calculated to convince common people and politicians worldwide to take steps to end (and hopefully reverse) global population growth.

Many readers will instinctively recoil from our proposal to reduce immigration into the United States. We understand and share many of your concerns.[4] Still, we contend that paeans to sustainability, or talk of other species having an intrinsic value that we need to respect, or reminders that God calls us to be good stewards of his creation, or earnest expressions of our strong environmental feelings, are all mere cant, when coupled with a blithe acceptance of the doubling or tripling of America's human population. And "think globally, *don't* act locally" is an unconvincing and hypocritical motto for U.S. population policy.

At a minimum, we insist that readers unwilling to reduce immigration into the United States own up to the demographic and environmental implications of their positions. If you support the immigration status quo of 1.5 million immigrants annually, then you also support increasing America's population to over 700 million people by 2100. If you support an immigration policy along the lines of Edward Kennedy and John McCain's bill of 2007 (as did both President Bush and then-senator Obama), which might have increased immigration to 2.25 million people annually, then you also support nearly tripling America's population to over 850 million people by 2100.

If you support these scenarios or anything like them, then you don't just support drastically increasing America's human population. You also support more cars, more houses, more malls, more power lines, more concrete and asphalt. You support less habitat and fewer resources for wildlife; less water in the rivers and streams for native fish; fewer forests, prairies, and wetlands; fewer wild birds and wild mammals (except perhaps for house sparrows, rats, and a few other human commensals). You support replacing these other species with human beings and our economic support systems.

In other words: if you support continued mass immigration, then you reject generous sustainability. In fact, given the grave dangers *to people* of continuing the endless growth status quo, if you support continued mass immigration, you cannot even plausibly claim to support a selfish, anthropocentric sustainability.

We need to face facts now: there is no time to lose. Immigration is currently the main driver of U.S. population growth. Continued U.S. population growth is incompatible with sustainability, nationally or globally. Therefore, environmentalists committed to sustainability should support reducing current high immigration levels, along with additional steps to promote population stabilization. Not just on pain of contradiction, but on pain of failure.

Americans must choose between sustainability and continued population growth. We cannot have both.

NOTES

This chapter first appeared as a longer article in the academic journal *Environmental Ethics* 31 (2009): 3–28.

　1. In fact, immigrants tend to have more children than native-born citizens, thus raising America's overall TFR. Since these projections hold TFR steady under all three scenarios, they almost certainly understate immigration's contribution to population growth. Thus they may obscure the ability of the United States to transition to a stable population, if we are willing to reduce immigration.

　2. Simple logic suggests that endless human population growth is incompatible with (in chronological order) generous sustainability, anthropocentric sustainabil-

ity, basic human happiness, and the laws of physics. Sooner or later, human beings will have to face population issues squarely. Better sooner!

3. Note, however, that even those holding narrower anthropocentric conceptions of sustainability should arguably advocate reducing U.S. immigration, for the good of future generations in the United States and abroad. Even if all you care about is people, you might think there can be too many of us.

4. See the second half of Cafaro and Staples 2009, an earlier, longer version of this essay, for an attempt to address some of the strongest objections to our proposal.

BIBLIOGRAPHY

Beck, Roy, Leon Kolankiewicz, and Steven Camarota. 2003. *Outsmarting Smart Growth: Population Growth, Immigration, and the Problem of Sprawl.* Washington, D.C.: Center for Immigration Studies.

Bouvier, Leon. 1998. "The Impact of Immigration on United States' Population Size: 1950–2050." Washington, D.C.: Negative Population Growth.

Cafaro, Philip. 1998. "Less Is More: Economic Consumption and the Good Life." *Philosophy Today* 42 (1): 26–39.

———. 2011. "Beyond Business as Usual: Alternative Wedges to Avoid Catastrophic Climate Change and Create Sustainable Societies." In *The Ethics of Global Climate Change,* edited by Denis Arnold, 192–215. Cambridge: Cambridge University Press.

Cafaro, Philip, and Winthrop Staples III. 2009. "The Environmental Argument for Reducing Immigration into the United States." *Environmental Ethics* 31 (1): 3–28.

Camarota, Steven A. 2002. "Immigrants in the United States—2002: A Snapshot of America's Foreign-Born Population." Washington, D.C.: Center for Immigration Studies.

Carbon Dioxide Information Analysis Center. 2010. "National Fossil Fuel CO_2 Emissions—All Countries." Washington, D.C.: U.S. Department of Energy.

Hansen, J., M. Sato, P. Kharecha, D. Beerling, R. Berner, V. Masson-Delmotte, M. Pagani, M. Raymo, D. L. Royer, and J. C. Zachos. 2008. "Target Atmospheric CO_2: Where Should Humanity Aim?" *Open Atmospheric Science Journal* 2: 217–231.

Hollmann, Frederick, Tammany Mulder, and Jeffrey Kallan. 2000. "Methodology and Assumptions for the Population Projections of the United States: 1999 to 2100." Population Division Working Paper no. 38. Washington, D.C.: U.S. Census Bureau.

Intergovernmental Panel on Climate Change (IPCC). 2007. *Climate Change 2007: Synthesis Report.* Geneva: IPCC. Accessed from www.ipcc.ch.

Kolankiewicz, Leon, and Roy Beck. 2001. "Forsaking Fundamentals: The Environmental Establishment Abandons U.S. Population Stabilization." Washington, D.C.: Center for Immigration Studies.

Natural Resources Conservation Service. 2001. "National Resources Inventory 2001, Urbanization and Development of Rural Land." Washington, D.C.: U.S. Department of Agriculture. Accessed from www.nrcs.usda.gov/technical/land/nri01/nri01dev.html.

Pimentel, David, and Marcia Pimentel. 1990. "Land, Energy and Water: The Constraints Governing Ideal U.S. Population Size." Washington, D.C.: Negative Population Growth.

President's Council on Sustainable Development. 1996. *Sustainable America: A New Consensus for Prosperity, Opportunity, and a Healthy Environment for the Future.* Washington, D.C.: Office of the President.

Singer, Peter. 2004. *One World: The Ethics of Globalization.* New Haven, Conn.: Yale University Press.

U.S. Census Bureau. 1900–2000. Decennial Censuses of Population. Washington, D.C.: Government Printing Office. Accessed from www.census.gov.

———. 2010. International Data Base, "Country Summaries." Accessed December 2010 from www.census.gov.

Wilcove, D. S., D. Rothstein, J. Dubow, A. Phillips, and E. Losos. 1998. "Quantifying Threats to Imperiled Species in the United States: Assessing the Relative Importance of Habitat Destruction, Alien Species, Pollution, Overexploitation, and Disease." *BioScience* 48 (8): 607–615.

World Commission on Environment and Development. 1987. *Our Common Future.* New York: Oxford University Press.

CHAPTER 16

Toward a New Armada

A Globalist Argument for Stabilizing the U.S. Population

JOSEPH BISH

THOUGH THE United States achieved a replacement-level fertility rate in the 1970s, its population has continued to increase rapidly, primarily due to the demographic effects of inward migration. The United States is the third most populous country on the planet, at 313 million, having added nearly 100 million people since 1970. Furthermore, it continues to grow rapidly with no end in sight and is expected to experience the fourth largest aggregate population growth of any country over the next forty years. Projections (Population Reference Bureau n.d.) are that by 2050:

- India will add 560 million people.
- Nigeria will add 168 million people.
- Pakistan will add 150 million people.
- The United States will add 113 million people.

In this essay, I argue that the U.S. population should be stabilized as one step on the road to creating a sustainable global society: one that leaves sufficient habitat and resources for nonhuman species on the American landscape and lessens our excessive global ecological footprint.

Some might ask why there should be concerns about population growth that results merely from migration, if the objective is to bring about stabilization of *world* population and achieve a sustainable human presence on Earth. Concentrating on lowering fertility in individual nations makes sense toward the goal of stabilizing the global population. But migration is the relocation of existing people, so stabilizing the population of the United States through reduced immigration would have no effect on the numerical growth of world population.

This conclusion fails to appreciate the power of the United States as an influential agent in the international system of nations. The goal of planetary population stabilization will be advanced by efforts to stabilize the population of the United States. Deriding citizen-led efforts to stabilize the population of any individual country, including the United States, can only subvert progress toward planetary population stabilization.

WHY STABILIZING THE U.S. POPULATION IS IMPORTANT

If one is committed to lessening the harmful impact of humanity on Earth's environment, one should be interested in the scale and scope of each and every country's impact on its own environments *and* its demands on ecological systems outside its national boundaries. Their combination quantifies the cumulative ecological harm a nation inflicts on planetary ecosystems. As Laurie Mazur notes in her introduction to *A Pivotal Moment*:

> The food we eat, the clothes we wear, our children's toys—all leave a trail of harm that spans the globe. The shrimp served at my local Red Lobster began life in a man-made lagoon in Thailand; to meet the growing demand for their products, shrimp farmers are destroying mangroves that provide essential protection from storm surges and tidal waves . . . about a third of all Chinese carbon dioxide emissions are the result of producing goods for export, mostly to the United States and other affluent countries. (Mazur 2009, 5)

Clearly, environmentalists here and abroad have a great stake in decreasing America's global ecological footprint. That means everyone should have an interest in slowing the growth of the U.S. population, which contributes significantly to that footprint. At a minimum, the topic deserves reasoned debate and principled position statements by anyone claiming to have global environmental concerns.

There are at least two reasons why stabilizing the U.S. population is necessary to planetary environmental goals. First, so long as the United States exists, the size of its populace will be an important variable in its environmental impact, locally and globally.

The population dynamics of the United States, or any nation, can vary independently of global population dynamics. If the world population were stable, for instance, the population of the United States could still be subject to decrease, increase, or stability. Given this fact, each nation must consider its population size in relation to its environmental impacts, now and in the future. Even in the absence of discreet nation-states—an unlikely scenario in the near future—there would remain important questions regarding the local and regional carrying capacities of distinct communities or bioregions.

In any case, America's ecological footprint is notoriously excessive. Stopping population growth and lessening our demands for resources are necessary steps to bring about long-term sustainability in this country. Fresh water, wilderness and biodiversity, forests, farmland, and many other renewable and nonrenewable resources are being depleted. Especially notable are measures of our waste products, such as municipal waste and carbon emissions, which tend to grow in tight correlation with population. For instance, while per capita carbon emissions in the United States leveled off in recent decades, between 1970 to 2004 America's population and its carbon emissions both rose by about 43 percent (Meyerson 2008).

Second, there is compelling need to stabilize the U.S. population as a tactic for helping end, or radically reform, the endless growth economy at the root of our ecological problems. Speaking in solidarity with the poor in the developing world, and citing social justice activist Adriana Varillas, Laurie Mazur writes:

> Around the world, people need alternatives to an economic system that . . .
> "promises prosperity but ignores the natural world on which prosper-
> ity depends; . . . which delivers wealth for a few, and grinding, inescap-
> able poverty for many more." That system, a brand of capitalism forged
> in the United States and exported throughout the world, has spawned
> great wealth and even greater inequality, while laying waste to the natural
> resources and processes that make the planet habitable. It is, therefore, un-
> sustainable—environmentally, economically, and morally. (Mazur 2009, 7)

Such frank assessments of our current system are important as we move toward sustainability and a more just world. (For a recent environmental critique of capitalism, see Speth 2008.) But we need to consider the extent to which the capitalist economy is fueled by population growth (Daly 1996). American capitalist Bill Gross (2010) writes:

Production depends upon people, not only in the actual process, but because of the final demand that justifies its existence. The more and more consumers, the more and more need for things to be produced. *I will go so far as to say that not only growth but capitalism itself may be in part dependent on a growing population.* . . . Currently, the globe is adding over 77 million people a year at a pace of 1.15% annually, but slowing. Still, that's 77 million more mouths to feed, 77 million more pairs of shoes to make, 77 million more little economic units of demand—houses, furniture, cars, roads, oil—more, more, more . . . *capitalism depends upon final demand and if there ever comes a time when population growth slows, then the world's most efficient economic system will be tested.*" (Emphasis added)

The contemporary brand of capitalism and mass consumption that environmental scholars like Mazur and Gus Speth decry is highly reliant on population growth for its continued growth and functioning. If its epicenter is indeed the United States, it seems no accident that the U.S. Chamber of Commerce, fielding the largest number of lobbyists in Washington, D.C., pushes relentlessly for ever-higher levels of immigration, or that the *Wall Street Journal* editorial page tends to cheer on their efforts.

Consciously ratcheting up the population of the United States—intentional policy changes have quadrupled legal levels of immigration in recent decades—hardly helps subvert the status quo of the U.S. growth economy. Rather, that economy is sustained and strengthened by population growth. Criticizing U.S.-based capitalism and the damage its resource consumption and wastes inflict on the global environment, while ignoring policies that lead to rapid domestic population growth, is strategically futile.

HARD CHOICES FOR FUNDAMENTAL CHANGE

Migration involves people seeking to improve their personal welfare or that of their loved ones. The significant demand for migration into the United States speaks clearly of unequal opportunities around the globe. The pent-up demand for immigration into the United States and its causes should not remain unexamined or unaddressed—but neither can this demand stand as a rationale for ignoring the effects on U.S. population levels, were that demand fully satisfied. A 2010 Gallop poll indicated that 165 million people would immigrate immediately into the United States if they had the means (Gallop 2009); this would result in an instant 50 percent increase in the American population. Beyond the obvious social and environmental ill effects this would cause—such as physical infrastructure being overwhelmed, skyrocketing unemployment, and great destruction of remaining wildlife habitat—there would also be adverse global implications, given Americans' high per capita consumption of global resources and the rise in carbon dioxide emissions and other pollutants concomitant with U.S. energy use.

Of course, environmentalists have long aspired to change Americans' consumer patterns and environmentally costly lifestyles. Yet there is little evidence that Americans are, as yet, willing to make significant changes in this regard. Studies of consumer patterns, such as those of sociologist Juliet Schor (1999), indicate a trend in the opposite direction: Americans continue to aspire to high levels of material prosperity and to equate well-being and happiness with consumer spending power and monetary wealth. The federal government, moreover, is determined to accelerate economic growth as quickly as possible: domestic consumption is approximately nineteen million barrels of oil per day (USEIA n.d.), greater than the combined total of the European Union and Japan just a few years ago (USCIA 2009). Greenhouse gas emissions were *accelerating* prior to the 2008 recession, and 7.2 million acres of land and the habitat it provided— an area nearly the size of Maryland—were developed between the years 2002 and 2007 (USNRCS 2009).

Unfortunately, it is a safe assumption that the majority of new Americans, whether native born or immigrant, will, in the foreseeable future, follow the ecologically destructive consumer patterns of today's Americans. It does not bode well for the U.S. environment, or Earth's, that there will be significantly more Americans in the twenty-first century if current population growth continues.

If we are serious about sustainability, we must consider the merits of U.S. population stabilization, partly through further limitations on immigration. I say "further limitations" because currently, huge as annual immigration is, the U.S. government provides only a fraction of immigrant invitations each year relative to the total demand. In other words, immigration is *already* limited. The question is where to set the levels, and it is a highly contentious one. Do we turn away even more people than we already do, as part of a comprehensive strategy toward demographic stability? Or do we accept more immigrants and acquiesce to massive domestic population increase, with all its environmental implications?

Many current environmental leaders appear to believe that the more people the U.S. accepts, the more equitable our nation is (Garcia 2003; *Scientific American* 2008). This perception, however, has been cogently challenged, considering how high immigration levels have damaged employment security and driven down wages for poor Americans in recent years (U.S. Commission 1997; Borjas 1999). Harming poor American citizens in order to help poor citizens from other countries, while benefiting wealthy American capitalists, seems ethically dubious (Macedo 2007). In any case, it is clear that key sustainability goals, such as slowing global climate change or setting aside sufficient habitat to prevent species extinctions, are either made more difficult or become impossible to achieve, in the context of an ever-growing American population.

Interestingly, many American environmental leaders who acquiesce in rapid domestic population growth continue to advocate for *global* population stabilization. A prime example is Carl Pope, former chairman of the Sierra Club (Pope 1998). The problem with global population stabilization as a stand-alone goal is that there is no way to deliver a program "globally," but only through discreet units such as nations or communities. What these advocates seek, then, is planetary population stabilization via fertility-related initiatives aimed at nations other than the United States. Supporting rapid population growth policies at home, along with policies to stabilize populations abroad, has yet to be explained in an ecologically coherent manner—and even appears hypocritical. It also suggests these leaders are operating under the assumption that achieving global replacement-level fertility will result automatically and finally in the stabilization of population in the United States. As previously explained, this assumption is mistaken.

There is an alternative position, however. In the last half century, prominent environmentalists such as David Brower and Gaylord Nelson have argued that the United States should support the stabilization or reduction of the global population, by *simultaneously* supporting noncoercive initiatives to reduce fertility abroad while curbing American population growth through reducing immigration levels. There is ample room to work on reducing *U.S.* fertility levels, too, through improved family planning services and other policy measures. Forty-six percent of pregnancies in the United States are unintended.

The United States remains an agent of great influence in the international community. Both through foreign aid and by setting stability goals for our national population, much could be accomplished to move the world toward population stabilization.

Self-identified cosmopolitans or "global environmentalists" contradict themselves when supporting policies that guarantee rapid population growth in the United States. Not only do such policies fail to force change on America as an influential agent in the international community, but they also fail to secure a massive landscape (45 percent of North America) and the conscious efforts of 310 million people in the global sustainability struggle. It is nonsensical to describe a planet-scale sustainability mission, which posits population stabilization as a fundamental component of that mission—and then immediately exempt a significant portion of the planet from that agenda.

CIVIL DEBATE

At this point, we should recognize the small-minded xenophobia shown by a certain constituency that supports decreasing immigration into the United States. Any commentary on immigration policy, even if—especially if—grounded in the worldview of sustainability, must openly condemn racism and unambiguously distance itself from it. Racism should find no friends among sustainability activists, including those who advocate for U.S. population stabilization as part of an international sustainability strategy.

In the last two decades, American population growth has become a virtually "untouchable" topic, since to advocate for admitting fewer people seems to risk being perceived as racist, xenophobic, or jingoistic. There are signs, however, that this tyranny is being broken. For example, prominent environmental leader Gus Speth, in his recent work *The Bridge at the Edge of the World*, articulated a (friendly) criticism of the failures of the environmental movement as a whole. Regarding American population growth, he notes:

> Another dimension of failure on the environmental front is U.S. population growth. The United States is the third most populous country in the world after India and China. The nation is now at three hundred million and slated to grow to 420 million by 2050. That's a huge increase. Natural increase will account for 60 percent of this growth; immigration, 40 percent. The problem, of course, is that each American has a huge environmental impact, the largest in the world. *By any objective standard, U.S. population growth is a legitimate and serious environmental issue.* But the subject is hardly on the environmental agenda, and the country has not learned how to discuss the problem even in progressive circles. . . . Environmentalists and others have got to learn how to reengage with this issue without seeming to join the vigilantes patrolling our southern border. (2008, 77–78; emphasis added)

Unfortunately, one need not look far to find racist rhetoric coming from some proponents of immigration reduction, confounding an important issue with superseded and dangerous racial ideologies. For instance, a quick perusal of the website of a group called the Council of Conservative Citizens makes clear that they are avowed racists. They oppose "the massive immigration of non-European and non-Western peoples into the United States that threatens to transform our nation into a non-European majority in our lifetime. . . . Legal immigration must be severely restricted or halted through appropriate changes in our laws and policies. We also oppose all efforts to mix the races of mankind" (Council of Conservative Citizens 2011).

The existence of racism among individual citizens and organizations, on both sides of the immigration issue, must be acknowledged and denounced. Racist arguments are neither meaningful nor relevant to a serious and civil debate concerning the environmental merits of stabilizing domestic population. Nor should the rest of us be confounded and debilitated by such racist xenophobia in our task to think through the crucial issue of population growth. Consider, for example, that many votes were cast in the 2008 U.S. presidential election by racists and xenophobes, yet this did not compel people to abandon free elections or the other institutions of democracy. The presence of racists in the immigration debate should not compel the environmental movement, in particular, to abandon investigation and open discussion of U.S. population growth.

Unfortunately, proponents of immigration expansion have seized the opportunity to attack any advocate for U.S. population stabilization as racist (for example, Poswolsky 2010). Tactics of ad hominem attack have been condoned and practiced at the highest levels of political and media leadership in the United States. It is, for example, a staple on the editorial page of the *New York Times* (2009), the most influential newspaper in the country and a relentless promoter of open borders. Such tactics, though intellectually dishonest, can work, because of the American cultural sensitivity and aversion to racism. They have played no small part in causing American environmental leaders to recoil fearfully from supporting U.S. population stabilization or even daring to discuss the topic of population growth (Meyerson 2004).

A derivative of the fear of racism associated with immigration restriction is the abuse of the term *anti-immigrant*. This pejorative label is applied in broad, indiscriminate brush strokes to any person or organization suggesting any downward adjustment in annual immigration levels (Kammer 2011). Rather than being reserved for people or organizations with a track record of demonstrated xenophobia, the term has been wielded as a defamation weapon by open-borders advocates. The only way individual environmental advocates or organizations can avoid being labeled *anti-immigrant* is if they resign themselves to supporting either the status quo or declaring an open-borders ideology, or tactfully avoid staking out a position on the topic at all.

As a short-term political tactic, such inflammatory abuses of language have been politically effective. In the long term, though, these cut-throat tactics are corrosive and subvert an informed and healthy democracy. Anyone who values democratic decision making should condemn the use of slander and abuse, both within the immigration debate and more broadly.

SINKING LIFEBOAT ETHICS AND THE RISE OF A NEW ARMADA

Stabilizing America's domestic population is a necessary step toward the larger goal of a stable planetary human population living sustainably on Earth. It is not the *only* step to reach that goal, but it is a necessary one (Brown 2006). Reducing domestic per capita overconsumption and developing appropriate green technologies are also vital requirements for the shift to sustainability. Still, the American environmental community's decision to accept policies that have ensured continued rapid domestic population growth for the past forty years remains a huge strategic mistake. It is an understandable failure, given the quandaries underlying massive demand for immigration into the United States and the confounding presence of racism in immigration debates. But it is a failure, nonetheless. Maintaining or increasing current immigration levels guarantees continued rapid population growth in the United States and the failure of the movement toward national and global sustainability.

Not only is America's immigration policy a violation of role-modeling principles (Why should Americans care about international population growth and support efforts to end it, if the growth of their own population is dismissed as irrelevant to environmental issues? Why should any other nation take population stabilization seriously, if Americans support continued population growth in their own country?). Support for rapid domestic population growth is also an abrogation of our duties to future generations, to other species, and to wild ecosystems at home and abroad,

which will suffer great harm as global ecological degradation increases, in
large part due to willfully engineered domestic population growth in the
United States.

The most responsible and brave decision U.S. environmentalists could
make would be to work for a gradual downward adjustment of U.S. citi-
zenship invitations, currently set at around one million annually. While
some argue (Hardin 1992) that immigration levels should be set at a "net-
zero" rate, with foreign entries into the United States set to equal the number of citizens who leave, I reject that proposal as overly aggressive and
politically counterproductive. A good compromise would be to slowly
reduce immigration, over the course of a decade or so, to the levels recommended by the Jordan Commission on Immigration Reform: roughly
550,000 people per year, or about 1,500 people per day (U.S. Commission
1997, 22). This will ensure that the United States remains a culturally vibrant, tolerant, and assimilative nation that is also committed to eventual
population stabilization.

To be fair, any downward adjustments to the number of people we invite into our country in any given year should be coupled with measures
that help people live better lives in their own countries: particularly increased foreign aid for family planning services, reworking unfair trade
agreements, and foreign debt forgiveness. It should also be joined with
policies that encourage Americans to consume less and with consistent
efforts to fight bona fide racism. Without these important qualifications
and accompanying policies, the management of the U.S. population
toward stabilization might rightly be classified as a kind of "lifeboat ethics"
(Hardin 1993) focused exclusively on Americans' own well-being.

This essay, however, does not suggest turning the United States into
such a self-serving lifeboat. Rather, the United States should be a lead
ship in a multinational sustainability armada, with the urgent mission to
ensure a sustainable future by acting in the present with all hands—all
nations—on deck. The face that should inspire us to launch these ships is
the face of Earth itself, including all the nonhuman life for which we must
act as stewards and caretakers.

Regardless of what population and immigration policies upon which
we democratically settle—45 percent of Americans wish immigration
decreased, while only 17 percent wish it increased (Gallop 2010)—one
thing is clear: Americans need substantial education regarding population

questions. We need public discussion, free speech, and principled debate about these matters, even if that proves difficult or opens up participants to special interest attacks or spurious, dishonest defamation campaigns. Confronting U.S. citizens about the size and growth of their own population, the drivers of that growth, and their options for remediating it is a necessary task for creating a sustainable future for the planet.

NOTE

I am a staunch supporter of immigration into the United States, especially as a source of cultural diversity and new ideas for sustainable living. I am always eager to discuss and reassess my views, especially with those who may doubt my pro-immigration advocacy position.

BIBLIOGRAPHY

Borjas, George. 1999. *Heaven's Door: Immigration Policy and the American Economy.* Princeton, N.J.: Princeton University Press.

Brown, Lester R. 2006. *U.S. Population Reaches 300 Million, Heading for 400 Million: No Cause for Celebration.* Washington, D.C.: Earth Policy Institute.

Council of Conservative Citizens. 2011. "Statement of Principles." Accessed June 2011 from http://cofcc.org.

Daly, Herman. 1996. *The Economics of Sustainable Development.* Boston: Beacon Press.

Gallop. 2009. "700 Million Worldwide Desire to Migrate Permanently." November. Accessed from www.gallup.com/poll/124028/700-million-worldwide -desire-migrate-permanently.aspx.

———. 2010. "Amid Immigration Debate, Americans' Views Ease Slightly." July. Accessed from www.gallup.com/poll/141560/amid-immigration-debate -americans-views-ease-slightly.aspx.

Garcia, Arnaldo. 2003. "Immigration, Population, and Environmental Justice." *Race, Poverty, Environment: A Journal of Social and Environmental Justice.* Accessed June 2011 from www.urbanhabitat.org/node/918.

Gross, Bill. 2010. "Privates Eye." *Investment Outlook* (blog). August. PIMCO: Your Global Investment Authority. Accessed from www.pimco.com/EN/Insights/ Pages/PrivatesEyeBillGrossAugust2010.aspx.

Hardin, Garrett. 1974. "Lifeboat Ethics: The Case against Helping the Poor." *Psychology Today*, September, 38–43.

————. 1992. "Zero Net Immigration as the Goal." *Population and Environment* 14 (2): 197–200.

————. 1993. *Living within Limits: Ecology, Economics, and the Population Taboos.* New York: Oxford University Press.

Kammer, Jerry. 2011. "The Carnegie Corporation and Immigration: How a Noble Vision Lost Its Way." March. Washington, D.C.: Center for Immigration Studies.

Macedo, Stephen. 2007. "The Moral Dilemma of U.S. Immigration Policy: Open Borders vs. Social Justice?" In *Debating Immigration*, edited by Carol Swain, 63–82. Cambridge: Cambridge University Press.

Mazur, Laurie, ed. 2009. *A Pivotal Moment: Population, Justice and the Environmental Challenge.* Washington, D.C.: Island Press.

Meyerson, Frederick A. B. 2004. "Policy View: Immigration, Population Policy, and the Sierra Club." *Population and Environment* 26 (1): 61–69.

————. 2008. "Population Growth Is Easier to Manage Than Per-Capita Emissions." *Bulletin of the Atomic Scientists*, January 17. Population and Climate Change Roundtable.

New York Times. 2009. "The Nativists Are Restless." Editorial, January 31.

Pope, Carl. 1998. "Moving On: Lessons from the Immigration Debate." *Sierra Magazine*. Sierra Club. Accessed from www.sierraclub.org/sierra/199807/ways .asp.

Population Reference Bureau. N.d. "Population Mid-2010" and "Population Mid-2050 (projected)." Accessed June 20, 2011, from www.prb.org.

Poswolsky, Rebecca. 2010. "Population and Fake Progressives." Imagine 2050, May 13. Accessed from http://imagine2050.newcomm.org/2010/05/13/ population-and-fake-progressives/.

Schor, Juliet B. 1999. *The Overspent American: Why We Want What We Don't Need.* New York: HarperPerennial.

Scientific American. 2008. "How Immigration May Affect Environmental Sustainability: Some Environmental Groups Are Taking on the Immigration Issue." September 26. Accessed from www.scientificamerican.com/article .cfm?id=immigrations-effect-on-evironment.

Speth, James Gustave. 2008. *The Bridge at the Edge of the World: Capitalism, the Environment, and Crossing from Crisis to Sustainability.* New Haven, Conn.: Yale University Press.

U.S. Central Intelligence Agency (USCIA). 2009. *World Factbook 2009.* Washington, D.C..

U.S. Commission on Immigration Reform. 1997. *Becoming an American: Immigration and Immigrant Policy.* Washington, D.C.: U.S. Government Printing Office.

U.S. Energy Information Administration (USEIA). N.d. "Oil: Crude and Petroleum Products Explained." Accessed June 20, 2011, from www.eia.gov/energy
explained/index.cfm?page=oil_home.

U.S. Natural Resources Conservation Service (USNRCS). 2009. *Summary Report:
2007 National Resources Inventory.* Washington, D.C.: U.S. Department of Agriculture.

CHAPTER 17

Perceiving Overpopulation
Can't We See What We're Doing?

RONNIE HAWKINS

I'VE BEEN TRACKING the public discussion, or lack thereof, regarding our surging population for almost half a century now, and I find it shocking that so little progress has been made in waking people up to the problem. I've gone from feeling a nagging worry about that ominous J-curve, to deep moral outrage regarding our species' ruthless destruction of other biospherical life, and finally to a cynical curiosity about just how the knife of natural selection will pare down our excessive numbers. My outrage sparks anew seeing us poised to construct yet another round of nuclear reactors, poison seas and wreck landscapes in a desperate grab for diminishing fossil fuels, and displace and destroy diverse organic life forms—all to maintain the growth of our burgeoning human project.

Is humanity really so ill-informed of its actual situation, so mesmerized by the imperative of infinite expansion, so deeply in denial of its suicidal trajectory, that it celebrates hitting seven billion this year and looks forward to adding another two or three billion by the end of the century? In what follows, I consider the underlying dynamics of our perilous situation and discuss why we have such difficulty perceiving it. My hope is that if we can come to *see* what we're doing, we will manage to apply the brakes in time to save much that is worth saving.

Fritjof Capra, physicist and systems theorist, speaks of humanity experiencing a "crisis of perception" on the way to a new worldview reflecting the ecological lessons we have learned in recent decades. He anticipates a shift to a new ecological paradigm that will recognize living organisms and their interrelationships as dynamic functional systems (Capra 1995). Arne Naess, the founder of deep ecology, has also addressed issues of perception, urging the adoption of what he calls a "gestalt ontology." Such an ontology not only recognizes that the whole is more than the sum of its parts but also distinguishes between the concrete contents of reality, which we experience spontaneously through gestalt perception, and "useful but immensely abstract structures" that help us understand the world and live in it intelligently (Naess 1995, 245). The concept of an ecosystem, for example, is an abstraction that is "*of* the world but not *in* the world," just as the map is not the territory, but its importance "cannot be overestimated" (Naess 2008, 78–79).

My recommendation is that we strive to see the abstract structures of which Capra and Naess speak, the theoretical concepts developed through empirical ecological investigation, within the workings of nature as if we possessed a kind of X-ray vision that would let us see them "in" the world, so as to more fully inform our day-to-day experience of nature's gestalt. Doing so will enable each of us to better connect our subjective, egocentric (centered on ourselves) viewpoints with the objective, allocentric (centered on other phenomena) perspectives taken by science. And, above all, we need to *see* the expansion of our growing human population—and the combined sum of all its frenetic activities—*into* the biosphere, so as to grasp the dramatic alterations that are taking place. Making the effort to do so may bump up our collective awareness enough for a critical mass of humanity to understand the gravity of our situation and take responsible action.

According to philosopher of science Norwood Russell Hanson, our perceptions are always theory laden, "threading knowledge into our seeing" (1958, 22). Hanson describes how Johannes Kepler, ushering in the Copernican Revolution, saw the sunrise as due to the rotation of the Earth on its axis; something Tycho Brahe, conceptually stuck in the ancient geocentric paradigm, was unable to see, even as his retinas took in the same sense data. Hanson provides a further example of a scientific apparatus viewed by a professional physicist, a schoolchild, and an infant: the physicist sees the object as an X-ray tube, *seeing in* the function of the glass and metal arrangement, while the child *sees that* the object would break if it fell to the floor, and the infant *sees only* an intriguing, shiny toy. Hanson says that these epistemic gradations of perception reflect differences of "conceptual organization" in the perceivers, but he maintains that these organizational differences are "'there' in the seeing," rather than interpretations second-arily imposed on raw visual experience (23).

Technologies for investigating and representing our common reality over an enormous range of scales now enable us to know much more than Brahe or Kepler, and once gained, this hard-won knowledge can be threaded into our seeing more widely. Deep understanding can some-times be conveyed simply and straightforwardly in words; for example, as when Aziza in Khaled Hosseini's *A Thousand Splendid Suns* tells her mother what she has learned from her tutor: "Water evaporates from the leaves—mammy, did you know?—the way it does from laundry hanging on a line. And that drives the flow of water up the tree. From the ground and through the roots, then all the way up the treetrunk, through the branches and into the leaves. It's called transpiration" (2007, 288). The Afghani child thus explains the coolness we all experience under the shade of a tree; we can envision the living processes at work all around us and give thanks for their relief on a hot summer's day. Knowledge can also be threaded into our perception by visual imagery that lets us see through surfaces; artist Alex Grey, for example, painting with the omniscience of the fabled "God's Eye View," helps us grasp the complexity of our living bodies beneath the skin (1990, 2001).

By now, most of humanity has seen pictures of the Earth from space, and many of us are adept at zooming in and out and all around this planet of ours with the disembodied eye of Google Earth. Both are examples of viewing something—in this case, the commonly shared biosphere—from an allocentric perspective, examining the globe we inhabit as if we were looking down on it. Yet all the while, we can continue to be aware of our connections to home in body, family, society, and biome. If we've read a little science, we can *see* our planet *as* a roughly spherical, rotating and revolving, three-dimensional object of a particular mass and extension, displaying certain geological, hydrological, and biological features. We can focus in on specific portions of this virtual Earth, observing patches of green and gray that we spontaneously *see as* forested lands, lands inten-sively exploited, urban and suburban structures, lands open to the sky. *Seeing in* what we've learned if we've done some more specific homework, our mind's eye can imaginatively trace the hydrologic flow of surface water from mountain to river to ocean, groundwater moving more slowly be-neath the soil, photosynthetic processes producing sugars and releasing oxygen from the leaves of plants, oxides of carbon, nitrogen, and sulfur rising from the tailpipes of cars. Thus we are able to envision the dynamic organization so eloquently described by Aldo Leopold:

> Plants absorb energy from the sun. This energy flows through a circuit called the biota, which may be represented by a pyramid consisting of layers. . . . A plant layer rests on the soil, an insect layer on the plants, a bird and rodent layer on the insects, and so on up through various animal groups to the apex layer, which consists of the larger carnivores. . . .
>
> Each successive layer depends on those below it for food, and often for other services, and each in turn furnishes food and services to those above. Proceeding upward, each successive layer decreases in numerical abundance. . . .
>
> Land, then, is not merely soil; it is a fountain of energy flowing through a circuit of soils, plants, and animals. Food chains are the living channels which conduct energy upward. (1949, 216)

Leopold's land pyramid is an abstract structure that I conceptualize, not a part of the concrete contents of my perception when I stand in the center of the degraded sand pine upland surrounding my home. Threading this sort of knowledge into the living landscape viewed from my window, however, I can *see why* there are many fewer red-tailed hawks than there are mourning doves. With a little more knowledge, I can also *see that* the hawks will bioconcentrate pollutants present in the system to a greater extent than will the doves, fat-soluble residues passing upward toward the pyramid's apex along with embodied energy. As a landowner, such knowledgeable perception can inform my decisions about whether or not to use pesticides, for example, as well as which type of bird could better withstand some human predation in a situation of food scarcity.

Taking the long view across time as well as space, integrating what we know from contemporary science, we humans can now *see* the abstract vertebrate body plan *in* every concrete tetrapod that walks, flies, or swims. We can see how much our own genomes, proteomes, and metabolomes share with all the other organisms that have evolved on this Earth since LUCA: our hypothetical last universal common ancestor of 3.5 billion years ago. With such epistemically engaged sensibilities, we can move from the allocentric and conceptual to the egocentric and immediate, feeling ourselves reverberating with the living beings in our midst, knowing that we are all interconnected components of Leopold's fountain of energy. The active perceptual process that I am urging is one of *seeing Life back "into" a world* from which it was erroneously deleted by the old Cartesian paradigm of a dead, mechanical nature passively awaiting exploitation by an alienated humanity. The new view is one of understanding oneself as a responsible part of this very complex living system that we call the biosphere, appreciating one's brief opportunity to know, love, and protect what has taken so long to evolve.

Most people seem blind to the anatomy, physiology, and long evolutionary history of our planet and its life forms, however. Nor do they seem willing to imaginatively project forward over time the inevitable consequences that continuing human population growth will have upon the larger system. I caught my first glimpse of our population's trajectory as a schoolchild and was frightened by the way the curve was approaching the vertical, seeing that we might someday fall off the tracks, so to speak, when they became too steep for our collective train to hold. The belief that grown-ups would surely, somehow, fix such a daunting problem was comforting, but still I voiced some worries.

Later, I remember being frustrated to the point of tears when a college roommate refused to even consider that our explosive population growth might have something to do with her own life. Like most of us most of the time, she navigated primarily by perceptions centered around her personal frame of reference. Not a biology major, she probably never created a terrarium or watched bacteria growing in a petri dish, nor was she given to the contemplation of spherical geometry. Rather, as a blossoming woman and dutiful daughter, having children was a central desideratum, and theoretical constructs held little relevance for the future she anticipated.

My own understanding of the workings of nature is more detailed now than it was then, but my orientation to that scary J-curve remains much the same: our species is on an unsustainable course. I did watch bacteria growing in a petri dish; once the colonies used up all their nutrients and started swimming in their own wastes, growth stopped and the population plummeted. I have also watched as the dime stores of my youth have transformed into big-box outlets with batteries of cashiers ringing up long lines of customers, the two-lane roads have morphed into multilane superhighways—connecting all this with our collective ascension along the y-axis. But I will admit that perception of these changes, from my situated egocenter, has often been easy to miss, like the gradual temperature rise for the lobster in the pot.

Making an effort to *see* humanity's growing population, with its increasingly voracious, competing national subgroupings, *into* the ecological framework that supports it, I can *see that* we have already far exceeded an appropriate human niche. Societies already eating at the highest levels of the Leopoldian pyramid are continuing to increase in numbers, while larger human populations strive to move up a trophic notch or two as their economies grow. The United States has not yet acknowledged a need to slow its population growth, let alone its material consumption, and India and China now aspire to achieve a similar level of consumerism. All together, we are using up petroleum at a rate of (at least) a thousand gallons a second (Kerr 2011). It is surely time to get past finger-pointing and admit this fact to ourselves: *it is the expanding scale of the whole human enterprise that is relentlessly destroying the biosphere*, the living system comprising all Life on Earth. Our human colonies are gobbling up more and more of the nutrients within our global petri dish, crowding out and killing off other species that kept our earthly terrarium in dynamic balance for millennia, and filling the vessel with our mounting wastes. Any rational assessment must conclude that we are trying to achieve the impossible: the part is attempting to become greater than the whole. Importing this abstract, allocentric view into my everyday, egocentric perception, I can *see* the workings of these unsustainable processes of growth *in* every new housing development I pass on my way to work.

At least part of the reason why we don't take our population problem seriously, then, is that most people don't yet know how to process it as a problem at the personal level (for an examination of social factors underlying a similar perceptual failure regarding climate change, including the psychological forces of denial at work, individually and collectively, see Norgaard 2011). There still remains the question, however, of why we are spurred on by such an intense drive toward *growth* in population and material consumption. In order to attempt an answer to this question, I would again solicit our powers of visualization.

We humans are primates, social animals who evolved through cooperative, small-group living. We still retain our proclivities for group identification and defense, which often meant not only offense against outsiders to the group but also a continual need to add more bodies to the defensive line. Beneath all this must lie a biological will-to-power, the urge toward growth and reproduction found in all living beings but kept in check in other species by pruning from without if not regulation from within. But while we share enormous biological commonality with the rest of life, we humans are distinctive in our facility with symbols: a talent largely responsible both for our evolutionary success in proliferating *and* for the present crisis of perception that holds us in thrall. I submit that it is our world of abstract symbols and their associated meanings, continually reinforcing an inherent biological drive for expansion, that has us locked us into a dangerously runaway feed-forward process. Escape from this vicious circle will require developing the reflexivity to see ourselves in the process of generating, and then buying into, the symbolic structures we create. It is time we changed their meaning and rearranged the feedback loops between abstraction and reality, so as to move in a more sustainable direction.

To explore this aspect of human population growth, we will need to scrutinize the relationship between the conceptual and the perceptual once again. Whereas my initial emphasis was on *seeing* the conceptualizations of science *into* our everyday perceptual world, in this case it is the importation of customary concepts into our spontaneous percepts that needs to be questioned. Contemporary science discloses that many of our representations of the world are badly out of sync with the way nature is constituted in actuality. In addition, symbolic meanings that intentionally misrepresent reality are being propagated with increasing desperation, while many more misperceptions designed to perpetuate the social status quo likely result from biasing processes we all share, often below the level of full consciousness. It seems there is a growing fear of what might happen should the current paradigm and the hierarchies it maintains finally shift.

One very powerful symbol at large within our culture today is that of money. Money is nothing in itself, of course; it is simply a symbol of abstract value, a quantified placeholder that must bottom out eventually in something concrete and desirable. Were it not for the fact that we have all learned to recognize, accept, and exchange money, to *see* it *as* something real and valuable, the bills and coins would hold little worth, and the electronic blips that currently symbolize great chunks of wealth or debt would be meaningless. Its importance in our current context lies in the fact that the rules of the elaborate language games that have grown up around the symbolic object of money, and our assumed need to continually maximize the amount of it that we "possess," individually and collectively, have come to encourage both continuing population growth and growth in our material consumption. The amplifying reflection back and forth between our abstract, money-focused symbol-world and our behavior reinforces various maladaptive practices, including those that promulgate ever-increasing growth along just about all major axes of the human enterprise.

Philosopher John Searle has analyzed the process by which we fashion our social worlds, using our talent for symbolization (1995, 2010). He explains how we "construct culture out of nature" (1995, 9), creating the social institutions that organize our activities through a series of linguistic acts, setting up elaborate systems of symbolic status that we all recognize and accept, and maintain through our acceptance. Searle's writings help us to achieve a kind of double vision, able simultaneously to understand the messages that our symbols carry and to visualize the relationships among the social agents encoding and decoding them. He points out that money and its associated symbolic entities like interest and debt are *ontologically subjective*: they exist only because we symbol-using social animals collectively believe them to exist. Their mode of existence is quite different from those things existing *concretely*, independently of human symbols like money and the beliefs, desires, and expectations that underlie them.

Since most of us have not yet developed the reflexivity to perceive our own agency in devising these symbols, however, the majority of human beings appear to be trapped in the behavioral mode of obeying the messages they convey, as if we had no choice in the matter. Moreover, we pay more attention to the linguistic content of these symbolic messages than to the concrete alterations of physical reality that our obedience to the former brings about.

To take a crucial example, only our fascination with symbols could have led us to accept the globalization of humanity's food supply, with its requisite steadily increasing fossil fuel consumption, pesticide application, and water depletion. Ecologically rational (Plumwood 2002) people would never have agreed to become dependent on their sustenance being shipped to them from thousands of miles away, even from continents on the other side of the planet. Instead of considering how large numbers of human beings might make a living from the land they inhabit, however—a consideration that would necessarily focus attention on the need to limit populations—we presently look to the circulation of abstract symbols in computer banks to keep it all working, millions of people turning billions of interconnected cranks, not because it makes functional sense to them, but simply in exchange for "money."

Similarly, our perception of living nature is filtered through an anthropocentric conceptual lens that reduces, abstracts, and quantifies, and we mistakenly take what is left for rock-hard reality. Consider, for example, the ontological difference between what is produced through the photosynthetic activities of green plants, which trap the energy of the sun in a form that supports all animal life, and what is "produced" by the calculation of compound interest, which is simply an abstract, mathematical operation creating nothing in the way of new material substance. We are taught to *see into* the tree, not the actual life-sustaining processes of transpiration and photosynthesis, but rather a quantity of board feet that in turn will net a certain number of dollars—and we make believe that exchanges of these symbols themselves will create something of value in the real world. But the real world, whose material and energetic exchanges are structured in accordance with the Leopoldian pyramid, is a world where a "dollar" is nothing but a concept in the head of a hungry primate.

Seeing through the layers of projected meanings right down to the agents who are doing the meaning construction and symbol manipulation, reconnecting our realm of abstraction with our biology, Searle observes: "governments have their origin in a series of primitive biological phenomena, such as the tendency of most primate social groups to form status hierarchies, the tendency of animals to accept leadership from other animals, and in some cases the sheer brute physical force that some animals can exert over others. . . . It seems to me these elements of primate biology are just as essential to understanding political philosophy as many of the features that are traditionally discussed, such as the social contract" (1995, 86).

The name of the particular form of human primate organization to which the vast majority of us currently submit is *patriarchy*. And as long as we configure ourselves into hierarchical arrangements that afford greater power to those in the upper echelons of a social pyramid, with powers that swell in proportion as the size of its base increases, it seems we are doomed to follow the growth imperative along multiple, interlocking dimensions all the way to the walls of our planetary petri dish. Under patriarchy, our species lives subdivided into a number of competing "superorganisms" variously called nations, corporations, religions, and similar large-scale patterns of grouping, as numerous human individuals channel their collective energies in ways that serve to maintain and enlarge the size and power of the social entity to which they feel they belong (Hölldobler and Wilson 2009).

There are many reasons why those positioned toward the apex of a social pyramid desire to see numbers at the lower levels grow: more consumers for their products; more laborers to keep wages low; more soldiers to sacrifice in the superorganismal conflicts necessary to secure the group cohesion that maintains the overall pattern. Most of us identify strongly with our respective superorganisms, and our cultural symbolism encourages us to conceptualize them as entities engaged in fierce competition with one another, perceiving increases in population or in socially constructed abstractions like "GDP" as indicators that we are "winning the game" against other such groupings. Granting enormous, destructive power to those at the top of our subgroup, moreover, allows group members to enjoy the comforting fantasy of absolute protection by a godlike father figure, all under the guise of "promoting national security." Need we ask why, under patriarchy, women must not be allowed agency over their own procreation, or why countries with the highest fertility rates are often the most overtly patriarchal? We continue to replay our evolutionary history, assuming that the fastest-growing, most ruthless competitors are somehow the fittest, using our entire planet as the backdrop for this drama. The necessary paradigm shift must therefore penetrate right down into our species' gendered core.

Twenty-five years ago, Arne Naess (1986) challenged "defenders of nature" to think our way through to the root causes of ecological degradation and work for an alternative way of life. Few of us rose to the challenge. We now inhabit a significantly more impoverished planet, one where we are destabilizing the climate and facing an increased likelihood of abrupt and painful population reduction. All the while, we have trusted in elders who weren't really "grown-ups" at all, but rather would-be patriarchs (and their supporters) pontificating about the evils of birth control and abortion to shore up their own positions within power hierarchies. The notion that one could claim to be "pro-life" while promoting further expansion of the human juggernaut, justifying the greatest destruction of planetary life Earth has seen in sixty-five million years, the accelerating extinction of nonhuman species that are being crowded right out of existence by a sprawling humanity (see Hawkins 1994), is one that deserves to be laughed right off the political stage. Isn't it time to begin a more adult conversation?

I close with an image from pioneer ecologist Charles Elton, who likened his first glimpse of that pyramidal flow of matter and energy to the functioning of a human village. As he observed, "when an ecologist says 'there goes a badger,' he should include in his thoughts some definite idea of the animal's place in the community to which it belongs, just as if he had said, 'there goes the vicar'" (Elton 2001, 64). We need to run the metaphor in the opposite direction now. Just as there is a limit to the number of badgers that can fill the badger role within a biotic community, there is a limit to the number of vicars—or bakers, or bankers—who will be useful and supportable within a functional human community. Unlike our symbols, human beings are ontologically objective. Once they come into existence, we can't "unthink" them if we end up with too many. This might be an important point to contemplate the next time a politician talks about "creating jobs." We need to ask, "Jobs doing what?" What kinds of jobs will bring our societies into ecological sustainability, and how many people will it take to fill them? We need a clear perception of the whole, and the place of our species within it, in order to visualize the goals toward which our collective human endeavors might intelligently aim.

BIBLIOGRAPHY

Capra, Fritjof. 1995. "Deep Ecology: A New Paradigm." In Sessions 1995, 19–25.
Elton, Charles. 2001. *Animal Ecology*. Chicago: University of Chicago Press. (Orig. pub. 1927.)
Grey, Alex. 1990. *Sacred Mirrors*. Rochester, Vt.: Inner Traditions International.
———. 2001. *Transfigurations*. Rochester, Vt.: Inner Traditions International.
Hanson, Norwood Russell. 1958. *Patterns of Discovery*. Cambridge: Cambridge University Press.
Hawkins, Ronnie Zoe. 1994. "Reproductive Choices: The Ecological Dimension." In *The Environmental Ethics and Policy Book*, edited by Donald VanDeVeer and Christine Pierce, 390–400. Belmont, Calif.: Wadsworth.
Hölldobler, Bert, and E. O. Wilson. 2009. *The Superorganism*. New York: W. W. Norton.
Hosseini, Khaled. 2007. *A Thousand Splendid Suns*. New York: Riverhead Books.
Kerr, Richard. 2011. "Peak Oil Production May Already Be Here." *Science* 331 (6924): 1510–1511.
Leopold, Aldo. 1949. *A Sand County Almanac*. London: Oxford University Press.
Naess, Arne. 1986. "Intrinsic Value: Will the Defenders of Nature Please Rise?" In *Conservation Biology: The Science of Scarcity and Diversity*, edited by Michael Soulé, 504–515. Sunderland, Mass.: Sinauer Associates.

————. 1995. "Ecosophy and Gestalt Ontology." In Sessions 1995, 240–245.

————. 2008. "The World of Concrete Contents." In *The Ecology of Wisdom: Writings by Arne Naess*, edited by Alan Drengson and Bill Devall, 70–80. Berkeley, Calif.: Counterpoint.

Norgaard, Kari. 2011. *Living in Denial: Climate Change, Emotions, and Everyday Life*. Cambridge: MIT Press.

Plumwood, Val. 2002. *Environmental Culture: The Ecological Crisis of Reason*. London: Routledge.

Searle, John. 1995. *The Construction of Social Reality*. New York: Free Press.

————. 2010. *Making the Social World: The Structure of Human Civilization*. Oxford: Oxford University Press.

Sessions, George. 1995. *Deep Ecology for the 21st Century: Readings on the Philosophy and Practice of the New Environmentalism*. Boston: Shambhala.

CHAPTER 18

Salmon in the Trees

AMY GULICK

*When we try to pick out anything by itself, we find it hitched
to everything else in the universe.*
—John Muir

CROUCHED ON A ROCK near a churning waterfall, I'm entranced
by thousands of salmon thronging in a pool. Fin to fin, tail to tail,
they sway against the current as one giant mob. I forget that they are individual fish until one springs from the crowded stream, hurling itself against
the foaming wall of water. And then another, and another. Fish after fish,
leap after leap, so much energy expended, so much energy delivered. The
long green arms of Sitka spruce and hemlock trees spread across the stream
as if to welcome the salmon back into their forested fold. Click, click,
click goes my camera in a frenzied attempt to freeze an airborne fish in my
frame. They're fast, much faster than my reflexes. I try again, and again.

Hours vaporize, like the mist rising into the forest from the spray of
the waterfall. But for the salmon every minute is precious because their
time is coming to an end. They've stopped eating. They're in their final
act—spawning—and they won't stop pushing upstream until they die.
Their instinctive drive to pass on their genes is hammered home to me
with every leaping fish. Click, click—lots of empty frames. I need to con-
centrate, but the distractions are many, and wonderful. The harpy screams
of ravens emanating from the forest jolt my soul. Bald eagles swoop from
treetops to rock tops, eyeballing the feast before them. Bears march into
the stream with purpose, causing me to stand at attention. They know
I'm here, but they seem focused on the fish at hand, or at paw. With one
eye pressed against the viewfinder, and one eye open for bears, I attempt
to focus on anything, but instead I just bask in the present. I've never felt

more alive. It's like I'm swirling in the middle of a wild performance with throbbing music, leaping dancers, and flashing lights. I have a front row seat to one of the greatest shows on Earth, one that plays out every year all over the Tongass National Forest of southeast Alaska.

Just a few days before, there wasn't a single salmon in this stream. In a few weeks, the only visible evidence of what took place here will be spawned-out carcasses littering the stream banks. The cleanup crews of birds, otters, and mink will scour the remains. Heavy fall rains will wash the fish bones out to sea, and bears will curl up in their dens as snow dusts the mountaintops. The show will be over, but the annual payout is rich. Bald eagles, fueled by salmon, will soar greater distances to find food during the lean winter months. Female bears, padded with fat reserves, will give birth in their dens and nurse their tiny cubs with salmon-enriched milk. The forest, fertilized with supercharged soil from decayed fish, will sprout new growth come spring. And the next generation of salmon is swaddled in the streams and incubated by the forest. The fertilized eggs will soon hatch, ensuring that the cycle of life is a circle, always flowing, never broken.

The Tongass boasts nearly a third of all that remains of the planet's rare old-growth temperate rain forests and contains the largest reserves of intact old-growth forest left in the United States. This magnificent slice of North America's coastline is home to one of the world's last remaining strongholds for wild Pacific salmon. Rarer still is that all of the pieces are here—ancient forests, wild salmon, grizzly bears, wolves, Steller sea lions, humpback whales, and more. The circle is whole. And we are part of it too, not strangers on the outside looking in. The Tongass is a place where people live with salmon in their streets and bears in their backyards. It's a land of remarkable contrasts. One of the world's largest densities of brown bears is twenty minutes by floatplane from the Internet cafes and thirty thousand residents of Juneau, the state capital. Cruise ships carrying more than two thousand passengers ply the same waters as mom-and-pop fishermen. That the modern world has arrived and hasn't yet broken the circle of life in the twenty-first-century Tongass is nothing short of astounding. But we're on our way to carving up this extraordinary forest, and it may just be a matter of time. We only have to look south to the once-magnificent salmon forests of Washington, Oregon, and northern California to see how quickly we can decimate ancient trees, wild salmon, and a rich way of life.

The original coastal temperate rain forest of North America once stretched intact along a narrow band between Alaska's Kodiak Archipelago and northern California. This rain-drenched ecosystem is capable of growing some of the largest, long-lived trees in the world. These mammoth trees, in part, are the reason why this region contains more organic matter per acre than any other ecosystem on the planet, more so than even the tropical rain forests near the equator. Abundance begets abundance, and it's no coincidence that the most complex indigenous hunting and gathering societies in North America lived here in some of the highest densities of First Nations settlements found anywhere on the continent. Thriving salmon runs, marine mammals, rich tidelands and estuaries, and upland forest mammals allowed the first peoples to establish permanent settlements and not rely on farming or herding for survival. More than sixty distinct languages were spoken between San Francisco Bay and the Kodiak Archipelago of Alaska. Archaeological evidence indicates that people occupied this bountiful region for more than 10,000 years. But during the past 150 years, modern man has drastically altered much of this once-glorious rain forest. How did this happen?

After Europeans arrived on the east coast of North America, they systematically expanded westward, logged virgin forests, ploughed native prairies, obliterated buffalo and grizzly bears from the Great Plains, and brought livestock to graze and alter the arid West. When they reached the misty northern Pacific coast, immense stands of trees dwarfed the newcomers. What did they do? They continued their pattern of destruction and toppled the towering trees, some that were alive before the birth of Christ. And they did it quickly. The mighty redwood forests of northern California were heavily logged by the late 1800s during the Gold Rush era. Moving north, the bulk of the once-great forests of Washington and Oregon were logged in the early 1900s for spruce, cedar, and Douglas fir to build airplanes and ships during World War I. As the forests fell, so went the forest dwellers—bears, eagles, salmon, indigenous people, and countless other species.

The greatest tragedy is that in many instances we don't even know what we've lost. We do know that of North America's original coastal temperate rain forest, 44 percent is gone, cut down in a mere 150 years for urban development, commercial logging, or farming, with most of this taking place from Vancouver Island in British Columbia south to northern California. And while all of this happened in the blink of a geologic eye, who among us today has a memory of what these primeval forests once contained? Crowded cities, sprawling suburbs, agricultural lands, and a giant spider web of roads now occupy former virgin forest lands, making it difficult for us to see how we used to live. If we care to look, we can find clues of our not-so-distant past in the dense second-growth forest stands. In these dark forests, the rotting stumps of trees that stood before Columbus stood on North America—stumps larger in girth than most living trees today, stumps that are now ghosts of their ancient selves—serve as tombstones marking a sad legacy to what once thrived for millennia.

To add insult to injury, we then turned our attention to the remains of these forests and what was left of the wildlife, and decided we could "manage," "control," and "improve" what nature had perfected. We put bounties on bald eagles and Dolly Varden trout, thinking we were helping salmon by killing their predators. We tidied and straightened salmon streams, not realizing that nature's chaos nurtures life. We built fish hatcheries and treated salmon like commodities instead of fine-tuned creatures that have carried their genetic message for millennia. We continued to clear-cut the remaining ancient forests, not heeding the wisdom written in all those growth rings of trees many centuries older than us. To be fair, we did much of this with the best of intentions, thinking we were doing the salmon, forests, and ourselves a favor. We know better today.

We now know that there are salmon in the trees. How can this be? In the last vestiges of rain forest in southeast Alaska and British Columbia, scientists have discovered high concentrations of a nitrogen variant in trees near salmon streams. This variant, called nitrogen-15, comes from the *ocean*. How did it find its way from the sea into the forest? It *swam* there, in the bodies of salmon loaded with marine nutrients from their time at sea. Pacific salmon are born in freshwater streams and rivers, migrate to the oceans to mature, and return to their birth streams as adults to spawn the next generation, bringing the rich broth of the ocean with them. But how exactly does nitrogen-15 make its way into the trees? Bears have a lot to do with this. In the Tongass National Forest of southeast Alaska, some of the world's highest densities of brown bears and black bears thrive on the millions of wild salmon that fill more than 4,500 spawning streams. Bears are not social animals, and to avoid trouble with each other they will catch fish and often carry them away from streams and into the forest. It turns out that bears move a lot of salmon into the forest. Researchers say that one bear can carry forty fish from a stream in eight hours. Toward the end of a good salmon season, bears can afford to be picky and usually target the richest parts of the fish and leave the rest behind. Other animals scavenge on these carcasses, spreading the nutrients farther throughout the forest. Guess what happens? All of this rich fish fertilizer decomposes into the soil, and the trees and other vegetation absorb it through their roots. Scientists have actually been able to trace nitrogen-15 in trees near salmon streams that they can link back to the fish. Not to be outdone, the trees return the favor by nurturing the salmon. Trees shade the spawning streams, keeping water temperatures cool for developing eggs. Their roots help stabilize the stream banks, preventing erosion from fouling the clean water and gravel beds the salmon need to lay their eggs. And fallen trees create protected pools and provide food for insects that in turn become food for the young salmon.

Salmon in the trees is a remarkable and yet perfectly natural phenomenon that has been taking place with or without us in this part of the world for many thousands of years. How fortunate we are that this beautiful web of life still exists somewhere and we have stumbled upon it. But will we heed it? Salmon link the land to the sea, and they can't survive if both aren't healthy. Neither can we. Salmon in the trees tells us that everything is connected. Not only in what remains of North America's coastal temperate rain forest, but in ecosystems worldwide. And if we start tossing away the pieces anywhere—salmon, trees, coral reefs, gorillas, plankton, or penguins—we eventually unravel the whole glorious show. We eventually unravel ourselves.

In North America, we can see the stark contrast between the intact ecosystem of the Tongass rain forest of southeast Alaska and its degraded counterparts in Washington, Oregon, and northern California. The once-thriving salmon streams in these areas have been dammed, dredged, and polluted. The once-bustling commercial fishing towns the former salmon streams used to support are now ghost towns, tourist destinations, or expensive retirement communities. The Alaska commercial salmon fishery, on the other hand, has been certified by the Marine Stewardship Council as one of the world's best examples of a sustainable fishery. Healthy salmon and trout populations in southeast Alaska support one in ten jobs and contribute close to a billion dollars to the region's economy. People can still make a living with their own small fishing boats. They also make a living by guiding visitors to see charismatic wildlife like grizzly bears, who can only be found on the West Coast of the Lower Forty-Eight on the California state flag, a fluttering symbol of a fleeting memory. Many people in southeast Alaska know how to catch fish, hunt deer, and distinguish between edible and poisonous berries, and their freezers are full of wild foods harvested close to their homes. In the Lower Forty-Eight, most people have freezers full of processed foods harvested on average more than two thousand miles from their homes. How much longer can we perpetuate this disconnect from nature?

The Tongass rain forest of Alaska serves as a shining reminder of the need to preserve wild places worldwide and to restore damaged ecosystems. Places like the Tongass and other naturally functioning parts of the world provide opportunities for people to live good lives while doing right by nature. I believe there's still time to get it right, not only for the future of the Tongass, but for the future of all nature and the well-being of humanity. If we stabilize and then lower our population and live within our natural means, nature has a chance to thrive and heal itself, and people can live in a world where enough is enough. Enough food, clean water, and clean air for everyone. Imagine.

But if the world's population and consumption levels continue to outpace the planet's capacity to replenish itself, then our own natural life support erodes and will eventually collapse. "Enough" will fade from the human vocabulary, as well as our collective memory. Technology may prolong the inevitable, but it will not save us. Long ago, we knew how to live within nature's constraints. Can we once again? *Will* we? Will we stop razing forests and cramming more homes for more people where streams flowed and bears grew fat on spawning salmon? Will we stop overfishing? Will we stop dumping chemicals into our waterways? Will we end efforts to "control" nature? Will we quit crowding the only home we have? Will we ever learn that growth, past a certain point, is not good?

As the planet has become more and more populated by humans, with our damaging industrial habits and our voracious appetites for natural resources, we are creating a different world. One with less resilience to withstand major events like droughts, flooding, and disease. A world where there isn't enough for all of us. A world of extremes—weather, poverty, wealth, and so on. Entire economies are based on the unsustainable model of infinite growth with finite resources. And it's catching up to us. As the late David Brower once said: "There's no business to be conducted on a broken planet." How can we expect rich countries to do with less, and third world countries to not want more? Is there reason for hope? Yes, there is.

There is a growing awareness worldwide that while we are part of the problem, we can also be part of the solution. It's only in the last several decades that we've realized the value to our own well-being of forests left standing, rivers flowing freely, and top predators roaming wild. We now know that all life on Earth depends on the planet's natural processes creating the most basic necessities—clean air and water, food, pollination, a livable climate, and so on. We are changing the way we view nature, do business, and live our lives. And if we can change our relationship with Earth, then we can change our population so as not to damage our life-support systems. Hope is everywhere and spreading. The rise of organic farming. The movement to buy local. Renewable and clean energy. Family planning. Empowerment of women. People worldwide demanding positive change from their leaders.

Along the panhandle of Alaska, in the ecologically intact Tongass rain forest, hope is an orange salmon egg pulsing with life in a clear stream. Muddy bear tracks meandering across a tidal flat. Ancient forests still standing, nourished by salmon that grew strong in the ocean and came home to spawn and die.

When the circle of life is whole, so are we.

PART IV

Solutions

CHAPTER 19

Trusting Women to End Population Growth

ROBERT ENGELMAN

O NE DAY IN THE mid-1980s, farmers in a village in the Himalayan foothills of Nepal gathered for a meeting organized by representatives of a foreign nongovernmental organization to prioritize community needs. The NGO representatives proposed a project to bring clean water from the headwaters of the nearby stream to a communal spigot to be constructed just above the village. The NGO would provide the pipe and other materials; the men of the village would supply the labor.

"Why would we want to do that?" members of the village council asked. "We don't have any problems with water here." When they came home from a day in the fields, the councilmen related, there were always jugs of fresh water in their homes. A water project was the last thing the community needed.

A farmer named Cansaman wondered about the council's response. Years earlier, he had been the village pioneer in undergoing a vasectomy, offered by a national family planning group. Cansaman went on to convince many other men that their families might thrive—and their manhood survive—if they underwent the simple operation. In the years afterward, vasectomies became widespread among the men of the village. No other effective contraceptives were easily available. As a result of his successful promotion of male sterilization, Cansaman became a favorite among the women of the village. He visited with several of these women after the needs assessment exercise, explained the NGO offer, and asked what they thought.

The women were enthusiastic. They were spending hours every afternoon trudging down the steep slopes of the valley to the streambed at its bottom and hauling up jugs of fresh water, all so that their husbands could refresh themselves in their homes each evening after a day in the fields.

"You tell the village council," the women instructed Cansaman, "that we will lay the pipe ourselves." Shamed by this remark, the village council assented to the project, and eventually women and men worked side by side to bring the water project to life.

As Cansaman related this story to me several years later, he stood on a low wall by the communal spigot and left it twisted open full bore. A steady column of water splashed noisily onto a concrete pad below his feet. I had to resist the temptation, born of habit from paying water bills and worrying about waste, to reach over and shut off the tap. But as I stood there listening, it dawned on me that we could just as well leave it wide open forever. Cansaman laughed when he ended his story. The liquid renewable resource poured off the pad, found its way back into the stream, and tumbled down the hillside on its long journey to the Bay of Bengal.

I have never returned to that village, but I would wager that the community is managing the stresses of poverty and environmental degradation better than most of its neighbors. Men and women had learned how to work cooperatively early on to manage natural resources in sustainable ways. Equally important, at least, couples in the community have been using contraception to plan their families for a quarter century. That has benefited not only their health and economic opportunities but also the village's population size. Poignantly, the gratitude of the community's women to one man for bringing them access to contraception was the key to a cooperative and sustainable response to water scarcity. If I'm right, the story may offer important lessons about how good gender relations and women's capacity to manage their own fertility—in this case with strong cooperation from their male partners—benefit us all.

Among policymakers, economists, and commentators in all media, it is an accepted truth that world population inevitably will grow from today's seven billion people to about nine billion by midcentury, then to ten billion by 2100—and no farther. The demographers say so, we are told, and since most of us know next to nothing about demography, the demographers must be right. Moreover, the peaking of world population will happen "on its own," with no need for "population control efforts" or any other initiatives. People will want roughly two children per couple on average, and that's what they'll have. Earth will provide. Demographically, all will be well.

Yet every aspect of this accepted truth is an illusion, based first on an error about the demographers' message and secondly on the future evolution of trends that not even experts can predict. The first error is easily corrected: world population is not, in fact, expected or projected to stabilize around ten billion in 2100. Population projections pointing to a ten-billion world population at the end of the century also project some continued population growth at that time—between five and six million people, effectively a new Boston metropolitan area each year, in the case of the United Nations medium projection (UNPD 2011).

Moreover, this projection assumes that women continue to have fewer children while life expectancy and mortality rates keep improving on roughly current lines. There's no room for the possibility of calamity stemming from climate change, peak oil, food shortage, a pandemic disease, violent conflict, or some combination of any or all of these—or for equally plausible scenarios in which women have many more or many fewer children than they are having today.

Finally, a peaking of world population is unlikely to "happen on its own." By midcentury, more than four billion women and men—give or take a few hundred million depending on which projection you use—are projected to be sexually active and reproductively fecund (UNPD 2011). Today, fewer than one billion couples are using effective modern contraception when they have sex (Haub 2010).

If two billion women are to prevent enough pregnancies to end up with about two children each, who will provide the contraceptives they and their partners need? Who will counsel them on how to safely and effectively prevent unwanted pregnancy? Are governments or contraceptive manufacturers mobilizing now to triple or quadruple production, distribution, and client counseling in just a few decades? Hardly. In fact, the financial assistance that wealthier countries give lower-income ones for voluntary family planning services was cut in half between 1995 and 2007, from $723 million to $338 million. In a world in which trillions of dollars move through currency markets on any given day, these shrinking dollar amounts are a pittance—but one that needs to turn around dramatically if population growth is to end for the right reason: lower birth rates. Yet no one can say when or even if that will happen.

What if, however, we could prove wrong the popular conviction that without coercive population control a future with nine billion people and a growing population is inevitable? Suppose we could demonstrate that world population size might peak earlier and at a lower level if government policies aimed not at reproductive coercion but at individual reproductive freedom? Suppose such policies aimed at allowing all women and girls to prevent all unwanted pregnancies and to conceive only when they themselves want to bear a child? The hypothesis this chapter probes may appear counterintuitive to those who assume most women, at least in developing countries, aspire to have large families and always will. If, starting at any moment, all pregnancies in the world resulted from individual women's intentions to give birth, human population would immediately shift course away from growth toward decline within a few decades to a peak in size, followed by gradual decrease.

Exploring this hypothesis matters because population size, growth, and distribution powerfully influence climate change, the loss of the planet's biological diversity, scarcities of natural resources, food and energy security, and even governance and security. While each of these claims is associated with some controversy, prominent groups of scientists have long acknowledged that population growth contributes significantly to humanity's environmental problems. In a joint statement in 1993, representatives of fifty-eight national scientific academies stressed the complexities of the population-environment relationship but nonetheless concluded: "As human numbers increase, the potential for irreversible [environmental] changes of far-reaching magnitude also increases. . . . In our judgment, humanity's ability to deal successfully with its social, economic, and environmental problems will require the achievement of zero population growth within the lifetime of our children" ("'Science Summit'" 1994). In 2005, the United Nations' *Millennium Ecosystem Assessment* identified population growth as a principal indirect driver of environmental change, along with economic growth and technological evolution (Reid et al. 2005).

The same three factors are predominant in human-caused climate change. Recently, a group of U.S. and European climate and demographic researchers published findings from an integrated assessment model calculating the impact of various population scenarios on global emissions of fossil-fuel carbon dioxide over the coming century. If world population peaked at close to eight billion rather than nine billion, along the lines described in a low-fertility demographic projection published by the UN Population Division, the model predicted there would be a significant emissions savings: about 5.1 billion tons of carbon dioxide by 2050 and 18.7 billion tons less by the century's end (O'Neill et al. 2005).

Such findings support the case that while alternate demographic futures would not on their own close the gap between environmental catastrophe and safety, they can help significantly. If this point is accepted, it suggests a next question: What can societies that value democracy, self-determination, human rights, personal autonomy, and privacy do to include demographic change among such strategies for environmental sustainability?

An important answer may lie in a relatively untested set of principles adopted by almost all the world's nations at a 1994 United Nations conference held in Cairo. The third of three once-a-decade governmental conferences on population and development, it produced a program of action that abandoned the strategy of "population control" by governments in favor of a focus on the health, rights, and well-being of women (UNPIN 1994).

An operating assumption of this program is that when women have access to the information and means that allow them to choose the timing of pregnancy, teen births are less frequent, intervals between births lengthen, and average family size shrinks. All of these improve maternal and child survival (World Health Organization 1995) and slow population growth.

Access to safe and reliable contraception has exploded since the mid-twentieth century. An estimated 55 percent of all heterosexually active women worldwide now use modern contraceptive methods, while an additional 7 percent use less reliable traditional methods (Haub 2010). As the use of birth control has spread, fertility has plummeted from 5 children per woman globally in 1950 to barely over 2.5 on average today (UNPD 2011).

While not necessarily sufficient to depress fertility on a population-wide basis, family planning is essential to the phenomenon. Women may begin sexual activity later in life and may resort to abortion to terminate unwanted pregnancies. But humanity's average family size could not have plummeted from 5 to 2.5 children per woman simply because women had diplomas, contractual rights, or confidence that their children would survive. To have small families, heterosexually active women and their partners absolutely need safe and effective contraception—in other words, modern birth control.

How many children will the average woman worldwide be having in 2050? How long will life expectancy be? We don't know. How could we? The year is nearly four decades in the future. But one possibility—among the most hopeful and inspiring available to a troubled world—is that population could peak before 2050 and be significantly below nine billion.

How would we arrive at such a point? The widespread belief that an earlier, lower population peak would require coercive "population control" is in error. *Decontrolling* population—specifically, removing from women the shackles of external reproductive control—would more quickly reduce birthrates worldwide than any other imaginable policy. Imagine this world: children are born only when both partners, but especially women, are freed from the pressure of others to give birth and want to raise a child to adulthood, and women have real autonomy in the productive as well as the reproductive spheres of their lives. In such a world, at this time in history, such a combination of circumstances would quite likely reverse global population growth soon and dramatically.

This is a strong statement, to say the least. The rest of this chapter will try to make its case, based on two lines of reasoning: the history of human reproduction and what we know about the gap between the pregnancies that women want and those they actually have. Both support confidence that a world of empowered women and intended pregnancies will fairly quickly reverse global population growth. And although this relates only indirectly to international migration, a theme of other chapters in this book, it seems logical that a sustainable world population will encourage sustainable national ones as well, on both sides of the development divide. That would logically reduce the desperation of so many people to leave the countries of their birth to escape conflict, environmental degradation, and the scarcity of resources, jobs, and hope.

"Every human society is faced not with one population problem but with two," anthropologist Margaret Mead wrote: "How to beget and rear enough children and how not to beget and rear too many. The definition of 'enough' and 'too many' varies enormously" (Mead 2001, 208).

It's easy to forget in an environmentally threatened world of seven billion humans that for most of human history, group survival rather than ecological overreach was often the key population issue. Working cooperatively with each other to birth babies and protect them from death by predators, accident, and disease to their adulthood, women deserve by far the lion's share of credit for making sure the key feat was performed. What feat? Raising more than two children per woman on average and becoming grandmothers. We have good reason to believe that midwives began their work almost as soon as hominids stood up on two feet, and their essential roles and the need to guide birthing women may have contributed mightily to the development of language (Engelman 2008).

Once midwives and mothers had partnered on safe delivery of babies, they and networks of related and unrelated female alloparents (assistant parents) honed their skills at collectively assuring child and adolescent survival. These skills assured third, fourth, and sometimes fifth or sixth children survived. And that led to secure populations—and then to growing ones. (None of this is to dismiss the importance of men in this process, especially in provisioning food and providing family defense. But in no known culture do men participate equally with women in the day-in, day-out task of raising children safely to adulthood.)

So give women credit, or most of it, for the hard work of growing their community's population, thus feeding a process that led *Homo sapiens* to occupy every continent on Earth other than Antarctica. But the story is more complicated than this. From the very beginning women needed to be strategic about their reproduction. If they gave birth too often in hostile environments, they risked ending their own line of descendants altogether. Pregnancy and birth are death-defying acts, especially in natural environments. The death of a mother even today, in some poverty settings, can condemn her progeny to early deaths. Moreover, even if she survives multiple births but she and her male partner and female alloparents cannot keep a large group of children fed, healthy, and protected from threats, the risk grows that any or all siblings will perish, or at least fail to succeed through good health and successful mating to become parents themselves.

What women are really after—at least when they have social permission to think about their own and their children's well-being—is not so much *more children* as more *for* the child or children they have. As both midwives and obstetricians know, a common question from a just-delivered mother is, "How can I make sure I don't get pregnant again, at least right away?" Indeed, history and recent fertility phenomena suggest the likelihood that women's interest in safely and effectively managing the timing of pregnancy and childbirth may be nearly universal among women and

that lack of education, affluence, and equality are simply barriers—along
with others related to patriarchal, pronatalist, and even medical cultural
norms—to existing aspirations to avoid unwanted pregnancies (Campbell, Sahin-Hodoglugil, and Potts 2006).

Women have sought and employed contraceptives since ancient times
to avoid unwanted pregnancy when circumstances were inauspicious for
the fifteen-to-eighteen-year parental commitment a new birth entails.
Egyptian papyri that are four thousand years old describe pessaries, ancient precursors to the diaphragm, made of acacia oil and crocodile dung
(Riddle 1992). Literature from Asia and North America documents herbs
used for centuries as emmenagogues, substances that induce immediate
menstruation and hence expel any recently fertilized eggs. In the Mediterranean during classical times, a booming trade in the contraceptive or
abortifacient silphium helped drive its source, a wild giant fennel, into
extinction. An ecclesiastical court record from 1319 preserves the personal
account of a young widow in southwestern France, who provided details
of her use of an herbal contraception during an extended affair with a
priest (Engelman 2008).

We know, too, that women and their partners historically have moder-
ated their reproduction in response to their external environments, natural
and economic (until modern times, these were generally the same thing).
In eighteenth- and nineteenth-century Sweden, for example, birthrates
neatly tracked the price of grain crops with a roughly nine-month delay
(Bengtsson and Dribe 2006). The population of late eighteenth-century
Japan declined during several decades of food scarcity—until a government propaganda campaign against infanticide (the dominant method of
family-size control at the time) pushed fertility well above replacement
levels in the nineteenth century, restoring demographic growth (Harris
and Ross 1987).[1]

Similar responses of fertility to external circumstances are evident today.
The high cost of housing in Japan is prominent among the reasons offered
by young people for delaying marriage and childbearing (Westley, Choe,
and Retherford 2010). In the United States, a 2 percent decline in the
country's birthrate in 2008 was attributed largely to the deterioration of
the economy (Stein 2010). It's ironic that so many economists assume that
economic growth is the greatest driver of fertility decline. The impression
depends in large part on the time scale examined: Over the past century
or two, the correlation between economic development and small families

is strong—though still not necessarily causal. But for much of human history, wealth and positive circumstances—including environmental ones—were associated with high fertility, while hard times often coincided with fewer births and smaller families. That pattern may be returning.

More important in fertility decline than the vagaries of economic circumstances, however, is a woman's capacity to decide for herself whether and when to become pregnant and deliver a child, coupled with the technological means and cultural permission to put her intentions into effect. Indeed, population growth rates and average family size worldwide have fallen by roughly half over the past four decades, as access to and the popularity of modern contraception have expanded. The average number of children born to each woman worldwide is no longer much higher than replacement fertility, the fertility average that would eventually end population growth altogether. Yet nearly 40 percent of all pregnancies worldwide are unintended by women and their partners, with—perhaps surprisingly—higher proportions of unintended pregnancies in developed than in developing countries.

As a thought experiment, consider how world population trends might change if the world somehow could be mobilized to bring the proportion of unintended pregnancies down to zero. No births except to children who are welcomed, sought, and hoped for by their parents from before conception. (Also, though it is less relevant to demographic outcomes: no abortions.) Such a world probably is not possible, but we could come a lot closer to it if enough people worked to bring it about. And our efforts would pay off not only for the well-being of women, their children, and their partners—unwanted pregnancy takes an immense toll on health and opportunities—but also for the natural world and nonhuman species, as population growth slowed and eventually reversed.

Just in the past year or two, data have become available that allow us to make tentative estimates of how fertility would be influenced by the success of a strategy that aimed to put women fully in charge of their own reproduction. Preliminary calculations based on conservative assumptions suggest that global fertility would immediately move slightly below replacement levels, putting world population on a path toward an early peak followed by gradual decline.

According to the Guttmacher Institute, an estimated 215 million women in developing countries have an "unmet need for family planning" (Singh, Darroch, Ashford, and Vlassoff 2009). The term applies to women who are sexually active and express the desire to avoid pregnancy, yet are not using contraception. This estimate derives from Demographic and Health Surveys conducted in certain developing countries every few years (these surveys, performed by ICF Macro for the U.S. Agency for International Development, can be accessed online at www.measuredhs.com). Many women in developed countries may be in the same circumstance, but data are insufficient in most cases to suggest their numbers.

In early 2010 researchers with the Futures Group in Washington, D.C., estimated the demographic impact of meeting unmet family planning demand in ninety-nine developing countries and one developed one. The researchers excluded China, on the assumption that government population policies aimed at limiting most families to a single child rule out births from unintended pregnancies. And they supplemented their country list with the United States, the world's most populous developed county and one for which there is some data suggesting the magnitude of the unmet need for family planning (Moreland, Smith, and Sharma 2010). Using accepted models for the impact of rising contraceptive prevalence on birthrates, the researchers concluded that satisfying unmet need for contraception in these one hundred countries—with a cumulative 2005 population of 4.3 billion—would produce a population of 6.3 billion in 2050. Under the UN medium projection, contrarily, the countries' population would be 400 million higher, at 6.7 billion. The average fertility at midcentury for the world's developing countries (whose populations overlap considerably with the country set the researchers studied) would be 1.65 children per woman, well below the population replacement fertility level—and continuing to fall.

These conclusions, if backed up by further research, are momentous. By implication, simply providing safe and effective contraceptive options to all sexually active women who do not want to become pregnant would end and then reverse world population growth. The effect is independent of any further fertility reductions that might occur as a result of greater educational attainment for women, improved child survival, and overall women's empowerment and economic advancement.

To some experts the idea that simply facilitating women's childbearing intentions would end population growth, without significant demand creation for family planning through cultural shifts and other means, goes against survey findings from many African and some Asian countries (see the Demographic and Health Surveys, previously mentioned).

These findings suggest that women's average desired family size in parts of these continents is as high as six or seven children. Wouldn't facilitating *these* women's childbearing intentions undermine any hope of ending world population growth? Not necessarily. For one thing, women expressing such high desired family sizes are at most a relatively small proportion of the world's population (albeit significant in Africa). But the more important point is that a high desired family size can easily coexist with high levels of unintended pregnancy that, if prevented, would result in significantly lower birth rates.

The reason for this is not hard to understand. Women's individual reproductive decisions arrive at their desired family size only cumulatively, if at all. Decisions about the desirability of pregnancy are made singly, in individual acts of sexual intercourse in which conception is possible. Whatever one's hopes for an eventual number of children, pregnancy decisions occur in the context of current personal, economic, and social circumstances. Desired family size can be compared to house size and the number of cars owned. We may wish to have a large house and many cars, but our circumstances may not allow for us to have either without endangering our finances and well-being. We decide moment by moment whether working toward that goal makes sense for us. So it is with reproductive intentions; every step of a woman and her partner's reproductive lives is governed by their immediate circumstances.

It seems likely that even in countries where women tell health surveys that they desire six or seven children, they would end up with fewer, possibly many fewer, if at each step of their reproductive lives they were able to choose precisely when to become pregnant. In some developed countries with low fertility, women express a desire to have two children yet have closer to one on average. With the right partner, the right job, the right apartment, and the right economic and social-support systems, for example, a woman in Japan might have the two children she desires. But with options to prevent or terminate pregnancies, many Japanese women have one child or none; the national average is 1.3 (Westley, Choe, and Retherford 2010).

All of this suggests the value of developing and testing the hypothesis that meeting the needs of women and their partners for personal control of pregnancy could lead to the end of population growth. Physician and reproductive specialist Malcolm Potts has found that in all countries where women can chose from a range of contraceptive options, backed by access to safe and legal abortion services, total fertility rates are at or below replacement fertility levels (Potts 1997).

If these findings can be borne out consistently by additional research, those who worry about the impact of global population growth on sustainability might usefully advocate for worldwide universal access to family planning services. The need for such access is enshrined in the second target of the fifth United Nations Millennium Development Goal, which calls for developing countries to "achieve, by 2015, universal access to reproductive health" (UNDESA 2010). This concept embraces more than family planning: a holistic state of sexual and reproductive well-being that includes maternal and child health, prevention of AIDS and other sexually transmitted infections, access to safe abortion services (where these are legal), and postabortion care.

The Futures Group study has not yet gained the widespread attention its findings merit. Among the reasons for this may be that the concept of "unmet need" for contraception is not one widely understood among the public, news media, and policymakers. Moreover, for reasons of lack of data, the Futures Group study excluded not only China, with a fifth of the world's population, but dozens of other developing countries—and all the world's industrialized countries other than the United States.

Newly available data on unintended pregnancy assembled by the Guttmacher Institute supports an alternative research approach to the question of the demographic impacts of births that result from pregnancies women never sought or wanted to have. These data, based on a range of surveys worldwide in more countries than included in the earlier study, provide the basis for beginning to answer the question: What would happen to world population growth if every pregnancy worldwide were the outcome of a woman's active intention to bear a child?

The Guttmacher Institute provides estimates, covering various years in the last decade, of the proportions of all pregnancies that women report as unintended in many developing and developed countries. More than 40 percent of pregnancies fall into this category in developing countries, and—perhaps surprisingly given much greater access to advanced health services—more than 47 percent do in developed countries such as the United States. Subtracting pregnancies that end in miscarriage, stillbirths, and induced abortion, Guttmacher researchers estimate the proportion of all births globally that result from unintended pregnancies: 22 percent in developed countries and just over 21 percent in developing ones. More than one in five human births, based on these survey results, is thus the result of a pregnancy that the woman involved did not want to happen (Singh, Wulf, Hussain, Bankole, and Sedgh 2009; Singh 2010).

Subtracting this proportion of births worldwide from the current total fertility rate of 2.53 would yield a global total fertility rate of slightly below 2 births per woman—well below the current replacement fertility rate of 2.35 and comfortably below any replacement rate that could be achieved even if all infants survived to reproductive age. Population would immediately reposition itself for a reversal of growth that probably would occur before 2050. The world's population would likely end up below the nine billion so often assumed for that year—especially as smaller-than-expected cohorts of future parents also succeeded in giving birth only after intended pregnancies.

Unfortunately for this calculation, however, many unintended pregnancies are *mistimed* rather than unintended for all time. Women became pregnant earlier than they had hoped to, giving birth to a child who otherwise might have arrived a year or two later. So the calculations have to allow for the possibility that preventing mistimed pregnancies could actually accelerate the arrival of later births from intended ones. There's no good way to estimate this proportion, except very conservatively—separating out mistimed pregnancies from never-wanted ones, where those data exist, and then extrapolating proportions of mistimed pregnancies to those populations in which the data do not distinguish among these pregnancies. For the sake of both caution and simplicity, we can add a biologically unlikely assumption: that any mistimed pregnancy that is prevented results in an intended *pregnancy in the same year*. Mistimed pregnancies thus "equal" intended pregnancies.

Putting all this together, what do the calculations show? Averaged over the seventy-three countries for which data exist (comprising 83 percent of the world's births), just under 10 percent result from pregnancies occurring among women who wanted never to have another childbirth. Even under the most conservative scenario, extrapolated globally with all births from mistimed pregnancies equivalent to births from intended pregnancies, a hypothetical world population in which women only became pregnant when they wanted to would reduce today's global total fertility rate to 2.29 births per woman. That figure is slightly below today's global replacement fertility rate—placing world population on a direct path toward future decline, albeit at a very slow pace given population momentum (and assuming neither future fertility decline nor improvement in mortality among young people). If we assume less conservatively that many prevented mistimed pregnancies never result in a subsequent intended pregnancy and birth, the total fertility rate could sink lower, resulting in a faster track toward a human population peak.

These calculations are, at best, first-order analyses of the impact on world population growth of an idealized scenario in which all births are the outcomes from intended pregnancies. More survey research and data on pregnancy intention among individual women in all countries would be needed to make a more robust determination of demographic impacts. Nonetheless, it is clear—and little known—that a successful global effort that assured all women the capacity to decide for themselves whether and when to become pregnant would also place world population on a path toward a peak followed by slow demographic decrease. Additional efforts to see that women have the educational, economic, legal, and political opportunities they deserve would accelerate this transition.

Frustratingly, only a major struggle backed by engaged publics around the world is likely ever to bring this world about. Contraception remains deeply sensitive and divisive. Religious authorities—especially those of the Catholic Church—do all they can to block access. Most cultures relegate the concerns of women, including reproductive concerns, to subordinate spheres. Throughout history, men have often been anxious to produce a multitude of future heirs, soldiers, laborers, farmers, and followers, while women have tended to be strategically concerned with the survival and well-being of each of their children (Engelman 2008). In most cultures, men's preferences hold sway. So does the conviction of many neoclassical economists that economic growth can continue indefinitely but requires equally endless population growth. Politicians often measure their self-worth based on the size of their electorates and are happy to side with the economists.

With all these factors in play, it is not surprising that the world's governments are nowhere close to allocating the resources the Cairo conference had estimated would be needed for all women in developing countries to have reasonable access to decent family planning services. This was roughly eighteen billion dollars in current dollars for the year 2010, a third of which was to be contributed by the governments of industrialized countries (UNPIN 1994). That's more than seventeen times what these governments actually spent on international family planning assistance in 2007, and assistance has changed little since the latter year.

Raising nine billion dollars a year from wealthy governments that currently spend just a few hundred million dollars on international family planning assistance shouldn't be as difficult as it is. As much money is allocated for a few days worth of military activities worldwide. A comparable or greater amount probably would be needed to assure that almost all pregnancies in wealthy countries are intentional, but this sum has never been estimated. Significant investments are also needed everywhere to educate young people on sexuality and reproduction; these amounts, too, remain unestimated.

Despite the unknowns, the point still holds: a world in which almost all births result from intended conceptions is possible. Yet due to contraception's sensitivity—complicated by a history pockmarked with episodes of contraceptive coercion in China, India, Peru, and a few other countries—environmentalists and advocates for women's rights and health have never succeeded in forging an activist alliance capable of raising the modest sums required for all to have access to family planning.

Several elements are needed if a global social movement to promote family planning and intentional pregnancy is ever to have its own birth. One is more research along the lines of the simple effort presented in this chapter to probe the likely population and environmental outcomes of a world of fully intended pregnancies—and the policies, programs, and costs that could lead to such a world. Another is agreement that any such policies and programs must be based on reproductive rights rather than coercion, and therefore the intentions of women and their partners rather than those of anyone else. And a third is the creativity to shape—or the courage to stand up to—the religious, economic, and other cultural forces that promote population growth and oppose the gender equity and reproductive health conditions that undermine it.

We can take heart, at least, from the experience of Cansaman and his female friends in Nepal more than two decades ago. It's a story duplicated in countries around the world in which women have gained access to contraception and have successfully demanded a voice in their own destiny and in civic life. There is nothing fated about a world of nine billion people—in 2050, or ever. While true control of population is beyond our aspirations and capacities, policy choices are available that will nudge our numbers closer to environmentally and socially sustainable levels. The choices are rooted in human development and human rights, specifically the right of all, and most directly of women, to decide for themselves when it is the right time to bring a child into the world.

NOTES

1. Replacement fertility is the number of children women in a population must have on average to bring a population with no net migration flows to a steady state. This occurs after some delay, due to the population momentum that ensues when large cohorts of youthful childbearers outnumber elderly people leaving the population by dying. Although commonly thought to equal 2.1 children everywhere—slightly more than 2 children because some young people die before reaching the age of parenting themselves—the global replacement rate is actually 2.35 children per woman. The extra "third of a child" needed to bring population equilibrium reflects still-high death rates among young people in many low-income families.

BIBLIOGRAPHY

Bengtsson, Tommy, and Martin Dribe. 2006. "Deliberate Control in a Natural Fertility Population: Southern Sweden, 1766–1864." *Demography* 43 (4): 727–746.

Campbell, Martha, Nalan Nuriya Sahin-Hodoglugil, and Malcolm Potts. 2006. "Barriers to Fertility Regulation: A Review of the Literature." *Studies in Family Planning* 37 (2): 87–98.

Engelman, Robert. 2008. *More: Population, Nature, and What Women Want.* Washington, D.C.: Island Press.

Harris, Marvin, and Eric Ross. 1987. *Death, Sex, and Fertility: Population Regulation in Preindustrial and Developing Societies.* New York: Columbia University Press.

Haub, Carl. 2010. *2010 World Population Data Sheet.* Washington, D.C.: Population Reference Bureau.

Mead, Margaret. 2001. *Male and Female: A Study of the Sexes in a Changing World.* New York: HarperCollins.

Moreland, Scott, Ellen Smith, and Sunita Sharma. 2010. *World Population Prospects and Unmet Need for Family Planning.* Washington, D.C.: Futures Group.

O'Neill, Brian, et al. 2005. "Impact of Demographic Change on Future Carbon Emissions: A Global Assessment." *Proceedings of the National Academy of Sciences* 107 (41): 17521–17526.

Potts, Malcolm. 1997. "Sex and the Birth Rate: Human Biology, Demographic Change, and Access to Fertility-Regulation Methods." *Population and Development Review* 23 (1): 1–39.

Reid, Walter, et al. 2005. *Millennium Ecosystem Assessment: Ecosystems and Human Well-Being: Synthesis.* Washington, D.C.: Island Press.

Riddle, John. 1992. *Contraception and Abortion from the Ancient World to the Renaissance.* Cambridge, Mass.: Harvard University Press.

"'Science Summit' on World Population: A Joint Statement by 58 of the World's Scientific Academies." 1994. *Population and Development Review* 20 (1): 233–238.

Singh, Susheela. 2010. Personal communication, September 16.

Singh, Susheela, Jacqueline Darroch, Lori Ashford, and Michael Vlassoff. 2009. *Adding It Up: The Costs and Benefits of Investing in Family Planning and Maternal and Newborn Health.* New York: Guttmacher Institute.

Singh, Susheela, Deirdre Wulf, Rubina Hussain, Akinrinola Bankole, and Gilda Sedgh. 2009. *Abortion Worldwide: A Decade of Uneven Progress.* New York: Guttmacher Institute.

Stein, Rob. 2010. "U.S. Birthrate Drops 2 Percent in 2008." *Washington Post,* April 7.

United Nations Department of Economic and Social Affairs (UNDESA). 2010. *The Millennium Development Goals Report 2010.* New York: United Nations.

United Nations Population Division (UNPD). 2011. *World Population Prospects: The 2010 Revision.* Population Database. New York: United Nations, Population Division, Department of Economic and Social Affairs. Accessed from http://esa.un.org/unpd/wpp/unpp/panel_population.htm.

United Nations Population Information Network (UNPIN). 1994. *Report of the International Conference on Population and Development (Cairo, 5–13 September 1994).* New York: United Nations, Population Division, Department of Economic and Social Affairs. Accessed from www.un.org/popin/icpd/conference/offeng/poa.html.

Westley, Sidney, Minja Choe, and Robert Retherford. 2010. "Very Low Fertility in Asia: Is There a Problem? Can It Be Solved?" *Asia Pacific Issues.* Honolulu: East-West Center.

World Health Organization. 1995. *The Health Benefits of Family Planning.* Geneva: World Health Organization.

CHAPTER 20

How Do We Solve the Population Problem?

WILLIAM RYERSON

I N 1992, SOME seventeen hundred of the world's scientists, including the majority of Nobel Laureates in the sciences, signed a "Warning to Humanity" written by the late Henry Kendall, chair of the Union of Concerned Scientists. The warning identified a range of critical stresses on the environment, including the atmosphere, water resources, oceans, soil, forests, species, and ecosystems, and stated the need to stabilize population numbers in order to alleviate these stresses and avoid potentially grave harms to people. "If we don't halt population growth with justice and compassion," wrote Kendall, "it will be done for us by nature, brutally and without pity—and we will leave a ravaged world." The report continues:

> The Earth is finite. Its ability to absorb wastes and destructive effluents is finite. Its ability to provide food and energy is finite. Its ability to provide for growing numbers of people is finite. And we are fast approaching many of the Earth's limits. Current economic practices which damage the environment, in both developed and underdeveloped nations, cannot be continued without the risk that vital global systems will be damaged beyond repair.
>
> Pressures resulting from unrestrained population growth put demands on the natural world that can overwhelm any efforts to achieve a sustainable future. If we are to halt the destruction of our environment, we must accept limits to that growth.
>
> No more than one or a few decades remain before the chance to avert the threats we now confront will be lost and the prospects for humanity are immeasurably diminished.

It concludes: "We the undersigned, senior members of the world's scientific community, hereby warn all humanity of what lies ahead. A great change in our stewardship of the Earth and the life on it is required, if vast human misery is to be avoided and our global home on this planet is not to be irretrievably mutilated" (Union of Concerned Scientists 1992).

Since the publication of this warning, the money spent by governments and NGOs on population stabilization has actually declined, and population has increased by over one billion people.

MERELY PROVIDING CONTRACEPTIVES CANNOT ACHIEVE
POPULATION STABILIZATION

There is widespread belief that increasing contraceptive supplies is all that is needed to solve the population problem. Of course, availability of family planning services is crucial, but lack of access to services is not the only major barrier to contraceptive use. The Demographic and Health Surveys carried out in numerous developing countries reveal that lack of access to services is infrequently cited as a reason for non-use. What other factors are at play?

A 1992 paper by Etienne van de Walle emphasizes one of the factors that affect the decisions of many women and men—fatalism. Many people simply have not reached the realization that reproductive decisions are a matter of conscious choice. Many who did not particularly want another pregnancy in the near future still reasoned that their deity had determined since the beginning of the universe how many children they would have, and that it did not matter what they thought or whether they might use a contraceptive, because they could not oppose God's will (van de Walle 1992).

For example, Pakistan's 2006–2007 *Demographic and Health Survey* found that the most common reason for non-use of contraceptives is the belief that God determines family size. This answer was given by 28 percent of the respondents. Since the fertility rate in Pakistan is 4.0 and the mean desired number of children among currently married women is 4.1, it is clear that family size norms are a major factor in driving high fertility (NIPS and Macro International 2008).

The tradition of large families is a deciding factor in fertility rates in most of sub-Saharan Africa. For example, the 2008 *Demographic and Health Survey* in Nigeria, Africa's most populous country with 162 million inhabitants, found that the average ideal number of children for married women was 6.7. For married men, it was 8.5. The fertility rate in Nigeria is 5.7 children per woman, which is below what people say they actually want. Of all births in Nigeria, 87 percent were wanted at the time, and another 7 percent were wanted, but not until later. Only 4 percent were unwanted. Nationwide, 67 percent of married women and 89 percent of married men know of at least one modern method of contraception, yet only 10 percent of married women report they currently use modern family planning methods. Of the non-users, 55 percent report that they never intend to use family planning. The top reasons given are opposition to family planning (39 percent), the desire to have as many children as possible (17 percent), fear of health effects (11 percent), and not knowing a method (8 percent). Lack of access and cost each were cited by only 0.2 percent of respondents (NPC and ICF Macro 2009).

In Ethiopia, the 2005 *Demographic and Health Survey* found that 87 percent of married women knew at least one modern method of contraception. Yet, only 14 percent of married women were using modern methods. Among non-users of family planning, 44 percent made it clear they had no intention to use family planning in the future. The top reasons for non-use were personal or religious opposition (24 percent), the desire to have as many children as possible (18 percent), fear of health effects (13 percent), and not knowing any method (9 percent). Only 3 percent said they did not know a source of contraceptives. As of 2010, the total fertility rate was 5.4 children per woman. That is just slightly higher than the average ideal number of children among married women, which is 5.1. Among married men, the average ideal number of children was 6.4 (Central Statistical Agency and ORC Macro 2006).

Clearly, one thing that could change the population dynamics of Pakistan, Nigeria, and Ethiopia is role-modeling small family norms and making them popular. Lack of access to contraception appears to be relatively minor by comparison to the norm of large families. The same pattern is found in many countries, including Benin, Botswana, Burkina Faso, Cameroon, Dominican Republic, Egypt, Ghana, Guatemala, India, Indonesia, Kenya, Liberia, Mali, Niger, Papua New Guinea, Peru, Senegal, Sierra Leone, Sri Lanka, Sudan, Tanzania, and Uganda.

Looking at several countries, Charles Westoff (1988) concludes that "by and large, contraceptive behavior . . . is not grossly inconsistent with reproductive intention." Only 1 to 2 percent of the women failed to use contraception in a manner consistent with their family size preference in Brazil, the Dominican Republic, Peru, and Liberia. According to Westoff (1988, 232): "The overwhelming majority of women who want no more children or want to postpone fertility, at least in the four countries discussed here, are behaving in a manner consistent with that goal."

World Bank economist Lant Pritchett, in a 1994 article in *Population and Development Review*, concluded that family size desire is the overwhelming determinant of actual fertility rates. "The conclusion that follows from the evidence and analysis we presented," he wrote, "is that because fertility is principally determined by the desire for children, contraceptive access (or cost) or family planning effort more generally is not a dominant, or typically even a major, factor in determining fertility differences" (39). According to Pritchett (1994), desired levels of fertility account for roughly 90 percent of differences among countries in total fertility rates. He argues that reducing the demand for children—for instance, by giving girls more education—is vastly more important to reducing fertility than providing more contraceptives or family planning services.

Yet another illustration of the importance of motivation is the fact that the contraceptive prevalence rate in Malawi (38 percent) is four times higher than it is in Macedonia (10 percent), but the total fertility rate in Malawi (6 children born during a woman's lifetime) is quadruple the rate in Macedonia (1.5) (Population Reference Bureau 2010).

Motivation to use family planning and to limit family size has been the key missing element in the strategy for population stabilization. While the percentage of non-users of contraceptives has declined, various studies indicate that the *number* of adults not using contraceptives is greater than it was in 1960, a fact stemming from the enormous increase in world population over the past fifty years. Approximately 44 percent of the roughly 2.3 billion people of reproductive age who are married or in long-term unions currently use no modern method of contraception at all. This means there are about 1 billion married adult non-users of contraceptive methods, plus an unknown number of sexually active unmarried individuals. It's time to focus some significant effort on motivating this group to use contraception for the purpose of achieving small family size.

The desired family sizes of the users of contraception will be very important in determining future population growth. In many countries, those who do use contraceptives still want more than enough children to replace themselves. Their goals, if achieved, will lead to continued high rates of growth.

I should make it clear that as a former employee of two Planned Parenthood affiliates, I have a strong belief in the importance of an ample supply of free or affordable contraceptive choices, delivered in a consumer-friendly way in the context of broad reproductive health care. I recognize there is a shortage of contraceptives in some countries and a need for new contraceptive technologies. I know that if those of us on the demand-creation side are successful, the demand for family planning methods will increase.

I support increased funding for the provision of family planning medical services. My point here is that the need goes beyond correcting a lack of access to contraception.

Many population planners measure progress on the basis of contraceptive prevalence rates. Use of effective family planning methods is critical but will not result in population stabilization if desired family size is five, six, or seven children. Similarly, delaying the first pregnancy and spacing children is important to the health of women and children—and to slowing population growth rates. But spacing seven children will still lead to a high growth rate. The data make it clear that there is a great need for better communication to increase family planning use where the barriers to use are cultural or informational.

CHANGING NORMS REGARDING FAMILY SIZE: THE KEY TO STABILIZING POPULATION

Throughout much of the world, people get their information and form many of their opinions from the mass media, particularly radio and television. Worldwide, the biggest audiences are to be found during evening (prime-time) hours, tuned in to entertainment programs. The most popular format by far is prime-time serial dramas, called *telenovelas* in Latin America. Unlike American soap operas, *telenovelas* have a beginning, middle, and end, and they run for a limited period of time.

Entertainment programs can reach large numbers of people very cost-effectively. Serial dramas are especially well suited to showing key characters' evolution from traditional attitudes toward modern attitudes regarding such issues as the role of women, family size decisions, and the use of family planning (Nariman 1993). Regarding such efforts, the Programme of Action from the 1994 Cairo Conference on Population and Development states:

> Governments, non-governmental organizations and the private sector should make greater and more effective use of the entertainment media, including radio and television soap operas and drama, folk theatre and other traditional media to encourage public discussion of important but sometimes sensitive topics related to the implementation of the present Programme of Action. When the entertainment media—especially dramas—are used for advocacy purposes or to promote particular lifestyles, the public should be so informed, and in each case the identity of sponsors should be indicated in an appropriate manner. (UNPIN 1994, Programme of Action, para. 11.23)

Mexico is the leading example of a country that has used serialized melodramas to lower fertility rates. Thomas Donnelly, with the United States Agency for International Development (USAID) in Mexico until 1983, wrote in a personal communication to the author in the 1970s: "Throughout Mexico, wherever one travels, when people are asked where they heard about family planning, or what made them decide to practice family planning, the response is universally attributed to one of the soap operas that Televisa has done." Donnelly also stated, "The Televisa family planning soap operas have made the single most powerful contribution to the Mexican population success story."

A vice president of Televisa, Miguel Sabido, created a methodology for using melodramas for social change. During the 1970s and 1980s, he created and broadcast five such programs addressing family planning, teenage pregnancy prevention, and related issues. Based on the social cognitive theory of Stanford psychologist Albert Bandura (who is a world's authority on how role models influence behavior), the Sabido programs created key characters who evolved from the cultural norm into positive role models for the audience on family planning use and related behaviors. The design elements of the Sabido approach are described in a publication on the Population Media Center website (Barker and Sabido 2005).

The methodology created by Sabido traveled to India, as Doordarshan (the Indian Television Authority) went on the air in July 1984 with India's first social-content soap opera, *Hum Log* (We People). The program included promotion of family planning and elevation of the status of women, through the words and actions of the key characters (Singhal and Rogers 1989).

Over seventeen months of broadcasting, this program achieved ratings ranging from 60 to 90 percent of the viewing audience. Research conducted by Arvind Singhal and Everett M. Rogers (1989) found, through a sample survey, that 70 percent of the viewers indicated they had learned from *Hum Log* that women should have equal opportunities; 68 percent had learned women should have the freedom to make their personal decisions in life; and 71 percent had learned that family size should be limited. Among other things, the program stimulated over four hundred thousand people to write letters to the Indian Television Authority and to various characters in the program, stating their views on the issues being dealt with or asking for help and advice.

A second Indian soap opera, *Humraahi* (Come Along with Me), produced by Roger Pereira of Bombay, went on the air in January 1992, airing at 9:00 p.m. once a week. The focus of the first fifty-two episodes was on the status of women, with particular attention to age of marriage, age of first pregnancy, gender bias in childbearing and child rearing, equal educational opportunity, and the right of women to choose their own husbands. By May 1992, *Humraahi* was the top-rated program on Indian television. A conservative estimate is that the program was seen by over a hundred million people each week.

In the series, a young girl who wanted to be educated and to become an attorney is instead forced into an arranged marriage at age fourteen by her father. Despite her pleas to her husband to delay consummating their marriage, she becomes pregnant and dies in childbirth. Following that key episode, the other characters lament what is happening to the young women of India and the tragedy of early marriage and pregnancy. A study of viewer response by the Annenberg School found many interviewees stating that after seeing the death of this character, they had decided not to marry their own daughters off at puberty, but to send them to be educated.

A longitudinal study of over three thousand people in the Hindi-speaking region of India, carried out by Marketing Research Private Group, Ltd., of Bombay, identified numerous significant shifts in attitudes while *Humraahi* was on the air, particularly related to the ideal age of marriage for women. The shifts in prosocial directions were dramatically greater for viewers than nonviewers (Ryerson and Sopariwala 1994).

A similar success story occurred in Kenya. After taking Kenyan television and radio personnel for training in Mexico, David Poindexter helped in the development of two programs: a television series, *Tushauriane* (Let's Talk about It), and a radio series, *Ushikwapo Shikamana* (If Assisted, Assist Yourself). Both programs went on the air in 1987. The programs were aimed at opening the minds of men to allowing their wives to seek family planning. The programs also effectively linked family size with land inheritance and the resulting ability or inability of children to support their parents in their old age.

These programs were the most popular programs ever produced by the Voice of Kenya. The television series ran for sixty episodes and then went into reruns. The radio series ran for two years at two episodes per week, with each episode playing twice during each day for most of the broadcast series.

By the time the series ended, contraceptive use in Kenya had increased 58 percent and desired family size had fallen from 6.3 to 4.8 children per woman. While many factors undoubtedly contributed to these changes, a study conducted by the University of Nairobi's School of Journalism at rural health centers found women saying that the radio program had caused their husbands to allow them to come in for family planning. In addition, a midpoint survey conducted during the radio series indicated that over 75 percent of the program's listenership had accepted the concept of smaller families.

The most extensive evaluation of the effects of a family planning serial drama occurred from 1993 to 1997 in Tanzania. There, Radio Tanzania broadcast a serial melodrama that attracted 55 percent of the population (aged fifteen to forty-five) in areas of the broadcast. In one region of the country, the area surrounding the city of Dodoma, a music program was substituted for the soap opera during the first two years of the project. Independent research by the University of New Mexico and the Population Family Life Education Programme of the government of Tanzania measured the effects caused by the program with regard to such issues as ideal age of marriage for women, use of family planning, and AIDS prevention behavior (Rogers et al. 1999). Because the population of the Dodoma comparison area was more urban than the rest of the country, a multiple regression analysis eliminated the influence such differences might have accounted for. Nationwide random sample surveys of three thousand people were conducted before, during, and after the broadcast of the program.

Among the findings were a significant increase in the percentage of listeners in the broadcast area who believed that they, rather than their deity or fate, could determine how many children they would have; an increase in the belief that children in small families have better lives than children in large families; and an increase in the percentage of respondents who approved of family planning. The study also provided evidence that the Tanzanian radio serial stimulated important behavioral changes. There was a strong positive relationship between listenership and the change in the percentage of men and women who were currently using any family planning method. Similar evidence was found for an increase in the percentage of Tanzanians who discussed family planning with their spouses and a decrease in the number of sexual partners for both men and women.

In regions where the show was broadcast, the percentage of married women who were currently using a family planning method increased by more than one-fourth, from 26 percent to 33 percent in the first two years of the program, while the average number of new family planning adopters per clinic, in a sample of twenty-one clinics, increased by 32 percent from June 1993 (the month before the show began airing) to December 1994. Over the same period, these percentages stayed roughly flat in the Dodoma control area. Independent data from Ministry of Health clinics showed that 41 percent of new adopters of family planning methods were influenced by the soap opera to seek family planning (Rogers et al. 1999).

Because entertainment programming attracts the largest audiences, it is particularly important to utilize entertainment media for disseminating information about family planning, family size issues, and gender relations. Radio and television programs can capture the attention of a large audience, because they are entertaining and can create characters with whom the audience can identify. They have great potential to provide role models that many audience members will emulate, as those characters evolve from traditional attitudes to modern attitudes regarding the status of women, family size decision making, and the use of family planning.

In terms of birth averted per dollar spent, mass media communications are probably the most effective strategy for reducing fertility rates. This is particularly true with entertainment broadcasting, where donor dollars play a catalytic role and commercial sponsorship underwrites the cost of airtime and production. Using the leverage of commercial sponsorship, as little as thirty-five million dollars a year in donor support—if spent properly—could lead to the development of highly effective motivational programs in all of the major developing countries of the world.

REDUCING BIRTHS THROUGH ELEVATING THE STATUS
OF WOMEN

There is substantial evidence that women who are educated have fewer children than those who are not, and that women who have opportunities to work outside the home similarly have lower fertility rates. Many governments and the United Nations have recognized the need to change the low status of women that exists in many countries, both because of the beneficial effect on fertility rates and the humanitarian mandate of improving women's lives.

The United Nations held global conferences on women's rights issues in Nairobi in 1985 and in Beijing in 1995. With the exception of a few very conservative countries, the world's governments agreed that the status of women and girls needed to be improved and that gender equity was an important goal in education, the economy, and family life. The plans of action that emerged from these conferences called for policy and legal changes regarding such things as freedom of choosing one's spouse, educational opportunities, freedom from domestic violence, the right to work outside the home, inheritance and property ownership rights, and improvement in maternal health services. Yet, very few of the delegates to these conferences discussed how to change the dynamics of family life. The right of a woman in Papua New Guinea to be free from beatings by her husband means nothing if she does not know that right exists, as is true in many villages where 100 percent of the women and 100 percent of the children report being beaten. The right of a school girl in Ethiopia to be free from marriage by abduction means nothing if her parents refuse to take her home once she's been raped and force her to live with her abductor.

As with decision making about family size and family planning, communication is *the* essential ingredient for improving the lot of women and girls worldwide. Beyond getting the policymakers to act, reaching people with information that causes social norms to change is key.

One of the thirty-five thousand letters received by Population Media Center–Ethiopia came from a woman in the southern region of Oromia. It thanked the writers for having tackled the issue of marriage by abduction. The woman's own daughter, she reported, had been abducted on her way to school and ended up married as a result. She and her husband were afraid to send their twelve-year-old girls to school for fear the same thing would happen to them. When the radio drama addressed the issue of marriage by abduction through the character Wubalem, the entire village, which was listening to the program, came together to enforce the law against marriage by abduction, which previously they did not know existed, and, the woman said, it was now safe to send their daughters to school.

One of the benefits of entertainment-education via the mass media as a strategy for addressing social norms is that it operates in a human rights context. The programs are not imported from outside the country, but instead they are locally managed, written, and acted in and are based on the policies of the host country. In addition, the programs refrain from telling people what to do. Traditional health messaging says, "Do this; don't do that." Instead, entertainment-education programs model various behaviors of positive, negative, and transitional characters in the context of the cultural realities of the country and show the realistic consequences of the choices these characters make. The audience is free to emulate their behaviors, but they are not instructed to do so. Clearly, many in the audience do follow the lead of key transitional characters, and many write letters to the producers thanking them for simultaneously educating and entertaining them.

Host governments of such programs like the approach as well. Many have been issuing public service announcements promoting social and health goals that have brought about little behavior change. Many ministers of health report that well in excess of 90 percent of their adult populations are aware of how HIV/AIDS is transmitted, but that too few people seem to be changing their behavior. An approach that reaches large numbers and stimulates healthful behavior change is welcomed by health authorities and those concerned with gender equity.

Such programs have been successful in changing attitudes and practices with regard to the practice of female genital mutilation, unassisted labor, the dowry system, the right of women to work in the workplace outside the home, the right of women to choose their own spouse, the right of women to play a role in determining how many children to have, and the right of girls to have equal educational opportunities with boys.

IS THERE ANY ROLE FOR COERCION?

Too often, women have been coerced into staying home from school, coerced into marriages with older men they do not even know, sometimes while they're still children, coerced into unwanted pregnancies, and coerced into staying in the home without economic opportunities. Some governments have imposed pregnancy coercion as well. In the 1970s, after hosting the first World Population Conference, Nicolae Ceausescu of Romania outlawed family planning in hopes of increasing Romania's population. More recently, the mayor of Manila outlawed the sale of contraception at the request of the Catholic Church, forcing thousands of Filipino women into repeated unwanted pregnancies. Indeed, much of the coercion that has occurred in the arena of women's rights and family planning has worsened women's lot and slowed progress in achieving population stabilization. Unfortunately, coercive cultural practices and norms that force women into repeated pregnancies and childbearing are rarely deplored as much as the more politically high-profile cases of coercive policies to slow down population growth—even though the former are egregious violations of human rights.

There have also been a few attempts at coercion by those trying to slow population growth rates. Indira Gandhi imposed involuntary sterilization in the 1970s with disastrous results, setting back attempts at voluntary family planning in India by decades. And China has used a combination of persuasion and coercion to bring about subreplacement fertility of the world's most populous country. But China is unlike most nations in that it has a very centralized government and a culture of people prioritizing what is good for the people as a whole. Yet, most of China's neighbors have achieved lower fertility rates voluntarily. This is a better way to operate, because it combines respect for human rights and success at reducing fertility rates, with both increasing people's well-being.

Brazil, Iran, Japan, Sri Lanka, and Thailand are all examples of countries that have achieved replacement fertility levels in a matter of a decade or so after strong government-backed communication campaigns were combined with readily accessible and affordable family planning services. That is what needs to be done globally. Indeed, the whole effort to improve women's lives and achieve sustainable population levels is part of a campaign to bring about a higher quality of life for people worldwide. Coercion has no useful role to play in that world.

CONCLUSION

Now that we have entered the ecological age, the goal of humanity should be to sustain a reasonable number of people on Earth, in comfort and security. Instead, we are recklessly pursuing an experiment to find out how many people can be supported in the short term, without regard to the impact on future generations of people or the consequences for other species. People have a unique ability to foresee the consequences of current activities, but our failure to use that ability with respect to our population growth may result in massive catastrophes.

It is clear our life-support systems are being overused. Otherwise, we would not have rising CO_2 levels, rising global temperatures, falling water tables, falling grain production per capita, degrading soils, disappearing forests, collapsing fisheries, growing energy shortages in many countries, and massive species extinctions.

Since we are living beyond the carrying capacity of the planet, we need to move quickly toward stopping population growth and then reducing our numbers. The actual long-term carrying capacity of Earth depends on our lifestyles and technologies, so it may be impossible to determine with any certainty what an optimal human population is. But what should be clear is that driving population numbers above carrying capacity risks long-term damage to Earth's natural systems and biodiversity and jeopardizes the ability to support future generations of people. Therefore, our goal should be to achieve a population well below the likely upper limit that can be sustained. Since the evidence is strong that the human species is currently in population overshoot, our goal as a global community should be to reverse our current demographic trends and reduce human numbers, until there is good evidence that our population is sustainable.

Solving the population problem will not be easy or inexpensive. Probably no one intervention will bring about rapid reductions in fertility rates; certainly none has to date. But the overall framework for population stabilization lies in the following four areas:

(1) The right of women and men to determine the number and spacing of their children; the right of girls, as well as boys, to be educated; the right of women to have equal opportunity for gainful employment; and the right of women, as well as men, to live free from violence and intimidation.

(2) Governmental policies that ensure the provision of high-quality, comprehensive reproductive health care, including family planning information and services, to all people who want it on a voluntary basis and, more broadly, provision of maternal and child health care that is affordable or free of charge.

(3) A social/cultural climate that motivates people to have small families, that allows women in particular to feel safe to express the desire
to have fewer (or no) children, and that enables women, as well as
men, to take the steps necessary to implement those desires. Communication campaigns that convey the relative safety of contraceptive use compared to early and repeated childbearing, the economic
benefits of small family size, the health benefits of child spacing,
and the dire environmental consequences of continued population
growth can help create such a climate.

(4) A new economic/political worldview that recognizes and works
within ecological limits. We must move away from economic
schemes based on perpetual population growth, material gain, consumer excess, the harsh exploitation of nature, and half-heartedly
cleaning up our worst messes after the fact. Instead we must create
a new kind of economy, based on clean and renewable energy
sources, on the conservation and preservation of biological diversity, and on working with natural systems to provide for a sustainable number of people.

BIBLIOGRAPHY

Barker, Kriss, and Miguel Sabido, eds. 2005. *Soap Operas for Social Change to Prevent HIV/AIDS: A Training Guide for Journalists and Media Personnel.* Shel-burne, Vt.: Population Media Center.
Central Statistical Agency and ORC Macro. 2006. *Ethiopia Demographic and Health Survey 2005.* Addis Ababa, Ethiopia, and Calverton, Md.
Nariman, Heidi. 1993. *Soap Operas for Social Change: Toward a Methodology for Entertainment-Education Television.* Westport, Conn.: Praeger.
National Institute of Population Studies (NIPS) and Macro International. 2008. *Pakistan Demographic and Health Survey 2006–07.* Islamabad, Pakistan: National Institute of Population Studies.
National Population Commission (NPC) and ICF Macro. 2009. *Nigeria Demographic and Health Survey 2008.* Abuja, Nigeria: National Population Commission.
Population Reference Bureau. 2010. *2010 World Population Data Sheet.* Washing-ton, D.C.: Population Reference Bureau.
Pritchett, Lant. 1994. "Desired Fertility and the Impact of Population Policies." *Population and Development Review* 20 (1): 1–55.
Rogers E. M., P. Vaughan, R. M. A. Swalehe, N. Rao, P. Svenkerud, and S. Sood.

1999. "Effects of an Entertainment-Education Radio Soap Opera on Family Planning Behavior in Tanzania." *Studies in Family Planning* 30 (3): 193–211.

Ryerson, William, and Dorab Sopariwala. 1994. "A Report on a Series of Three Surveys in the Hindi-Speaking Region of India to Test the Effect of the Television Serial, *Humraahi*, as a Vehicle of Social Change." Shelburne, Vt.: Population Media Center.

Singhal, Arvind, and Everett M. Rogers. 1989. *India's Information Revolution*. New Delhi: Sage.

Union of Concerned Scientists. 1992. "World Scientists' Warning to Humanity." Union of Concerned Scientists. Accessed from www.ucsusa.org/about/1992-world-scientists.html.

United Nations Population Information Network (UNPIN). 1994. *Report of the International Conference on Population and Development (Cairo, 5–13 September 1994)*. New York: United Nations, Population Division, Department of Economic and Social Affairs. Accessed from www.un.org/popin/icpd/conference/offeng/poa.html.

van de Walle, Etienne. 1992. "Fertility Transition, Conscious Choice and Numeracy." *Demography* 27 (4): 487–502.

Westoff, Charles. 1988. "Is the KAP-gap Real?" *Population and Development Review* 14 (2): 225–232.

CHAPTER 21

A Post-Cairo Paradigm

Both Numbers and Women Matter

DON WEEDEN AND CHARMAYNE PALOMBA

S EVERAL YEARS AGO, Steven Sinding, then secretary general of the International Planned Parenthood Federation and a long-time USAID population official, made the bold, candid assertion that "the 'population movement' is to all intents and purposes dead" (2006). According to Sinding and other insiders, the fatal blow was struck at the International Conference on Population and Development (ICPD) at Cairo in 1994. There, societal goals such as reducing population growth for poverty alleviation and environmental sustainability were supplanted almost entirely by individual goals defined in terms of sexual and reproductive health and rights (SRHR).

Much of the Cairo Agenda was very positive. It recognized that SRHR services alone were insufficient to ensure women's reproductive health autonomy and called for greater attention to girls' education and women's empowerment through economic development and other means. Cairo also codified and endorsed proven strategies and principles that had already become part of the mainstream, such as greater attention to client needs, particularly concerning the quality of reproductive health services. Cairo recommended doing away with program numerical targets such as family planning acceptor quotas, which were unnecessary and often counterproductive. For example, India decided shortly after the Cairo conference to drop all such targets from its reproductive health program. Such changes were good and necessary. But the Cairo paradigm clearly excluded concerns about population growth, a shift that continues to impede discussion and progress on this critical issue nearly two decades later.

According to Sinding, two main factors were responsible for the exclusion of population concerns at Cairo. First, a determined alliance of feminists and social justice activists had succeeded in creating an overblown and, indeed, inaccurate image of international family planning programs as coercive and violating women's rights. Second, there was a growing but false sense that the "population problem" was largely solved (Sinding 2006). The insider's view is that a politically astute feminist and social justice lobby successfully undermined the old-guard populationists by rendering "population control" politically incorrect. This perception played into the political process typical of such international conferences. As two analysts wrote of the Cairo Conference: "In the search for consensus, [such] conferences are . . . likely to be excessively sensitive to the 'political correctness' of the day. This tendency exemplifies what has been called the 'mobilization of bias,' meaning that some issues are organized into politics while others are organized out" (McIntosh and Finkle 1995, 252). Despite nearly forty years of international concern and mobilization surrounding the consequences of population growth, the "P" in ICPD was effectively "organized out" of international discourse.

By the early 1990s, the success of the family planning "revolution"—which achieved replacement fertility in much of the developed world and nearly halved fertility in developing countries—had led some to believe that world population was no longer exploding, and a confused media often went along with this belief (Wattenberg 1997). However, demographic data undermine this complacency. Global population continues to increase by more than 75 million per year, as it has for the last four decades. The United Nations expects global population to continue to grow, with medium variant projections reaching 9.3 billion by 2050 and 10.1 billion by the end of the century (UNDESA 2011).

To many experts concerned about growing human numbers, the Cairo conference not only chose to ignore the considerable scientific data on the widespread harmful impacts of population growth but also failed to evaluate the demographic implications of the new sexual and reproductive health paradigm. This new paradigm added a wide range of services to previously separate family planning programs, which could clearly weaken family planning services. But the conference "winners" simply didn't care. The Cairo conference was imbued with the same taboo that has thwarted serious public discussion about population growth over the last few decades—that is, that international population stabilization policies are coercive and ultimately violate women's rights. Thus, representatives from the feminist and social justice movement became strange bedfellows of the Vatican and other conservative religious advocates (Kissling 2009, 386).

This result came about in part because there were few nongovernmental population organizations at Cairo supporting the demographic rationale for population activism. Years before, so-called mainstream population groups such as the Population Council and Pathfinder International had drifted away from population stabilization and environmental concerns, as the old guard was replaced by those with a women's health and rights perspective. At one time, such groups had joined forces with national environmental organizations in the hope that concerns about global environmental issues would rally support for population stabilization and family planning services.

Prior to Cairo, the environmental community had also become increasingly disengaged with population work, and the Cairo Agenda accelerated this trend. According to Frances Kissling, a long-time reproductive health activist, "For environmentalists, the shift was a mind bender. They had entered the field of population out of concern for the effect of population size and growth on the environment. If addressing the relationship was now considered unethical, was there any reason for them to stay in the field? Within a few years after Cairo, most environmental groups bowed out of population work" (Kissling 2009, 387). Today, the few environmental groups that do engage population issues promote the Cairo Agenda almost exclusively. The National Wildlife Federation's (NWF) population program is a good example. An interview with NWF staff convinced one observer that female empowerment—as opposed to reduced birthrates and population stabilization—was their population program's end goal (Kolankiewicz and Beck 2001, 22).

The combined departure of the population and environmental groups left the advocacy community with virtually no major voice explicitly calling for population stabilization. In the decade and a half following Cairo, the pervasive silence on the population issue extended to other key players, including development institutions, donors, country health programs, and universities. The word *population* had become an anachronism, taboo, and virtually unspeakable. Among the politically correct left, "anything remotely resembling demographic [concerns and objectives] was racist, anti-woman, anti-poor, and flirting with eugenics" (Weld 2011).

However, as often happens when a viewpoint is unfairly ostracized, the social barometer has begun to move back toward the center. The fact that demographic concerns have begun to resurface in the mainstream media demonstrates that ideology cannot ultimately trump legitimate, reality-based concerns. Population growth is once again being discussed in the environmental context, particularly in connection with climate change and biodiversity destruction, as discussed below.

U.S. media coverage of the population-environment connection has quadrupled in the past few years (Mazur 2010, 16), spurred to some extent by an increasingly vocal group of concerned scientists and population-specific nonprofits such as the Optimum Population Trust (UK) and the Population Institute (U.S.). Widely discussed books with population themes have recently been published, such as Jonathan Franzen's *Freedom* and Alan Weisman's *The World without Us*, and well-known bloggers such as Andrew Revkin of the *New York Times* have frequently commented on population-environment concerns. In his 2009 film *How Many People Can Live on Planet Earth?* David Attenborough examines the dangers of overpopulation. National Geographic, the PBS NewsHour, and the Pulitzer Center on Crisis Reporting launched a collaborative series on population issues in early 2011. In the past two years, researchers at the London School of Economics (Wire 2009) and Oregon State University (Murtaugh and Schlax 2009) have reported, in separate studies, that family planning is a far more cost-effective climate change intervention than most green technologies.

Not surprisingly, this renewed attention to demographic concerns has stirred reactions from many of the same feminist and social justice activists who helped to torpedo population concerns fifteen years ago, along with some from a new generation. It appears they collectively fear that overstatements (in their view) of the environmental impacts of population growth will justify coercive programs and take attention away from the hard-earned gains of the Cairo Agenda. However, this is not to say that reactions from feminist and social justice activists have been monolithic.

At one end of the spectrum are the "population naysayers," who believe that demographic arguments represent a false, quick fix to our environmental problems. From their perspective, the primary solutions include reducing consumption in developed countries and countering environmental degradation at the hands of corporations. Those who espouse this view essentially deny the connection between population and environmental degradation and therefore reject the need for family planning for ecological reasons.

One of the best-known advocates of this view, Betsy Hartmann, wrote recently: "In many ways, this focus on population control threw the American environmental movement off track. By shifting the blame elsewhere, to the proverbial dark-skinned Other, it prevented many Americans from taking a deeper look at their own role, and the role of the U.S. government and corporations, in causing environmental degradation at home and abroad" (Hartmann 2010). Hartmann's arguments deal far more with the purported *consequences* of recognizing population as a driver of environmental degradation than the fundamental question of whether population actually *is* a primary driver. Recognizing population growth's contribution to environmental harm is by no means tantamount to letting high-consumption societies "off the hook," as Hartmann claims. Rather, it is an acknowledgment that reducing *per capita* consumption while aggregate consumption continues to climb (as a function of population) is an exercise in futility. In the face of today's unprecedented environmental problems, we can ill afford such spurious arguments. Indeed, the myopic focus of Hartmann and others on the high rates of consumption in the West as the culprit in climate change and other environmental concerns essentially implies that those in countries with low per capita consumption are virtuous as long as they remain poor.

A primary concern among some feminists and social justice advocates is that women's reproductive health will become a means to an end (of population stabilization), rather than an end itself, thereby negatively impacting the cause of women's rights. On the other hand, population advocates believe that the renewed interest in demographic concerns, if married to the objectives of the Cairo Agenda, could accomplish just the opposite. Funding and interest in reproductive health has steadily declined since Cairo, and many old-guard populationists feel that a primary factor driving this decline is the shift away from the larger frame of population. (Other reasons include the vast increase in HIV/AIDS budgets, which siphoned off funding from family planning, and continuing opposition from the religious right.) A partnership between population and reproductive health proponents could bring about greater interest and funding for the Cairo Agenda, while more aggressively addressing global and U.S. population growth. There appears to be interest on both sides in forming such a partnership that would constitute an approach in which "both women and numbers matter" (Kissling 2009, 388).

Among those feminist and social justice thinkers cautiously exploring links among these various issues, Laurie Mazur stands out. In her recent edited anthology *A Pivotal Moment: Population, Justice, and the Environmental Challenge* (2009b), she asks her colleagues not to fear the "P" word. The publisher describes the book as developing an "equity and rights-based" approach to population advocacy. It has much to recommend it, including a number of solid chapters written by well-known reproductive health advocates. Unfortunately, the book is riddled with many of the distortions and unfair attacks of the past, thus failing as a "bridge" between the population and social justice communities.

Mazur accepts population as a factor in environmental problems. However, her book downplays its importance, warns against a return to "population control" approaches almost as a mantra, and excoriates population and environment advocates who suggest that the United States should stabilize its own population by reducing historically high immigration numbers. This book warrants attention because of its strong sections, but also because many of its views are indicative of the wide gap that remains between population and social justice advocates.

Mazur acknowledges that "there is a lot of fear—and outright hostility to—talking about population and environment in the same breath," and she appears bent on making concessions to the social justice "population naysayers" at nearly every turn, perhaps in order to get them to at least acknowledge that numbers matter. The book puts feminist and social justice concerns—particularly the Cairo Agenda—out front, while grudgingly acknowledging population growth's environmental role as a background factor. Mazur, clearly conflicted about this issue, writes: "Human numbers are not a primary cause of environmental degradation, but they do magnify the harmful effects of unsustainable production and consumption" (Mazur 2009a, 2).

THE CASE OF GHANA: POPULATION OR CORPORATE GREED?

Mazur's arguments essentially follow those of the social justice movement, which blames the global environmental crisis almost exclusively on Western consumption and corporate power and marginalizes the impact of population growth. She cites Ghana as a typical example of the devastation wrought on developing countries' natural resources by the corporate-driven global market. Ghana's primary rainforests have been reduced by 90 percent in the past fifty years, with nearly a third of this loss occurring in the past fifteen years. In 1996, a U.S. Department of Commerce article described Ghana (a country smaller than Oregon) as one of the most populous countries of sub-Saharan Africa; at the time, it had eighteen million people (Adlakha 1996). Today the population is almost twenty-five million, representing a fourfold increase since 1960, and the population density is three times that of Venezuela and twice that of Tanzania (Population Reference Bureau 2011). With an average of 3.5 children born per woman and an annual growth rate of 1.8 percent, Ghana's population continues to grow rapidly (USCIA 2011). While Mazur acknowledges the challenge Ghana's high population growth presents in terms of localized environmental stress, she pins the majority of the blame for the country's massive deforestation on multinational logging companies and illegal loggers feeding the global market.

There is no doubt that Ghana's recent drive to increase commodity exports has contributed to environmental degradation within the country. But to depict population size and growth as unimportant factors in deforestation misrepresents the situation both within Ghana and elsewhere. For developing countries generally, subsistence agriculture is the most significant direct cause of deforestation. One study found subsistence farming responsible for 48 percent of tropical deforestation and commercial agriculture for 32 percent (UNFCCC 2007, 81). While commercial agricultural land use varies from country to country, much of this land is used for grain production for domestic consumption, particularly in countries like Ghana, where high urban growth rates increase demand. As is the case in most sub-Saharan African countries, over half the population of Ghana is engaged in agriculture, mostly at the small-scale subsistence level (USCIA 2011).

A comprehensive 2005 study on deforestation in Ghana discusses the inevitable "adverse ramifications" of the high rate of population growth on the problem of deforestation (Asante 2005, 89). As the demand for farmland increases in proportion to the population, so too do rates of forest clearance—a trend exacerbated by the fact that subsistence agriculture causes farmed land to lose its natural fertility within several years. Increasing yields (as an alternative to increasing farmland area) has proved challenging, due to the prohibitively high costs of fertilizer and lack of requisite local knowledge of high-yield farming practices (Appiah et al. 2009, 481). In her discussion of Ghana, Mazur emphasizes that subsistence farmers cutting into forest reserves for food and fuel have been "displaced" in favor of land use for export industries. The implication seems to be that if it were not for those industries, the subsistence farming of an exploding population would not in itself place an unbearable burden on Ghana's forests. The facts do not support such a claim.

In addition to subsistence farming, other population-driven pressures on Ghana's forests include the increasing demand for construction materials for housing and for fuel wood. More specifically, 89 percent of Ghanaians—and 94 percent in rural areas—use solid fuels (wood fuels and charcoal) for cooking, 90 percent of which comes directly from natural forests (Asante 2005, 92). If population growth rates and fuel usage continue unabated, it is estimated that Ghana will consume upwards of twenty-five million tons of wood fuel by 2020, far outpacing yields (Peprah 2010, 2). These fuels serve as the major energy source for Ghana's poor, who are unable to afford alternatives such as kerosene. In a 2011 article on the devastating effects of fuel wood cultivation on Ghana's forests, a native cocoa farmer laments that while rapid deforestation for wood fuels is "an alarming issue that demands serious attention, the solution to that would take forever because most of us cannot afford kerosene always to light our homes" (Mensah 2011).

Ghanaians themselves recognize the pivotal role population growth plays in deforestation. According to a 2007 survey of Ghanaian households in three forest districts, the most highly ranked cause of deforestation was poverty-driven agriculture. The third highest cause cited was household population levels (Appiah et al. 2009, 479). The study notes that these perceptions indicate a marked shift away from past tendencies to blame "logging companies and government policies" for deforestation. While there is no doubt that commercial logging's contributions to deforestation must be abated, no effective policy can come from an approach that ignores the central role of Ghana's rapid population growth on deforestation, especially in a country that has lost 90 percent of its forest cover in fewer than fifty years and continues to do so at an estimated 3 percent per year (IUCN 2006).

Despite a brief recognition that population plays a role in pushing subsistence farmers into forest reserves for food and fuel, Mazur insists that population growth is "not to blame for Ghana's poverty or environmental problems" (Mazur 2009a, 7). She correctly recognizes that the wealth generated by export-oriented World Bank and International Monetary Fund (IMF) policies has done little to lift Ghanaians out of poverty. But by no means does the fact that Ghana has suffered the ravages of these policies diminish the impact of the country's high population growth rate on deforestation and other environmental problems.

The larger point is that population growth in developing countries does have considerable local and regional environmental impact. Some environmental and social justice leaders try to argue that population growth is not an issue because 95 percent of future growth will be in developing countries, whose carbon footprints are a fraction of that of the developed world. This is not even true in terms of climate change, because necessary development will almost certainly increase per capita carbon emissions in poorer countries, at least in the middle term. But marginalizing the role of population is doubly false when one turns to environmental issues as a whole, since it ignores the pressure that developing countries' increasing populations exert on local resources and wild nature. These pressures ultimately lead to chronic and growing problems such as water scarcity, overfishing, deforestation, wildlife hunting and poaching ("bushmeat"), desertification due to overgrazing, farmland erosion, river siltation, and biodiversity destruction.

Leading conservationist Dave Foreman discusses the need to look at environmental impact at both the global and the local levels. He argues that some people, "such as middle class Americans, draw raw goods from the whole Earth." Those in developing countries, on the other hand, "draw little from elsewhere in the world, but may hack deadly wounds in their neighborhoods" (Foreman 2011, 48). Such localized population effects exert huge impacts on biodiversity, as most of the world's biodiversity "hotspots" (which collectively contain 40 percent of the world's known species) are located in developing countries. Virtually every review of biodiversity loss lists population growth as one of the primary root causes behind on-the-ground direct causes such as habitat disturbance and fragmentation, pollution, and overhunting (Cincotta and Engelman 2000, 41).

IS COERCION NECESSARY TO CARRY OUT POPULATION POLICIES?

Another argument that runs through Mazur's book is the familiar historical revisionism that pre-Cairo population programs were often coercive, and that we need to be extremely careful in resurrecting the population issue so that we do not return to such dangerous solutions. This is the same myth that helped to derail population concerns at Cairo. One contribution to the book states that "human rights abuses are likely where reproductive health services are seen as a means to an end, rather than as an end in themselves" (Alvarado and Echegaray 2009, 292). In other words, concern for population growth will likely lead to coercion.

The myth of widespread coercion in family planning programs persists in part because the charge has been repeated so often; the coercion myth is also self-serving for feminists and social justice activists who oppose population concerns. However, scholars and practitioners within the population field know better. Even contributors in Mazur's book recognize that "coercion was—and is—rare in population and family planning programs" (Bruce and Bongaarts 2009, 270). Population analysts Martha Campbell and Kathleen Bedford drive home the same point: "A myth was developed in Cairo . . . [that] everything that had happened before 1994 . . . was population control—the term itself being unquestionably derogatory. This myth was framed in such a way as to exclude any mention of the numerically more common and successful voluntary family planning programs that had been developed between the 1950s and 1990s" (Campbell and Bedford 2009, 3105). Sinding (2006) has written: "The vast majority of programs in developing countries were based on carefully protected principles of voluntarism. A tiny minority of countries, all in Asia, at one time or another violated these principles and two of them, India and China, are indeed, very large. But it is seriously misleading to condemn an entire movement because of the missteps of a few."

This is not to underplay the importance of preventing coercion; rather, it is to demonstrate that such violations do not, by any means, follow from the institution of demographic concerns in national family planning policies. Of the scores of countries in the world with such policies, only a handful of countries are anomalies in instances of coercion, and each must be considered in light of its own peculiar circumstances.

With its one-child family policy, China is considered the most egregious example, but it is a mistake to consider the policy itself or instances of its abuse as typical in any way of other population programs. Historically, societal concerns have taken precedence over individual concerns in most areas of policy in China, and population/family planning is no exception to that general rule. In the face of explosive population growth resulting from Mao Zedong's Great Leap Forward, China instituted the one-child policy in urban areas for the ethnic Han majority (with ethnic minorities, those living in rural areas, and others exempted from the policy) in an attempt to curb the population growth it recognized as a threat to its economic prosperity. It should be noted that despite widespread international condemnation, a recent opinion poll shows that 76 percent of Chinese approve of the policy (Pew Research Center 2008, 5). In addition, it is estimated that the policy has prevented a minimum of 250 million births (Fitzpatrick 2009)—not an insignificant number in a country whose total greenhouse gas emissions are the highest in the world, and whose resource-intensive economy continues to grow rapidly.

India's forced vasectomy campaign during Indira Gandhi's "Emergency" period in the 1970s is another example pointed to by those opposing demographic objectives in family planning. It has often been reported that "millions of poor men and women" ("Population, Women's Rights" 2009) were victims of forced sterilizations, but reliable investigations conducted soon after the event concluded that such abuses "were concentrated in a few parts of the country relatively close to New Delhi" and that thousands—not millions—experienced, in some cases, forced vasectomies and otherwise "unpleasant treatment at the hands of police and other government authorities." It was also noted that these actions were the result of local bureaucratic initiatives "outside the formal policy process" (Gwatkin 1979, 37, 48). The period in which these abuses took place was relatively brief—a few weeks at most in any one location—and represents an aberration in India's sixty-year-old population program, which on the whole can be more legitimately criticized for its lackluster family planning program performance. While the number of actual abuses during the Indian Emergency has been overstated, it is important to note that the *fear* of coercion, widely disseminated through rumors in the Indian countryside, was damaging in its own right, as millions of people "altered their normal activities" in response to perceived threats (48). But the claim that millions underwent forced sterilizations is a gross exaggeration.

It is important to put the Indian and Chinese abuses—as well as perhaps some isolated instances in countries such as Peru—in their proper perspective. *Far* more women across the developing world have suffered and died as a result of a *lack* of access to family planning information and services than as a result of coercive programs. Indeed, historically, far more coercion has been used in *preventing* access to contraception, including decades of religiously motivated banning of family planning methods in Latin America and the recent outlawing of contraceptive sales by the mayor of Manila. According to the Demographic and Health Surveys (DHS) conducted in most developing countries around the world, there are "215 million sexually active women who do not want another child in the next two years, or ever, yet they are not using a modern method of contraception" (Campbell and Potts 2011, 21). Meanwhile, one in sixteen women die in childbirth, and infant mortality and malnourishment rates, related to inadequate birth spacing or large numbers of children, remain startlingly high. Furthermore, as Madeline Weld of the Population Institute of Canada has stated, "No population control program in any country has ever come close to inflicting upon women the horrors that millions of them have experienced during the environmental and social collapse of some of the world's most overpopulated and conflict-ridden regions" (Weld 2011).

Coercive measures such as forced sterilization or abortion, or penalties for "excess births" such as loss of educational opportunities or food supplements, represent egregious human rights violations. They should not be tolerated. These instances of coercion have set back progress in voluntary family planning programs at both national and global levels. However, strong family planning programs that include demographic objectives do not need to resort to coercive measures. Numerous national-level programs based on population stabilization policies have demonstrated that individual reproductive health needs and societal concern for population growth can be effectively addressed together.

In 1989, Iran recognized that high population growth was putting a strain on the economy and environment, and the government instituted a family planning program. The multipronged effort included using the media to raise awareness of available family planning services, offering modern contraception free of charge, and even requiring couples to take a course on contraception before marriage. The government actively encouraged people to limit themselves to two-child families, and from 1987 to 1994, Iran saw its population growth rate reduced by half, one of the fastest declines in history. Concomitantly, Iran put resources into women's education, and in thirty years the female literacy rate went from 25 percent to 70 percent (Brown 2011, 16).

Thailand saw a similarly impressive drop in population growth—from seven children per woman to just below replacement rate—after their demographically driven government program made contraceptives widely available by setting up distribution by midwives and nurses within communities. Thailand's population policies broadened access for women and prevented an estimated 16.1 million births between 1972 and 2010 (Speidel et al. 2007). Other examples of strong effective country programs include Korea, Tunisia, Morocco, Colombia, Mexico, Costa Rica, Singapore, Bangladesh, certain states in India (such as Kerala) and Indonesia (Bongaarts and Sinding 2009, 42; Speidel et al. 2007).

THE IMMIGRATION DEBATE

Yet another area of conflict between populationists and social justice advocates involves immigration. Many population advocates believe that the primary responsibility to deal with population issues falls to individual countries and their citizens, and that this responsibility encompasses immigration policy. From their perspective, immigration typically needs to be limited, primarily to avoid undermining efforts by receiving countries to stabilize their populations, but also to pressure high emigration countries to face their responsibilities to reduce their own population growth.

However, social justice advocates reject this logic. They criticize those making environmental arguments for stabilizing U.S. population growth, or reducing immigration levels, as unjust and "anti-immigrant." One author in Mazur's book writes that "blaming immigrants fails to address the root causes of complex problems" (Gibbs 2009, 61), referring to the global drivers of migration that, from a social justice perspective, never seem to include people having too many children. Sierra Club leader Carl Pope, who lobbied back in the 1970s for the U.S. Congress to limit immigration in order to stabilize America's population, wrote in the 1990s that "population growth is a global problem, while immigration is merely a local symptom" (Pope 1998). Laurie Mazur opines: "The anti-immigrant groups misrepresent the nature of environmental challenges we face today. They imply that we are in a lifeboat with limited resources, and if too many people get in, we will all sink. . . . We may be in a lifeboat but it is not the United States. It's our planet, and we are in it all together" (Mazur 2009a, 16).

Apparently, the long-time environmental adage, "think globally, act locally," does not apply to population growth! But surely, treating the entire planet as a global village, or one open commons, is a formula for inaction and failure. Deforestation is a global problem, desertification is a global problem, climate change is a global problem. All these problems would benefit from strong international cooperation, in conjunction with strong national policies that address them as well. No one seriously suggests that international efforts should *take the place of* national policies to address these issues—international efforts are instead designed to fund and facilitate national programs and to coordinate them so as to maximize their effectiveness. The need for action at a variety of levels is acknowledged in the case of every other major environmental issue on the international agenda. No one has ever explained why population growth should be treated differently. In fact, if population growth is a serious environmental problem—and it is—then it should *not* be treated differently. Action is needed at all levels, but especially at the level of national governments. This is where effective population policy mostly will be made, including upholding reproductive freedoms (or not), incentivizing responsible child-bearing (or not), and setting sustainable immigration policies (or not).

In advocating historically high immigration into the United States and other wealthy Western nations, social justice advocates have a weak hand to play, if the focus remains on the actual ecological impacts of such immigration. Hence the often-used ploy of "straw man" arguments, claiming that immigration reductionists "blame immigrants" for environmental problems, or that they fixate on immigration as the *sole* cause of environmental degradation in the United States. If such attempts fail, critics will often play the race card.

A contributor to Mazur's book, Priscilla Huang, claims the goal of demographically focused environmentalists is to "maintain the population status quo and preserve the white American majority" (Huang 2009, 358). Bolstering her arguments with ad hominem McCarthyesque attacks, Huang describes environmental concerns about immigration-driven population growth as the "greening of hate." She and others making such claims ignore the historically strong support for U.S. population stabilization by the environmental movement of the 1970s and 1980s by such environmental icons as David Brower, Gaylord Nelson, and E. O. Wilson, and by two presidential commissions on population growth and sustainability. Moreover, they ignore the fact that long-time environmentalists established major immigration reduction groups, such as FAIR and NumbersUSA. They also ignore the bipartisan recommendations of the Jordan Commission, which consisted of five Democrats and four Republicans and was chaired by the late African American congresswoman Barbara Jordan, a liberal Democrat from Texas. The commission recommended that in order to protect the wages and employment security of some of America's most vulnerable workers, including those with low levels of skills and education and recent immigrants, immigration levels should be halved. Indeed, the Pew Hispanic Center has found that recent immigrants tend to favor lower levels of immigration, in part because of high rates of unemployment in the United States and the wage suppression they generate. But it seems that immigration is such a social justice "sacred cow" that any suggestion regarding immigration reduction, no matter how reasonable, will be strenuously, even viciously, attacked.

All told, Mazur's criticism of many population advocates—depicted as overzealous, prone to coercion, unnuanced, and in some cases insensitive to racism—is counterproductive. A partnership requires respect and trust. Mazur's book falls short on both. This is a shame, because she and her colleagues have the credibility and intelligence to play an important "bridging role."

CONCLUSION

In the end, we need to affirm that both women and numbers matter. The core of the Cairo Agenda involves meeting women's unmet reproductive health needs, while respecting and facilitating the right of couples to choose how many children to have. However, the latter tenet is clearly an inadequate response to ending population growth as quickly as possible. Many demographers and reproductive health experts have noted that providing universal access to contraceptives and reproductive health services will not likely suffice to reach population stabilization in developing countries, particularly where fertility preferences remain high (Meyerson 2008b; Bongaarts and Sinding 2009, 40; Ryerson 2011). Many argue that it is also necessary to increase the demand for family planning by effectively communicating the benefits of smaller families. For example, targeted communications strategies such as television and radio serial dramas have proved effective in changing social norms regarding family size (as discussed in Bill Ryerson's essay in this volume). Programs that help to overcome cultural barriers to contraceptive use—particularly the desire for large families—are of utmost importance.

We need to proceed with a sense of urgency reflective of the environmental crisis we face. Fred Meyerson, in discussing the twin goals of population reduction and lower CO_2 emissions, writes: "Voluntary programs to modify individual behavior tend to fall short of intended goals. In such cases, legislation, programs, and incentives that encourage responsible parenting and sustainable resource use must be mandated in order to achieve population stabilization and climate change mitigation." However, Meyerson (2008a) adds, "there is agreement . . . about the need to provide Family Planning/Reproductive Health . . . and related education to everyone on the planet . . . in a non-coercive way." As noted above, a number of countries have implemented successful, noncoercive population programs.

At a fundamental level, many feminists and social justice advocates appear to be open to population stabilization arguments concerning eradication of poverty, food security, and environmental sustainability. But we need to do away with the myths that environmental degradation is caused solely by Western overconsumption, that concerns regarding population lead inexorably to coercion, or that support for immigration reduction can only be based on racist or nativist motives. We need to join forces as natural allies and get on with the urgent business of stabilizing (and ultimately reducing) population, both globally and nationally.

BIBLIOGRAPHY

Adlakha, Arjun. 1996. "International Brief Population Trends: Ghana." Washington, D.C.: U.S. Census Bureau. Accessed June 27, 2011, from www.census.gov.
Alvarado, Susana Chávez, and Jacqueline Nolley Echegaray. 2009. "Going to Extremes: Population Politics and Reproductive Rights in Peru." In Mazur 2009b, 292–299.
Appiah, Mark, et al. 2009. "Dependence on Forest Resources and Tropical Deforestation in Ghana." *Environment, Development and Sustainability* 11 (3): 471–487.
Asante, Michael. 2005. *Deforestation in Ghana: Explaining the Chronic Failure of Forest Preservation Policies in a Developing Country.* Lanham, Md.: University Press of America.
Bongaarts, John, and Steven Sinding. 2009. "A Response to Critics of Family Planning Programs." *International Perspectives on Sexual and Reproductive Health* 35 (1): 39–44.
Brown, Lester. 2011. "Smart Planning for the Global Family." *Reporter* 43 (2): 14–17.
Bruce, Judith, and John Bongaarts. 2009. "The New Population Challenge." In Mazur 2009b, 260–275.

Campbell, Martha, and Kathleen Bedford. 2009. "The Theoretical and Political Framing of the Population Factor in Development." *Philosophical Transactions of the Royal Society B* 364: 3101–3113.

Campbell, Martha, and Malcolm Potts. 2011. "Our Profound Choice: 7 Billion Reasons to Invest in Family Planning." *Reporter* 43 (2): 18–24.

Cincotta, Richard, and Robert Engelman. 2000. *Nature's Place: Human Population and the Future of Biological Diversity*. Washington, D.C.: Population Action International.

Fitzpatrick, Laura. 2009. "China's One-Child Policy." *Time Magazine*, July 27.

Foreman, Dave. 2011. *Man Swarm and the Killing of Wildlife*. Durango, Colo.: Raven's Eye Press.

Gibbs, Susan. 2009. "People on the Move: Population, Migration, and the Environment." In Mazur 2009b, 53–65.

Gwatkin, Davidson. 1979. "Political Will and Family Planning: The Implications of India's Emergency Experience." *Population and Development Review* 5 (1): 29–59.

Hartmann, Betsy. 2010. "The Greening of Hate: An Environmentalist's Essay." Southern Poverty Law Center. Accessed May 20, 2011, from www.splcenter.org.

Huang, Priscilla. 2009. "Over-Breeders and the Population Bomb: The Reemergence of Nativism in Anti-Immigration Policies." In Mazur 2009b, 353–364.

International Union for the Conservation of Nature (IUCN). 2006. "Forest Landscape Restoration to Meet Ghana's Deforestation Challenges." February 8. Accessed from www.iucn.org/about/work/programmes/forest/fp_our_work/fp_our_work_thematic/fp_our_work_flr/?732/Forest-Landscape-Restoration-to-meet-Ghanas-deforestation-challenges.

Kissling, Frances. 2009. "Reconciling Differences: Population, Reproductive Rights, and the Environment." In Mazur 2009b, 383–391.

Kolankiewicz, Leon, and Roy Beck. 2001. *Forsaking Fundamentals: The Environmental Establishment Abandons U.S. Population Stabilization*. Washington, D.C.: Center for Immigration Studies, 2001.

Mazur, Laurie. 2009a. Introduction. In Mazur 2009b, 1–23.

———, ed. 2009b. *A Pivotal Moment: Population, Justice, and the Environmental Challenge*. Washington, D.C.: Island Press.

———. 2010. "Population Matters: Why Population Growth Is So Hard to Talk About and Why We Should Talk about it Anyway." *Conscience* 21 (2): 13–18.

McIntosh, Alison, and Jason Finkle. 1995. "The Cairo Conference on Population and Development: A New Paradigm?" *Population and Development Review* 21 (2): 223–260.

Mensah, Kent. 2011. "Fuel Wood Consuming Ghana's Forest." *Ghanaian Chronicle*, April 12.

Meyerson, Frederick A. B. 2008a. "Reducing Unintended Fertility Should Be a Top International Climate Priority." *Bulletin of the Atomic Scientists*, "Population and Climate Change Roundtable," February 15. Accessed from www.thebulletin.org/web-edition/roundtables/population-and-climate-change.

————. 2008b. "Stabilize Global Population and Tax Carbon to Reduce Per-Capita Emissions." *Bulletin of the Atomic Scientists*, "Population and Climate Change Roundtable," March 19. Accessed from www.thebulletin.org/web-edition/roundtables/population-and-climate-change.

Murtaugh, Paul, and Michael Schlax. 2009. "Reproduction and the Carbon Legacies of Individuals." *Global Environmental Change* 19 (1): 14–20.

Peprah, Peter Takyi. 2010. "Wood-Fuel for Cooking and Its Effect on the Environment." Paper presented at the 2010 Conference on Official Statistics and the Environment, Santiago, Chile, October 20–22.

Pew Research Center. 2008. *The 2008 Pew Global Attitudes Survey in China: The Chinese Celebrate Their Roaring Economy, as They Struggle with Its Costs.* Washington, D.C.: Pew Research Center.

Pope, Carl. 1998. "Think Globally, Act Sensibly: Immigration Is Not the Problem." *AsianWeek*, April 2.

Population Reference Bureau. 2011. "2011 World Population Data Sheet." Accessed July 26, 2011, from www.prb.org/pdf11/2011population-data-sheet_eng.pdf.

"Population, Women's Rights, and Sexual and Reproductive Health." 2009. Population Justice Project, October 1 (posted by Liz). Accessed October 20, 2011, from http://mazur.vernalfroth.com/2009/10/page/5/.

Ryerson, William. 2011. "Unmet Need—Lack of Access or Lack of Cultural and Informational Support?" Website for film *Mother*, March 15. Accessed June 30, 2011, from www.motherthefilm.com/unmet-need.

Sinding, Steven. 2006. "Population and Sexual Reproductive Health and Rights: State of the Field and Some Suggestions for Future Program Actions." Policy brief prepared for the Packard Foundation Population Program Review Task Force, January.

Speidel, J. Joseph, Deborah C. Weiss, Sally A. Ethelston, and Sarah M. Gilbert. 2007. "Family Planning and Reproductive Health: The Link to Environmental Preservation." *Population and Environment* 28 (4/5): 247–258. Bixby Center for Reproductive Health Research and Policy, University of California, San Francisco, October 17. Accessed May 20, 2011 at http://bixbycenter.ucsf.edu.

United Nations Department of Economic and Social Affairs (UNDESA). 2011. "World Population Prospects: The 2010 Revision." New York: United Nations.

United Nations Framework Convention on Climate Change (UNFCCC). 2007. "Investment and Financial Flows to Address Climate Change." October. Accessed June 27, 2011, from http://unfccc.int/resource/docs/publications/financial_flows.pdf.

U.S. Central Intelligence Agency (USCIA). 2011. *The World Factbook 2011*. Washington, D.C.

Wattenberg, Ben. 1997. "The Population Explosion Is Over." *New York Times Magazine*, November 23, 60–63.

Weld, Madeline. 2011. "Deconstructing the Dangerous Dogma of Denial: The Feminist-Environmental Justice Movement and Their Flight from Overpopulation." *(We) Can Do Better*, February 24. Accessed June 27, 2011, from http://candobetter.net/node/2373.

Wire, Thomas. 2009. *Fewer Emitters, Lower Emissions, Less Cost: Reducing Future Carbon Emissions by Investing in Family Planning: A Cost/Benefit Analysis*. London: London School of Economics.

CHAPTER 22

Confronting Finitude

RICHARD LAMM

IT IS OFTEN OBSERVED that the hardest challenge in public policy is to change a policy that has been successful. There is good reason for this. Success deserves respect, and the burden of proof ought to be on those who seek to change a policy that has produced success. Don't abandon what works until the evidence is clear and convincing that it no longer does. Success thus creates a heavy but not insurmountable assumption in favor of the status quo. But "new occasions teach new duties," and time does make "ancient good uncouth."

Clearly, immigration has been good for America. We peopled this continent with immigrants, assimilated groups who had fought each other for centuries in the Old World, and created one of the world's most harmonious and bountiful nations. Why change one of the main pillars of our past success? The answer is that we must change our immigration policies, because reality has changed. Past success can be a trap, blinding us to new realities. When the Statue of Liberty went up in 1886, America had about 60 million people—compared to 310 million today. Immigrants arrived into a "sink or swim" society and prospered using the raw materials of a naturally rich geography.

But that reality is long gone. Americans now live in a cash-wage industrial society with no more virgin land. A cash-wage society needs capital and creativity. We can still take limited numbers of immigrants, but we must make sure their numbers and skill sets make sense in terms of today's economy and the interests of our own citizens. Our immigration policy must fit into other, broader policy goals. We can no longer blindly assume that all immigrants benefit America.

This is not a new thought. Congresswoman Barbara Jordan and the U.S. Commission on Immigration Reform warned us in 1997 that high immigration levels were hurting our own poor by driving down wages and pushing less-skilled, less-educated citizens out of the workforce. The commission argued that we should better synchronize our immigration policy and our labor policy. Recent research confirms that mass immigration costs poor Americans dearly and has played an important role in increasing economic inequality over the past four decades (Borjas 1999, 2004). When you add discouraged workers to our 9 percent unemployment rate, you get a true unemployment rate of nearly 17 percent. Do we not have an important moral duty to set labor policy to benefit our own workers?

America in 2011 had no more jobs than it had in 2000, yet it has taken in 13.5 million immigrants since 2000. We have had zero net job growth in those ten years, yet we have tried to absorb millions of new people. As I write these words, there are six Americans looking for jobs for every new job created. Yet our immigration policies are on automatic pilot, bringing in over a million legal immigrants year after year. Policies forged in a far different economic atmosphere need rethinking.

When change is called for, paradigms should shift. At some point, additional demographic and economic growth run into environmental constraints and turn from assets into liabilities. Then we should consider reining in growth—or accept that nature may rein it in for us. If we stick our heads in the sand today, global warming, peak oil, or some other trauma still may upend our existing social and economic thinking tomorrow. Science and technology may delay but cannot help us avoid the consequences of finiteness; in fact, the science and technology that many point to as our salvation could be part of the problem. They certainly have instilled in us a deep hubris that all human problems are solvable from within current thinking and behavioral patterns.

Public policy and most of our institutions, as presently structured, assume boundless resources and no ecological limits. As a nation, we confidently proclaim that there are no limits that cannot be overcome, and around the world, endless growth also seems an assumption beyond challenge. It will be hard to change our thinking, but we must because we are bumping up against the reality of ecological limits. Nature has a different set of rules, and the larger ecosystem is totally indifferent to human moral codes. Millions of people have died in the past, the just and the unjust, when societies have pushed nature too hard (Diamond 2011).

I think we can better plan for the future by heeding the warning that infinite growth cannot take place in a finite world. The fact that we have been so successful in pushing back certain limits should not dissuade us from believing that limits are real. Human civilization is presently living on the upper shoulders of some incredibly steep geometric growth curves. We have used more resources since 1950 than in all preceding human history. The globe is warming, forests are shrinking, icecaps are melting, coral reefs are dying, fisheries are becoming depleted, species are vanishing, deserts are growing, and freshwater is under more and more demand from agriculture, industry, and burgeoning cities. These are warning signs of a world having breached its carrying capacity.

In 1992, over seventeen hundred of the world's leading scientists, including a majority of Nobel Laureates in science, published a statement called the "World Scientists' Warning to Humanity." It read, in part:

> Human beings and the natural world are on a collision course. Human activities inflict harsh and often irreversible damage on the environment and on critical resources. If not checked, many of our current practices put at serious risk the future that we wish for human society and the plant and animal kingdoms, and may so alter the living world that it will be unable to sustain life in the manner that we know. Fundamental changes are urgent if we are to avoid the collision our present course will bring about. . . .

> The Earth is finite. Its ability to absorb wastes and destructive effluent is finite. Its ability to provide food and energy is finite. Its ability to provide for growing numbers of people is finite. And we are fast approaching many of the Earth's limits. Current economic practices which damage the environment, in both developed and underdeveloped nations, cannot be continued without the risk that vital global systems will be damaged beyond repair. (Union of Concerned Scientists 1992)

When our best scientists tell us this, perhaps we should listen. It is time to give up our faith in technofixes and instead change our mental map of the world, our culture, and our economy, and confront finitude.

⚘

How might an appreciation of limits change long-held views regarding ethics and public policy? Perhaps we might have to change or reinterpret cherished concepts of individual rights, including reproductive rights; at a minimum, we will have to consider trade-offs that we thus far have mostly avoided. For example: the rights to eat sufficient food, drink pure water, and breathe clean air could conflict—arguably already do conflict in many places—with the right to have as many children as one wants. The human rights to sufficient food, water, and other necessary resources may conflict—arguably already do often conflict—with the rights of nonhuman species to those same resources, which they need in order to survive. Human reproductive rights may conflict—arguably already do conflict—with nonhuman reproductive rights, which nonhuman species need in order to avoid extinction. These are difficult practical problems. It is no exaggeration to say that public policy analysts have barely begun to consider them.

Our standard of living, our economic system, our political stability, all require expanding use of energy and resources, and our political, economic, and social thinking largely assumes the indefinite expansion of population and economic activity. We all feel entitled to grow richer every year. Our ideals of social justice require an expanding pie to share with the less fortunate. Progress is identified with growth, and the economies of all nations endeavor to achieve steady increases in consumption. The uncritical and pervasive mindset of growth underlying all these trends and entitlements is manifestly unsustainable and must change. We must reevaluate our trajectory toward ever expanding numbers of people consuming ever greater amounts of resources. The world must learn to live with finitude.

Take immigration and population policy, for example. In the 1990s, two key national commissions were charged to look into these matters in the United States. In 1990, President Bush appointed iconic civil rights leader and congresswoman Barbara Jordan to chair the bipartisan U.S. Commission on Immigration Reform. In its report to Congress, the Jordan Commission noted the value of immigration to the United States, yet it warned: "There are costs as well as benefits from today's immigration. Those workers most at risk in our restructuring economy, low-skilled workers in production and service jobs, are those who directly compete with today's low-skilled immigrants" (U.S. Commission 1997, 2–4). The commission affirmed the need and the right to set immigration policy in the national interest, and with that in mind, it suggested halving current immigration levels, back to 550,000 annually. It also argued forcefully against continued toleration of illegal immigration and for strong measures to combat it.

In 1993, President Clinton convened the President's Council on Sustainable Development; again, a bipartisan group of cabinet officers and business and labor leaders. The council explored many key aspects of ecological sustainability, including, commendably, population growth. As it put matters in its 1996 report to the president: "Managing population growth, resources, and wastes is essential to ensuring that the total impact of these factors is within the bounds of sustainability. Stabilizing the population without changing consumption and waste production patterns would not be enough, but it would make an immensely challenging task more manageable. In the United States, each is necessary; neither alone is sufficient." One of the council's ten major suggestions for creating a sustainable society was: "Move toward stabilization of U.S. population" (President's Council 1996). Although the council was too delicate to say so, in a country where immigration accounts for about two-thirds of annual population increase, "moving toward population stabilization" would necessarily involve reducing immigration.

One of the most interesting aspects of the findings of both the council and the commission was the way they moved inexorably from good progressive goals—sustainability, fair wages for workers—to recommendations to reduce immigration. Their analyses suggest that liberals must rethink our knee-jerk support for mass immigration if we want to achieve key political goals. Indeed, such arguments can be pushed further. If we want to sustain or strengthen safety net programs, we must restrict the benefits to those legally in the country. If we want to protect or expand the amount of habitat, water, and other resources available to other species, we will have to limit immigration-fueled population growth. The price of compassion is restriction. You cannot have Social Security, food stamps, and other safety net programs open to a world of seven billion people. You cannot provide resources for other species if you have already given them away to people, no matter how deserving. Liberal programs demand borders, and sustaining an achieved quality of life means respecting limits (Daly 1996, 145–157).

Today, *illegal* immigration is having heavy economic, social, demographic, and environmental impacts, and it is past time to make the liberal case for controlling illegal immigration. I first got interested in illegal immigration when a Colorado packing plant fired a group of Hispanic Americans and replaced them with illegal immigrants. A small group of the fired workers came to me, as governor, to complain. There was little I could do. I called the president of the packing plant, who nicely told me to mind my own business and claimed that all his new workers had green cards, which indeed they had, bought in the underground market along with fake Social Security cards for twenty-five dollars apiece. Sometime later, the Immigration and Naturalization Service raided the plant, but the workforce evaporated during the raid, to return (or to be replaced by other illegal immigrants) shortly thereafter. The plant continued to employ many illegal workers, until it was bought out and closed ten years later.

It is easy to see why this underground workforce is attractive to employers. The owner of this particular packing plant essentially told me he was not going to pay legal workers sixteen dollars an hour, plus benefits, when he could hire illegal workers at ten dollars an hour without benefits. This type of reasoning will forever lock the bottom quartile of our American wage earners into poverty, for how are they ever to obtain a decent wage when employers have access to endless pools of illegal unskilled labor? Illegal immigrants are generally good, hard-working people who will quietly accept minimum wage or less, don't get or expect health care or other benefits, and, if they complain, can easily be fired. Even the minimum U.S. wage is attractive to workers from countries whose standard of living is a fraction of ours.

But that is not to say this is "cheap labor." It may be "cheap" to those who pay the wages, but for the rest of us it is clearly "subsidized" labor, as taxpayers pick up the costs of education, health, and other municipal costs imposed by this workforce. These costs have become substantial as illegal immigration has increased and as more illegal workers stay longer and raise families. Such "cheap" illegal labor is even more expensive for those working-class Americans who are driven from their jobs by unfair competition, or who see their wages decline in flooded job markets.

My own position is that the federal government should set immigration levels (and enforce immigration laws) so as to benefit American workers in ways that reduce, rather than increase, economic inequality in our country. Some of my fellow Democrats may disagree, and instead choose to set those levels so as to benefit poor people from other countries. That is fine, but I insist that it is a choice. Whatever choice we make, it should be based on a realistic understanding of limits and on the likely consequences of the choices made.

❦

Even more important, we must consider ecological sustainability and our moral duties in the crowded, damaged world human beings are busy

creating. In my twenty years of elective office and forty years following the
political polls in Colorado, population growth or environmental problems
have always been among the top three issues of concern. Coloradans are
extraordinarily protective of their local environments, and most understand that preserving wild nature and sufficient natural resources means
limiting population growth, at both state and federal levels. But how
should we think about our nation's moral obligations to other nations that
have exceeded their carrying capacities? If a nation is having trouble feeding its own people, what duties does *it* owe to other nations? Can we even
look into such a public policy black hole?

One scholar who has explored these matters, Herschel Elliott, sees
chaos ahead and warns that we are unlikely to be the first species in the
world to be exempt from ecological limits. He doubts whether growth
can permanently solve growth-driven problems; we must move to sustainability, but this will require us to reject much of the paradigm on which
the human-centered ethical thinking of the Western world is based (Elliott
1996, 2005).

Elliott believes that traditional, abstract ethics assumes an infinite
world. But in a finite world, public policy must make not only moral sense
but also ecological sense. No ethics can demand what the ecosystem cannot support. We cannot have a moral duty to supply something whereby
the act of supplying it further harms the ecosystem and undermines life on
this Earth, leaving a mess behind for future generations to deal with. We
cannot disregard the factual consequences of supposedly moral behavior.

Elliott sees excessive abstraction and anthropocentrism as the twin obstacles to sustainability. He points out that however laudatory and well
meaning in human terms, the ecosystem will not give priority to humans
over every other living kind. And he insists that neither religion nor conventional ethical thinking can trump ecological limits, stating:

> The first duty of moral behavior is to preserve the endurance and the
> resilience of the Earth's system of living things. This principle cannot be
> justified by appeals to reason or the infallible revelations of God. It cannot
> be justified by valid inferences from a human-centered definition of value
> or from moral principles which are merely assumed. Furthermore, it can-
> not be refuted by appeal to public opinion or to the great moral traditions
> of the Western World. It is not subject to scholarly rebuttal by profession-
> als in moral philosophy. Rather, it has a physical and biological necessity.
> (Elliott 2005, 18–19)

I believe that Elliott is right—that we should commit ourselves foremost to preserving the endurance and resilience of life on Earth. We must reconcile our thinking and culture to the ecological system that surrounds us. Those who passionately believe that there are no limits and that population growth or economic growth can go on indefinitely should at least consider what we should do if this belief is proved wrong. Once again: we are living on the shoulders of some steep and clearly unsustainable geometric curves of demographic, economic, and resource-consumptive growth. No ethical code should demand of people duties and behaviors that the natural world—the very ground of our livelihood and well-being—cannot support. We need to construct an ethical code based on both human rights and ecological sustainability.

We should start this exploration now. Moral codes, no matter how logical, and human rights, no matter how compassionate, must live and make sense within the limitations of the ecosystem. Moral life cannot be constructed solely in a thought-world. But to state that the old rules and rights have to be rethought does not mean that no rules apply. Geopolitics requires that we help deal with problems that, at least in the case of global warming, we helped to cause. Few argue with the principle that a nation owes its first duty to its own citizens. But we also cannot be an island of plenty amid a world of chaos. We have done very little thinking to address what happens when global warming or peak oil manifest themselves in societal breakdown. We need to get on with it. Our public policy must adapt to our ecological system. At a minimum, we should all be able to agree that our economic system ought not destroy our ecological system. Yet that is what it is doing now.

BIBLIOGRAPHY

Borjas, George. 1999. *Heaven's Door: Immigration Policy and the American Economy.* Princeton, N.J.: Princeton University Press.
———. 2004. "Increasing the Supply of Labor through Immigration: Measuring the Impact on Native-Born Workers." Washington, D.C.: Center for Immigration Studies.
Daly, Herman. 1996. *Beyond Growth: The Economics of Sustainable Development.* Boston: Beacon Press.
Diamond, Jared. 2011. *Collapse: How Societies Choose to Fail or Succeed.* Rev. ed. New York: Penguin Books. (Orig. pub. 2004.)

Elliott, Herschel. 1996. "The Absurdity of a Human-Centered Ethics." *Population and Environment* 17 (5): 427–436.

———. 2005. *Ethics for a Finite World: An Essay Concerning a Sustainable Future.* Golden, Colo.: Fulcrum.

President's Council on Sustainable Development. 1996. *Sustainable America: A New Consensus for Prosperity, Opportunity, and a Healthy Environment for the Future.* Washington, D.C. Accessed from http://clinton2.nara.gov/PCSD/Publications/TF_Reports/amer-top.html.

Union of Concerned Scientists. 1992. "World Scientists' Warning to Humanity." Accessed May 4, 2011, at www.ucsusa.org/about/1992-world-scientists.html.

U.S. Commission on Immigration Reform. 1997. *Becoming an American: Immigration and Immigrant Policy: Executive Summary.* Washington, D.C.: U.S. Commission on Immigration Reform.

CHAPTER 23

For a Species Right to Exist

WINTHROP STAPLES III AND PHILIP CAFARO

T HE LEAD AUTHOR of this article first started thinking about species rights when still a child. One day, when I was eleven, I heard
heavy machinery and looked out the front door. A bulldozer was scrap-
ing the trees off the undeveloped land on the other side of our street. I
asked my dad what they were doing, and he replied that the workers were
going to build houses in the woods where I hiked and set box traps for the
animals that I always released. I asked why they had to build the houses.
Dad answered, "People need houses to live in, and there are always more
people." I think I surprised both of us when I heard myself say, "Why
do there always have to be more people?" and "Where are the animals
supposed to live?" I clearly recall this as one of the few times my dad, a
World War II veteran, carpenter, and engineer who genuinely did know
just about everything, could not answer one of my questions.

Watching the destruction, I knew, deep down, that those animals be-
longed there, that they had a *right* to those woods, and that what I was
seeing was wrong. As I learned more about the history of the place where I
lived, I also remember feeling deprived, because the Blue Hills Reservation
and other wooded areas in Randolph, Massachusetts, did not have deer
with enormous antlers, or what our colonial ancestors called "catamount"
sneaking around, trying to kill them. I knew that the deer and cougar
should be there, and felt as if some members of my family were missing.

In the decades that followed, I traveled the world, learning about many
species and working to protect them: lynx in Alaska, chestnut trees in

New England, Amur leopards in the Russian Far East, black bear in the American South. After a lifetime of studying and working to protect wildlife, I am more convinced than ever that other species have a right to continue to exist here on Earth and that future children have a right to know and appreciate them. As we argue below, defending other species' right to exist is the right thing to do—for them and for us. In what follows, we maintain that species have a *moral* right to continued existence free from untimely anthropogenic extinction, and that this should be guaranteed as a *legal* right under national and international law. We also consider the practical implications of recognizing such a right, one of which is a commitment to reducing human populations.

AN INTRODUCTION TO RIGHTS

Rights center on "the three *R*'s": respect, restraint, and resources. To assert a right is to claim that people should respect some person (or other entity), act with restraint toward him or her (or it), and allow him or her (or it) a fair share of resources.

Historically, as Cass Sunstein reminds us, "rights are a product of concrete historical experiences with wrongs" (2004, 35–36). Biologists tell us that humanity is currently extinguishing species at a rate approximately one thousand times faster than the historical background rate (Reid et al. 2005). We have set in motion the sixth great extinction event in the history of Earth—originally as the unconscious byproduct of demographic and economic growth, but now, more and more, due to conscious and deliberate political and economic policies. This is an immense wrong, which we should resist with all the tools at our disposal, including the conceptual and legal tool of rights.

As Ronald Dworkin (1984) has noted, in the modern world, "rights are trumps." Rights talk is the way we articulate our most important moral claims today, and well-established rights claims are hard to override. As mass extinction accelerates, claims asserting species rights therefore seem necessary to properly articulate our moral duties vis-à-vis other species. Practically, because rights are the legal coin of the realm in modern constitutional democracies, establishing a species legal right to exist can help to reduce anthropogenic species extinctions (Stone 1996) and move us toward a more just and sustainable world.

To focus discussion, let us define *rights* in more detail. Any such definition engages complex philosophical issues. But at their core, rights are *entitlements* that people act in certain ways toward us and *entitlements* to key resources that we need for our well-being. They are *justified claims* on others, with correlative *duties* that they act (or refrain from acting) in certain ways. They promote and preserve certain *interests and achievements* that we judge to be of great value. Rights also promote *freedom to* be what we want to be and *freedom from* unwanted or harmful actions of others. Finally, rights are *trumps*: powerful claims that tend to outweigh nonrights claims.

Currently there are two main ways that political philosophers try to justify moral rights and determine which moral rights people have (Wenar 2010). *Status theories* argue that because of what people are, we should respect them by accepting rights that limit how we may treat one another. *Interest theories* argue that rights are tools for protecting, maximizing, or fairly distributing some essential or primary goods. We believe that status theories and interest theories both capture important aspects of rights, and that they should be brought together in a more comprehensive *eudaemonistic theory* of rights (Sen 1994; Nussbaum 2006, 284–291). In this approach, rights are key tools for enabling human flourishing. We should uphold rights (rights have normative force) because of what people are and can be. People as people deserve respect, and we show that respect by upholding their rights and promoting their interests. But we only appreciate the full value of rights and understand how to balance rights when they conflict by pressing on to specify a full account of human flourishing and by showing how promoting rights furthers this flourishing in various ways.

ARGUMENT FOR A SPECIES MORAL RIGHT TO EXIST

Of course, *flourishing* is an organic metaphor (from *flower*). Other species can flourish, too. In a world where people continue to appropriate more and more of the habitat and resources all species need, we face an obvious question: Do we want other species to continue to flourish on Earth? If the answer is yes, then we need to affirm their right to do so. Such an affirmation is needed to wake humanity up to our moral responsibilities toward other species and to provide the legal and rhetorical tools necessary, as a practical matter, to preserve species from extinction (CELDF n.d.).

The authors value the existence and achievements of other species. We thus expand the claim "rights are key tools for enabling human flourishing" as follows: "Rights are key tools for enabling the flourishing of *all* life, human and nonhuman." We further assert that natural species have a right to continued existence free from anthropogenic extinction.

In his article "Are There Any Absolute Rights?" Alan Gewirth (1981) argues that all persons have an absolute right against homicide, or unjust killing. Whether such a right really is absolute, in theory or practice, is debatable, but clearly the right to life is a fundamental human right. Without it, our lives and projects hang by a thread. Without it, other rights have little point or purpose. Before we can talk about how rights improve our lives, we must secure life itself. So the right to life is the first and most important right for persons.

In the same way, the right to continued existence is the first and most important right to uphold on behalf of other species. The right against untimely extinction is paramount. A genuine commitment to this right entails others, such as the right to a certain amount of resources and habitat and the right to continue to evolve without human interference.

To return to our definition of rights, embracing a species moral right to exist means affirming *entitlements* that people refrain from activities (particularly economic activities) that endanger species; and *entitlements* that we secure to all species the habitat and resources they need to survive and thrive. It means making *claims* on people that we take to be rationally *justified*, with correlative *duties* that they act through their governments to secure the habitat and resources needed by other species; that they refrain from consuming in ways that over-appropriate other species' essential resources; and that the corporations that provide them with goods and services be compelled likewise to act with restraint. While it does not mean ascribing a conscious *interest* to other species in their continued existence (Sandler and Crane 2006), it does mean recognizing their persistence in reproducing and refining a natural kind that we identify as a good kind— and recognizing this as an *achievement* of great creativity and lasting value. It involves promoting other species' *freedom to* be what they are and to evolve into what they will be, and *freedom from* untimely human extinction or unnecessary human interference. Finally, such a right to continued existence is a powerful *trumping* claim that should outweigh nonessential human interests. Just as the presence of sick, uninsured children in a nation justifies taxing citizens' private property to provide those children with health care, so the presence of an endangered species, reduced to its last population or last few members, outweighs a real estate developer's right to build on a plot of land or a community's right to dam a river or build a new power plant.

What ultimately justifies a species' moral right to exist? Recall that status theories argue that because of what *people* are, we should respect them, by accepting rights that limit how we may treat one another. Key characteristics that many philosophers have argued mandate such respect are human rationality, free will, autonomy, and creativity. These are indeed wonderful capacities that deserve to be respected, preserved, and enhanced through securing people's rights.

In the same way, we can argue that we should respect other species for what *they* are. In general, species are the primary examples and repositories of organic nature's order, creativity, and diversity. They represent many thousands and often millions of years of activity and achievement. The organisms comprising a species show incredible functional, organizational, and behavioral complexity. Every species, like every person, is unique, with its own history and destiny. All this supports the view that species generally possess great intrinsic value (Rolston 1988; Agar 2001) and hence (we argue) that they possess certain rights that help affirm and defend that value.

In particular cases, species may be keystone predators or humble detritivores; flashy birds-of-paradise or exquisitely camouflaged sparrows; towering redwoods, home to myriads of other species, or diminutive mites, inhabiting the interstices of the bristles of a particular bird species' feathers. These particularities, too, may support species' rights. Arguably, we should preserve the cheetah's right to exist because it can run up to seventy miles per hour while bringing down gazelles. We should preserve chimpanzees in the wild because they engage in complex social interactions, tool making, and the rudiments of language, in addition to being our closest nonhuman kin. We should preserve horseshoe crabs because of their extreme longevity as a species, perhaps four hundred million years in essentially the same form; and the Arctic tern because its peregrinations tie together the Earth's Arctic and Antarctic regions (two times a year!).

All these species are what they are, and what they are is good. It is a fatal mistake to take human beings as the template for all natural goodness and decide what has importance or ultimate value, what shall live or die, based on their similarities to us. It is simply another form of unjustified self-partiality and anthropocentrism to do so.

The possession of rights defines membership within modern societies. Rights holders are members of the moral community and must be treated with respect and restraint. Non–rights holders are not members and may be treated as mere means to genuine community members' ends. The proposal to recognize a species right to exist is thus also a proposal to extend the bounds of our moral community. As Aldo Leopold put it, the goal is to establish a "land ethic" that "enlarges the boundaries of the community to include soils, waters, plants, and animals, or collectively, the land." Such an ethics affirms the "right" of other species "to continued existence, and, at least in spots, their continued existence in a natural state" (Leopold 1949, 239–240). It is no accident that Leopold asserts a "biotic right" against untimely species extinction several times in *A Sand County Almanac*. In the end, affirming such rights and affirming a "land ethic" come to essentially the same thing.

POSSIBLE OBJECTIONS

A number of objections are possible to this ascription of a species moral right against untimely extinction (for a fuller discussion of possible objections, see Staples 2009). Many center on the seeming strangeness of applying the term *rights* in such a novel way. Rights are typically ascribed to individual human beings: not to larger wholes, and not to nonhuman beings. Stating a version of this objection, Tom Regan writes: "The rights view restricts inherent value and rights to individuals. Because species are not individuals, the rights view does not recognize the rights of species to anything" (Regan 2004, xxxix). Similarly, Bryan Norton writes: "It might be suggested that rights of species are somehow generated from the interests of species, but the concept of interest of species is not at all clear. Individual lives are bounded by birth and death, and these parameters guide judgments of individual interest. Anything that threatens to cause the death of an individual is clearly against that individual's interest, other things being equal. But [the same cannot be said about the end of a species]" (Norton 1992, 170–171). Ronald Sandler largely concurs:

> For something to have interests, it must be goal or end directed, otherwise it is difficult to substantiate claims about its being harmed or benefited. [Individual] organisms are goal directed—they are organized towards accomplishing things like avoiding predators and reproducing—so an organism is harmed (or benefited) when its capacity to pursue its good is impaired (or improved). . . . Species fail to satisfy the conditions for having interest-based intrinsic value even when they are conceived as individuals, rather than collectives. (Sandler 2009, 426–427)

In response to these kinds of objections, proponents have argued convincingly that species are not just random collections but real entities, with a persisting, historical (if open-ended) identity (Hull 1976; Rolston 1989a). They have noted that biologists often speak and write about human actions *harming* species (e.g., "the failure in recent decades to preserve sufficient sage grouse habitat has harmed the grouse, and led to a steep decline in its numbers"). In a bit more of a stretch, some have argued that species' persistence through time, instantiating forms generation after generation, is analogous to individual organisms' goal-directedness; and thus, that species manifest a sort of interest in their own persistence (Johnson 1983). Much has been written about whether ascriptions of harm, interests, goal-directedness, or a good-of-their-own are true or false, or whether they are literally true or merely metaphorically suggestive, when applied to species.

This debate, however, appears to rest on a mistake: the anthropocentric mistake of taking our paradigm rights holder as an unquestionable template for the wider ascription of rights. The true criterion for moral rights holding is whether the extinction of a species is an immense and preventable wrong, which destroys an entity of great objective intrinsic value. It is and it does. Therefore, we propose, species have a moral right to continued existence.

Nothing turns on whether asserting such a right "seems odd" or "sounds funny" to our ears, any more than the truth of antebellum abolitionists' claims that African Americans had a right to freedom depended on how those claims sounded to slave owners. Such claims for species' rights are bound to seem strange, precisely because our relationship to nature has been so selfish and unjust. Eventually, we may hope that like the claim that African Americans deserve to be treated with respect, claims regarding other species' right to exist will come to seem true to most people and then, eventually, *obviously* true.

Justifying a species right to exist does not depend on making the case that species have interests or on showing that the extinction of a species harms it in the way that an individual organism may be harmed. There is more to value in the world than tightly integrated individual organisms, and just as a hawk is not a handsaw, an individual sharp-shinned hawk is not the species *Accipiter striatus*. Similarly, nothing of ethical import depends on the degree to which a species' evolutionary trajectory is a function of an internal goal-directness or "will" to a certain kind of order, as opposed to environmental factors, or mere chance. Answering such questions may be important for a scientific understanding of particular species, or of the evolution of species in general. But the answers seem unlikely to alter our views regarding whether or not species should be preserved from untimely extinction due to the actions of rational moral agents.

The bottom line is that these natural kinds are good kinds. The flourishing of the diversity of life is a great good, while the anthropogenic extinction of species, ripping great holes in the tapestry of life, is a great and preventable evil. Hence these species have a moral right to continued existence. Restricting rights to human beings—setting ourselves up as the be-all and end-all of Earthly existence—is selfish and lacks any convincing rational justification.

ARGUMENT FOR A SPECIES LEGAL RIGHT TO EXIST

In addition to arguing for a species *moral* right to continued existence, we also contend, in agreement with Favre (1979), Stone (1996), and the Community Environmental Defense Fund (CELDF n.d.), that the nations of the world should create *legal* rights against untimely species extinction through national legislation and binding international treaties. They should do so, in part, as a means to uphold species' moral right to exist. But they should also do so to further *human* interests and to uphold future generations' moral right to know and experience wild nature. We believe both human and nonhuman flourishing would be furthered by creating and enforcing a species legal right to exist.

Legal rights are purely conventional. They are human creations, and we may deploy them creatively, if that furthers our goals. If granting legal rights to species can further human flourishing, this in itself seems sufficient justification for creating them. Doing so would no more depend on showing that species have interests or can be harmed than granting corporations rights to own property depends on proving that corporations are conscious or sentient.

Legal rights have proven powerful tools in helping create societies where human beings can flourish, and there is solid evidence that securing species' rights can help them to do likewise. Baird Callicott and William Grove-Fanning (2009) argue plausibly that the U.S. Endangered Species Act (ESA), passed in 1973, created a de facto species legal right to continued existence. The legal protections provided by the ESA have prevented numerous species from going extinct; making such a right explicit and strengthening its provisions for protecting critical habitat could help many more species in the United States recover and thrive.

In 2008, the people of Ecuador added a new chapter on the rights of nature to their national constitution (Revkin 2008). The additions, proposed by a constitutional convention and ratified by popular vote, included the following:

> Article 1. Nature or *Pachamama*, where life is reproduced and exists, has the right to exist, persist, maintain itself and regenerate its own vital cycles, structure, functions, and evolutionary processes.

> Article 3. The State will motivate natural and juridical persons as well as collectives to protect nature; it will promote respect towards all the elements that form an ecosystem.

> Article 4. The State will apply precaution and restriction measures in all the activities that can lead to the extinction of species, the destruction of ecosystems, or the permanent alteration of natural cycles.

While enacting legal rights for nature will not preserve species all by itself, it does place new tools at the disposal of environmental groups (Doctorow 2010). Along with other political and economic reforms—and perhaps helping to spur them forward—securing rights for nature could play an important role in preserving species in Ecuador. At a minimum, such examples of de jure or de facto species legal rights show that there are no insurmountable "conceptual" difficulties in assigning rights to species.

In judging proposals to extend legal rights, we should look closely at the nature of the putative rights holders and ask whether we can make sense of assigning rights to them. On the other hand, we should also look to the potential impacts of new rights claims on other individuals *and on the community as a whole*. For new legal rights create new kinds of communities. That is their goal—along with protecting particular rights holders. We agree with Joseph Raz (1992), who argues that particular rights, when justified, are justified with reference to their impacts on society as a whole, and that the proper scope and reach of rights should be specified with reference to their wider impacts on society.

Our full brief for establishing a species legal right to exist would attempt to consider all its important potential impacts, on people and on other species, and show how a society that upheld such a right would be superior to one that did not, all things considered. Such a brief is beyond the scope of this essay. But our argument for establishing a species legal right to exist, in outline, runs as follows:

(1) Nonhuman species have a moral right to continued existence free from untimely anthropogenic extinction.

(2) All human beings, present and future, have an equal moral right to experience and connect to wild nature.

(3) Establishing a species legal right to exist would not unduly burden human beings.

(4) Establishing a species legal right to exist could act as a valuable brake on economic growth, which currently threatens both human and nonhuman well-being.

We should establish a species legal right to exist.

Each of these premises stands in need of clarification and justification; the previous section began to provide this for premise (1). Regarding premise (2), many people believe their lives would be significantly worse without opportunities to explore and experience wild nature. Expressing this belief in the language of rights comes naturally to environmentalists. "Who has decided," Rachel Carson asked in *Silent Spring*:

> who has the *right* to decide, for the countless legions of people who were not consulted, that the supreme value is a world without insects, even though it be also a sterile world ungraced by the curving wing of a bird in flight. The decision is that of the authoritarian temporarily entrusted with power; he has made it during a moment of inattention by millions to whom beauty and the ordered world of nature still have a meaning that is deep and imperative. (1962, 118–119, emphasis in the original)

Future human flourishing arguably depends, in many ways, on access, appreciation, and connection to the natural world (Rolston 1989b; Cafaro 2001). In an address to journalists, Carson affirmed: "I am not afraid of being thought a sentimentalist, when I stand here tonight and tell you that I believe natural beauty has a necessary place in the spiritual development of any individual or any society. I believe that whenever we destroy beauty, or whenever we substitute something man-made and artificial for a natural feature of the earth, we have retarded some part of man's spiritual growth" (1998, 160). This "spiritual growth"—which following Carson we may interpret broadly as humanity's emotional, artistic, scientific, moral, and overall cognitive development—arguably depends on common citizens' continued equal access to a full, diverse, wild nature, not a world of mere scraps and tatters.

About one hundred years before Carson spoke, reflecting on the diminished ecological landscape around him in Concord, Massachusetts, Henry Thoreau wrote in his journal on March 23, 1856: "When I consider that the nobler animals have been exterminated here, I cannot but feel as if I lived in a tamed, and, as it were, emasculated country. . . . I take infinite pains to know the phenomena of the spring, thinking that I have here the entire poem, and then, to my chagrin, I hear that it is but an imperfect copy that I possess and have read, that my ancestors have torn out many of the first leaves and grandest passages, and mutilated it in many places" (1962, 2:985). Like Thoreau, many of us believe that our descendants will "wish to know an entire heaven and an entire Earth." We believe they have a right to explore and know the great beauty, grace, and wisdom contained in wild nature. We should do all we can to safeguard that right.

Regarding premise (3), we need to acknowledge that establishing a species legal right to exist necessarily involves *some* burdens on people—limiting our freedom of action; bringing economic costs as well as benefits—and that such a right *could* be interpreted or applied so stringently that it would indeed result in unacceptable burdens. But the same is true for any legal right. Individual rights only find their proper scope and limit within a system of rights, interpreted intelligently, with reference to their overall purpose. We believe such intelligent interpretation is possible for a species right to exist and attempt to provide it in the following section of this essay. Those who believe our suggestions go too far, or not far enough, are free to propose alternative implementation strategies.

At the same time, those who reject a species right to exist, due to the supposed burdens it places on people, should do so explicitly, in full knowledge of the depauperate world they are helping to justify and create. Just as those who propose a new right have considerable explaining to do, so do those who oppose such a right (if it is at all plausible). How do the burdens of setting aside sufficient habitat and resources for other species compare to the losses, human and nonhuman, that will occur under the moral status quo? By all means, take your stand for or against creating a species legal right to exist. Then imagine your position being accepted and acted upon by your society. Then imagine explaining the results to your descendants, one hundred or five hundred years from now.

Regarding premise (4), we note that many individuals and corporations oppose measures to protect endangered species because such measures cost them money, while a main reason given by political opponents of such measures is that they impede economic growth. Defenders typically respond by pointing to the small economic costs of endangered species protection relative to the economy as a whole and by supporting efforts to compensate individuals who are disproportionately impacted by protection efforts: for example, reimbursing ranchers who lose livestock to wolves. We support such practical arguments and policies.

In addition, we argue that future human well-being depends on slowing economic growth, not accelerating it. The benefits of further economic growth in wealthy, overdeveloped societies such as the United States are negligible (Kasser 2002; Layard 2005), while such growth is the main driver of climate change and other global ecological catastrophes that threaten to undermine the key ecosystem services on which we all depend (Speth 2009). Contemporary societies and their governments are so blinded by orthodox economic ideology that they find it hard even to consider slowing economic growth, much less taking concrete steps to do so (Cafaro 2011). Therefore, measures that slow growth indirectly—such as workers' rights to generous vacation time, or unemployment compensation, or a species right against extinction—may be doubly valuable in achieving their direct purposes and in slowing toxic economic growth.

In summary, a comprehensive argument for a species legal right to exist depends at least as much on exploring a more intelligent, less materialistic conception of human flourishing and defending the rights of future generations as it does on affirming ethical limits to humanity's claims on Earth's resources. It depends as much on justice for people as on justice for other species. It depends on a more idealistic view of how much we *should* take from nature, but also on a more realistic view of how much we *can* take from nature. Reason's twin voices of justice and prudence speak in harmony, we believe, in favor of our proposal.

IMPLICATIONS OF ACKNOWLEDGING A SPECIES RIGHT
TO EXIST

What actions would be necessary to implement a species legal right to continued existence? The most important would be to preserve sufficient habitat for other species. Only 11.5 percent of Earth's land area is presently within protected areas (Kunzig 2008), with much less protected in the oceans, and wildlands are being developed or degraded rapidly in many parts of the world. Island biogeography's species-area theory predicts that if 90 percent of worldwide habitat is lost for wildlife—roughly the same percentage now outside protected areas—then approximately half of Earth's species will be driven extinct (MacArthur and Wilson 1967; Primack 2010, 145–150).[1] Current trends make a future "build out" or appropriation of all habitats outside protected areas highly probable: above all, humanity's continued failure to stabilize our population. United Nations demographers have recently revised upward their projections for world population growth, with human numbers expected to balloon to 9.3 billion by 2050 (UNPD 2011). It is hard to imagine people restraining their conversion of terrestrial and marine habitats, when they will need to expand the number of houses, grow and harvest more food, produce more energy, and satisfy the many other demands an ever-growing population will make.

If we want to preserve species, then, we must end this demographic onslaught as quickly as possible (Foreman 2011). At the same time, we must set aside habitat. Species-area theory predicts that placing 50 percent of every major habitat type in protected area status—and sufficiently limiting pollution and climate change so that this habitat remains useful to wildlife—should ensure that approximately 85 percent of existing species survive into the twenty-second century (Wilson 2002). Combined with species reintroductions and extra protection for biologically rich areas, that percentage might be pushed up to 90 percent or higher, and the overwhelming majority of nonhuman species could be preserved (Primack 2010, 351–360). An additional benefit of moving quickly to greatly increase designated wildlife habitat is that limiting the land available for development would force people to confront limits to growth that much more quickly.

As a start toward operationalizing a species legal right to exist, we would propose the following:

(1) a 50/50 sharing of Earth's terrestrial and marine ecosystems, including its most productive ecosystems, between human and nonhuman beings, with half of such landscapes set aside for biodiversity protection and evolutionary viability (Schmeigelow et al. 2006); and

(2) a further targeting of the richest terrestrial and marine ecosystems for extra preservation and recovery of extirpated species populations.

Thus we would preserve habitat, the sine qua non of species protection. But we also need to make sure that habitat remains usable by other species, and that they have all the resources they need to flourish. Hence we would further propose that people

(3) strictly limit their use of the other key resources on which nonhuman species depend—above all, in terrestrial ecosystems, fresh water; and that we

(4) strictly limit air, water, and other types of pollution to keep habitat and resources in sufficiently good condition for other species (and us) to use.

By taking these steps we would preserve sufficient resources overall. But we also need to make sure that we preserve habitat and resources for other species *over the long term*. Hence we further propose that human societies

(5) transition from endless growth economies to steady-state economies (Daly 2007); and

(6) humanely stabilize and then gradually reduce the human population (Grant 2001).

Today the global population stands at seven billion and climbing. As general targets, we might seek to end population growth within fifteen to twenty years, peaking at eight billion, reduce the global population to six billion people by the end of the twenty-first century, and reduce it further to two or three billion people by the end of the following century.

Thus we might preserve sufficient resources for ourselves and other species, in perpetuity. Thus *and thus only*, we claim, will we have any chance to create genuinely sustainable societies. As a bonus, population reduction would improve the lives of billions of the world's poorest people. As several recent reports on progress toward achieving the United Nation's Millennium Development Goals convincingly show, high birth rates and overpopulation are key factors undermining efforts to boost well-being in the developing world (APPG 2007; United Nations Population Fund 2009).

Proposals (1)–(4) or something roughly like them are necessary to operationalize a species legal right to continued existence and flourishing. But we doubt that (1)–(4) are achievable without proposals (5) and (6). In the long run, the continued imperative to grow economically or demographically will derail the most earnest and rigorous efforts to accomplish (1)–(4) (Czech 2002). Hence establishing a species legal right to exist and flourish implies acting on proposals (5) and (6) as well.

In addition, it is not clear that humanity can escape enacting proposals (5) and (6) even if it chooses to write off other species' rights. Ever more people and ever more human economic activity are impossible to square with sustaining the resources and ecosystem services necessary for *people* to lead comfortable and enjoyable lives in the future. That is the clear, if largely unacknowledged, lesson of climate change and other examples of planetwide environmental degradation (McKibben 2007). So even on a selfish, anthropocentric definition of sustainability, where we ignore proposals (1)–(3) and only pursue proposal (4), pollution abatement, as far as is good for ourselves, we likely will have to move on proposals (5) and (6). Humanity must face up to limits to growth.

This is no cause for lamentation. We believe acknowledging other species' right to exist and adopting proposals (1)–(6) would create a better world than the one we are constructing by blindly pursuing the demographic and economic status quo; for other species, certainly, but also for people. It would be a world where people are less likely to suffer hunger, sickness, resource wars, and other ills stemming from the overuse and collapse of ecosystems. It would be a world where the human right to experience and celebrate wild nature is more widely ensured. It would be a world with significant room for human activity, but also one where we set aside places where such activity is largely absent; where we cultivate wisdom as well as cleverness, and self-restraint as well as self-development. Thus it would be a world with happier, freer, more just—and fewer—people; one where, when children asked their parents, "Where are the animals supposed to live?" they could answer, honestly and proudly: "Right here, next to us, forever."

NOTES

1. Some question whether extinction estimates given by calculations using the species-area curve are too high (He and Hubbell 2011), but "the model has been empirically validated to the point of acceptance by most biologists" (Primack 2010, 146). Even skeptics acknowledge that a huge wave of species extinctions due to habitat loss is underway. If traditional species-area theory overestimates likely species extinctions due to habitat loss, this error is probably more than compensated for by other factors that undermine species survival worldwide. These include greatly increased chemical pollution, competition from invasive species, emergent diseases, rapid anthropogenic climate change, and the fact that some of the most biologically productive habitat types have been almost totally developed.

BIBLIOGRAPHY

Agar, Nicholas. 2001. *Life's Intrinsic Value: Science, Ethics, and Nature.* New York: Columbia University Press.

All Party Parliamentary Group on Population, Development and Reproductive Health (APPG). 2007. *Return of the Population Growth Factor: Its Impact upon the Millennium Development Goals.* London: House of Commons.

Cafaro, Philip. 2001. "The Naturalist's Virtues." *Philosophy in the Contemporary World* 8 (2): 85–99.

———. 2011. "Beyond Business as Usual: Alternative Wedges to Avoid Catastrophic Climate Change and Create Sustainable Societies." In *The Ethics of Global Climate Change*, edited by Denis G. Arnold, 192–215. Cambridge: Cambridge University Press.

Callicott, Baird, and William Grove-Fanning. 2009. "Should Endangered Species Have Standing? Toward Legal Rights for Listed Species." *Social Philosophy and Policy* 26 (2): 317–352. DOI: 10.1017/S0265052509090268.

Carson, Rachel. 1962. *Silent Spring.* New York: Fawcett.

———. 1998. *Lost Woods: The Discovered Writing of Rachel Carson.* Edited by Linda Lear. Boston: Beacon Press.

Community Environmental Legal Defense Fund (CELDF). N.d. "Rights of Nature." Accessed June 2011 from www.celdf.org/section.php?id=42.

Czech, Brian. 2002. *Shoveling Fuel for a Runaway Train: Errant Economists, Shameful Spenders, and a Plan to Stop Them All.* Berkeley: University of California Press.

Daly, Herman. 2007. *Ecological Economics and Sustainable Development: Selected Essays of Herman Daly.* Cheltenham, U.K.: Edward Elgar.

Doctorow, Cory. 2010. "BP Sued in Ecuador for Violating the 'Rights of Nature.'" *Democracy Now*, November 29.

Dworkin, Ronald. 1984. "Rights as Trumps." In *Theories of Rights*, edited by Jeremy Waldron, 153–167. Oxford: Oxford University Press.

Favre, David. 1979. "Wildlife Rights: The Ever-Widening Circle." *Environmental Law* 9: 241.

Foreman, Dave. 2011. *Man Swarm and the Killing of Wildlife*. Durango, Colo.: Raven's Eye Press.

Gewirth, Alan. 1981. "Are There Any Absolute Rights?" In *Theories of Rights*, edited by Jeremy Waldron, 81–109. Oxford: Oxford University Press.

Grant, Lindsey. 2001. *Too Many People: The Case for Reversing Growth*. Santa Ana, Calif.: Seven Locks Press.

He, Fangliang, and Stephen Hubbell. 2011. "Species-Area Relationships Always Overestimate Extinction Rates from Habitat Loss." *Nature* 473: 368–371.

Hull, David. 1976. "Are Species Really Individuals?" *Systemic Zoology* 25 (2): 174–191.

Johnson, Lawrence. 1983. "Humanity, Holism and Environmental Ethics." *Environmental Ethics* 5: 345–354.

Kasser, Tim. 2002. *The High Price of Materialism*. Cambridge, Mass.: MIT Press.

Kunzig, Robert. 2008. "Are Hotspots the Key to Conservation?" *Scientific American, Earth 3.0*, special issue, 42–49.

Layard, Richard. 2005. *Happiness: Lessons from a New Science*. New York: Penguin.

Leopold, Aldo. 1949. *A Sand County Almanac: And Sketches Here and There*. New York: Oxford University Press.

MacArthur, R. H., and E. O. Wilson. 1967. *The Theory of Island Biogeography*. Princeton, N.J.: Princeton University Press.

McKibben, Bill. 2007. *Deep Economy: The Wealth of Communities and the Durable Future*. New York: Henry Holt.

Norton, Bryan. 1992. *Why Preserve Natural Variety?* Princeton, N.J.: Princeton University Press.

Nussbaum, Martha. 2006. *Frontiers of Justice: Disability, Nationality, Species Membership*. Cambridge, Mass.: Harvard University Press.

Primack, Richard. 2010. *Essentials of Conservation Biology*. 5th ed. Sunderland, Mass.: Sinauer Associates.

Raz, Joseph. 1992. "Rights and Individual Well-Being." *Ratio Juris* 5 (2): 127–142.

Regan, Tom. 2004. *The Case for Animal Rights: Updated*. Berkeley: University of California Press.

Reid, Walter, et al. 2005. *Ecosystems and Human Well-Being: Synthesis*. Millennium Ecosystem Assessment series. Washington, D.C.: Island Press.

Revkin, Andrew C. 2008. "Ecuador Constitution Grants Rights to Nature." *New York Times Dot Earth*. September 29. Accessed from http://dotearth.blogs.nytimes.com/2008/09/29/ecuador-constitution-grants-nature-rights/.

Rolston, Holmes, III. 1988. *Environmental Ethics: Duties to and Values in the Natural World*. Philadelphia: Temple University Press, 1988.

———. 1989a. "Duties to Endangered Species." In *Philosophy Gone Wild: Environmental Ethics*, 206–219. Buffalo: Prometheus Press.

———. 1989b. "Values in Nature." In *Philosophy Gone Wild: Environmental Ethics*, 74–90. Buffalo: Prometheus Press.

Sandler, Ronald. 2009. "The Value of Species and the Ethical Foundations of Assisted Colonization." *Conservation Biology* 24 (2): 424–431.

Sandler, Ronald, and Judith Crane. 2006. "On the Moral Considerability of *Homo sapiens* and Other Species." *Environmental Values* 15 (1): 69–84.

Schmeigelow, F. K. A., S. G. Cumming, S. Harrison, S. Leroux, K. Lisgo, R. Noss, and B. Olsen. 2006. "Conservation beyond Crisis Management: A Conservation-Matrix Model." Beacons Discussion Paper #1. Edmonton: University of Alberta. Accessed from http://natureneedshalf.org/news-item-4/.

Sen, Amartya. 1994. "Women's Empowerment and Human Rights: The Challenge to Policy." In *Population: The Complex Reality: A Report of the Population Summit of the World's Scientific Academies*, edited by Francis Graham-Smith. London: Royal Society.

Speth, Gustave. 2009. *The Bridge at the Edge of the World: Capitalism, the Environment, and Crossing from Crisis to Sustainability*. New Haven, Conn.: Yale University Press.

Staples, Winthrop. 2009. "For a Species Moral Right to Exist: The Imperative of an Adequate Environmental Ethics." Master's thesis, Colorado State University.

Stone, Christopher D. 1996. *Should Trees Have Standing? and Other Essays on Law, Morals and the Environment*. Dobbs Ferry, N.Y.: Oceana.

Sunstein, Cass. 2004. *The Second Bill of Rights: FDR's Unfinished Revolution and Why We Need It More Than Ever*. New York: Basic Books.

Thoreau, Henry. 1962. *The Journal of Henry D. Thoreau*. Edited by Bradford Torrey and Francis Allen. New York: Dover.

United Nations Department of Economic and Social Affairs, Population Division (UNPD). 2011. "World Population to Reach 10 Billion by 2100 If Fertility in All Countries Converges to Replacement Level." Press release, May 3. New York: United Nations. Accessed from http://esa.un.org/unpd/wpp/Other -Information/Press_Release_WPP2010.pdf.

United Nations Population Fund. 2009. *State of World Population 2009: Facing a Changing World: Women, Population, and Climate*. New York: United Nations.

Wenar, Leif. 2010. "Rights." *Stanford Encyclopedia of Philosophy*. Accessed from http://plato.stanford.edu/entries/rights/.

Wilson, E. O. 2002. *The Future of Life*. New York: Knopf.

CHAPTER 24

Island Civilization

A Vision for Human Inhabitance
in the Fourth Millennium

RODERICK NASH

> *What we call wildness is a civilization other than our own.*
> —Henry David Thoreau

> *We are the most dangerous species of life on the planet, and*
> *every other species, even the earth itself, has cause to fear our*
> *power to exterminate. But we are also the only species which,*
> *when it chooses to do so, will go to great effort to save what it*
> *might destroy.*
> —Wallace Stegner

T HE NEW, THIRD millennium we are just entering affords an excellent opportunity to think big about the history and future of
wilderness and civilization on planet Earth. Of course a millennium is
an entirely artificial concept. Measuring time in thousand-year units only
began in 1582 when Christian officials arbitrarily fixed a date for the birth
of Christ. So there was nothing special about December 31, 999; it was not
even recognized as the end of the first millennium. But we made a big deal
about the end of the second one a thousand years later. Here is an opportunity to transcend our species' characteristic myopia. Rarely do humans
make plans more than a few years in advance, and we don't do history very
well, either. We do not often think in the wider angles that encompass our
species as a whole, but now is an excellent time to begin.

One way to look at the opportunity and the responsibility we have with
regard to the environment is in terms of legacy. As a historian, I am con-

cerned about how the future will regard what happened to the planet on our watch. What will my great-grandchildren (and theirs) think when they learn the truth about passenger pigeons, salmon, whales, and coral reefs?

My mission in this essay is to review the history of human-Nature relations and to extend the discussion into the distant future. I want to stretch our minds a bit. What could the human tenure on Earth be like a thousand years from now—at the start of the fourth millennium? My proposal involves some really major changes. I expect it to be controversial. At first glance you may think Island Civilization is crazy and impossible, but do not stop with criticism. The whole purpose of this essay is to advance for discussion a strategy for inhabiting this planet that will work in the very long run and for the global ecosystem. This is simply the greatest challenge facing our species. If you disagree with my vision of an Island Civilization, create your own. If you think staying the present course is the way to go, put forward your evidence and reasoning. The essential thing is that we occasionally lift our eyes from everyday details and five-year plans to the far horizons of planetary possibility. Having such a goal is a vital first step to solving problems. Without it we lack direction and the means to evaluate options as they come into focus.

As a starting point let's consider wilderness. It's a state of mind, a perception rather than a geographical reality, and prior to the advent of herding and agriculture about ten thousand years ago, it didn't exist. But after we began to draw mental lines between ourselves and Nature, and to place walls and fences on the land, the idea of controlled versus uncontrolled environments acquired meaning. The root of the word *wilderness* in Old English was something that had its own will. The adjective that came to be used was *wild*: for example, wildfire, wild (undammed) rivers, and wildcats. The other important part of the word, *ness*, indicates a condition or place. So *wilderness* literally means "self-willed land," a place where wild, undomesticated animals roam and where natural processes proceed unencumbered by human interference.

After humans created farms, and literally bet our survival on them instead of on hunting and gathering, uncontrolled nature became the enemy of the new civilization. Pastoral societies, like those that produced the Old and New Testaments, became obsessed with making the crooked straight and the rough places plain. For thousands of years the success of civilization seemed to mandate the destruction of wild places, wild animals, and wild peoples. The game plan was to break their wills. In the Bible, wilderness was the land God cursed. Its antipode was called *paradise*. Adam and Eve lost it when they angered God and found themselves banished into the wild. The first European colonists of the New World carried in their intellectual baggage a full load of bias against wilderness. The last thing settlers of the eastern seaboard had in mind was protecting wild nature or establishing national parks! Indians were savages who needed to be "civilized" or eliminated. After a rocky start, these pioneers became very good at breaking the will of uncontrolled land and peoples. Axes, rifles, and barbed wire—and more recently railroads, dams, and freeways—were the celebrated tools of an environmental transformation that left the wilderness in scattered remnants.

Lost in the celebration of westward expansion, however, was the possible irony of the project. When does success in too great a dose produce failure? We always thought of growth as synonymous with progress, but bigger is not better if it creates a civilization that is unsustainable. What needs to be conquered is not wilderness, but rather our capitalist-driven culture in its cancer-like tendency to self-destruct.

Americans began to explore these revolutionary ideas as the second millennium drew to a close in the nineteenth and twentieth centuries. As early as 1851, Henry David Thoreau thought that wildness held the key to the preservation of the world. George Perkins Marsh, a well-traveled diplomat who spoke twenty-one languages, explained in his remarkable book *Man and Nature*, published in 1867, that with their improved technology, uninhibited by ethical concerns, humans had become a new and destructive force of nature. He suspected that what humans assumed to be victory against the forest primeval would result in floods, droughts, and desertification, finally defeating their dreams of progress and prosperity. Beginning in the 1870s, John Muir reversed thousands of years of Judeo-Christian attitudes by publicizing mountain forests as temples and cathedrals. What shocked Americans of this generation the most was the U.S. census pronouncement in 1890 that there was no more frontier. With the Native Americans crushed, the buffalo almost gone, and industrial cities losing their luster, it was possible to think that the cherished civilizing process could go too far. The appearance in the early twentieth century of best-selling books with a primitivist slant—like Jack London's *The Call of the Wild* (1903) and Edgar Rice Burroughs's *Tarzan* (1914)—indicated that the relative valuations of wilderness and civilization were changing.

With the onset of the twentieth century, a scarcity theory of value began to reshape the relative importance of wilderness and civilization in the United States. It explains the national angst over the closing of the frontier. The dominant attitude toward wilderness was passing over a tipping point from liability to asset. Wilderness appreciation and later preservation began in the cities, where wild country was perceived as a relative novelty and substantially less threatening.

The rationale of the early movement for wilderness was almost entirely anthropocentric. Scenery, recreation, and the economics of a new nature-based tourism underlay the growing popularity of wild places. More sophisticated, but no less utilitarian, were ideas of wilderness as a sanctuary, a museum of national history, a stimulant for unique art and literature, and a psychological aid for stress relief. These were good arguments for their time and underlay the establishment of the first national parks and wilderness. The Wilderness Act of 1964 was revolutionary, but—make no mistake—its point was the benefit of people.

A new, biocentric rationale for wilderness emerged in the last fifty years of the second millennium. At its core was the idea that wilderness has intrinsic value, and that its protection is not about *us* at all. Rather, it is a place where our species can take a badly needed "time-out" from our ten-thousand-year-old obsession with controlling and modifying the planet. In honoring wilderness, we manifest a capacity for restraint. Preserved wilderness is a gesture of planetary modesty, a way to share the spaceship on which all life travels together.

The roots of this valuation of wilderness run back in the United States to Henry David Thoreau's belief that "wildness is a civilization other than our own." John Muir wrote about "the rights of all the rest of creation" that civilized humans had consistently ignored. The case for the rights of certain animals had been vigorously made in England in the nineteenth century, and in 1915 Albert Schweitzer extended the ideal to "reverence for life." The ideal here and in Cornell University botanist Liberty Hyde Bailey's book *The Holy Earth*, also 1915, was not just being a good manager or steward of nature, but respecting it as an ethical equal because it had been created by God. As Bailey put it, humans should "put our dominion into the realm of morals. It is now in the realm of trade." This theological holism, which has a long history in Western thought and an even longer one in Asian cultures, received major support from the new science of ecology. The phrase *food chains* first appeared in 1927 and *ecosystem* in 1935.

Focusing on interdependencies, ecologists provided scientific ground to the belief that nature is a community to which mankind belongs, not a commodity it possesses.

In essays written in the 1920s and 1930s, and particularly in his 1949 book *A Sand County Almanac*, wildlife ecologist Aldo Leopold became the major American articulator of the celebrated "land ethic." Wilderness preservation was one of Leopold's highest priorities. It constituted, Leopold argued, "an act of national contrition" on the part of a species notorious for "biotic arrogance." In the 1960s the emergence of Leopold's book as a best-seller, along with the popularity of ecologist Rachel Carson, particularly her *Silent Spring* (1962), evidenced a changing American attitude toward Nature. *Conservation*, around as a term since 1907, had been strictly utilitarian in its emphasis on national strength and prosperity. *Preservation*, a term that Muir favored, implied human benefit from uncontrolled and unutilized environments. A new 1960s word, *environmentalism*, took a broader view of utility, popularized the term *pollution* (which impacts many species), and added momentum to the idea of the rights of Nature. Theologians and philosophers joined environmentalists in arguing that the nation's natural rights tradition, which had extended the moral community in the past to include African Americans, native peoples, and women, should now turn to the task of liberating another oppressed minority: Nature. The phrase *deep ecology* appeared in 1973 to describe a belief in the right of every life form to flourish in a shared ecosystem. Some philosophers extended their application of natural rights to land forms, like rivers and mountains, and to ecosystems.

This line of ethical thinking suggested that just as John Locke's "social contract" mandated restrictions on individual freedom in the interest of creating a just society, so an "ecological contract" might restrain the human species in its relations to the ecosystem. The passage of the Marine Mammals Protection Act (1972) and the Endangered Species Act (1973) was remarkable in that they endowed nonhuman species with rights to life, liberty, and the pursuit of happiness (in appropriate terms, of course). Significantly, many of the species protected were not considered cute or useful to humans in any way; their value was intrinsic and their membership in the biotic community indisputable.

The appearance of biocentrism and environmental ethics was encouraging, but an avalanche of evidence has revealed that civilization continues to wreck natural rhythms and balances in the third millennium. Awareness of the problems has penetrated deeply into contemporary thought and discussion. Accelerated human-caused destruction of biodiversity amounts, in the evaluation of biologists, to a sixth mass extinction. More humans were alive in 1950 than had previously lived in the entire history of the species, and population subsequently surged upward by a billion every fifteen years. Sprawling into open space at the rate of six thousand acres each day in the United States alone, people dominated most of the preferred locales in the temperate latitudes. Climate change, fresh water scarcity, soil depletion, deforestation, and food issues make headlines daily. Lurking just over the horizon are concerns over massive epidemics, food shortages, and the specter of a climate-change episode that could devastate life on the planet.

Civilization, in a word, appears vulnerable. Making the point explicitly, Jared Diamond's 2005 book *Collapse* underscores the ecological unsustainability in many human cultures over the last ten thousand years and suggests strongly that we are not exempt. There will be a resolution of environmental problems, he argues; if not by intelligent choice, then by ecological disaster and social disintegration. My proposal for Island Civilization responds to the concerns Diamond and others have raised.

As for wilderness, where most of the thirty-odd million species sharing Earth reside, it is now *itself* an endangered geographical kind. Only about 2 percent of the contiguous forty-eight states are legally wild, and about the same amount is paved! Much of the American landscape has been modified to some degree. Ironically, the United States has been a leader in national parks and wilderness preservation and is only a little more than a century beyond its frontier era. In other, older regions—France and Japan come to mind—human control of natural environments is near total. At least in the temperate latitudes, we are dealing only with remnants of a once-wild world, and we now face irreversible decisions about their future on a planet that suddenly seems small and vulnerable. In a century, wilderness could completely disappear or become so fragmented as to be ecologically meaningless. Some now view this not just as a violation of the rights of humans to enjoy wild nature but as a violation of the rights of other species and of self-willed environments themselves.

Looking toward the fourth millennium, a thousand years ahead, there seem to be several ways that the natural world in which we evolved could end. A *wasteland scenario* anticipates a trashed, poisoned, and used-up planet that can support only a pathetic remnant of its once-miraculous biological diversity. Humans have proved to be terrible neighbors to most of the rest of life on the planet. We did not share well. Growth was confused with progress. Centuries of deficit environmental financing of a too large and sprawling civilization has brought the ecosystem, ourselves included of course, to its knees. Maybe, in the height of ingratitude and irresponsibility, we have abandoned and discarded this planet. A vanguard of humans, no wiser for their history, treks through the stars seeking new frontiers to plunder. Perhaps wilderness conditions eventually return to what Alan Weisman (2007) calls "the world without us," but the setback to evolution would be profound and millions of years in healing.

The second possible future is the *garden scenario*. Imagine by the fourth millennium that human control of nature is total, but this time, it's "beneficent." Our species has occupied and modified every square mile and every planetary process from the oceans to weather to the creation and evolution of life. It is finally, as some feared, all about us. We're no longer part of nature: we've stepped off, or more exactly, over the biotic team. Scores of billions of people occupy this planetary garden. Dammed rivers flow clean and cold (but without much diversity of life), and waving fields of grain stretch to the horizon. The only big animals around are those we eat! Maybe such a world could be made sustainable for a few species, but the wilderness, and the diversity of life that depends on it, are long gone. So may be environmental health long thought linked to the normal and natural functioning of ecosystems. The gardeners of this man-made "Eden" may not be quite as *sapient* apes as they imagined, but in the aftermath of their violent, myopic takeover of Earth they become victims of homogenization, biotic impoverishment, and their own excessive appetites.

There is a third scenario that has captured the imagination of some thoughtful environmental philosophers. It might be called the *future primitive*. It involves writing off technological civilization as a ten-thousand-year experiment gone awry. Either by choice or necessity, small numbers of humans resume the kind of hunter and gatherer existence that indeed worked quite well for our species for millions of years. But the downside of this scenario is that the extraordinary achievements and potential of civilization are lost. A better goal, I feel, was articulated by Henry David Thoreau, who stated that he wished "to secure all the advantages" of civilization "without suffering any of the disadvantages." Don't humans have as much right to fulfill their evolutionary potential as other species? The vital proviso is that in so doing, we do not compromise or eliminate the opportunity of other members of the biotic community to fulfill theirs. This means not discarding technology but using it ethically and responsibly—indeed, *wisely*.

The fourth scenario for the fourth millennium I call *Island Civilization*. It is a dream, to borrow from Martin Luther King, and it involves human clustering on a planetary scale. Boundaries are drawn around the human presence, not around wilderness. Advanced technologies permit humans to reduce their environmental impact. For the first time in human history, better tools mean peace rather than war with Nature. Of course, Island Civilization means the end of the idea of integrating our civilization into Nature. The divorce that began with herding and agriculture is final! Since we proved clever enough to create our separate environments, rather than adapt to what Nature provided, we take that option to the logical extreme. We impact only a *tiny part* of the planet. The rest is self-willed. The matrix is wild—not civilized.

Of course a change like this one involves compromises with human freedom. On a finite planet, shared with millions of other species, only limited numbers of humans can enjoy unlimited opportunities. The first step toward Island Civilization is to check population growth and decrease the human population to a total of about 1.5 billion. Of course this can be done! Here's one problem for which we know the cause and the solution. It is the motivation that is thus far lacking. A new, expanded Earth ethic, coupled with plain fear about the crash of a bloated species, might turn things around. The essential first step is to put Nature above people: "Earth First!" was the name Dave Foreman, Mike Roselle, and their colleagues gave to their platform in 1980. As it is, humans increase and multiply at the rate of ten thousand per hour, a rate that wipes out any gains made by today's friends of wildlife and wilderness.

The other need for restraint is in the realm of living space. We have historically demanded too much of a planet we share with other species. We've pushed the wild things into the least desirable corners of the environment. It's time our species settled some of the more biologically "marginal" lands—which we can modify with our intelligence—and left the biologically richer ones to wild nature. The fact is that we've been atrocious roommates in the Earth household. What other species would support an Endangered Species Act for us?

One version of Island Civilization might direct that the 1.5 billion people live in five hundred concentrated habitats, scattered widely over

Earth. Food production, energy generation, waste treatment, and cultural activities take place within hundred-mile closed-circle units supporting three million humans. "Cities" cannot begin to describe the new living arrangements that the architects and engineers of the fourth millennium could create. They might be on the poles, around mountains, underground, or undersea. Rivers might run through some of them. Some of the islands might float in water or in the air. There would be cultural exchange, of course—but little to no global trade in food, energy, or materials among the islands. Economies would be relocalized: the concept of "hundred-mile meals" would essentially be a reality. We would get back to an arrangement that worked well on a small scale for Greek city-states, medieval monasteries, and the pueblos of the Southwest. Sure, wild nature will be severely altered on the islands we occupy, but isn't that fairer and better than a planetwide sacrifice to a single species? The concept of an island means that human impact is completely contained. The kind of sprawl from which the planet suffers today would be gone.

Exciting as the possibilities are for this new way for humans to live, it is what's outside the islands that is especially compelling. Human presence has imploded. Fences are down. Dams are gone. Roads, railroads, pipelines, telephone lines, ocean-going ships, indeed all terrestrial forms of transportation could be unnecessary in a millennium. I'm counting on amazing new technology to make all this possible. Nuclear fusion may be just the tip of the new technological iceberg. Utopian science fiction? Well, consider what was said about television and computers a century ago. And the pace of technological change is accelerating dramatically. Of course, I can't prove marvels such as transportation by teleportation will exist in a thousand years, but by the same token, you can't show they won't. Turn our best minds loose on the technological challenges of Island Civilization, and miracles will happen. It is not necessary to go back to the Pleistocene to live with a low ecological impact. Technology, I would argue, is essentially neutral; it's what kind of technologies we develop and what we do with them that is the problem. So why not expand our ethics, end mind pollution, and take the high-tech road to minimal impact? The result could be the preservation dream. The frontier reappears, and this time it is permanent. Rivers are full of salmon, and the deer, buffalo, and antelope play on the plains. The big predators are back too and, without human interference, perhaps are evolving into something resembling the Pleistocene megafauna we never got to know. As we were before herding and agriculture, ten thousand years ago, humans by the year 4000 are once again good neighbors within the ecological community. *Homo sapiens* is healthy and enjoying its version of liberty and the pursuit of happiness, and so are all the other creatures and components of the natural world.

But what, the question frequently arises, are your options if you don't want to live on densely populated islands in a matrix of wilderness? The short response is that if you wanted to live a high-technological lifestyle in 4000, you wouldn't have a choice. According to the terms of a new, ecological contract, we'd surrender some freedoms like herding cows on the open range or living in sprawling ski resorts. (If you wanted to ski, you'd choose to live on the island built into, say, part of the Alps.) But you could leave the islands to enjoy minimum-impact vacations in high-quality wilderness. You could even live out there for a while—or forever. The condition is that you'd have to do it as part of the wilderness. That means a resumption of the old pre-pastoral ways. No herds or settling down, no towns and walls, not even cottages in the woods. Those who opted off the island would take only what they needed from Nature; profits and growth would not figure into the equation. We would have finally learned what the 1964 Wilderness Act meant about people being *visitors who do not remain* in someone else's home.

Perhaps humans of the distant future will be able to choose on a seasonal basis between ways of life centered on computers or campfires. Young people in these societies might be encouraged to undertake a two-year mission or vision quest into the wild. Completely out of contact with the civilized islands, they could learn the old hunting and gathering ways and the old land ethics. Here is where some humans might go back to the Pleistocene and choose to live in the future-primitive way I described earlier. But is it possible people could support themselves out there for that long, living off the land? The answer is of course they could, because the healthy land and seas on which our ancestors built sustainable cultures for hundreds of thousands of years would be back again.

Island Civilization is a response to the history of *Homo sapiens* on Earth. For some five million years of our species existence the planet was self-willed. Humans were just another hunter and gatherer, and population remained relatively small and stable. It was a successful lifestyle that weathered just as severe climate changes as the one that scares us now. About ten thousand years before the present our species began to experiment with controlling nature and reshaping our habitats. More precisely, humans stopped adapting to their environment and began to destroy and re-create it. Parts of this experiment resulted in impressive pinnacles of evolutionary achievement. But over time, irony kicked in. Human success, especially the idea that bigger was better, carried the seeds of its own destruction as well as that of many other life-forms. From the standpoint of the rest of life, the growth of our civilization amounts to a cancer in the ecosystem. We no longer belong to the ecological team: we've checked off the biotic ark! Isn't this exactly what biologist Edward O. Wilson (1993) meant by saying, "Darwin's dice have rolled badly for Earth"? Island Civilization makes the needed correction. It permits human beings to realize their cultural and technological potential, while safeguarding the same right of self-realization for all the other beings.

I have long been a supporter of the wilderness preservation movement and, more recently, of conservation biology and the rewilding idea. But it seems increasingly evident that the admirable scientists, philosophers, and public servants involved in these efforts shy away from the full implications of their own ideas. Worrying about fragmentation of wildlife habitat, they neglect the option of fragmenting us! Trying to create connections between wild islands, they pass up the possibility of making civilization an island on a wild Earth. It is hard for me to see the important goals of conservation biology being realized without a radical restructuring of human lifestyles and ambitions. The beauty of Island Civilization is that it permits humans to fulfill their evolutionary potential without compromising or eliminating the opportunity of other species to do the same.

Biologists warn us that evolution has discarded thousands of promising starts such as ours, and that we should be worried about the future of our present lifestyle. The upward-trending curves cannot be sustained. There will be major changes. The rub is whether they will be made deliberately, haphazardly, desperately. The stakes are enormously high: nothing less than the future of life on Earth. And that, of course, includes ours too.

So we stand at a crossroads not merely of human history but of the entire evolutionary process. Life evolved from stardust, water, and fire over billions of years, until one clever species developed the capacity to bring down the whole biological miracle. But amid the fear associated with this reality of a sinking ark, there is one comfort. Earth is not threatened as in the age of the dinosaurs by an errant asteroid, a death star. Now *we* are the death star, but we are also capable of changing its course. And it may be appropriate at this point to observe that up until now, the environmental movement has been mostly negative. It is against things. With Island Civilization I am not just talking about problems. Island Civilization is something to be *for*.

Imagine, in conclusion, this planet, in the desperate frame of mind contemporary conditions warrant, putting a "personals" advertisement on a hypothetical, intergalactic cyber-dating service, a kind of E-Harmony.com for the universe:

TEMPERATE BUT ENDANGERED PLANET

ENJOYS WEATHER, PHOTOSYNTHESIS, EVOLUTION, CONTINENTAL DRIFT

SEEKS CARING LONG-TERM RELATIONSHIP WITH COMPASSIONATE LIFEFORM

Well, maybe it could still be us! Maybe biocentric ethics and respect for self-willed nature—along with a healthy dose of fear for our future—could turn us from cancerous to caring. Maybe we should answer that personals ad. Earth might just be ready to receive a proposal for Island Civilization.

BIBLIOGRAPHY

Bailey, Liberty Hyde. 1915. *The Holy Earth*. New York: C. Scribner.
Burroughs, Edgar Rice. 1914. *Tarzan of the Apes*. New York: A. L. Burt.
Carson, Rachel. 1962. *Silent Spring*. New York: Fawcett.
Diamond, Jared. 2005. *Collapse: How Societies Choose to Fail or Succeed*. New York: Viking.
Leopold, Aldo. 1949. *A Sand County Almanac: And Sketches Here and There*. New York: Oxford University Press.
London, Jack. 1903. *The Call of the Wild*. New York: Macmillan.
Marsh, George Perkins. 1867. *Man and Nature*. New York: C. Scribner.
Weisman, Alan. 2007. *The World without Us*. New York: St. Martin's Press.
Wilson, Edward O. 1993. "Is Humanity Suicidal?" *New York Times Magazine*, May 30.

Epilogue

Is Humanity a Cancer on the Earth?

PHILIP CAFARO

ORTY YEARS AGO, at the dawn of the modern environmental movement, it was common to hear humanity's rapid population growth spoken of as "cancerous"—dangerous and out of control—and even occasionally of humanity itself as a cancer threatening life on Earth. Since then, such rhetoric has largely disappeared from environmental discourse, along with serious attention to human overpopulation.

The notion of "humanity as cancer" grated. Who wants to think of themselves, or their children, as part of a sickening, life-threatening disease? Many of us know people who have suffered from cancer. The whole way of speaking seems in bad taste.

Yet environmentalists back then at least had the clarity to realize that overpopulation was a problem, and the courage to say so. Today we are ever so much more sensitive, well behaved, well spoken. And we are failing utterly to protect wild nature or future human generations from overpopulation.

In one area after another, the contributors to *Life on the Brink* document what Dave Foreman so aptly describes as "the Man Swarm" overwhelming biodiversity. They lament the losses and call for human restraint in our appropriation of the habitats and resources of the world. And they know that such restraint is impossible without curbing human numbers.

The ability to restrain ourselves lies at the core of humanity's ostensible superiority over the rest of nature. Immanuel Kant laid it out clearly over two hundred years ago: rationality = choice = freedom = morality.

Our ability to reason allows us to distinguish different courses of action and choose one over another. This constitutes a limited, yet real, freedom, which in turn demands that we act with justice and generosity in a world that we have so much power to influence, for good or ill.

We do not expect wombats, redwoods, or cancer-causing viruses to respect rights or appreciate limits. We do expect this from people. The claim is that humanity is different precisely because we can act with foresight, planning, restraint, and higher ends in view. But can we? Can people act intelligently and with restraint *as a species*, a global community, which collectively holds the fate of Earth in its hands? That is far from clear.

Humanity gives every indication of being "out of control" in terms of its use and appropriation of the biosphere (Hern 1990, 1999). It is clear that rapid economic and demographic growth is the primary, fundamental cause of our major environmental problems. The IPCC's Fourth Assessment Report of 2007 shows this unequivocally for global climate change; several overviews in recent years document it for the ongoing worldwide mass extinction of species (Secretariat of the Convention on Biological Diversity 2010); and the comprehensive multivolume *Millennium Ecosystem Assessment* published in 2005 documents it for ecological degradation as a whole. Growth in human numbers and economic activity is causing these problems. Yet it is precisely growth that cannot be stopped or even slowed under the current economic regime, or questioned by the reigning economic ideology.

Economists—the secular priests of the current age—have developed an elaborate theology in which perpetual growth is necessary, good, and inevitable, and those who acknowledge limits to growth are deemed pessimists who oppose human progress. They justify the rejection of limits by appeal to a view of human nature as greedy and insatiable and to a definition of freedom that (unlike Kant's) limits the use of reason to the instrumental pursuit of arbitrary ends, rather than seeing the recognition and pursuit of higher ends as key to real freedom. They have developed a metaphysics in which everything that is "not us" has value exclusively as a resource *for* us.

Modern economic theory reads as if cancer had found a voice. Why, here it is now, in the person of Larry Summers! In the late 1990s, as U.S. Treasury secretary, Summers declared that the Clinton administration "cannot and will not accept any 'speed limit' on American economic growth. It is the task of economic policy to grow the economy as rapidly, sustainably and inclusively as possible." Earlier, he had confidently stated that "there are no . . . limits to the carrying capacity of the Earth that are likely to bind any time in the foreseeable future. There isn't a risk of an apocalypse due to global warming, or anything else. The idea that we should put limits on growth because of some natural limit is a profound error" (McKibben 2007, 9, 24). Profiles of Summers habitually refer to him as highly intelligent. So, reading the words above, you might assume that he had actually explored whether rapid growth really is sustainable and found good evidence that the answer is "yes," or that his "foreseeable future" stretched out past the next quarterly earnings reports or election cycle, say fifty or a hundred years out, when our children and grandchildren will be alive. But such is not the case. Summers literally does not know what he is talking about, and words like "sustainably" or "the foreseeable future" are merely there for their soothing rhetorical effect. They are an invitation to not think about limits to growth, and a subtle preparation to accept lost species and ecological degradation as inevitable.

The contributors to this anthology decline the invitation. We are committed to the idea that the human race can be more than an ever-gaping mouth swallowing the world. We want to work toward a future in which humanity limits its appropriation of the biosphere, and wild nature continues to flourish. In this way, I believe, we stand up for what is best in humanity.

In the world our contributors seek to create, polar bears continue to hunt seals along the Arctic pack ice. Sperm whales fight unseen duels-to-the-death with giant squids, a mile below the ocean's surface. Arctic terns knit together the North and South Poles in their twice-yearly migrations, covering forty-four thousand miles annually. The great forests of the Amazon, Borneo, and the Congo remain standing, remain *breathing*, remain overflowing with life, and are not cut down to accommodate displaced peasants or to grow sugarcane to fuel an ever-growing world auto fleet. In that world, many of the biosphere's grasslands are restored as wild ecosystems brimming with wildlife. Rivers are allowed to run free of dams, overexploitation, and pollution, so they can become again—in the language of the Song of Solomon—"living waters." Sea turtles and sharks are brought back from the precipice of extinction. Large land animals, from wolves and cougars to tigers and elephants, are also restored and granted the unbroken expanses of untrammeled nature they require to live and evolve. In the world we envision, we stop cutting old growth, period;

indeed, we leave many of the world's forests alone, because our need for pulp, wood, land, and fuel is so vastly reduced.

In the world we seek to create, our children's and our grandchildren's right to enjoy natural beauty remains secure, rather than being sacrificed on the altars of greed, materialism, or desperate need. They can explore and enjoy wild nature, in parks and open spaces close to home, or backpacking and canoeing across great wilderness areas. Their pictures and memories need not become memorials to what has been lost, as so many of our own have become. Instead, they may share the experiences and the places they have loved with their own children and grandchildren, and so on, in perpetuity.

Since most of the contributors to *Life on the Brink* are Americans, many of us have a special concern to preserve wild places in the United States, and we do not apologize for that concern. That is how environmentalism works, when it works, with people standing up and fighting for those places that are near and dear to them. But we do not seek to preserve our own beloved landscapes by displacing the ecological costs of Americans' excessive consumption elsewhere. Instead, we strive to reduce such consumption ourselves and try to convince our fellow citizens to do likewise. At the same time, we decline to support the folly of nations that have high fertility rates by encouraging them to send their excess inhabitants to the United States. The American frontier closed long ago; we are "full up." The ecological damage to the North American continent has already been exorbitant, and it is time to conserve the wild nature and nonhuman species that remain, many of which are in decline. Meanwhile, from a global ecological perspective, the last thing the world needs is hundreds of millions more Americans.

This volume's contributors recognize that no country can preserve wild nature in the context of endless economic *or* demographic growth, nor can the world as a whole. Either of these tsunamis, by itself, will wash away the wild species and wild places we love, and will threaten essential ecosystem services. Hence we are committed to ending the endless growth economy, and we support the family planning, abortion, women's empowerment, tax, and immigration policies necessary to stabilize and then reduce populations around the world and in the United States. Anything less is neither ecologically sustainable nor fair to the rest of nature. For these reasons, we reject suggestions from the Left to focus on reforming the economy while ignoring population growth (Angus and Butler 2011), and suggestions from the Right to limit population growth, through reduced immigration, while maximizing per capita economic growth. Such recommendations betray a weak commitment to sustainability and a shallow understanding of what is necessary to achieve it.

We thus are committed to an end to conventional economic and demographic growth. But we do not seek the creation of some static, unchanging reality. Humanity can and should continue to grow in all sorts of ways: morally, intellectually, spiritually, creatively. It would be great if we grew in our understanding and appreciation for nature and in our willingness to share the world with other species. But cramming ever more people onto the landscape is not compatible with this sort of moral and intellectual growth. Such growth has clearly become toxic to the ecosystems on which human beings, for all our technological achievements, remain dependent for our survival and flourishing. It is time to consciously work to *decrease* humanity's physical presence on Earth.

Human beings have a legitimate place on our home planet, of course, in rural and urban landscapes, and even in wild landscapes, in small numbers. But our place is not everywhere. As Rod Nash, Win Staples, and other contributors suggest, we need to redress a growing imbalance between human-dominated and natural landscapes. The human footprint needs to shrink. And again, lessening the human footprint is inseparable from limiting the number of human feet.

Whether our contributors' visions will be achieved, for a future that includes the flourishing of biodiversity, remains to be seen. Perhaps humanity really is a cancer on the biosphere, unwilling or unable to control ourselves. We will likely prove or disprove the hypothesis this century; above all, perhaps, by whether we can consciously and conscientiously limit our own numbers.

BIBLIOGRAPHY

Angus, Ian, and Simon Butler. 2011. *Too Many People? Population, Immigration, and the Environmental Crisis.* Chicago: Haymarket Books.

Hern, Warren M. 1990. "Why Are There So Many of Us? Description and Diagnosis of a Planetary Ecopathological Process." *Population and Environment* 12 (1): 9–39.

———. 1999. "How Many Times Has the Human Population Doubled? Comparisons with Cancer." *Population and Environment* 21 (1): 59–80.

Intergovernmental Panel on Climate Change (IPCC). 2007. *Climate Change 2007: Synthesis Report.* (Fourth Assessment Report.) Geneva: IPCC.

McKibben, Bill. 2007. *Deep Economy: The Wealth of Communities and the Durable Future.* New York: Henry Holt.

Millennium Ecosystem Assessment. 2005. 5 vols. Washington, D.C.: Island Press.

Secretariat of the Convention on Biological Diversity. 2010. *Global Biodiversity Outlook 3.* Montreal: Convention on Biological Diversity, United Nations Environment Programme.

SELECT BIBLIOGRAPHY

We list here important recent writings on population and environmental issues, as well as several key books exploring alternatives to the endless growth economy. In addition, a valuable *Bibliography of Population and Environment Sources* can be found on the website of the Center for Environment and Population under "Publications," while a good list of "must-read articles" is posted under the "Resources" tab on the website for the group Howmany.org.

All Party Parliamentary Group on Population, Development, and Reproductive Health. 2007. *Return of the Population Growth Factor: Its Impact on the Millennium Development Goals.* London: Her Majesty's Stationery Office.

Beck, Roy, Leon Kolankiewicz, and Steven Camarota. 2003. *Outsmarting Smart Growth: Population Growth, Immigration, and the Problem of Sprawl.* Washington, D.C.: Center for Immigration Studies.

Brown, Lester R. 2004. *Outgrowing the Earth.* New York: Norton.

———. 2011. *World on the Edge: How to Prevent Environmental and Economic Collapse.* New York: Norton.

Butler, Tom. 2002. *Wild Earth: Wild Ideas for a World out of Balance.* Minneapolis: Milkweed Press.

Cafaro, Philip. 2012. "Climate Ethics and Population Policy." *WIREs Climate Change* 3 (1): 45–61.

Camarota, Steven. 2007. "100 Million More: Projecting the Impact of Immigration on the U.S. Population, 2007–2060." Washington, D.C.: Center for Immigration Studies.

Cincotta, Richard, and Robert Engelman. 2000. "Nature's Place: Human Population and the Future of Biological Diversity." Washington, D.C.: Population Action International.

Crist, Eileen. 2007. "Beyond the Climate Crisis: A Critique of Climate Change Discourse." *Telos* 141 (Winter): 29–55.

Czech, Brian. 2002. *Shoveling Fuel for a Runaway Train: Errant Economists, Shameful Spenders, and a Plan to Stop Them All.* Berkeley: University of California Press.

Daly, Herman, and John Cobb. 1994. *For the Common Good: Redirecting the Economy toward Community, the Environment, and a Sustainable Future.* 2nd ed. Boston: Beacon Press.

Ehrlich, Paul, and Anne Ehrlich. 2004. *One with Nineveh: Politics, Consumption, and the Human Future.* Washington, D.C.: Island Press.

———. 2009. *The Dominant Animal: Human Evolution and the Environment.* Washington, D.C.: Island Press.

Engelman, Robert. 2008. *More: Population, Nature, and What Women Want.* Washington, D.C.: Island Press.

———. 2010. *Population, Climate Change, and Women's Lives.* Washington, D.C.: Worldwatch Institute, 2010.

Foreman, Dave. 2004. *Rewilding North America: A Vision for Conservation in the 21st Century.* Washington, D.C.: Island Press.

———. 2011. *Man Swarm and the Killing of Wildlife.* Durango, Colo.: Raven's Eye Press.

Grant, Lindsey. 2001. *Too Many People: The Case for Reversing Growth.* Santa Ana, Calif.: Seven Locks Press.

———, ed. 2006. *The Case for Fewer People: The NPG Forum Papers.* Santa Ana, Calif.: Seven Locks Press.

Hardin, Garrett. 1993. *Living within Limits: Ecology, Economics, and the Population Taboos.* New York: Oxford University Press.

———. 1999. *The Ostrich Factor: Our Population Myopia.* Oxford: Oxford University Press.

Imhoff, Daniel, ed. 2010. *CAFO (Concentrated Animal Feeding Operation): The Tragedy of Industrial Animal Factories.* Sausalito, Calif.: Foundation for Deep Ecology.

Jackson, Jeremy, Karen Alexander, and Enric Sala. 2011. *Shifting Baselines: The Past and Future of Ocean Fisheries.* Washington, D.C.: Island Press.

Jackson, Tim. 2009. *Prosperity without Growth? Economics for a Finite Planet.* European Union Sustainable Development Commission. London: Earthscan.

Jensen, Derrick. 2006. *Endgame*. Vol. 1: *The Problem of Civilization*. Vol. 2: *Resistance*. New York: Seven Stories.

Kolankiewicz, Leon, and Roy Beck. 2001. "Forsaking Fundamentals: The Environmental Establishment Abandons U.S. Population Stabilization." Washington, D.C.: Center for Immigration Studies.

Kolankiewicz, Leon, and Steven Camarota. 2008. "Immigration to the United States and World-wide Greenhouse Gas Emissions." Washington, D.C.: Center for Immigration Studies.

Kunstler, James. 2005. *The Long Emergency: Surviving the Converging Catastrophes of the Twenty-First Century*. New York: Atlantic Monthly Press.

Markham, Victoria. 2006. *U.S. National Report on Population and the Environment*. New Canaan, Conn.: Center for Environment and Population.

Mazur, Laurie, ed. 2009. *A Pivotal Moment: Population, Justice and the Environmental Challenge*. Washington, D.C.: Island Press.

McBay, Aric, Keith Lierre, and Derrick Jensen. 2011. *Deep Green Resistance: Strategy to Save the Planet*. New York: Seven Stories.

McKee, Jeffrey. 2003. *Sparing Nature: The Conflict between Human Population Growth and Earth's Biodiversity*. New Brunswick, N.J.: Rutgers University Press.

McKibben, Bill. 1998. *Maybe One: A Case for Smaller Families*. New York: Penguin.

———. 2007. *Deep Economy: The Wealth of Communities and the Durable Future*. New York: Henry Holt.

Moore, Kathleen, and Michael Nelson, eds. 2010. *Moral Ground: Ethical Action for a Planet in Peril*. San Antonio, Tex.: Trinity University Press.

Moreland, Scott, Ellen Smith, and Suneeta Sharma. 2010. *World Population Prospects and Unmet Need for Family Planning*. Washington, D.C.: Futures Group.

Murtaugh, Paul, and Michael Schlax. 2009. "Reproduction and the Carbon Legacies of Individuals." *Global Environmental Change* 19 (1): 14–20.

O'Neill, Brian, Landis Mackellar, and Wolfgang Lutz. 2005. *Population and Climate Change*. Cambridge: Cambridge University Press.

Roberts, Callum. 2007. *The Unnatural History of the Sea*. Washington D.C.: Island Press.

Singh, Susheela, Jaqueline Darroch, Lori Ashford, and Michael Vlassoff. 2009. *Adding It Up: The Costs and Benefits of Investing in Family Planning and Maternal and Newborn Health*. New York: Guttmacher Institute, 2009.

Smail, Kenneth. 2002. "Remembering Malthus: A Preliminary Argument for a Significant Reduction in Global Human Numbers." *American Journal of Physical Anthropology* 118 (3): 292–297.

Speidel, Joseph, Steven Sinding, Duff Gillespie, Elizabeth Maguire, and Margaret Neuse. 2009. *Making the Case for International Family Planning Assistance*. New York: Population Connection.

United Nations Department of Economic and Social Affairs, Population Division.
    2011. *World Population Prospects: The 2010 Revision.* New York: United Nations.
    (Note: a valuable annual report.)
United Nations Population Fund. 2011. *State of World Population 2011: People and
    Possibilities in a World of 7 Billion.* New York: United Nations. (Note: a valuable
    annual report.)
Weisman, Alan. 2007. *The World without Us.* New York: St. Martin's Press.
Wilson, Edward O. 2002. *The Future of Life.* New York: Alfred Knopf.
Wire, Thomas. 2009. *Fewer Emitters, Lower Emissions, Less Cost: Reducing Future
    Carbon Emissions by Investing in Family Planning: A Cost/Benefit Analysis.* Lon-
    don: London School of Economics.

RESOURCES

If you share our conviction that overpopulation is an important environmental problem, we urge you to continue to educate yourself and others about the issue and to join in some of the many ongoing efforts to reverse course. Below we list useful websites to explore, as well as organizations that are working to reduce population growth and preserve wild nature. For up-to-date demographic information, two particularly valuable resources are the websites of the United Nations Department of Economic and Social Affairs, Population Division (www.un.org/esa/population), and the United States Census Bureau (www.census.gov).

Apply the Brakes (http://applythebrakes.com). Compelling personal statements by U.S. conservation leaders on the need to stop unsustainable population growth, both at home and abroad.

Australian Conservation Foundation (http://acfonline.org.au). Australia's leading environmental advocacy group, with a dedicated campaign to limit population growth in Australia.

Californians for Population Stabilization (www.capsweb.org). Working to formulate and advance policies designed to stabilize the population of California and the United States at levels that will preserve a good quality of life for all.

Center for the Advancement of the Steady State Economy (http://steadystate
.org). Educating and advocating for the steady state economy, including stabilizing both population and consumption.

Center for Biological Diversity (http://biologicaldiversity.org). Working through
science, law, and creative media to secure a future for all species—with a dedicated campaign on overpopulation and species extinction.

Center for Environment and Population (http://cepnet.org). Ensuring that the
best available science-based knowledge regarding population is integrated into
U.S. environmental debates and policies; CEP features an excellent information-
packed website.

Center for a New American Dream (www.newdream.org). Helping Americans
reduce and shift their consumption to improve quality of life, protect the environment, and promote social justice.

Earth Policy Institute (www.earth-policy.org). Dedicated to planning for a sustainable future and to providing a roadmap for how to get there from here.

Foundation for Deep Ecology (http://deepecology.org). Supporting education
and advocacy on behalf of wild Nature, including efforts to rethink present assumptions about economics, development, and the place of human beings in the
natural order.

Guttmacher Institute (www.guttmacher.org). Advancing sexual and reproductive
health and rights through an integrated program of research, policy analysis, and
public education.

HowMany.org (http://howmany.org). Working to remove the obstacles that
keep population from being seriously and rationally discussed; a terrific website,
packed with news and information.

Institute for Population Studies (http://ifpops.org). Dedicated to raising awareness about how world problems are tied to a growing population and to combating the fallacy that we cannot do anything about population growth except
accommodate it.

International Planned Parenthood Federation (http://ippf.org). A leading advocate of sexual and reproductive health and rights, providing contraception and
family planning advice throughout the world.

Negative Population Growth (http://npg.org). Unique among U.S. environmental groups in advocating for a reduction in U.S. population, rather than just population stabilization.

New Economics Institute (http://neweconomicsinstitute.org). Working to develop and lead the transition to a new economy that gives priority to supporting human well-being and Earth's natural systems.

Northwest Earth Institute (www.nwei.org). Helping lead the curious and motivated to take responsibility for Earth through classes and activities designed to promote connection, reflection, and action.

NumbersUSA (www.numbersusa.com). Largest and most effective organization working to reduce immigration into the United States; D.C.-based, with an active and engaged membership.

Optimum Population Trust (http://populationmatters.org). Working to reduce birth rates globally and in the United Kingdom and to balance immigration and emigration to prevent population increases in the UK.

Population Action International (http://populationaction.org). Securing funding and developing programs to ensure women access to contraception, to improve health, to reduce poverty, and to protect nature.

Population Connection (www.populationconnection.org). Formerly the leading U.S. group advocating for population stabilization, under the name Zero Population Growth.

Population-Environment Research Network (http://populationenvironment research.org). Advancing academic research on population and the environment by promoting online scientific exchange among researchers.

Population Institute (http://populationinstitute.org). Educating policymakers and the general public about population issues and promoting universal access to family planning.

Population Media Center (www.populationmedia.org). Using entertainment-education strategies, such as serialized radio and television dramas, to improve the health and well-being of people around the world.

Population Reference Bureau (www.prb.org). Providing timely and objective information on U.S. and international population trends and their implications; excellent, informative website.

Progressives for Immigration Reform (www.progressivesforimmigrationreform .org). Educating Americans about mass immigration's roles in furthering income inequality and driving rapid, ecologically unsustainable population growth.

Rewilding Institute (http://rewilding.org). Working to provide a long-term, hopeful vision for conservation in North America and to create and implement the North American Wildlands Network.

Sea Shepherd (www.seashepherd.org). Using innovative direct-action tactics to expose and confront illegal activities in order to end habitat destruction and wildlife slaughter in the world's oceans.

Sustainable Population Australia (http://population.org.au). Dedicated to ending habitat loss and species extinctions driven by human population growth, in Australia and throughout the world.

United Nations Department of Economic and Social Affairs, Population Division (www.un.org/esa/population). Responsible for monitoring a broad range of demographic trends; website gathers a great deal of useful information.

United Nations Population Fund (http://unfpa.org). International development agency working to reduce poverty and ensure that every pregnancy is wanted and every birth is safe; another very useful website.

United States Census Bureau (www.census.gov). Website allows access to a great compendium of demographic statistics and analyses, not just for the United States but for the world as a whole.

Wildlands Network (http://twp.org). Working to create large, protected land corridors across North America, provide sufficient habitat, and safeguard wildlife through the twenty-first century and beyond.

Worldwatch Institute (www.worldwatch.org). Independent research institute developing and disseminating solid data and innovative strategies for achieving sustainable societies worldwide.

CONTRIBUTORS

Albert Bartlett joined the faculty of the Department of Physics at the University of Colorado in Boulder in 1950. He has a talk on the arithmetic of growth that he has given an average of once every nine days between 1969 and 2011, and he has published many articles on the problems of growth and on the fundamentals of sustainability. He is past president of the American Association of Physics Teachers and a fellow of the American Physical Society and of the American Association for the Advancement of Science.

Joseph Bish holds a master of science in environmental advocacy and organizing from Antioch University New England. He has professionally advocated on environmental issues including ocean conservation and alternatives to nuclear power. He now works on global population advocacy for the Population Institute. His views are his own.

Lester Brown, founder and president of the Earth Policy Institute and founder of the Worldwatch Institute, has authored or coauthored fifty books, which have appeared in some forty languages. He is the recipient of many prizes and awards, including twenty-five honorary degrees, the 1987 United Nations Environment Prize, and the 1994 Blue Planet Prize for his "exceptional contributions to solving global environmental problems."

Tom Butler, conservation activist and writer, serves as the editorial projects director of the Foundation for Deep Ecology. He was a founding board member and is current president of the Northeast Wilderness Trust, the only regional land trust in the northeastern United States focused exclusively on protecting forever-wild landscapes.

Philip Cafaro is professor of philosophy at Colorado State University in Fort Collins, Colorado, and author of *Thoreau's Living Ethics*, also published by the University of Georgia Press. He is president of the International Society for Environmental Ethics and president of the board of Progressives for Immigration Reform.

Martha Campbell is the founder and president of the nonprofit Venture Strategies for Health and Development. A political scientist, she lectures in the School of Public Health, University of California, Berkeley, focusing on population growth, conflicting perspectives on fertility as they influence international policies, and barriers limiting women's ability to manage their childbearing.

William R. Catton Jr., a World War II navy veteran, taught sociology at universities in the United States, Canada, and New Zealand, and is now a Washington State University professor emeritus. His two most important books are *Overshoot: The Ecological Basis of Revolutionary Change* and *Bottleneck: Humanity's Impending Impasse.*

Eileen Crist teaches at Virginia Tech in the Department of Science and Technology in Society, where she is advisor for the undergraduate program Humanities, Science, and Environment. She is author of *Images of Animals: Anthropomorphism and Animal Mind* and coeditor of *Gaia in Turmoil: Climate Change, Biodepletion, and Earth Ethics in an Age of Crisis.*

Anne Ehrlich has written extensively on population and environmental issues and has coauthored ten books, including *The Population Explosion, Betrayal of Science and Reason*, and *One with Nineveh*. She has served on the board of directors of Friends of the Earth, the Rocky Mountain Biological Laboratory, and the Sierra Club, and has received numerous honors and awards.

Paul Ehrlich, author of *The Population Bomb* and numerous other influential works, is Bing Professor of Population Studies and professor of biological sciences at Stanford University. He is a member of the National Academy of Sciences and a recipient of the Craford Prize, the Blue Planet Prize, and numerous other international honors.

Robert Engelman is president of the Worldwatch Institute in Washington, D.C., and has written on population, environment, and gender issues for more than twenty years. In 2008 the Population Institute awarded his book, *More: Population, Nature, and What Women Want*, its Global Media Award for Individual Reporting.

Dave Foreman has worked since 1971 to save wilderness and wildlife, cofounding Earth First!, The Wildlands Project, New Mexico Wilderness Alliance, and the Rewilding Institute. His books include *Confessions of an Eco-Warrior, Rewilding North America*, and most recently *Man Swarm and the Killing of Wildlife*. In 1998, he was picked as one of Audubon's 100 Champions of Conservation.

Amy Gulick, a fellow with the International League of Conservation Photographers, has received the Daniel Housberg Wilderness Image Award from the Alaska Conservation Foundation, a Lowell Thomas Award from the Society of American Travel Writers Foundation, and the Voice of the Wild Award from the Alaska Wilderness League. Her book *Salmon in the Trees: Life in Alaska's Tongass Rain Forest* won a 2011 Nautilus Book Award and a 2010 Independent Publisher Book Award.

Ronnie Hawkins recently retired from the University of Central Florida, where she taught environmental philosophy, bioethics, philosophy of science, and existentialism. She has always held the position that a truly "pro-life" stance respects all Life on Earth and therefore entails recognizing the moral imperative of voluntarily limiting human procreation as well as our consumption of planetary resources.

Leon Kolankiewicz is a consulting wildlife biologist and senior environmental planner who has prepared many comprehensive conservation plans for U.S. national wildlife refuges and managed environmental impact statements on numerous controversial projects. He is a former vice-president of the Carrying Capacity Network, a former Peace Corps volunteer, and the author of *Where Salmon Come to Die: An Autumn on Alaska's Raincoast*.

Richard Lamm is codirector of the Institute for Public Policy Studies, a professor at the University of Denver, and a former three-term governor of Colorado. As a first-year legislator, he drafted and succeeded in passing the nation's first liberalized abortion law, and he was an early leader of the U.S. environmental movement.

Jeffrey McKee is a biological anthropologist conducting research on hominin evolution and paleoecology, with applications to contemporary effects of humans on biodiversity. He has directed excavations at the South African early hominin sites of Taung and Makapansgat and has authored books including *Sparing Nature— The Conflict between Human Population Growth and Earth's Biodiversity.*

Stephanie Mills is an author, lecturer, and longtime bioregionalist. Her books include *Tough Little Beauties, Epicurean Simplicity, In Service of the Wild,* and most recently *On Gandhi's Path: Bob Swann's Work for Peace and Community Economics.* She is a fellow of the Post Carbon Institute and holds an honorary doctorate from her alma mater, Mills College.

Roderick Nash is professor emeritus of history and environmental studies at the University of California, Santa Barbara. He is the author of *Wilderness and the American Mind* and *The Rights of Nature: A History of Environmental Ethics.*

Tim Palmer is the author and photographer of twenty-two books about the environment, river conservation, and the American landscape, including *Rivers of America* and *The Heart of America: Our Landscape, Our Future.* Formerly a land-use planner, he has won numerous book awards and conservation honors, including the National Wildlife Federation's Conservation Achievement Award for Communications.

Charmayne Palomba was until recently a research assistant at the Weeden Foundation and has a long-standing interest in conservation and the role of population growth in species loss and environmental degradation. She did her graduate work in environmental philosophy at the University of North Texas and now attends the New York University School of Law, where she plans to focus on environmental and natural resources law.

William Ryerson is president of the Population Media Center and chair and CEO of the Population Institute. A forty-year veteran of the population issue, he has specialized in use of entertainment media to promote family planning and small family size in three dozen countries worldwide.

Winthrop Staples III is a former Special Forces officer, an endangered species biologist, and an environmental philosopher whose research thesis was titled "For a Species' Moral Right to Exist." He has conducted field research on Alaskan lynx and Amur leopard, among other species, and is currently revising a science fiction screenplay with a species rights theme.

Captain Paul Watson helped found Greenpeace in 1972 and the Sea Shepherd Conservation Society in 1977, leading it for the past thirty-four years as it has evolved into the world's most active marine nonprofit organization. His books include *Sea Shepherd: My Fight for Whales and Seals*, *Cry Wolf*, *Ocean Warrior*, *Earth Force* and *Seal Wars*.

Don Weeden has worked in the international population field for over twenty-five years, serving in various overseas and management positions for Columbia University, International Planned Parenthood Federation, and other nongovernmental organizations. He is currently executive director of the Weeden Foundation, whose mission to protect biodiversity includes efforts to stabilize domestic and global population growth.

George Wuerthner is the ecological projects director for the Foundation for Deep Ecology, where he does research and writes about environmental issues. For many years he was a full-time freelance photographer and writer and has published thirty-five books on natural history, conservation history, ecology, and environmental issues.

and progress, 164–169, 306–307; in
self, culture, and moral character,
versus material wealth, 317; taboo
on questioning, 167–168; as
undermining human flourishing,
294
—endless, 191, 253; as economists'
religion, 314; need to end, to protect
biodiversity, 296, 316
—exponential, 30–33, 101–102;
bacteria example of, 36–37; pond
example of, 101–102
—sustainable, 30, 37. *See also*
sustainability
growth rate, formula for calculating, 35
Guttmacher Institute, 234

habitat loss, and population
pressures, 85–86, 295. *See also*
biodiversity: loss of: caused by
overpopulation
HANPP (human appropriation of net
primary production), 84
Hanson, Norwood Russell, 203
Hardin, Garrett, 96, 155
Hartmann, Betsy, 259
Hayden, Tom, 3
Hays, Samuel, 58
Hernandez, Omar, 76
Holy Earth, The (Bailey), 304
Homo colossus, compared with *Homo
sapiens*, 22–25, 84
Honduras, 75–78, 111
Hosseini, Khaled, 204
*How Many People Can Live on Planet
Earth?* (film), 151n2, 258
*How Many People Can the Earth
Support?* (Cohen), 4
Huang, Priscilla, 268
human supremacy, 143–145; as
mistaken, 130–132; as shown

in restraint, 313–314. *See also*
anthropocentrism
Hum Log (We People), 245–246
Humraahi (Come Along with Me),
246
hunger, overpopulation's impacts on,
xiii
Hurricane Katrina, 108
Hurricane Mitch, 111
hypocrisy, 134, 194

immigration, U.S., 102–106, 267–
269, 277–279; Americans want
decrease in, 198; as chief cause of
U.S. population growth, 64–65,
102–103, 189, 278; economic effects
of, 103–106; encouraged by wealthy
capitalists, 103, 194; as encouraging
irresponsible overprocreation,
134–135, 185; environmental impacts
of, 98–99, 103, 176–181, 191, 193;
and equity issues, 193–194; history
of, 274; illegal, 278–279; as means
to secure cheap labor, 279; rates of,
64–65
immigration reduction: arguments
against, 268; arguments for, 106,
172–186, 198; policy proposals to
achieve, 183–185; and racism, 195–
197, 268; as related to progressive
political goals, 278
India, 63–64, 245–246, 251, 265
inequality, economic, increased by
mass immigration, 104, 194, 275,
279
intrinsic value of nature, 304. *See also*
biocentrism
invasive species, and population
growth, 86
IPAT formula, 78–79, 81–83
Iran, 146–147, 266